TRIANGLE C

ILLUMINATING THE GAY AND

And the Band Played On
by Randy Shilts

The Autobiography of Alice B. Toklas
by Gertrude Stein

The Beebo Brinker Chronicles
by Ann Bannon

Bertram Cope's Year
by Henry Blake Fuller

A Boy's Own Story/
The Beautiful Room Is Empty
by Edmund White

Brideshead Revisited
by Evelyn Waugh

The Celluloid Closet
by Vito Russo

City of Night
by John Rechy

Dancer from the Dance
by Andrew Holleran

Death in Venice
and Seven Other Stories
by Thomas Mann

Family Dancing
by David Leavitt

The Family of Max Desir
by Robert Ferro

Giovanni's Room
by James Baldwin

The Lure
by Felice Picano

The Naked Civil Servant/How to Become a Virgin/
Resident Alien
by Quentin Crisp

Olivia
by Olivia

Oranges Are Not the Only Fruit
by Jeanette Winterson

Orlando
by Virginia Woolf

The Picture of Dorian Gray
by Oscar Wilde

The Price of Salt
by Patricia Highsmith

Rubyfruit Jungle
by Rita Mae Brown

A Single Man
by Christopher Isherwood

The Sophie Horowitz Story/Girls, Visions and Everything/
After Dolores
by Sarah Schulman

Surpassing the Love of Men
by Lillian Faderman

The Well of Loneliness
by Radclyffe Hall

What Is Found There/An Atlas of the Difficult World/
The Fact of a Doorframe
by Adrienne Rich

Zami/Sister Outsider/Undersong
by Audre Lorde

THE NAKED CIVIL SERVANT

HOW TO BECOME A VIRGIN

RESIDENT ALIEN

THE NAKED CIVIL SERVANT
HOW TO BECOME A VIRGIN
RESIDENT ALIEN

QUENTIN CRISP

With a
New Preface and Afterword
by the Author

QUALITY PAPERBACK BOOK CLUB
NEW YORK

Printed in the United States of America

Contents

PREFACE

THIS IS THE SECTION OF A MASSIVE tome that no one ever reads, not even a conscientious member of the book club. It begins, "I would like to thank . . ." The eyes glaze. The heart sinks. Fortunately, in my case, this is just a few short paragraphs.

First, I wish to thank Mr. David Rosen of Quality Paperback Book Club/Triangle Classics, who has made it possible for me to produce a book with very little work. And I must say, work is a four-letter word that I never use in mixed company.

I also wish to thank my agent, Mr. Stedman Mays. He is a very kind and gracious gentleman who rules the Clausen, Mays & Tahan literary agency with consummate skill and humor. Certainly, I must owe him an amazing lot, because I am sure it is he who convinced Mr. Rosen to print this book. And I must praise Miss Mary Tahan for her diligent handling of my chaotic affairs.

I also thank Mr. Phillip Ward for all his kind help and friendship. In my waning years, he has made it all very easy for me. Mr. Ward has helped me rewrite my one-man show, *An Evening With Quentin Crisp*, and is helping me prepare the manuscript of my next book. He is like your friendly innkeeper, adroitly steering me through much of life's chaos and complexities.

This volume of my collected memoirs is the story of my life, from the time I was born to the present moment. The pages you are about to read might frighten you, but I hope not. This is not my intention.

The first part of what follows is called *The Naked Civil Servant*, which is a bad title because everywhere I go I have to explain that I was never a civil servant. It was a joke on how boring being a model had become. For nearly thirty years, I worked as a life model, posing nude, in an English art school. I earned sufficient money for a living, but it did grow tiresome. As a young man, I could sit perfectly still while students studying to be artists would paint me or sculpt me. But thirty years on, my bones began to creak. It was time to make a move. The book was written about 1966, before I ever knew I would reach the Big Time, and is the story of my life before moving to America when I was seventy-two years old.

The second part of this collection is called *How to Become a Virgin*, which refers to my own re-virgination—my own fresh rebirth as a new persona—through television when I reached America. I was so overwhelmed by America, where everyone is your friend, that I could have wept for joy in the streets! I am now busy trying to become an American citizen. I have always been an American in my heart.

The third part is called *Resident Alien*, another bad title, referring to my status as a foreign citizen living in New York. I have not had very good luck with titles. The book is a compilation of my diaries printed in the *New York Native*, a newspaper published by a charming man called Mr. Thomas Steele. His courage to print my diary is to be rewarded by being mentioned in this book.

So, dear reader, enjoy traveling through the pages ahead. Once you have made it through all the curious misadventures of this book, I'll catch you at the other end. There I will bring you up to date from where *Resident Alien* left off. Have a fine read!

Thank you,

Quentin Crisp

THE NAKED CIVIL SERVANT

Preface by Michael Holroyd

Preface

It is a brave writer who attempts a preface to this book. In one sense *The Naked Civil Servant* needs no introduction: It says everything with extraordinary precision and force. Mr. Quentin Crisp has been well-known to himself for so long that he may suspect he is now internationally famous as one of London's works of art. He may be unlikely to recognize the need for an introduction to American readers.

Yet he first came to the attention of the American public only in the fall of 1976, when a dramatic documentary of his life blazed across American television screens. This program produced an astonishing reaction, and rightly so, since it had been based on this most astonishing autobiography. I was in New York the week after it was shown and everyone seemed not simply to be talking about it, but asking me about him. I told them nothing. A writer is like a weighing machine: Words come only when you put money in. This is a condition of literature which Mr. Crisp has had no difficulty in grasping.

In fact, I told them nothing not through professionalism, but ignorance. I have never met Mr. Crisp. Although I am introducing him to you, no one has introduced him to me. This is proper. I am not doing a friend a favor: I am attempting to do you one.

You may never meet Mr. Crisp. When he wrote this book he didn't believe in "abroad" except as a nightmare place where everyone makes absurd sounds all around you until, once you have moved out of earshot, they revert to standard English. On his travels, wherever he may have imagined he was going, he appears never to have reached much beyond High Wycombe (a hamlet thirty miles from London). So his gaunt and mincing figure will never pitter-patter in menacing retreat from you on the sidewalk; you will never be dazzled by the blue hair, orange face, and vermilion lips, or deafened by the roar of his amulets. You are safe from having ludicrously to feign indifference, from being tempted into philistinism or savagery. You meet him in his most convenient shape, which nevertheless conveys the essence of the man. For though he represents himself as a diseased oyster, he has here produced his pearl.

It is open to you to see Mr. Crisp as uniquely English, the Queen of Queer Street and a most vivid embodiment of the Era of Eccentricity that followed the decline of the British Empire. If it were only that, his story would be part of history and of sociology, and no more. Unfortunately, he writes so well that his life grafts itself onto ours. If we are not affected by these pages then we must be partly dead. For Mr. Crisp does not write exclusively of homosexuality, but of the outcast state in whatever form it may take anywhere at any time. Like King Lear, he has exposed himself to "feel what wretches feel"; and we have taken too little care of that. He challenges our response to anything we think is deeply and unfashionably non-conventional.

The response to him in Britain has been terrible, and this has afforded Mr. Crisp some satisfaction. It is his form of revenge. The wonder (and for himself the disappointment) is that he is still alive. God knows how, though his frail body is full of stamina and his spirit wrapped around with cunning and iron politeness. But he should have been killed: That would have ended the business in the most logical way. Fielding's London lives again in these pages, with its squalor and violence.

Civilization retreats as Mr. Crisp daintily steps forward.

The Naked Civil Servant was first published in Britain in January, 1968, and it is interesting now to see what reviewers made of it there. They came, certainly not to praise the book, but to bury it with respectability. Simon Gray in *The Listener* called it "a brave little tale"; Paul Bailey in *The Observer* thought it "entertaining"; John Whitley gave it marks for "candor" and "charm" in *The Sunday Times.* There is bravery, entertainment, candor, charm. But the discomfort of those critics who did not like the book was preferable to the tepidity of many who did. B. A. Young in *Punch* called it "a book full of self-pity"; the critic of *The Times Literary Supplement,* revolted by the "intolerably arch and jaunty manner," read it with "total absence of compassion"—as did Mary Conroy in the London *Times.* Accepting it "without emotion," she complimented the author on having exploited so well his gift for unpopularity. These critics had felt the threat. Best of all was *The Scotsman,* which optimistically placed it among the week's fiction. Only Irish reviewers recognized the bleak wit and insight, and did not look away; and it is with an Irish writer that I see *The Naked Civil Servant* having affinities. To the English, Mr. Crisp has appeared as one of the more flamboyant inventions of Evelyn Waugh; but his world is closer to that of Samuel Beckett:

> My relations with Jackson were of short duration. I could have put up with him as a friend, but unfortunately he found me disgusting, as did Johnson, Wilson, Nicholson, and Watson, all whore-sons. I then tried, for a space, to lay hold of kindred spirits among the inferior races, red, yellow, chocolate, and so on. And if the plague-stricken had been less difficult of access I would have intruded on them too, ogling, sidling, leering, ineffing and conating, my

heart palpitating. With the insane too I failed, by a hair's breath.

Mr. Crisp would, I believe, recognize this scene as being very near to his own life. He shares with Beckett this desolation and disgust and the wonderful ability to free it from all sentimentality, to breathe vitality and humor into it, to give it style. Mr. Crisp is a master of the inverted cliché. He stands the world of the "dead normals" on its head; he makes it truly dead.

In his first sentence, Mr. Crisp refers to himself as having been "disfigured" by homosexuality. He has not hidden this disfigurement, but tried to find a way of turning guilt and humiliation, fear, hatred, and all his other crippling disadvantages into enviable assets. He converted his body into a fantastic vehicle called "Quentin" (he had been christened Denis), fashioned for propaganda and amusement. If he could not command love, at least he could get attention. By dressing up so as to attract maximum hostility, he transferred the guilt and hatred to ordinary conventional people. He set great store by their bad opinion and became a connoisseur of different classes of enmity. "Nobody escapes my love," he tells us—but almost everyone has tried. There are "no sympathetic characters in real life."

In the 1920s Mr. Crisp became a walking tutor to London and was kept going by his evangelical zeal. Though girls could be boyish, men still had to be men, and homosexuality was felt to be something classical and far distant, vaguely Greek. Mr. Crisp brought it up to date and gave it a bad name—like cancer. Freud's works were then for the first time being translated into English, and as the climate changed Mr. Crisp hurriedly jumped off the bandwagon and switched from reform to entertainment. Peace came to him with the Second World War. Utopia had temporarily arrived—imported by Americans in uniform. Mr. Crisp "adores"

Americans. "I was by nature American," he writes. So over to you.

Since the war the Quentin vehicle has apparently overshot its mark. By the 1960s fancy dress had become *de rigueur*, and it was only by advertising himself as a grotesque and aging caricature of the new teenager that Mr. Crisp continued to attract adequate contempt. The book stops in 1967, the year in which legislation following the Wolfenden Report on Homosexual Offences and Prostitution was introduced. This legal relaxation came too late to make much difference to him except as an obstacle to gaining that state of alienation he sees as desirable.

To bring the story up to date. Mr. Crisp, now in his seventieth year, has risked his self-sufficiency by becoming a cult personality. People commiserate with him on the number of parties to which he's invited, but he tells them it's wonderful. He has achieved his purpose of making the enemy appear harmlessly eccentric. When they telephone and threaten him with death, he gives them an appointment. They know where to find him. He has been living in the same Chelsea room now for thirty-three years; since the first four, the dirt and dust have got no worse. He receives cake from a distant admirer in Hampton Court; he gives Wine and Crisp Evenings, "a Straight Talk from a Bent Speaker." He has two television sets at "Cinerama" angles to each other; one is inert and the other "comes off the water supply"—but no one is fooled. For the truth is that Mr. Crisp has reached his prime in the television age. In an interview in *The Guardian*, he told Alex Hamilton that people are continually informing him that they have seen him on television—"rushing up to you in the street to say it, when you think they would hurry by with their faces averted. The essence of style is to be predictable and television rapidly established predictability. People say, 'Oh, you would say that,' or quote you and add, 'as you would say,' and if this is what they like, you must do it. If people can predict you, they own you, and they love you."

If he had known what television would do, he confessed to Alex Hamilton, he would have told his mother that he didn't mean to learn to read and write. He would wait for television.

Mr. Crisp's career has been a strange boxing match with this world, where each blow that struck him counted as a point scored in his favor. The rules were his and he has come out an easy winner. But the contest is over now. At the end of this book he threatens to commit a murder; instead, he has been led away into success and is now ready for America.

This monster of depravity is also the author of a poem about a kangaroo, a novel on the Welfare State, and a volume on window-dressing. Does this *oeuvre* have any message for us? I think there is one: that we should all have the courage to develop our own feelings and form our own opinions, and not take on second-hand thoughts and emotions. Mr. Crisp stands for postjudice *versus* prejudice.

But if you want to irritate him, if you can't resist it, then, bearing in mind his hostility to all "culture," join me in proclaiming *The Naked Civil Servant* a classic of autobiography.

—MICHAEL HOLROYD

Chapter I

From the dawn of my history I was so disfigured by the characteristics of a certain kind of homosexual person that, when I grew up, I realized that I could not ignore my predicament. The way in which I chose to deal with it would now be called existentialist. Perhaps Jean-Paul Sartre would be kind enough to say that I exercised the last vestiges of my free will by swimming with the tide—but faster. In the time of which I am writing I was merely thought of as brazening it out.

I became not merely a self-confessed homosexual but a self-evident one. That is to say I put my case not only before the people who knew me but also before strangers. This was not difficult to do. I wore makeup at a time when even on women eye shadow was sinful. Many a young girl in those days had to leave home and go on the streets simply in order to wear nail varnish.

As soon as I put my uniform on, the rest of my life solidified around me like a plaster cast. From that moment on, my friends were anyone who could put up with the disgrace; my occupation, any job from which I was not given the sack; my playground, any café or restaurant from which I was not barred or any street corner from which the police did not move me on. An additional restricting circumstance was that the year in which I first pointed my toes toward the outer world was 1931. The tidal wave, started by the fall of Wall Street, had by this time reached London. The sky was dark with millionaires throwing themselves out of windows.

So black was the way ahead that my progress consisted of long periods of inert despondency punctuated by spasmodic lurches forward toward any small chink of light that I thought I saw. In major issues I never had any choice and therefore the word regret had in my life no application.

As the years went by, it did not get lighter but I became accustomed to the dark. Consequently I was able to move with a little more of that freedom which T.S. Eliot says is a different kind of pain from prison. These crippling disadvantages gave my life an interest that it would otherwise never have had. To survive at all was an adventure; to reach old age was a miracle. In one respect it was a blessing. In an expanding universe, time is on the side of the outcast. Those who once inhabited the suburbs of human contempt find that without changing their address they eventually live in the metropolis. In my case this took a very long time.

In the year 1908 one of the largest meteorites the world has ever known was hurled at the earth. It missed its mark. It hit Siberia. I was born in Sutton, in Surrey.

As soon as I stepped out of my mother's womb onto dry land, I realized that I had made a mistake—that I shouldn't have come, but the trouble with children is that they are not returnable. I felt that the invitation had really been intended for someone else. In this I was wrong. There had been no invitation at all, either for me or for the brother born thirteen months earlier.

A brother and sister seven and eight years older than I were presumably expected though hardly, I imagine, welcome. Before any of us were born there were bailiffs in my parents' house in Carshalton.

When they moved to Sutton we by no means lived in poverty. We lived in debt. It looks better, and keeping up with the Joneses was a full-time job with my mother and father. It was not until many years later when I lived alone that I realized how much cheaper it was to drag the Joneses down to my level.

As soon as I was a few days old I caught pneumonia. I was literally as well as metaphorically wrapped in cotton wool. From this ambience I still keenly feel my exile. When I was well again, I saw that my mother intended to reapportion her love and divide it equally among her four children. I flew into an ungovernable rage from which I have never fully recovered. A fair share of anything is starvation diet to an egomaniac. For the next twelve years I cried or was sick or had what my governesses politely called an "accident"—that is to say I wet myself or worse. After that time I had to think of some other way of drawing attention to myself, because I was sent to a prep school where such practices might not have seemed endearing.

In infancy I was seldom able to vary the means by which I kept a stranglehold on my mother's attention, but on one occasion I managed to have myself "kidnapped." Everybody in the family always used this word to describe the incident but there were no ransom notes. I did not at that time sit on the knees of golden-hearted gangsters while they played poker in rooms with the windows boarded up. The whole drama was in one act.

Our nurse told my brother and me that we were about to be taken for a lovely walk. I began as usual to deploy delaying tactics such as keeping my arms as rigid as a semaphore signaler's while she tried to put my coat on. Then as now I didn't hold with the outer world. Tired of these antics, nurse took my brother downstairs and they hid. Not knowing that they were doing this, my mother, when I asked her where they were, told me I might go just as far as the front gate to look for them. I went not only to the gate but out into the street and down to the corner of the Brighton

Road. There I met a rag-and-bone man who offered me a lift in his handcart.

I was found on Sutton Downs two or three miles from home by one of my mother's friends. Only about two hours had passed, but the whole neighborhood had been stirred up and my mother had telephoned the police. This was nice. Unfortunately the doctor who examined me on my return advised my mother never to question me about the incident. That was a pity, for now I can remember nothing of my journey.

For many years I was troubled by two half-formed memories. In one the ground is covered with crumpled newspapers. I put my hands on these and move them about but I never lift any of them up. Underneath is something unpleasant. To this day I have no idea whether this has something to do with my ride in the handcart or not. Perhaps one should regard the kidnapping as just the first instance of my being picked up by a strange man at a street corner.

The other memory was of drawing something long—a thin tube, a piece of cord—between my finger and thumb. I felt that there were lumps inside the tube. The sensation was faintly nasty. One day when I was at least forty I was lying in bed having another go at my half-buried past when I saw in detail the coverlet that had been on my cot when I was a baby. This had ribs of twisted white wool running across it, and around the edge was a lace border with small loops in it that I felt if I pulled the coverlet up to my chin. At the same time that I saw these details, I remembered that in this cot I slept beside my parents' bed. One night I heard my parents whispering. Then my mother called my name tentatively—experimentally. I knew that on no account must I answer. The whispering began again and, after a while, my father gave a long, despairing groan. I was surprised at this because I had expected, not him, but my mother to be hurt. It is a pity that I cannot say that, when I recalled all this, the scales fell from my eyes and the meaning of my life was suddenly clear. I merely experienced a pleasant relief as though I had solved a clue in a long-abandoned crossword puzzle. The only practical use I ever found for this revelation was that it enabled me to answer with certainty one of the questions that doctors and psychologists always asked me. Did my parents ever make love after I was born? I never know how they imagined I would be able to answer, but I could.

Sad to say the greatest scandal in Sutton during my childhood came and went without my being able to convert it to my own use, though I perched on the knee of its central character. Moreover, while I sat thus, he powdered my face and declared openly that I was his favorite. A production of *A Midsummer Night's Dream* was being put on at the preparatory school to which my two brothers went. To give it a professional gloss, a down-and-out actor, who showed us photographs of himself wearing nothing but a bunch of grapes, had been engaged as director.

It is an instance of my mother's spasmodic indulgence of me that I was allowed to appear in public wearing a wreath of roses and a green tulle dress in a show that was in no other way transvestite. The play was not being acted solely by the boys of the school. My sister had a walk-on part and a Miss Benmore, draped in mauve chiffon, sat in the middle of the stage on a seat that at home was called the "rug box" and usually stood in our hall. I danced myself silly but only when I fought with another fairy for a place that I felt was really mine did the applause become as loud and as sincere as I felt it should be.

The London actor had evidently played Bottom in more senses than one, for next day he was seen by my sister on Sutton station in handcuffs. Later, the headmaster of my brothers' school telephoned my mother and begged her not to let any of us see the local papers. The actor had been charged with seducing one of the boys. I was too young to know that I had lived a little while.

While I spent all my time at home, my mother can hardly have known ever a short spell when she was not worried about me. Sometimes she tried cosseting me and sometimes she tried upbraiding me while, after one of my "accidents," she washed my stinking knickers. I wept but I never really felt guilty. I thought my vomit, my feces, my tears were love gifts to my mother—no more disgusting, after all, than a broken heart.

My lust for praise was inordinate. Only the servants made any attempt to satisfy it. For them I danced incessantly and recited poems that I made up as I went along. I did not realize, when they applauded me, that clapping might merely be a welcome change from dusting. If my mother called me down from some upper room that the housemaid was supposed to be cleaning, I did not obey until she was really angry. Then I could cry.

My father did not like me. My presence was insistently physical. He was a fastidious man. He dusted the chair on which the cat had been lying before occupying it himself. He ate a banana with a knife and fork—to modern minds a dead giveaway if ever there was one. In later years I had to supply various subsidiary kinds of fuel for the furnaces of his hatred. In infancy my existence was enough.

So my parents and I constructed between us the classic triangle for all the world as if we had read the right books on psychology, but although (or because) my mother was so close to me, she did not realize that I was gradually coming to require not love so much as unconditional obedience.

Chapter 2

Even in childhood I was mad about men in uniform.

As in a silent movie, when thirty long years had passed, I went back to the place of my birth to pose in the art school there. Passing through the railway station, I saw, with that inward eye that is the curse of solitude, my sister squatting by the ticket office to play with a baby bear that a sailor held on a lead. He stood for a while watching my sister and I watched him.

I also remember the soldiers that were billeted in private houses in Sutton during the First World War. To most people they presented a domestic inconvenience bravely borne but to me they were emotionally disturbing. When they marched away to Flanders, the girls lined the streets and, with delicious sadness, threw sweets to them. It all seemed wistful and romantic at the time. I had never then heard any of the things men say about women making fools of themselves.

When the First World War was about half over and people had given up saying that it would only last a few weeks and taken to prophesying that it would go on forever, my father suffered his first defeat in the presence of the Joneses. He moved us all into a smaller house on the opposite side of the road. The only thing that worried me here was that I lost my captive audience. There were no rooms and, presumably, no money for servants who lived in. In the modern world where servants are extinct it is difficult to realize that to my parents this change in their circumstances must have been rather like the Fall. The only thing that made the situation bearable for them was that, because it was wartime, all economies could be made to look like patriotic gestures.

We moved into this new home when I was seven and out again when I was ten, and it is here that my definite childhood recollections begin. Of the two houses that I had lived in previously my memories are sharp, but have no chronology. Their background is hazy or even false, but if anyone were to utter the name of our wartime house, all the quality of my life there would come back to me. This house was almost the last in the road. My memory always looks toward the empty fields and the poplar trees standing along the mauve-gray paths that zigzagged slightly uphill toward Belmont and the school to which I then went. The sky is sunless, the earth unpopulated; and, to my waking eyes, this landscape is forever in a state of pause without the least hint of expectancy. This is also the setting for my most persistent childhood dream and in the nightmare foreboding is everywhere. I look at each poplar tree in turn until I catch a glimpse of a figure hiding behind one of them—a woman in a black hat and a gray cloak. As soon as I see her, she starts to come toward me along the path. She travels at great speed, but her cloak gives no sign that her legs are moving. I do not cry out; I do not run away. The dream has no ending.

Although I did not think about this nightmare during the day, I seldom went out of doors wantonly. If I left the house by myself it was usually to visit one or other of two girls of about my own age. I had no friends who were boys because boys wanted to fight. I knew I would get hurt and not win. Also they would not play my games of make-believe. But girls could be made to do as I said if I shouted at them or hit them or, in the last resort, deserted them. In case the desertion might come as a relief, I always remembered to cry loudly as

I ran through their front gates so that someone would hear and scold them for not being a "good little hostess." All the games I played with these little girls were really only one game. We dressed up in their mothers' or even grandmothers' clothes, which we found in box rooms and attics, and trailed about the house and garden describing in piercing voices the splendors of the lives that in our imaginations we were leading. "This wheelbarrow is my carriage. I gather up my train as I get in. Get in the other side, you fool. I nod to the servants as I leave. No. I ignore them. I am very proud and very beautiful." This kind of monologue I could keep up for whole afternoons.

I cannot say whether my mother led me into this lifelong exotic swoon because it was secretly her own ideal or whether, finding me already there, she sustained me in it as a way of keeping me quiet. Undoubtedly she allowed me to feel that it was a taste we shared. The first grown-up entertainment to which she ever took me was *Chu Chin Chow*. In this play a certain Miss Brayton, wearing saucers on her breasts and a kind of dirty-clothes basket on her head, walked up and down stairs with her hands at the utmost horizontality. I nearly fainted with delight. The first paintings that I consciously looked at were Lord Leighton's classical mock-ups. My introduction to literature was of a piece with these other cultural initiations. My mother read to me from *The Lady of the Lake* and the *Idylls of the King*. She used the "poetry" voice but she read extremely well—possibly because she was made to read the same pieces so often. When she decided that it was time for me to read to myself she handed me fairy stories, and from them I graduated to the works of Mr. Haggard. Having exhausted these I gave up reading altogether and from then on held a view of literature which I can best express by this anecdote.

A friend of mine had a landlady who, when she saw him putting on his hat and advancing toward the front door, would say, "Going out." Should she find him at the sink, holding his kettle under the running tap, she would say, "Filling your kettle." These and other such phrases were not questions; they were statements. Because they were made with a smile, they were meant to show that she approved and was, in a remote way, taking part in his life. One day she entered a room where he was sitting with his eyes turned toward an open novel. She said, "Waiting."

Once while I was engaged in sharing my gauzy internal dream with one of my little friends, a faint breath of criticism ruffled the garden where we played. A quite unnecessary cousin of my playmate was present and she suggested that, to bring a little true romance into our game, she should stand on the veranda and watch with green eyes while her lover (me) walked by with my friend on my arm, talking and laughing and paying no heed. For a moment I was absolutely disorientated. I realized an effort was being made to edge me into the disgusting role of a handsome prince. Then my hostess said, "Oh, Denis (as my name was before I dyed it) never plays the part of a man." I do not recall that she had any difficulty in saying this or that her cousin took more than a moment to reply, "Oh well, I'll be the prince and he can stand on the veranda." The moment passed and I moved back into the dream.

Occasionally I tried to drag my brother into my world of make-believe. I rarely succeeded. No wiles of mine—not even my tears (and tears were to me what glass beads were to African traders)—could buy his companionship for long. I learned very early in life that I was always going to need people more than they needed me.

To most children I suppose there is a difference in degree between their imaginary and their real lives—the one being more fluid, freer, and more beautiful than the other. To me fantasy and reality were not merely different; they were opposed. In the one I was a woman, exotic, disdainful; in the other I was a boy. The chasm between the two states of being never narrowed.

At home I managed to make my life miserable more or less unaided. At school this was done for me. Teachers could not refrain from scoring off me as soon as they perceived that I had no armor. When some of the pupils had gone into Sutton to take a music examination, I happened to be the last to come back into the school. The headmistress asked me if I thought that I had passed. I replied that I did—that the exam had been quite easy. There was a roar of laughter from everyone. Only then did I realize that I ought, as a formality, to have said the exam was difficult.

Finding myself the constant object of amused attention was hateful to me, yet I don't remember feeling the slightest embarrassment at arriving from time to time at school with my upper half awash with tears and my lower half dripping with excrement.

At my preparatory school I won a very poor scholarship to a public school on the borders of Staffordshire and Derbyshire. Before I went there, during a routine fit of weeping, my mother warned me that I would not be able to go on like that at boarding school. I never did. I was half-starved, half-frozen, and humiliated in a number of ways, but I never felt the faintest desire to cry. Fear and hatred do not seem to find expression in tears.

This school was on the top of a hill so that God could see everything that went on. It looked like a cross between a prison and a church and it was.

For about a year I was preoccupied only with survival—learning the rules, lying low under fire, and laying the blame on others. When at length these things became second nature to me, I had a timorous look around and saw that the whole school was in an even greater ferment of emotion than my prep school had been, but here the charge ran from the older to the younger boys rather than between the staff and the pupils.

For details of the love life of the prefects, which was one of our abiding preoccupations, you could ask one of the boys whose vocation was to carry notes from the prefects to the ordinary boys. (They were forbidden to speak to one another.) I was once in a class when the master said to one of these procurers, "What's that?" A piece of paper was handed over my head from the boy to the master. When he saw it, he said, "What are these names? Why are they bracketed together?" "They're just names," said the boy and this he repeated to all the questions that were fired at him. Finally the paper was handed back and the class continued. At length, the great scandal, that we had all so longed for, occurred. It was to the school what the Mrs. Simpson affair was to England.

The ground plan of the college was an "H." Four classrooms were on each of two opposing arms of this figure and there were two dormitories on each of the two floors above these rooms. Thus there were four "houses" on each side of the building—an irresistible Romeo and Juliet setup.

One night, though Montague arms reached out to him from three dormitories besides his own, a boy descended two flights of stairs, traversed the crossbar of the "H," and climbed two flights of stairs on the other wing to keep a tryst with a Capulet. Now, in the winter of my life, feeling that Shakespeare's Romeo might just as well have married the girl next door, I realize that these two schoolboys could have met behind some dreary haystack almost any afternoon. What the older boy did, he did not for love alone, but in order to defy the authorities with all the world on his side. He was caught. By lunchtime the next day the whole school knew every detail of this mad escapade.

His sin was the occasion of the only public beating that I have ever witnessed. The entire school was assembled in the big hall and seated on benches on either side of the room. In the open space in the middle the modern Romeo bent over and the headmaster ran down the room to administer the blows. After the first two strokes the younger brother of the victim left the room. Even now I can't help wishing that we had all done the same. What made this exhibition so disgusting was not the pain inflicted. Today a go-ahead schoolmaster would say, "This delights me more than it delights you." In many parts of London, such goings-on are just another way of making a party go with a swing. What was almost insufferable was that a simple form of self-gratification should be put forward as a moral duty. Before that day I had disliked the head; afterward I hated him.

I think that all the boys felt a little shaken, frightened, degraded. At least no one seemed to regard what they had seen as right. Some of us enshrined the culprit in our hearts as one of the saints of Aphrodite. He was, of course, expelled at once to prevent a snowstorm of "fan" notes, but he had the nerve to turn up again at a later date. I don't think that I ever spoke a word to him, but now, when I saw him throwing a cricket ball about with some other boys (well out of sight of any member of the staff), I watched him greedily. He was a thick-set young man with black hair growing low on his forehead. His expression was brutish and mocking—very desirable.

Unlike our Miss Capulet I myself never lured any of the boys to their doom. This was not for want of trying but for lack of any physical advantages. I was very plain. My rich mouse hair was straight but my teeth were not. I wore tin-rimmed spectacles. In spite of this formidable natural chastity belt, I did spend one night in bed with another boy. He was the only Indian in the school and, when his arrival in our dormitory was heralded, I hoped that he might be some unimaginable animal given to fits of terrible rage. This was not so.

Sexually he was a little more precocious than the other boys and went with prostitutes during the holidays but in all other respects, he was only as dangerous as the rest. Our sleeping together was part of the thinly spread orgy that was a ritual on the last night of every term. The occasion could only be described as a success inasmuch as the object of the exercise was to do it and to be known to have done it. These ends were achieved. I did not expect any pleasure and there was none. I did not even experience a sense of sin. The intimations of immorality had come and gone some time back.

As soon as I was old enough to wash myself, I had begun the habit of staying in the bath until my body passed from lobster-pink to scum-gray. While lying in one of these semi-submerged trances, in a boarding house in Queen's Gate to which my parents moved temporarily, I discovered the only fact of life that I have ever fully understood. Masturbation is not only an expression of self-regard: it is also the natural emotional outlet of those who, before anything has reared its ugly head, have already accepted as inevitable the wide gulf between their real futures and the expectations of their fantasies. The habit fitted snugly into my well-established world of make-believe.

When I awoke the morning after my first orgasm, I remembered it instantly and wondered if I should die, go mad, or contract some incurable disease. After a few days it became obvious that I was to experience no noticeable physical ill-effects. Coziness was restored. About my immortal soul I did not worry. Vice is its own reward. It is virtue which, if it is to be marketed with consumer appeal, must carry Green Shield stamps. The greenest of these is the "sweet bye-and-bye." For me this stamp is not negotiable. The one thing I would not wish on my worst enemy is eternal life.

I think I can say that effeminate homosexuals are among those who indulge least in sex acts with other boys at school. They seem to realize that these jolly get-togethers are really only a pooling of the carnal feelings of two people who deep down are interested in their dreams of girls. Otherwise they tend to be self-congratulatory pyrotechnical displays of potency.

Certainly I felt this to be so. I longed to be the subject of a school-shaking romance, but relationships in which personality was not involved were valueless to me. What I wanted most of all was to use sex as a weapon to allure, subjugate, and, if possible, destroy the personality of others. Holding this view I was naturally more interested in the masters than in my mere equals. I tried to seduce them all the time. I worked hard at lessons or at least hard enough to shine. Thus I forfeited all friendship with the other boys. This scarcely mattered as most of them disliked me so much already.

Worst of all from their point of view, I was openly eager to take exams. Possibly exams are more difficult now than they used to be. At my school the early ones could be passed by an effort of memory alone. I used to go into the examination room with pale lips mumbling whole vocabularies of Latin military words and come out again thoroughly relaxed, knowing nothing. Even geography could be dealt with in this way. I learned by heart the names of the towns on the L.M.S. Railway. Of course, if a dot had been missing from the map, I would have arrived in Edinburgh with a town in hand, but the examiners were seldom as unkind as that. With their generous help I got into the sixth form when I was fifteen.

Once this standard had been achieved, I felt the tide beginning to turn. I do not mean that at last the boys started to respect me but that now the masters began to hate me too. I had reached the limit of my educability. It slowly dawned on the staff that they had spread their brooding pinions over a boy who had no more than a crossword-puzzle mentality. I was the opposite of a chimpanzee. I could memorize but I could not infer results from causes. Out of sheer disillusionment, the masters allowed themselves to be hoodwinked by the specialization racket. I went to the Latin master and said, "I'm afraid I'll have to give up Latin this term, sir—dear old Latin—but I've so much geography to do." Then I went to the geography master and said, "I'm afraid I'll have to give up geography—dear old geography, etc." After a lot more speeches of this kind, my timetable became an arid waste. For my final two years I sat in a Nissen hut and read trashy novels by Susan Glaspell.

I was at boarding school for four years. During that time I learned only one thing that I was ever able to use in adult life. I discovered that my great gift was for unpopularity. At first I would have done anything to shed it. I tried feverishly to develop protective coloring. Then these endeavors became fitful, alternating with essays in deliberate provocation. Finally I mastered my medium. It became an armor—almost a weapon. I had passed that barrier of which Mr. O'Connor speaks in the *Memoirs of a Public Baby*. I had learned consciously to achieve an effect that originally I had produced by accident. I must have been very unpopular indeed. To this day I have a tiny mark on my wrist where boys sawed through the flesh with a jagged ruler. For this and other reasons, I hated school but it was as well that I went there. It provided a dress rehearsal for the treatment that I was to receive in the streets of London in a few years' time.

During my last term my father had written a desperate letter (doubtless dictated by my mother) to my classics master asking him what on earth was to be done with me. The reply stated that I had not the makings of a scholar. I suppose that a classical training helps one to put things mildly. It was suggested that, as I seemed to have an ability to write, I should try to enter the field of journalism. The teacher had to say something positive and, having no knowledge of anything that had happened in the world since Thermopylae, did not understand that I was totally unsuited to this profession. Above all else, a journalist must be able to get on with strangers. Nevertheless I went to London University to take a course in journalism.

I did not protest at the absurdity of this. I dared not. I had nothing to suggest in its place and I knew that, while I sat dreaming through the lectures, at least I was putting off for another two years my terrible confrontation with the outer world.

Chapter 3

I was now eighteen and beginning to feel really uneasy about the future—openly on the grounds that I was so inadequate to earn a living, and secretly because I suspected that sexually I was quite unlike anyone else in the world. Friends were starting to ask me questions about my private life. Their intention was not unkind, but I was filled with misgiving.

"Are you keen on this girl you talk so much about?" a friend of my mother asked. "Good God, no," I replied putting on a face as though I had just stepped in something. Then I hastily embarked upon a cynical diatribe against all human sentiments. This was the kind of conversation that my mother's friend loved, but I now think that I wasted a rather wonderful woman. If I could simply have told her that, to my bewilderment, I did not think that I was ever going to be able to take a sexual interest in any girl, I'm sure she would have listened. This would have been at least a thin rope flung from my tiny island toward the mainland.

She would not have believed me, because in those far-off days a homosexual person was never anyone that you actually knew and seldom anyone that you had met. She would have thought that I had chosen at random a peculiarity that would make me more interesting, but she would not have been shocked. She was my first glimpse of the *vie de bohème.*

Her name was Mrs. Longhurst, a big striding strident person of about forty. ("I'm longing for one of those bonnets with jet beads on them"). By profession she was a stewardess and sometimes a portrait model ("Who cares as long as it brings in some money?"). She lived in Charlotte Street ("I adore all foreigners") in a room whose walls were covered with African knives. Her other room she had let to a nurse who had attended my mother during her four years in various nursing homes. After a while this nurse came to dislike Mrs. Longhurst, but at first she thought her a "real character." She introduced her as such to my mother and me. Mrs. Longhurst took to me at once and allowed me to visit her constantly to play pontoon and talk about myself. Her mode of speech was the most exaggerated that I had ever heard. These are the words with which she warned my mother (who longed to leave Battersea) not to try Hampstead: "Don't live in Hampstead. That's where the parents lived and they were crippled with rheumatism—bed-ridden. They moved and what happened? Within a week they were dancing in the streets of Maida Vale." This woman did not fly to extremes; she lived there. I also soon became an adept at this mode of talk and, with the passing of the years, came to speak in this way unconsciously.

Mrs. Longhurst's attitude to homosexuality, as to most things, was a mocking curiosity but she was never savage. The rest of the world in which I lived was still stumbling about in search of a weapon with which to exterminate this monster whose shape and size were not yet known or even guessed at. It was thought to be Greek in origin, smaller than socialism but more deadly—especially to children. At about this time *The Well of Loneliness* was banned. The widely reported court case, together with the extraordinary reputation that Tallulah Bankhead was painstakingly building up for herself as a delinquent, brought Lesbianism, if not into the light of day, at least into the twilight, but I do not remember ever hearing anyone discuss the subject except Mrs. Longhurst and my mother. If one is not going to take the necessary precautions to avoid having parents, one must undertake to bring them up. This was what, very cautiously, I was beginning to do with my mother. My father remained invincibly ignorant.

When I left King's College, London (needless to say without a diploma in journalism), I could at first find no better occupation than sitting at home getting on my parents' nerves. I became so listless that my mother thought it only polite to regard me as ill. She sent me to her doctor. Without making even the most cursory examination of me he declared that all I needed was a lesson in life. My father was very annoyed. He realized that he would have to pay a consultation fee for these few glib words. He was lucky that psychology had not yet reached the middle classes. He might have had to pay much more for less. At the time, my own reaction to the doctor's remark was blank incomprehension. Later when, to vary the monotony of my existence, I took to wandering about the streets of the West End, I stumbled on the very truth that was just what the doctor had ordered. I learned that I was not alone.

As I wandered along Piccadilly or Shaftesbury Avenue, I passed young men standing at the street corners who said, "Isn't it terrible tonight, dear? No men about. The Dilly's not what it used to be." Though the Indian boy at school had once amazed us all with the information that in Birmingham there were male prostitutes, I had never believed that I would actually see one. Here they were for all the world to recognize—or almost all the world. A passer-by would have to be very innocent indeed not to catch the meaning of the mannequin walk and the stance in which the hip was only prevented from total dislocation by the hand placed upon it.

The whole set of stylizations that are known as "camp" (a word that I was hearing then for the first time) was, in 1926, self-explanatory. Women moved and gesticulated in this way. Homosexuals wished for obvious reasons to copy them. The strange thing about "camp" is that it has become fossilized. The mannerisms have never changed. If I were now to see a woman sitting with her knees clamped together, one hand on her hip and the other lightly touching her back hair, I should think, "Either she scored her last social triumph in 1926 or it is a man in drag."

Perhaps "camp" is set in the 'twenties because after that differences between the sexes—especially visible differences—began to fade. This, of course, has never mattered to women in the least. They know they are women. To homosexuals, who must, with every breath they draw, with every step they take, demonstrate that they are feminine, it is frustrating. They look back in sorrow to that more formal era and try to relive it.

The whole structure of society was at that time much more rigid than it has ever been since, and in two main ways. The first of these was sexual.

The short skirts, bobbed hair, and flat chests that were in fashion were in fact symbols of immaturity. No one ever drew attention to this, presumably out of politeness. The word "boyish" was used to describe the girls of that era. This epithet they accepted graciously. They knew that they looked nothing like boys. They also realized that it was meant to be a compliment. Manliness was all the rage.

The men of the twenties searched themselves for vestiges of effeminacy as though for lice. They did not worry about their characters but about their hair and their clothes. Their predicament was that they must never be caught worrying about either. I once heard a slightly dandified friend of my brother say, "People are always accusing me of taking care over my appearance."

The sexual meaning of behavior was only sketchily understood, but the symbolism of clothes was recognized by everyone. To wear suede shoes was to be under suspicion. Anyone who had hair rather than bristle at the back of his neck was thought to be an artist, a foreigner, or worse. A friend of mine who was young in the same decade as I says that, when he was introduced to an elderly gentleman as an artist, the gentleman said, "Oh, I know this young man is an artist. The other day I saw him in the street in a brown jacket."

The other way in which society in the twenties was rigid was in its class distinctions. Doubtless to a sociologist there were many different strata merging here and there but, among the people that I was now getting to know, there were only two classes. They never mingled except in bed. There was "them," who acted refined and spoke nice and whose people had pots of money, and there was "us," who were the salt of the earth.

Mitford's First Law had not then been formulated. I could have put the words "toilet," "mirror," and "perfume" all into one sentence. None of the boys on the game would have noticed. I would still have been "them" because my slight cockney accent had been flattened out a little. But they forgave me for my unfair advantages because I was in the same sexual boat as they. I took to them like a duck to ducks.

Between these twin barriers of sex and class, we sat huddled together in a café called the Black Cat. (We were not putting up with any such nonsense as "Au Chat Noir," which was written over the window.) This was in Old Compton Street. It looked like a dozen other cafés in Soho. It had a horseshoe bar of occasionally scrubbed wood, black-and-white checked, linoleum on the floor, and mirrors everywhere. The deafening glass boxes in which nowadays customers sit and eat with their ankles on view to the public had not then been built. In that happier time all was squalor and a silence spangled only with the swish of knives and the tinkle of glass as the windows of the Black Cat got pushed in.

Day after uneventful day, night after loveless night, we sat in this café buying each other cups of tea, combing each other's hair, and trying on each other's lipsticks. We were waited on with indulgent contempt by an elderly gentleman, who later achieved a fame that we would have then thought quite beyond him, by being involved in a murder case. Had the denizens of the Black Cat known he was such a desperate character, they would doubtless have done much more to provoke him. As it was we only bored him by making, with ladylike sips, each cup of tea last as long as a four-course meal. From time to time he threw us out. When this happened we waltzed around the neighboring streets in search of love or money or both. If we didn't find either, we returned to the café and put on more lipstick. It never occurred to any of us to try to be more lovable. Even if it had, I do not think we would have adopted a measure so extreme. Occasionally, while we chattered on the street corner, one of our friends would go whizzing past crying, "They're coming." At this we would scatter. It meant that, while being questioned, one of the boys had bolted and his inquisitors were after him. At such times, if a detective saw his quarry escaping, he would seize upon the nearest prey, however innocently that person might be behaving. We treated the police as it is said you should treat wild animals. As we passed them, we never ran but, if they were already running, we spread out so that only one of our number would die. Policemen in uniform were not classed as man-eaters. I had no idea what the rules were but they never seemed to give chase; they only moved us on.

The perpetual danger in which we lived bound us together. In the café there was a lot of stylized cattiness, but this was never unkindly meant. Nothing at all was meant by it. It was a formal game of innuendoes about other people being older than they said, about their teeth being false and their hair being a wig. Such conversation was thought to be smart and so very feminine. It was better, I need hardly say, to seem like a truly appalling woman than not like a woman at all. Unfortunately in this game there seemed to be very few cards in the pack, and a whole evening spent playing it became monotonous. When we were not thus engaged, we talked about our sufferings, and this I greatly preferred. Soon I had learned by heart almost every argument that could be reared in the climate of that time against the persecution of homosexuals. We weren't doing any harm; we couldn't help it; and, though this was hardly watertight from a legal point of view, we had enough to bear already. Some speakers even went so far as not merely to excuse our sin but to glorify it, making it a source of national culture. The great names of history from Shakespeare onward were fingered over and over like beads on a rosary. We did not see that it might particularly be the offense of soliciting that was being condemned. It is hardly a matter for amazement that we did not understand this. Confusion on this point was everywhere.

The attitude of the law was arbitrary—bordering on slapdash. Boys arrested for soliciting were found guilty before they had spoken. If they did get a chance to say anything, the sound of their voices only caused the presiding magistrate to increase their sentences. I think the boys were right in assuming that they were being condemned for effeminacy. They also put forward the argument that they went on the streets because they were poor and that they were poor because they were sacked from jobs if their employers discovered them to be queer. Undoubtedly this was partly true but not entirely so. Many of the boys from the Black Cat had other jobs by day—truly improbable ones in some cases. One frail little thing was a plumber's mate. About this were many arch jokes and much rolling of blue-lidded eyes. Young men like this one were prostitutes by vocation—blessed in infancy with gifts for serving the community in a special way.

I have known female whores who spoke very bitterly of their calling. "If they don't like my face, they can put a cushion over it. I know it's not *that* they're interested in." But to the boys this profession never seemed shameful. It was their daytime occupations for which they felt they needed to apologize. In some instances, these were lower class or humdrum or, worst of all, unfeminine. At least whoring was never that.

The average woman, unless she is particularly ill-favored, regards loving and being loved as a normal part of life. If a man says he loves her she believes him. Indeed some women are convinced they are adored by men who can be seen by all to be running in the opposite direction. For homosexuals this is not so. Love and admiration have to be won against heavy odds. Any declaration of affection requires proof. So many approaches made to them are insincere—even hostile. What better proof of love can there be than money? A ten-shilling note showed incontrovertibly just how mad about you a man is. Even in the minds of some women a confusion exists between love and money if the quantity is large enough. They evade the charge of mercenariness by using the cash they extort from one man to deal a bludgeoning blow of humiliation upon another. Some homosexuals attempt this gambit, but it is risky. The giving of money is a masculine act and blurs the internal image.

I have always held the view that the union of two hearts whose incomes are equal is a complete waste of time. If anyone offered me money in exchange for sex I accepted it gladly, and by money I mean seven shillings sixpence. I still lived at home where two shillings sixpence a week was all the pocket money that I received. Early in life I learned that I was not going to be able to afford to set a value on myself. In consequence I have never had the bother of taking offense but can decide afresh each time that anything is offered to me whether I want it or not. Apart from my need for small change, there was another reason for accepting money. It absolved me from the charge of enjoying sex for its own sake. At home it had been explained to me that I must never say that I loved food—hardly that I liked it. How much greater the disapproval would have been for admitting that I liked sex I could only infer, as the subject was seldom mentioned. To some people an offer of money is so insulting that they can accept a book token for ten shillings but not a ten-shilling note. I never needed to be offered a love token. The cash would do nicely. So far from feeling humiliated, I felt in some measure compensated for all the insults (which carried no fringe benefit of money) that I daily received from other directions.

I disliked the coarseness of the situations in which I found myself. Courtship consisted of walking along the street with a man who had my elbow in a merciless grip until we came to a dark doorway. Then he said, "This'll do." These are the only words of tenderness that were ever uttered to me.

The venality of my predicament I took calmly. Unlike Desdemona, I could perform the deed but not say the word.

Chapter 4

My outlook was so limited that I assumed that all deviates were openly despised and rejected. Their grief and their fear drew my melancholy nature strongly. At first I only wanted to wallow in their misery, but, as time went by, I longed to reach its very essence. Finally I desired to represent it. By this process I managed to shift homosexuality from being a burden to being a cause. The weight lifted and some of the guilt evaporated.

It seemed to me that there were few homosexuals in the world. I felt that the entire strength of the club must be prepared to show its membership card at any time, and, to a nature as dramatic as mine, not to deny rapidly became to protest. By the time I was twenty-three I had made myself into a test case. I realized that it did no good to be seen to be homosexual in the West End where sin reigned supreme or in Soho which was inhabited exclusively by other outcasts of various kinds, but the rest of England was straightforward missionary country. It was densely populated by aborigines who had never heard of homosexuality and who, when first they did, became frightened and angry. I went to work on them.

The message I wished to propagate was that effeminacy existed in people who were in all other respects just like home. I went about the routine of daily living looking undeniably like a homosexual person. I had had a lot of practice at school in being the one against the many but, even so, I was not prepared for the effect my appearance had on the great British public. I had to begin cautiously.

I was from birth an object of mild ridicule because of my movements—especially the perpetual flutter of my hands—and my voice. Like the voices of a number of homosexuals, this is an insinuating blend of eagerness and caution in which even such words as "hello" and "goodbye" seem not so much uttered as divulged. But these natural outward and visible signs of inward and spiritual disgrace were not enough. People could say that I was ignorant of them or was trying without success to hide them. I wanted it to be known that I was not ashamed and therefore had to display symptoms that could not be thought to be accidental.

I began to wear make-up. For a while I still went on as before at home and never mentioned to my mother anything about the life I lived in the outer world. She once protested that I never brought home any of my friends. I explained, quite truthfully, that she would hate them if I did. She never mentioned the matter again, which I took to be a sign that the protest was formal and that secretly she would be glad to hear no more on that subject.

Once outside the flat, I hurried like a wrong hushed up to the nearest public lavatory and put on my war paint. Then I proceeded calmly wherever I was going. If I wasn't going anywhere, I tried to look as though I was. It became harder and harder to think of places to go and things to do as it slowly dawned on me that sex was definitely out—a realization that usually leaves people with a lot of spare time. If I was to become Miss Arc's only rival, it wouldn't do to allow myself to be picked up by strange men. This would give people the opportunity to say that I had only adopted an effeminate appearance for this purpose. Actually, from the moment that I began to look really startling, men ceased to make propositions to me. They found it too risky or too distasteful. But even the idea that this might be my intention must be eliminated. I began to walk faster and learned never to look strangers in the eye. Frequently in the street I swept past people I knew quite well. I once did this to my brother. This was just as well. He was with a girl who said, "Did you see that?" to which he replied, "Yes. Matter of fact, I've seen it before."

Without knowing it, I was acquiring that haughty bearing which is characteristic of so many eccentrics. What other expression would you expect to find on the face of anyone who knows that if he turns his head too quickly, he will see on the faces of others glares of stark terror or grimaces of hatred? Aloofness is the posture of self-defense, but even people who quite liked me said that I felt superior to the rest of the world. I felt scared and before long I was to have good cause.

By constantly complaining that the Battersea flat was sunless, my mother induced my father to buy a house outside High Wycombe. I could not do otherwise than go with them. My sister was by this time married; one of my brothers was abroad and the other was soon to go. Abroad was thought in those days to have some special advantages for young men of the middle classes and in this connection the word "scope" was on everybody's lips. As in childhood I had evinced so much distaste for even going outside the front door, my parents made little attempt to send me overseas. In this they were very wise. I don't hold with abroad and think that foreigners speak English when our backs are turned.

Even High Wycombe to me was like a desert at the edge of civilization. As I roamed the fields adjacent to the house, forced by my mother to take her chow for a walk, between the hedges my starved eyes would see mirages of the London Pavilion or the Marble Arch and I would stumble toward them with little cries. My great fear was that here I might live and die and not matter. Just how distasteful my life was at this time cannot have been apparent to others. A friend of my sister, rushing in where even devils would have feared to tread, remarked, "I wonder what you'd have been like if you'd been a woman. I suppose you'd have lived in the country and kept a dog and played bridge." I was too choked with fury to be able to defend myself against this charge. Among other objections to this image of me was the fact that I hated animals. I still do. I have enough dumb friends without them.

In childhood I had longed to be taught dancing but nothing ever came of this. In a characteristic fit of indulgence my mother went so far as to buy me a pair of blocked ballet shoes (she did not know or care that no male dancer, except Mr. Dolin in *Train Bleu*, had ever worn such things), but she never dared to mention to my father the idea of my becoming a dancer. It would have made him difficult to deal with for days. After the failure of journalism, she hammered away at commercial art as the last door through which it might be possible to push me into the outer world. I was sent to an art school in High Wycombe.

I had already done one term at Battersea Polytechnic before we left London and there had drawn a frog that the principal had thought was a piece of drapery. I don't think that I was taught anything. The only good that came of my attendance at this school was my meeting there with a girl who was to remain my friend for more than twenty years. She had been crippled by polio and wore a metal splint on one leg. At every step the whole side of her body had to be swung forward by a great effort from the shoulder. Despite this she was determined not to be left out of things. Her willpower was formidable. Because of her handicap, she was sympathetic to all deformity and was especially drawn to anyone she felt to be worse off than she. I came into this category.

The school at High Wycombe was, naturally, further

out of touch with reality than the one in Battersea. Furniture design was well taught there because the town was the home of that industry which many years later formulated the "G" plan. All other subjects were thought to be rather beside the point. None of the three or four men who comprised the staff had ever worked in an advertising agency or made free-lance commercial art into a paying profession. They would have been secretly ashamed to do so. Advertising was considered in those days a disgraceful trade. As no one felt confident to teach or even control me, I did more or less as I liked.

"What are you going to do this morning?"

"Oh, I don't know. A poster."

"What of?"

"Coty's Ashes of Roses." All my posters were exotic.

I very much doubt if, at the end of such a piece of dialogue as this, I was shown any advertising that M. Coty had recently put out, or, if I was, that I was warned that I must follow closely the existing line. I was encouraged to be original with some very far-fetched results. As I was now twenty-one and in a class full of girls in gym slips, I seemed by comparison a genius and behaved like one. I went to school, as one might say, in mufti, but my hair and my fingernails were long enough to cause comment from strangers on the way there and back.

Chapter 5

My father hated me chiefly because I was revolting but also because I was expensive. Sometimes he would turn on me at the dinner table and hiss, "Don't eat so much butter on your bread." To such injunctions I paid even less heed than usual, for our life now seemed to be luxurious. I have since decided that with the move out of London my father had abandoned common sense altogether and plunged into a financial gamble that in his own way he was shortly to win.

We occupied what I would now call a very ordinary four-bedroom house and employed a housemaid and a gardener. This last feature of opulence was due not so much to the size of the garden as to the fact that nothing would have induced me to till or even to scratch the soil. I don't hold with flowers even when they are as good as artificial ones.

We also had a car but this could hardly be looked upon as a status symbol. Every car that my father bought was broken down. He chose them like this deliberately so that he could spend almost all the weekend in the garage repairing them. This was a way of avoiding being with his family. Man goes and buys a car and lies beneath. When he was not tinkering with it, he was making the car the subject of one of our recurring Strindberg dramas. Every Sunday afternoon he asked my mother if she would like to go for a drive. She, who had learned her lines perfectly, said that she would.

"Where would you like to go?"

My mother then ploughed her way conscientiously through the list of places that were within driving distance. She was told that they were too far away or at the top or bottom of hills that were bad for the car. Then she was allowed to say, "Well, anywhere. I don't mind."

"If you don't care where we go," my father would conclude, "we might as well stay at home."

But we didn't and the whole afternoon was hell.

About eighteen months after we moved to High Wycombe, the dreary ritual of our lives was interrupted by my mother going away for a few days. What caused this to happen, I can't remember. Perhaps she left in self-defense. This was a very rare occurrence as neither my father nor I could boil a kettle unless conditions were favorable. This was further evidence of the rigid sexual structure of the world at this time. Men fetched coal from cellars and hammered nails; women boiled kettles. You knew where you were even though you hated it.

My father and I got on shakily but, to my amazement, not badly. We spoke to each other. He asked me what I intended to do with my life and at last I understood that the future was now. Neither of my parents ever said to me, "You're mad but, when you go out into the world, you will doubtless meet people as mad as you and I can only hope that you get on all right with them." Such words as these would have been a great help. Instead, my mother protected me from the world and my father threatened me with it. My feeling of inadequacy increased steadily. I remember a day when my mother and I stood beside the road at Loudwater station and waited for my father to emerge from the London train. As we stood there, a stream of men in dark suits and bowler hats went by us. I thought, "I'll never be able to get into step with them." I felt as I had in childhood when two other children turned a skipping rope and urged me to run under it and start jumping. I couldn't do it.

Hateful was the dark-blue serge . . . O, why should life all labor be? Perhaps I was a born lotus-eater suffering from permanent symptoms of withdrawal.

At the end of one of the ominous but not hostile conversations with my father that took place during my mother's absence, he said, "The trouble is you look like a male whore."

This cheered me up a little as I had not then taken my final vows. I was in a twilit state between sin and virtue. The remark was the first acknowledgment that he had ever made of any part of my problem. In gratitude I promised that when I went up to London at Christmas, I would try not to come back.

Chapter 6

At the Black Cat (which by this time honored me by turning me out) there had been one young man who had come in for a certain amount of notoriety by boasting that he was not on the game. In proof of this claim he carried books under his arm and occasionally snubbed the other members of the clientle with snippets of literature—chiefly by Michael Arlen. He was the least likable of the lot. It was inevitably him that I got to know best. Being at the losing end of human relationships does not necessarily mean that you are perpetually climbing toward a vanishing ideal. After a while your despondency may bring you to a halt where you can be overtaken by absolutely anyone who wishes to know you. If I was standing still and he was reaching up to me, he must have come from depths that only Dante could calculate. I didn't think of this. He was the only person of my own age whom I knew well and who lived by himself in London. Whenever I had saved up enough pocket money to pay the fare from High Wycombe, I went to stay with him for weekends. Once I even allowed myself to be nagged into inviting him for a day or two to my parents' house. He was short, with black hair ending in a staccato manner at the back, and his thumbnails were wider than they were long. When my mother saw them she made the special face that people make when they hear a knife skidding across a tin plate. She was very good at this expression. Toward the end of her life, she went into it whenever fingernails were even mentioned. She was halfway there by nature, having a high bridge to her nose, hooded eyes, and lips that were made for sucking a lemon.

When the time came for me to leave home for good, with a red handkerchief full of cosmetics tied to a birch rod over my shoulder, it was toward these thumbnails that I turned my steps. The world lay all before me—like a trapdoor.

In letters so voluminous that the postman scarcely had strength to deliver them, we had made our plans. My friend had taken a flat in Baron's Court, which we shared for three months. He seemed genuinely pleased that we were going to live together. I am so constituted that if I am told someone does not like me, I say, "Why?" but, if I am told that they do, I only put my head on one side and lower my eyelids. I therefore never asked myself what on earth this man hoped to gain by setting up house with me. We were not lovers and soon we were not friends, but he never told me to go, though within weeks it transpired that I was a dead loss. I had no capacity to survive. He had probably guessed that if our lot was to be improved he would have to drag me forward, but after living with me for a week, he knew that if our affairs were merely to stay the same he would have to hold me up.

He had visited my home and seen that I was invincibly middle class or worse (my mother had a faint cockney accent), but I may have seemed to him to be of high degree. Perhaps he thought that one day something must come of all talents I claimed by implication to possess. I never stopped quoting my own stories, plays, and poems. If he did think this, it would have carried great weight, for what Mr. Haggard was to me, Mr. Arlen was to him. He lived in an all-pervading dream about the well-born, the well-paid, and the well-publicized. About the worship of talent and fame there is something gay and forward-looking. A neophyte may one day achieve some measure of these things for himself but I can never help flinching from a display of undue reverence for titles. It seems so hopeless and self-wounding. This young man fell upon the thorns of class; he bled. Nothing would induce him, he once told me, to have his shoes cleaned in the street. It was such a cruel display of the master-servant relationship. When we were camping, one sunny day, with some men laying pipes in Hyde Park, he was shattered because one of the workmen said of a roll of putty that he was manipulating, "The more you play with it, the longer it gets. It's like a navvy's prick." While I was trying to pretend that I had not heard this affront to my maidenly modesty, Thumbnails was recovering from the pain of having heard a laborer pierce himself to the heart by calling himself a "navvy."

For whatever prestige he hoped my companionship would bring him my companion paid a punishing price. It was 1931. I had no job and most of the time he had none. We were driven to some dodgy expedients, and he had not only to run risks on my behalf but also to put up with my unconcealed disgust for the methods by which he provided food that my moral compunction never prevented me from eating. As we all know from witnessing the consuming jealousy of husbands who are never faithful, people do not confine themselves to the emotions to which they are entitled.

Our great money-saving device was used on the chain teashops—A.B.C., Lyons, etc. We patronized them (or should I say they patronized us?) only during rush hours, going in separately but sitting together. We ate fast so as not to use up all the rush hour and asked for separate bills so that we could leave one at a time. We took it in turns to go first. Whoever did this went to the pay desk and changed sixpence into coppers to make a telephone call so that the manageress would see him speak to the cashier. If he was challenged, he said his friend was paying. Whoever remained behind could try anything. He could pass the cash desk in the crowd; he could say his friend had paid; he also could ask for pennies to make a telephone call, but against this move there would in any chess book be a bracketed question mark; he could pay his own bill; or he could admit defeat and pay both. This almost never happened. In six months, we nearly always ate one or two free meals a day.

I did not object to these felonies because they were against the law. My very existence was illegal. I was embarrassed by their pettiness and cross because, if I were apprehended in connection with any of them, the snow-white brand image of a homosexual person, toward which I had begun intermittently to work, would be dimmed. So far, however, I couldn't really afford virtue, so I settled for indignation with vice. It served roughly the same purpose and was much cheaper.

While I was still living in Baron's Court, my father won his great gamble with the future. He died. On hearing of the death of anyone I have known well, I have usually experienced a slight thrill of pleasure. Another witness to my stupidity or weakness has been silenced. When the telegram announcing my father's death arrived, I felt nothing except irritation at the thought of having to go home, attend the funeral, and come back. Though I loathed my life in London, I knew that this was what I must do. If I stayed away, the same nagging from my family would begin all over again. Not that I was free from being nagged in London. Indeed reprimands constituted almost the whole of my flat-mate's discourse—especially when we were in public. While we sat in the various teashops or walked along the streets, smiling and nodding so as to seem to strangers to be talking airily of this and that, he was saying, "You look terrible. Push your hair back from your forehead. Not abruptly as though I had mentioned it. Casually. That's a bit better. And for

God's sake don't look so crushed. Smile." This kind of nagging I hardly minded at first. It made everything I did or said or looked a matter of importance, but as feelings of hunger, hopelessness, and hatred began to weaken even my interest in myself, I started to long to get away. Freedom did not come for six months. Before then my talent for attracting public ridicule was to be put to the greatest test so far. I went on the stage.

One evening Thumbnails, introducing himself as a journalist, arrived in the dressing room of the specialty dancer of a pantomime in Hammersmith. One of her numbers had included a few hit-or-miss *fouettés*. He told her that if, on a given night, she were to do thirty-two of these steps, it would constitute a record and be worth mentioning in the papers.

On the night in question the pantomime dancer, in fact, shuddered to a halt after barely beginning her marathon, but journalism, like the Light of Lights, looks on the motive not the deed, and the story was printed just the same. When the papers came out everybody kissed everybody and the dancer was so grateful that she allowed herself to be persuaded to take part in a charity matineé at the Scala Theater, in aid of some hospital or other. In order to stay on stage, for more than a two-minute solo (which she fully intended to do, for her charity toward hospitals must not be doubted), the dancer explained that she must have a partner to wave his arms while she changed her costume and got her breath back. My flat mate assured her that he knew just the person for the job.

Except for fighting with my little friend on the stage of Sutton Town Hall and playing the part of a madman in High Wycombe amateur theatricals, I had had no previous stage experience whatsoever, but by this time, my whole life was an unsympathetic part played to a hostile audience. I felt that I had already done sufficient basic training. For the part of the act that involved me, the dancer had decided to do an acrobatic solo that she knew by heart, with me as a sort of visible stage hand. This number showed her as an idol enthroned on an altar and me as a slave—the Oriental equivalent of a church brass cleaner. With matters arranged thus, a few sketchy rehearsals were thought to be sufficient.

When the curtain went up on this part of the bill, I was revealed with my back to the audience in I can't remember whose pyjama trousers with my upper half sporadically coated with "slave white." I looked like an insufficiently basted chicken. As I moved one arm commanding a second layer of curtains to part, there was a deafening roar of laughter. I took this calmly. To me it was just like Piccadilly Circus. My partner must have been a bit surprised. She went bravely on, however, twisting, turning, writhing while I ran about the stage or clung to her for support, liberally streaking her unattainable whiteness with my orange makeup. As long as I was moving, the audience kept on laughing. When the curtain came down, we could have continued to bow until our discs slipped. The audience would have applauded forever.

Chapter 7

By this time my companion and I were living in King's Cross, a much more fertile region than the one we had just left. Baron's Court had been a no-man's-land in which the houses were blind with stained glass and, on the pavements, raw trees no thicker than your arm stood in straitjackets of chicken wire wincing at every breath of wind. Our new location was loud with the noise of steam trains and lousy with teashops that had a well-defined rush hour.

Things were better without, but they had grown worse within. We now shared a double room for which the rent was eleven shillings each and we were almost never apart. My roommate's idea of companionship included having me sit on the edge of the bath while he cleaned his teeth. My aversion caused me to live in a state of tension every moment that I was not alone, but the middle-class morality in which I had been so carefully reared prevailed. I hissed but I almost never shouted. I don't expect that this self-restraint would have lasted indefinitely but it didn't have to. After three months in King's Cross, news reached me from my mother which broke the siege.

My mother had a genius for making and keeping friends. This talent was instinctive and was exercised without a hope of profit. It was merely my good fortune that at least twice she was able to turn it to my account. The woman who many years before had introduced us to Mrs. Longhurst now, for my mother's sake, persuaded one of the directors of a vast firm of consulting electrical engineers to give me employment. I was absolutely amazed. He paid me two pounds ten shillings a week for eighteen months before coming to his senses. Until I had been in work long enough to become eligible for the dole (fifteen shillings threepence a week) I almost held my breath. After that point was passed, my relief became evident in my general demeanor and particularly in the returning length of my hair and my fingernails.

Even greater than my joy at the prospect of one day being able to draw unemployment insurance was my ecstasy at moving into a room of my own. Once I had achieved this I was happy. All the reactions that other people have described to me when at last they found someone to live with—the heightened perception of the world around them, the inability to refrain from taking little skips as they walked—all these were mine on realizing that I might with luck never have to live with anyone again.

I was happy. The room I took (and even this I couldn't find without the help of the roommate I was so gladly leaving) was in darkest Pimlico. It had Nottingham lace curtains at the window, corned-beef linoleum on the floor, and a brass bedstead in one corner. Some of my friends said how lucky I was to have been let in, while others laughed the room to scorn and implored me to chi-chi it up. I didn't listen. I was happy.

At work I never once understood what I was doing. In theory I was employed as an engineer's tracer. This was one of the many kinds of work at which I could never hope to become proficient. Accuracy is alien to my nature. Many years later a woman asked me what a "point" was. When I told her it was a seventy-second part of an inch, she said, "But there isn't such a thing, really. Is there?" That is what I have always secretly thought. When I was given plans to trace, I copied the mistakes as well as the revisions and neither of them properly; when I was told to transfer the positions of electric pylons from one map to another I did so with such a jolly laugh that construction men telephoned from distant shires to ask what on earth was going on at head office. If any housewife has a pylon among her rose bushes, if any country clergyman has a pylon sticking up through his church roof, if any borough surveyor has a pylon blocking his main thoroughfare, may she or he read here that I apologize. May it comfort them to know that I was happy.

When I was not at work, I sat in my room and wrote plays, poems, libretti, stories, which were never to see the light of publication. The crippling weakness of all these works was that the ideas they sought to embody were far too highbrow for my sub-Tennysonian style. This is the main fault in all the writings that I have ever read in manuscript. The poverty from which I have suffered could be diagnosed as "Soho" poverty. It comes from having the airs and graces of a genius and no talent. But I was happy.

On evenings when I felt that I could write no more I went to visit friends, boys from the cafés who had rooms in houses where no landladies fly, or girls with whom I had been at art school. The journey there and back I nearly always made on foot to show that I could. It was getting harder all the time.

Exhibitionism is like a drug. Hooked in adolescence, I was now taking doses so massive that they would have killed a novice. Blind with mascara and dumb with lipstick, I paraded the dim streets of Pimlico with my overcoat wrapped around me as though it were a tailless ermine cape. I had to walk like a mummy leaving its tomb. At every step one foot had to land directly in front of the other. My knees ground together. After about a mile of walking thus, my trousers began to wear out between the knees; after two miles I began to wear out. Sometimes I wore a fringe so deep that it completely obscured the way ahead. This hardly mattered. There were always others to look where I was going.

As my appearance progressed from the effeminate to the bizarre, the reaction of strangers passed from startled contempt to outraged hatred. They began to take action. If I was compelled to stand still in the street in order to wait for a bus or on the platform of an Underground railway station, people would turn without a word and slap my face; if I was wearing sandals, passers-by took care to stamp on my toes; and once a crowd had started to follow me, it grew and grew until no traffic could pass down the road. If I didn't put a stop to this quickly, by getting on a bus or going into a shop, the police had to deal with it. Barging his way through the yelling crowd or coming at me from a side street, the constable would say, "You again. Move on." Then, turning on the rabble with raised arms, he would tell them that it was over—that there was nothing to see (both of which statements were untrue). In a weary voice, he would implore them to pass along the pavement. I was excited, exhausted, and worried by these crowds but, because I had never yet been savaged by them, I was not frightened. Because I still believed that I could educate them, I was happy.

Chapter 8

Homosexuals have time for everybody. This is not only an instance of the known law that all outsiders are polite to insiders because at best they secretly revere them or at worst fear that they may one day need them. Homosexuals are sincerely interested. They will sit for hours on stairs while chars complain about their rheumatism; they will stand at street corners while postmen rage against the handwriting of correspondents; they will pay extra fares to hear conductors rail against their wives. Every detail of the lives of real people, however mundane it may be, seems romantic to them. Romance is that enchantment that distance lends to things, and homosexuals are in a different world from the "dead normals" with many light years dark between. If by some chance an hour of pointless gossip makes fleeting reference to some foible, some odd superstition, some illogical preference that they find they share with the speaker, homosexuals are as amazed and delighted as an Earthman would be on learning that Martians cook by gas.

I have this lust for small talk. Nobody escapes my love. When I was not writing my interminable manuscripts or stalking the streets, I was scrabbling away with my bare hands at the hearts of all the people who couldn't get away. At this time my friends were few because of the difficulties attendant upon knowing me. Many I could never visit because they had resident husbands, fathers, or landladies; others I could visit occasionally but not meet in public because it was too embarrassing. On the other hand there was a handful who hardly liked my company at all but loved to cling to my arm in the street and fracture themselves with merriment while housewives hissed and workmen spat upon the ground before my gilded toes.

All were welcome in my room in Denbigh Street. Among my visitors were the student from High Wycombe and the student from Battersea whose cousin, when alone with me, flung herself on the floor at my feet and said she wasn't worthy of me. This was true but I never understood why she brought the subject up. A male prostitute (renamed Greta on account of his reverence for Garbo) used to call, and a model whom I had met in Hyde Park who brought with him a Czech gentleman with an unspellable name. But my most faithful guests were an Irish boy, his friend who was a deserter from the Seaforth Highlanders, and a girl who ran a shuttle service between them.

My friendship with the Irishman was a sexless variation on a well-known theme. I have no doubt that I met him at the Marble Arch. In those days there must have been a picture of this monument and a map of the surrounding streets on the wall of every gentlemen's lavatory in Cardiff, Glasgow, Belfast, and points west, for whenever a ruined Celt arrived in London, this is where he came to rest—or should I say work? And the sort of man who liked that sort of thing could go there and pick one of these boys from the wall as though he were plucking a peach—which, indeed, some of the specimens resembled.

If these down-and-outs were innocent when they arrived and merely stood about at Marble Arch in order to be with their countrymen, they soon learned to tap the steamers and before long to aim for the rich-looking homosexuals. It was especially the Irish who concentrated on these. They felt that with them they could run up and down the scales of flattery without a hint of *pianissimo*. Though they did this for venal ends, they also enjoyed it. It was the exercise of their native genius. As Italian is the language of song, Irish is the voice of flattery. From the lips of these young men I have heard phrases so archaic and hyperboles so florid that even Mr. Synge could not have used them without a giggle. When they gave it up you knew they liked you. This was the stage in our friendship that the Irish boy and I had reached by the time he was my guest in Pimlico.

Though mercifully the flattery dies, the hard-luck story never fades. If I were asked what the word "con" meant, I would say that it was something done by impecunious Irishmen to English queers.

So the reason why the Irishman, his friend, and their girl called on me so often was because they were always in need of sixpence. Knowing someone poorer than myself when I only earned two pounds ten shillings was a luxury, and I usually tried to indulge myself as well as them. Their own description of the situation was that they "tapped me unmercifully," but if I refused them a loan they never turned nasty, and when I gave them something I never asked for it to be returned or suggested that they should do anything to deserve it. In this way our friendship was kept pleasant for a great many years. It faded gracefully as time and the world intervened.

While I lived in Pimlico and worked at my first job, I did not reach that state of terrible gaiety that I was to achieve later. To some extent I still lived in the future—a habit which is the death of happiness. I wrote a play about Helen of Troy and looked forward to the day when it would be published along with a lot of other works. I still hoped to find tolerance for my kind and love for myself, though I now saw that this could not be reached by means of sex. It would be less true to say that I saw through sex than to say that I no longer saw through it. It had ceased to be a door to a sustaining relationship. It had become its slightly distasteful self. For many years I was at least happy enough to live without sexual encounters at all. Sex is the last refuge of the miserable. All the same I indulged in fantasies of living the public life of a famous writer, painter, or actor combined with the private life of a clean-up odalisque. When I switched these dreams off and came to terms with my true expectations, I could not avoid seeing that I was always going to have a very circumscribed life. If traveling to Ealing was like embarking on a crusade, I could be fairly sure that I was never going to Rome or Paris or New York; if it had taken me twenty-two years to crawl into a job that I could only do badly, I was never likely to live the briefcase life. I must not expect that I would ever have money or influence. I had better decide on some one small thing that I really wanted and aim to achieve some measure of that. I chose happiness and, like Bernard Shaw's serpent, I set about willing what I had imagined and creating what I had willed.

The essence of happiness is its absoluteness. It is automatically the state of being of those who live in the continuous present all over their bodies. No effort is required to define or even attain happiness, but enormous concentration is needed to abandon everything else.

Graham Greene has boasted that wherever we can show him happiness, he will show us ignorance, selfishness, and greed. Had his words been written forty years ago, I would have known that much sooner that happiness was something for which I was naturally equipped. Unfortunately there are two other requirements—good health and solvency. The first of these prerequisites I have enjoyed almost continuously since people ceased to look after me, but the second has failed me at several periods of my life. One such wave of penury was to engulf me within a week of leaving my job with the electrical engineers.

Chapter 9

When I was swept down into this second trough of destitution, I found myself in general worse off than when I had first come to London, but there were a few respects in which my lot was improved. I lived on my own. It is hard enough to share wealth without being involved in undignified scenes; shared poverty consists of nothing else. Alone, I could spread the little money I had to cover—or almost to cover—my vital needs and I could decide, without that irksome effort toward consistency which I always make in the presence of others, just which underhand dodges I would attempt and which were so risky as to be beneath me. After a while my morality came to rest at a level at which it has remained ever since. If I saw someone ahead of me in the street drop a pound note, I would overtake him and give it back, but if I found a pound note in the gutter and had no idea to whom it had belonged, I would certainly not take it to the nearest police station. I imagine most people come gradually to some completely illogical code of this kind and describe themselves as reasonably honest.

Another way in which things were now better than they had been in King's Cross was that instead of receiving every week fourteen guilt-edged shillings from my mother, I drew fifteen shillings threepence from the taxpayers who, though they complained more, could afford it better. Getting the money was one of the ways in which life was harder.

The Pentonville Labour Exchange looked like a vast one-story barn and issuing appropriately from it I always heard a bellowing sound. This was the noise which, as soon as I appeared on the horizon, was set up by the four-deep queue that permanently surrounded the building. The lowing was sustained *fortissimo* during the whole time that I was inside the building and only died away as I disappeared around the corner of the street. To such a din I was already more or less inured. What came as a shock was having what modern tube travelers call the "rush hour technique" practiced in a spirit of mockery upon my person. While I was in the middle of the queue, both hands were fully occupied in fending off the fumblers who were busy fore and aft. It was a mercy that I was able to press my genital organs firmly against the counter at the moment when one hand had to be released for the purpose of signing the book. Only the eternal presence of two policemen, one at each door of the building, prevented a fight.

One day, after weeks of this ritual, a solemn but benign figure appeared on the other side of the counter and beckoned me. The tumult and the shouting died; the moving fingers left my fly buttons. A clerk lifted up the flap of the counter and pointed toward the doorway through which the manager had receded. His office was very small and, apart from his own desk, crowded with at least three others. At these clerks sat with their heads bowed and their pens poised a fraction of an inch above their work. I do not think a single figure was written while I was in the room.

The ruler of the Labour Exchange motioned me to sit on a chair in front of his desk and began to address me in a magisterial but kindly voice. "I came out to see what all the noise was about," he said. "I suppose you know it's on account of you."

Me: Yes, sir.

Ruler: I see we have you down as an engineer's

tracer. Do you think, looking as you do, that you are likely to get work of this kind?

Me: I would like to find work as a commercial artist.

While employed by the electrical firm I had attended evening classes in life drawing and illustration at the Regent Street Polytechnic. (The principal of St. Martin's School of Art had refused to admit me, saying that it was a miracle that I had a job at all and that I had better not try to change it.) I now mentioned these studies in the hope of seeming serious-minded. I said it might be a little less unlikely that I would find work in a studio than in an office. My inquisitor agreed. He couldn't stop himself from asking why I had adopted such a peculiar appearance. Then not only the pens but the pulses of the surrounding clerks stood still.

Ruler: Why do you go about looking as you do?

Me? Because this is the way I am. I wouldn't like you or anyone else to think I was ashamed.

He must have been a truly enlightened man for, though we were still stumbling through the sexual darkness of 1933, he did not ask me what I meant. He said, "I think you're making things very difficult for yourself." Then he rose to his feet and I to mine. "You had better go out by this door," he added kindly, escorting me to a staff entrance. When I turned in the doorway to thank him he said, "If it all gets too much for you, come and see me again. I will see what I can do." As he uttered these words he placed his hand on my shoulder, a gesture which, in the circumstances, amounted to a daring vote of confidence. He was the first official ever to treat my problem as at least real to me.

The fifteen shillings threepence which through his beneficence I drew from the Labour Exchange for six months had to be eked out very carefully.

I took a room, the rent of which was six shillings a week, in a Clerkenwell house which belonged to a superannuated policeman and his wife. They were typecast. I could almost see on her hands the flour from the first pie with which she had lured her husband from his beat down the area steps into her kitchen. The attic which they let to me was long enough to lie down in but would not have been wide enough for that purpose and was too low to stand up in. A six-foot man would have died of lumbago. The furniture consisted of a bed as narrow as a coffin (though not as peaceful), beside which stood a wash-stand with a jug and basin on it. At the foot of the bed was a little table with a chair placed so that a man of no cubic capacity whatsoever could sit there. But not only could no one, however starved, have made use of the chair where it stood; he could also not sit on it anywhere else. It could not be extricated from its position without the whole place being dismantled. The room had a window through which I could squeeze myself onto the roof. Here in the better summer weather I used to lie on the foot-wide parapet that ran around the top of the house. I hoped I would go to sleep and fall into the street below. I never did. Even a cheap death is hard to come by.

After paying my rent, I had nine shillings threepence left, of which a shilling a day was spent on food. On week days I could eat a midday meal for this amount in a dining room near Euston Station. It was run by a big blonde woman whose conversation was a sort of ad lib trailer for *Coronation Street*. I used to go to her restaurant after the lunch-hour crowd had left and before the food had had time to get cold. She gave me whatever food she wanted to get rid of, saying that all the other dishes written on the blackboard had not turned out very nice. "Cut it on the bias," she screamed down the service-lift shaft to her husband. This he certainly did. At every meal I leveled to the ground two pyramids of food that would have daunted a Pharaoh.

Throughout my early life, the amount of food I ate was a cause for incessant criticism by my friends. At first I used to point out in a whimpering voice that most of my acquaintances only saw me in cafés where, since I sat in them from noon to nightfall and sometimes beyond, the least I could do to appease the proprietors was spend money. Later I grew tired of defending myself. I take it to be axiomatic that people are revolted by witnessing the shameless gratification of an appetite they do not share.

To this rule the proprietress of the 1s. diner-restaurant was an exception. If the place was empty she abandoned the work of clearing up to sit and watch me eat. Her kindness was an absolutely genuine emotion based on the snobbery of the times.

In spite of my astonishing disdain, I had still not succeeded in shaking off my former roommate. This was just as well. He had discovered both the attic and the dining room which now made my existence possible. We often ate together but, though his airs and graces were far less pronounced than mine, the proprietress did not like him. She fed him well but spoke of him badly. "It's different with you, luv. But him! Why, some of the lads around here went to school with him." She felt that he should have spoken the same language as they and not tried to deceive her into treating him with respect. This attempted imposture made him unworthy of extra helpings of jam roll. I have no way of knowing that she did not disparage me to him when he was there alone but, as far as I could see, she was pleased with me. I was a real gentleman. This by itself would have been but little recommendation. What mattered was that I was of high degree but at low ebb. Every ladleful of mashed potato that she sloshed on to my plate, in her heart she flung into the face of the existing social order. Not with imprudence but with a kindness that not even Christ (the gentleman with the longest hard-luck story of them all) could disapprove, she became for a moment the superior of her superiors.

This attitude of mind was one of the two great snobberies by which I was amazed to find that I could profit. The second was the common man's reverence for the arts.

Art, by which the people who used the word always meant painting, was in those days sacred. It had not yet fallen into disrepute by becoming a game that any number could play. It was not a profession by which a great deal of money could be made. It was still a divine madness which caused the possessed to grow their hair long and lead lives of unalleviated poverty. Once, when I fainted in an Express Dairy, the manageress almost carried me downstairs to a part of the restaurant that was not used in the evenings. There she fed me with her own hand as though I were a pigeon—only rarer. "You're an artist, I expect," she murmured. "You don't always remember to have regular meals." I gave a wan smile of gratitude and, touched by her sweetness, paid my bill.

Later, when I lived in Chelsea (which was proof positive that I was not of this world), this deference to art often saved my skin. As I stood pressed against the railings of some dim London square with a stranger's hand at my throat or my crotch or both, another member of the gang would whisper, "But he's an artist. I seen him in Chelsea." Immediately the grip on my person would loosen and, in a shaken voice, my aggressor would say, "I didn't know."

The art that I practiced at this time consisted of rearranging the position of the words "Sea View" on the letterhead of some boarding house in Brighton. This it did not seem necessary to mention.

When I had eaten my sixth huge meal of the week in the dining room by Euston Station, there was, in theory (if no disaster such as having to buy a piece of soap had overtaken me), three shillings threepence left for buying Sunday dinner. When, many years after this time, a friend of mine went to Israel to keep house for a doctor, she wrote and asked if I knew of any recipes that required no stove and no food. I couldn't help her, and I couldn't help myself when I lived in Clerkenwell. I had no idea how to live cheaply. I used to buy a loaf of bread, a pint of milk, and a hunk of black chocolate so hard that the confectioner could only break it with a small axe which possibly he kept solely for this purpose. These provisions I consumed lying on my bed, which I seldom left for the whole weekend (unless lured out by other people's food). It is easier to starve supine than erect.

That was how I spent Saturday and Sunday when things had gone well. Quite often I had by this time already been bullied by the local boys into parting with several pennies or, worse, a sixpence. Even those who had seen me at the Labour Exchange were not above begging from me.

In spite of my intense interest in these men I never came fully to comprehend the attitude they adopted toward me and my kind. This may partly have been because I feared and desired and sentimentalized them. It may also not have been their intention that I should understand them. If I was busy trying to seem mysterious and aloof to them, we must not rule out the possibility that they were reciprocally engaged.

This denomination of the homosexual religion is quasi-normal, and the same exaggerated and oversimplified distinction that separated men from women in the outer world ran like a wall straight and impassable between the "roughs" and the "bitches." I was over thirty before, for the first time, I heard somebody say that he did not think of himself as masculine or feminine but merely as a person attracted to other persons with male sexual organs. A confession of this nature would still bewilder and, perhaps, anger some of my homosexual friends. Quite recently a male prostitute of my acquaintance, on one of his amateur nights, picked up a young soldier only to find at the crucial moment that he had lumbered himself with a passive sodomite. "And, all of a sudden, he turned over. After all I'd done—flitting about the room in my wrap, making him coffee. You know, camping myself silly. My dear, I was disgusted. I made him get up and put on his clothes again." Whether he did in fact make the soldier get out of bed the instant the awful discovery was made is beside the point. The speaker wished all those who heard this tale to appreciate how clear a moral distinction there was between him and certain other people to whom sex is a mere pleasure mechanism. This point would have been understood immediately by the homosexuals I knew in my Clerkenwell days.

They were all pseudo-women in search of pseudo-men. To this idea the roughs undoubtedly pandered, either permanently because it was part of some self-congratulatory idea they had of themselves, or temporarily whenever they were with us. They consciously tried to embody the myth of the great dark man which haunts the dreams of pathological homosexuals and is the cause of one of their dilemmas.

This problem is similar to the one that confronts heterosexuals who happen to be ever so for virgins.

Recently a letter was published in one of the women's papers asking how the writer should deal with her young man. He had told her that he would only happily marry a virgin. He pointed out that he could not possibly know for certain that she was pure unless he had sexual intercourse with her. This letter may, in fact, have been written by the editor, but it poses a riddle that men are only slowly ceasing to try to solve. The parallel problem that confronts homosexuals is that they set out to win the love of a "real" man. If they succeed, they fail. A man who "goes with" other men is not what they would call a real man. This conundrum is incapable of resolution, but that does not make homosexuals give it up. They only search more frantically and with less and less discretion for more and more masculine men, and because they themselves are, however reluctantly, to some extent masculine, their judgment in these matters is for the most part physical. If you ask a homosexual what his newest true love is like, you will never get the answer, "He is wise or kind or brave." He will only say, "It's enormous."

Though, in the heterosexual world of the twenties and thirties, masculinity was sacred, the brand image of it had not come to its fullest flower in the minds of women. Their heroes were Rudolph Valentino and, later, Ivor Novello. It would have been delightful to know how the latter spoke in private of the parts which in public he played with such dash. In one play, to show how virile he was, he spat a piece of apple he was chewing onto the floor before demanding a kiss from a wicked woman in a low café in Montmartre.

Wicked Woman: But we don't love each other, do we?

Mr. Novello: What the hell do we care! (*They kiss.*)

Curtain.

This was masculinity stalking toward the deliciously quivering stalls.

Another thing that may have prevented women from coming out openly in favor of unretouched masculinity was that love and marriage in those days were still confused in their minds. They could only stretch out one hand toward the untamed male. With the other they were preventing the escape of someone whom they regarded as a suitable husband—a person of the same class, size, age, and nationality as they. Homosexuals do not need to divide their attention in this troublesome way. They can clutch with both hands at the myth of the great dark man. Their choice, unless they suffer from some subsidiary kink, is guided by the desire to bolster up, with a number of contrasts, that dream of themselves which it is their one increasing purpose to maintain.

To understand what kind of man they most admire it is only necessary to guess what they wish they themselves were—young, frail, beautiful, and refined. Hence their predilection is for huge, violent, coarse brutes.

Any of these characteristics that the roughs did not possess by nature, they could put on at a moment's notice as mating plumage. But they, too, had a problem.

The exotic had for them a great lure based on its rarity. The idea of the orchidaceous woman was everywhere. Greta Garbo and Marlene Dietrich leaned down from the screen and shamelessly poured sequins over the heads of the dreamers in the cheap front rows, but from the real lives of working-class men this element was almost totally lacking. The girls available to them were just like home. Parents in those days still had some say in what their daughters wore. Only prostitutes at the social level wore vermilion hair, gold eyelids, and green fingernails. The girl next door had to make a necessity of virtue.

Men appeared to go along with this idea but it was noticeable that, whenever pansies were in bloom, they couldn't resist doing a little window shopping. They must never admit to themselves or to God or to one another that they even liked the company of homosexuals—let alone that "trade" with them was a pleasurable pastime. Any attention that they paid to us had to be put in the form of an infliction. Such gestures as running their fingers through our hair were accompanied by insults about what a bloody awful mop it was. If they wished to make any more definitely sexual advances, these must be ruthlessly stripped of any quality of indulgence. I have known at least one heterosexual man who told me that, to be really satisfactory, all sexual intercourse must preserve the illusion of rape, so I was never able to decide how much of the inordinate interest taken in me by the Clerkenwell boys was due to sexual curiosity and how much was what it seemed—hatred. I longed to know, but I soon had to deprive myself of the strong stimulus that their proximity provided. The danger was too great.

Keeping out of their way was not easy for topographical reasons. A partial solution to the problem of how to avoid trouble at the hands of roughs would have been never to go out at a time when decent people were in their beds. Decency, however, must be an even more exhausting state to maintain than its opposite. Those who succeed seem to need a stupefying amount of sleep. Even by ten o'clock at night the streets of all the slum districts I ever lived in were empty of every living thing but toughs. To reach home at all after this hour I had to pass some of them.

The shortest route between the strictly comparative safety of the main road and my front door lay to the north, but this was the most densely populated part of the neighborhood. Therefore in a sense it was the most dangerous. If I had recently met with any trouble there, I used to try coming home through the quieter area to the south by walking up Rosebery Avenue and nipping into any of the dark turnings on the left when I judged that I was not being watched. The disadvantage of this plan was that, unless I went a very long way around indeed, I had to pass at the corner of Farringdon Road a coffee stall around which there was always a crowd of young men.

One night, when I had just risked this hazard, I became aware that I was being followed by more than one person. I was in trouble.

I lived every moment that I was out of doors in a state of feverish awareness. It covered only a limited area of human experience. Outside the field of my own safety I was the least observant person. I could never give people correct street directions nor describe places with any accuracy, even if they were landmarks that I passed every day, but if I heard strangers walking along the road behind me, I knew at once whether they just happened to be there or whether they were pursuers. I could usually gauge how many members of the hunt were present even though they might all be marching in step precisely for the purpose of deceiving me on this point. I could tell if there was a woman among them. The presence of a girl almost always meant that the situation was going to be less grim.

Once I had made up my mind about all these details, there were automatically a number of rules that must be followed. I must never look back; I must on no account run but must increase my rate of progress gradually. A pace of more than four miles an hour eliminates half-hearted murderers. Serious ones will, at this point, break into a run. You will then know for certain that your predicament is of the worst kind.

Even when overtaken and addressed (with some such words as "Who the hell do you think you are?"), I seldom ceased to walk fast until I was forcibly stopped. Then I would stand absolutely still and look at the person holding my arm. Sometimes a look (which must never be haughty) was enough to make them let go of my sleeve. If it was not, I would try an offer of money, whether they asked me for any or not. As of necessity the amount proffered was small, my aggressors frequently knocked it out of my hand. I was left with no other pacifying strategy than speech. I spoke very slowly and very quietly. This had the effect of compelling my enemies to listen but it was at best only a delaying tactic. While I talked, they remained silent if only to enjoy the luxury of hearing themselves called "Sir." But even I could not prolong a filibuster indefinitely. As soon as I paused for breath or by mistake asked a question, they started to work themselves into a frenzy by shouting, swearing, and laughing—a device that I am told is standard procedure in bayonet practice.

One night this ritual had just begun when a taxi

came down the street. I raised my arm and to my amazement the taxi stopped, but as soon as I got into it and the boys began to surge around, the driver realized what the situation was and, getting down from his seat, ordered me out of his cab. This was not what always happened. I have on other similar occasions known a taxi driver to run considerable risk to himself and his vehicle by moving slowly but persistently forward through dense crowds that hammered with their fists on the sides of the cab while inside I pulled, as though they were reins, at the leather straps which in those days held the windows of taxis shut.

The taxi driver in Rosebery Avenue, either from caution or moral indignation, had no intention of making a gesture in my favor. He stood in the road and continued to demand that I get out. This I did not immediately do. One of the boys started to drag me out. It was foolish of me to allow this to happen as, by resisting, I became part of the battle. As soon as I was in the street once more, the whole gang started to hit me from all sides. Almost immediately I fell on to my hands and knees in the gutter. For a second, I wondered whether I could stay there forever, but, fearing that I might be kicked, I staggered to my feet and was at once knocked across the pavement by a single, more carefully aimed blow. As I leaned against the front of Finsbury Town Hall covering my own equally ornate façade with my hands to try to prevent rivers of mascara from running down my cheeks, I said, "I seem to have annoyed you gentlemen in some way."

At this there was a sound of genuine amusement quite unlike the barking noise emitted by a lynching party. I knew that this was the moment to try to move away, though I could hardly see where I was going. As I lurched along the wall, voices shouted after me but no one followed. Apparently whatever point my enemies had wished to make had been established.

The mysterious thing in all such occurrences was not

that strangers, sometimes without a word being uttered on either side, attacked me. It was that they never killed me. Certainly fear did not restrain them. I never made even a pretense of defending myself (not because my behavior was modeled on Christian ethics but because to try would only have provoked redoubled ferocity from my aggressors), and no one ever came to my aid. Also, these young men must have known that whatever they did to me, there would have been only the most perfunctory police inquiry into the incident, yet though on two occasions I have lain for a few seconds unconscious on the pavement, I was never damaged beyond repair. My assailants did not apparently require my death nor even my disfigurement. This was why I concluded that a large part of their motive for attacking me was to release their sexual curiosity in a manner consistent with their heavily guarded idea of manliness. They were only slightly concerned with forcing me to accept their superiority. If this latter was their whole aim, then all those street brawls were a waste of time. I regarded all heterosexuals, however low, as superior to any homosexual, however noble.

Chapter 10

This skirmish must have occurred toward the end of my stay in Clerkenwell. By this time I was once again in a job. I remember that I had difficulty in forcing myself to go to work the following day. This was not because I felt ill. To my surprise I found, when I awoke the next morning, that I was not suffering even from the slightest headache. My reluctance to step outside the front door was due to the fact that when I looked in the looking glass (which I did the moment I was fully conscious) I saw that one side of my face was an ashy gray and the other the color of blackberry juice. I ought not to have worried about the comment that this might cause in the office. I should have known that I could rely on the Englishness of the English. No one said a word. This was probably not from lack of curiosity. One of the travelers for this firm told me that when the directors had given him lunch in the public house next door, the sole topic of conversation had been "whether I did or whether I didn't." Nevertheless they would have died rather than hear any of the details of my private life from my own two lips. They guessed—and they were right—that if they questioned me at all, no matter how flippantly, they would have had the whole truth forced upon them.

This new job, like my first, was found for me by my mother. Digging ever deeper through older and older strata of friendship, she had unearthed the wife of a publisher whom we had all known in Sutton. (I had been to one of their hateful parties during which, rather than play games in which somebody had to kiss somebody, I had sat in another room and played patience with cards which I had had the forethought to bring with me.) My mother, in a fragment of the voluminous correspondence which, now that she lived in farthest Devonshire, was her chief hobby, pleaded with this woman, who nagged her husband, who coerced a printing firm with whom he did a lot of business to employ me in their art department.

I was not a success. I sat in an upper room and tried to adapt myself to the whims of a man so moody that most days passed in a silence unbroken even by greeting or valediction. On others he danced and sang with such vigor that, even if there had been any work to which my talents were equal, I could not have done it. The swinging of the lamps and the shaking of the floor would have prevented me. Some of his moodiness was, I think, due to his red hair, but more was caused by the burden that he carried on my behalf. As the head of our department, one of his duties was to take whatever work I did downstairs to the directors and explain it if he could. Doing this always brought down upon him humiliations that he could hardly bear. As a commercial artist, I was as hopeless as I had been as a tracer. Indeed, the qualifications were the same for both occupations—a slow pulse, good eyesight, and a minimum of ideas. The word "slick," now a term of contempt, was then the highest praise. In all the long dark years that I was in or on the fringe of advertising, my work never attained any noticeable degree of this quality of high gloss. I was always compelled to spend hours retouching my lettering and hours more retouching the retouching until the paper was embossed with white paint. The words I had written could only be read by the blind.

After a year of watching me doing this, the red-haired artist gave notice. As he left he said, "I feel I ought to say something—give you some advice—but the thing for you to do is to carry on just the way you do now. You're as meek as a bloody lamb, but down there" (he jerked his fifteen-amp hair toward the floor, meaning in the board room—not in hell) "they know you don't care a damn about any of them and there's just nothing they can do about it."

He was wrong. I liked the directors; I had arranged to do so. I was secretly shocked to see stalking toward me naked what, in my first job, I had only seen heavily veiled—the senseless and implacable hatred that workers feel for their employers. This hostility was something to which I never grew accustomed. In my whole life, the only relationships with individuals (as opposed to crowds) that I took seriously were those that I managed to establish with the people for whom I worked. They paid me and this raised them higher in my esteem than any amount of praise or protestation of affection ever could. In return I was their slave. To the amazement and sometimes the disgust of my co-workers in various studios I never attempted to introduce any quality into my work that might be over the head of my boss. Nay, I executed drawings that I knew to be of the utmost banality with positive gusto, for whatever is done for money is sacred.

For the first three months in the printing firm, my employers and I were only engaged—not actually married. Explaining that I was on approval, they paid me nothing. Three times a week I was given permission to walk across London (it would have been madness to have spent a penny each way on fares) and sign on at the Labor Exchange. This was but one of the bewildering flashes in which the dark core of the mind of accountancy was revealed to me.

On one of the many days on which there was little that I could profitably do sitting at my desk, I was sent out to buy a pair of scissors. I went to Selfridge's department store, which I felt that I understood. It was thence that my snacks had been sent to me at boarding school. I bought some scissors for five shillings. When I returned and told the girl who kept the petty cash book how much they had cost, she became distraught. "I can't put down 'Scissors, five shillings,' " she wailed. "You can buy a pair in Woolworth's for sixpence." I tried to calm her by enumerating the ways in which the article I had bought was superior to anything sold by Woolworth's. While doing this, I happened to utter the words "paper shears." Her ivory brow smoothed out immediately. "Oh," she sighed, "I can put down 'Paper shears, five shillings.' That's quite all right."

I was delighted with this incident, but certain other features of the firm's economy were burdensome to me. The art department was supposed to "pay its way." Its share of the rent, light, and heat of the building was added to my wages and the cost of art materials. This sum, I was warned, ought to be covered by the prices charged for the work, although we all knew that these "art" fees were frequently lowered until they were out of sight, to make the printing estimate acceptable. The layouts were really nothing but appetizers. This and other monetary equations I endeavored to take seriously. I worked my brushes to the ferrule. As the other members of the staff clattered down the stairs in the evening, they called back over their shoulders, "Are you staying all night?" The first person to arrive in the morning, finding me already there, asked, "Have you been here all night?" I gave a mocking laugh, but I had. The solvency of the art department so worried me that I tried not to sharpen my pencils too often. Such flights into the absurd may have been launched partly by the trance of malnutrition in which I permanently floated. Friends prophesied that I would be blown away by the first winds of winter. I swayed obligingly but I did not grant their wish. I went on living.

I went on working.

The job meant a lot more to me than salvation from

the fumblers' queue at the Labor Exchange. It hushed, even if it could not silence, the terrible things said about me by my relatives which, though I never heard them directly, reached me slightly blurred on the great family intercom. Also I felt that commercial art might become a permanent means of getting by. Being employed by the electrical engineers had only taught me how to ask where the gentlemen's lavatory was without blushing. Now I was learning something which might be really useful. I never thought of work as something that would one day earn me a lot of money. Squalor was my natural setting. I did not hope that a job would extend me to the limit of my talents. I hadn't any. What I wanted to wrest from regular employment was something with which to bargain with the heterosexual world for acceptance as a homosexual. This evangelical zeal was the real motive for everything I did. It would subside for a while and then flare up again—especially if my employer had recently called me into his office and made another attempt to coerce me into altering my appearance. Without looking at me and moving the papers on his desk from side to side, he would say, "Fact of the matter is we don't particularly like employing people with plucked eyebrows and pointed fingernails." For a week or two my eyebrows, which usually marched across my forehead in single file, were allowed to form fours and the style of my fingernails was changed from Gothic to Norman.

Surprisingly, I was not dismissed. On the contrary, the day came when I was given an assistant. Thinking only of the havoc that an extra two pounds a week in wages would wreak on the firm's economy, I at first protested at this daring expansion. The directors, laughing heartily, pointed out how inconvenient it would be for them if, while I was the only member of the art department, I were to become ill or get run over by a bus. I asked them to provide me with a female assistant. I foresaw that there would be mutiny if a man were ever placed in a position where he had to do as I said. Whether my employers saw the sense of this I never knew, but they pandered to my whim and engaged a charming girl with whom I worked happily for about a year. This was the first time I had ever been in the position of a master instead of a slave. I tried to behave with the utmost tact so as not to inflict on my assistant any of the humiliations that had been heaped on me. One day, however, presumably because of some special pressure of work, when she held a drawing up for my approval, I said, "Yes. That's all right but the feet are bad." No sooner had these harsh words passed my momentarily unguarded lips than I hastened to soften their directness with chivalrous obliquities. "What I meant was," I began, "that certain superficial critics might say . . ." At this point she cut me short. "Thank God," she sighed. "You've said what you really mean at last."

In all I was four years with this firm, earning for my last few months there three pounds a week. Then the business was sold and I sensed that, for all their courtesy, my new bosses were waiting for me to go. For the first time in a long while I took a look at the outside world. To my delight, I found that the storm had largely abated. Jobs were no longer hard to get.

Now they were only hard to keep.

Chapter II

While I had not been watching, a number of tiny studios had sprung up at the tops of narrow buildings in Fleet Street and Chancery Lane. They had rather intimidating names like The Twentieth Century Advertising Service or The New London Studios. If I burst into any of these offices, I usually found two people playing table tennis in a nest of dirty teacups and the crumpled drawings of forgotten art students. One of the players would turn out to be the managing director and the other his staff. They didn't look pleased with my interruption of the day's business, but now they would nearly always give me their attention for a few minutes, though this was frequently directed more at the art work I had done on my face than at anything in my book of specimens. When I had first come to London, I had seldom got as far as undoing the arm-splitting portfolio I then carried.

During the next two winters I worked in some of these studios, whose staff could hardly be seen with the naked eye. In the summer the tide of advertising always mysteriously receded, leaving all firms but those with the deepest roots high and dry. In this period of drought someone from all these smaller concerns had to be asked to leave. This was always me. My feelings on being dismissed were a mixture of indignation and relief. By the time I was twenty-eight, I had tired of this experience. I easily found a way of preventing its recurrence. I gave up work.

I became a free-lance commercial artist. I reached the Canaan of all the more optimistic art students of that time. Unlike modern students, none of those who were with me at Battersea Polytechnic ever thought of becoming a teacher. The girls gloomily guessed that they would go into lampshade factories and die there unless, before the red-sailed sampan or the pear with russet leaf got them, they managed to marry. They seemed to realize that this was a desperate choice. To St. Paul marriage was barely preferable to hell. To women, though these two states may be the same, either was more to be desired than work. The male students tried to creep into studios or agencies, but only as a steppingstone to those bright fields where they would work for themselves. From the very first week of their employment they started to collect printer's pulls of every brush stroke that they made—a tailpiece, a decorated initial. These they kept under their drawing boards and fingered when the barrage of contemptuous criticism was loudest.

I cannot claim that from this moment I was always happy but, from the age of twenty-eight, I never did for long anything that I didn't want to do—except grow old.

I was elated by my freedom but I was anxious. Being a free-lance commercial artist would be taxing for anyone; for a person with no talent, it was hazardous.

I became a little man around the corner of advertising. I called on all the clients listed by all the studios I had ever worked in and offered to produce the same style of drawing as that to which they were accustomed, but more cheaply, more quickly, and worse. This ruse worked admirably then. It would be of no avail now. During the course of my lifetime, advertising has altered completely.

In that happy time when I first became a free-lance artist, advertising was a disgraceful trade. The confession that it was your chosen profession was received as though you had said, "I'm in burglary." It was run by businessmen who were presumed to have failed in more reputable concerns and staffed by artists and copywriters who felt that they were exiles from fine art and literature. Their function was to think up the atrocious pictorial and verbal puns, jokes, and riddles (Sheila Dore drinking Oxo) that appeared on the billboards. Then, at some time during the next few years, advertising became the great tax evasion racket and everything began to change. Instead of nagging their agencies to do more for less, manufacturers began to implore them to think up ways of using up their vast "appropriations." Even I, who never worked in any large advertising concern, was later to attend a meeting at which a client said, "But even if these counter dispensers are invoiced at two pounds each and we foist one of them on every one of our concessionaires, that will only use up about two thousand pounds. We must get rid of twenty thousand before the beginning of April." When this way of thinking became fashionable, advertising began to grow rich and attract an entirely different kind of employee—university graduates who brought with them a new ambience of fatuous elegance. If today you call on an up-to-date agency to hand in some copy for a two-inch single-column insertion in the daily press, you trudge through carpets as thick as pampas grass into a room lined with gilt mirrors. There a young man waits to extend toward you in perfunctory greeting at least four inches of cuff, transfiguration white. It is quite hard to remember that you have not come to have your hair waved.

In the sixties, if you tell anyone that you are a practitioner of advertising, you will still be treated as though you had said you were in burglary, but morality has changed. The increased scale of your operations will lend you respectability. Who, except possibly the

Postmaster General, would refuse to shake hands with one of the Great Train Robbers?

If, during my brief career as a commercial artist, any of these complexities were beginning to proliferate in advertising, they disturbed the atmosphere at a level far above my head. I merely ran in and out of business premises, studios, and printers' works trying to persuade people to change their catalogue covers, posh up their letterheadings, or decorate their leaflets with catchphrases or thumbnail sketches. My problems were small and mostly purely personal.

For anyone whose appearance is highly eccentric it is usually first meetings that are a special ordeal. In the days when I had looked for regular employment I had only the initial interview for each job to negotiate. Now that I was free-lancing, I had to face several such challenges every week. Since I depended for my livelihood on the goodwill of whomever I had come to see, these situations needed to be handled with much greater care than confrontations with strangers in the street. I found it necessary to develop a technique for being interviewed. This came into operation the moment I arrived at the reception desk. It began with not evincing any surprise as all the office boys fled through the doors nearest to them, firstly in order to fall about the corridors laughing without restraint and secondly so that they might spread to distant floors of the building the news of my advent. Then, while I waited for my appointment, I had to invent some artificial occupation for my attention so that it would seem natural for me not to look up as each member of the staff, carrying a meaningless piece of paper, came to speak to the receptionist. Finally there was the interview itself. At the start of this I must, by what actors call some piece of "business," allow my client a good look at me while I was not looking at him. I did not always succeed in giving him time to put his eyes back in his head before I turned my gaze upon him.

Once the initial shock of seeing me had worn off, my interviewer was sometimes so relieved to find that I was not actually mad or even in any other way unconventional that he gave me work out of simple gratitude. A second visit was usually quite easy at top level, though by this time all lesser personnel knew what to expect and the glass panels of whatever doors gave on to the route that I must travel were cloudy with the feverish breath of typists. It was now that I realized fully that, while I was apprehensive of strangers, any of the girls who might be forced to come close enough to me to hand me an envelope were trembling so that they could hardly stand. I never found anything except time that would remove this reaction of stark terror. In order at least to reduce it to a minimum, I cultivated an air of politeness bordering on subservience. Very slowly I was starting to go through that process that usually only convulses adolescents. I was learning not merely to confront people but to communicate with them.

In the outer world in which I was now struggling to make a living, prosperity was gradually returning to England. In the inner world in which I lived more intensely, things were getting worse. Possibly the two opposing trends were connected. It was only in the idealistic dreams of H. G. Wells that people became nicer as they acquired wealth. What in fact happened was that, as soon as men were released by affluence from the need for any unethical conduct themselves, they felt free to swoop down from their newly attained moral elevation upon the turpitude of others. To restore the self-esteem of which poverty had temporarily deprived them, the force of their condemnation exceeded the violence of any opprobrium that was formerly heaped upon them. In accordance with this rule, the fair name of vice was now being dragged through the mud by the English newspapers. It was hard to make dreary old fornication and adultery into news, so the press directed the hostile gaze of the public toward the deviates. About the private lives of these more and more facts and pseudo-facts were coming to light every week. At first I imagined that this increase of knowledge would herald the dawn of a new day when the butch lion would lie down with the camp lamb. To my disappointment I now realized that to know all is not to forgive all. It is to despise everybody.

The first rumors about homosexuality that were now spread abroad brought only fear. They suggested that it was a much larger monster than had originally been suspected, devoring not only all ballet dancers and a few actors but thrusting one claw in at the front door of the homes of apparently quite ordinary citizens. The cry went up that England was going to the bitches. The police, to show that they took this prognostication seriously, began to clean up the West End.

Even when I had first discovered the Soho cafés certain older male prostitutes were taking their amber cigarette holders from their lips to declare that nothing was what it used to be—that the police had ruined Piccadilly; but in those days detectives chased me and my friends through the streets chiefly to satisfy their own hunting instincts. That their quarry was supposed to be a menace to civilization was incidental. They mentioned it only as, when blood sports are being denounced, huntsmen drag in the fact that foxes are a nuisance to farmers. We were not taken seriously. We were thought to be the exposed part of a very small iceberg. The general estimate of the number and kind of men who might be interested in us was even less realistic. One of the first policemen who ever questioned me at a street corner, when he had decided to stand a little closer and change his bullying tone to accents of fatherly concern, warned me that the only people who would go with boys were men suffering from venereal disease. They would be ashamed to communicate this to a woman. He may not have believed this story himself but he certainly expected me to.

Such naive ideas as this were now no longer in fashion. Police methods were growing very much grimmer. The decoy system became a nightly routine. Those of my friends who had previously dreaded that they might be hounded into jail now began to fear that they might be vamped into it.

The main field of operations for this particular strategy were the dimly lighted public lavatories in the less populous areas of London. While one detective in plain clothes wandered about with vigilant unconcern on the opposite side of the street, his accomplice, selected by his superiors because his natural endowments made him specially suited to the work, stood inside the urinal "flashing"—demonstrating his do-it-yourself apparatus to anyone who happened to come in. (One cannot imagine how the kit inspection that would precede a stint of this duty would be conducted.) This trap worked well and by it many of the most unlikely people were lured to their doom. In modern times, when everyone knows about these maneuvers, they are falling into desuetude. Common knowledge robs them of their effect. They also offend the sporting instinct of the British people. It is thought to be a dodge comparable with deliberately placing a diamond bracelet on the pavement and pouncing from ambush upon anyone who picks it up. Almost exclusively it ensnared borderline cases. Those whose idea of a lovely way to spend an evening was to wander from one "gents" to another quickly learned to recognize a copper even by braille. It was persons who had never heard of homosexuality, but whose perfectly natural curiosity was aroused by any odd manifestation of human behavior, who were in such danger from these police techniques. One can be sure that, even on a good night, merely to ask the constable what on earth he was doing would lead to an arrest; on a bad evening, a brief glance in his direction would be enough. But the worst result of the decoy system was that, in a policeman who did not happen to favor queers, being given the chore of making himself attractive to them rapidly turned his dislike into ferocious disgust. In return homosexuals who originally feared the police, which some would consider to be a good thing, came to despise them.

From the law's point of view the only weakness of the decoy system was that it took two constables to apprehend one sexual offender. This was a waste of manpower. The police thought of homosexuals as North American Indians thought of bison. They cast about for a way of exterminating them in herds. With the aid of informers they discovered where the great drag dances were being held and turned their attention thither.

These balls were organized by private individuals and held in any of the large banquet rooms that can be hired for parties. They couldn't, of course, be advertised, but no publicity was needed. The network always managed to reach anyone who might want to go and had half-a-crown to spare for a ticket. About three-quarters of the men who attended these dances were in drag.

In a raid a hundred or more screaming, shrieking, fighting, kicking boys in feathered headdresses and diamanté trains could be scooped, pushed, or flung into vans by a relatively small squad of policemen.

Once, when I lived in Baron's Court, I traveled by Underground to Piccadilly Circus wearing a black silk dress and some kind of velvet cape. I went to the Regent Palace Hotel, had a drink, and talked airily of this and that with my escort, who was, I think, in a dinner jacket. Then I returned home. The evening was a triumph, in that it was boring; nothing happened. Since then I have never worn drag. Its only effect on me is to make me look less feminine. In women's clothes even a faint Adam's apple, even slightly bony insteps, are harshly conspicuous. I never attended one of these transvestite dances, but I very much doubt whether the charge brought against most of the guests—aiding and abetting an immoral performance—was founded on evidence. I suspect that they were very similar to the two or three drag parties that I have known. These were all exactly like one another. At none of them was there much sin. There was only a great deal of hysteria. I have sadly to say that to me everything about homosexuals was endearing except their gaiety. Being at a party at which they were having a really good time was like seeing a silent film of the twenties (with all the staccato haste and all the frantic mime) accompanied by a sound track recorded in the parrot house at the zoo. I do not expect such parties are given anymore. There is no need. Fancy dress has become national costume.

When these dances ceased to be given because they became too dangerous to be worth the pleasure, the police began to bend their ireful brows on the queer clubs.

To these no one in drag was ever knowingly admitted. An evening spent in one of them would almost always be quiet—even cozy. They were said to be places of assignation. They were to exactly the same extent as are all public houses, clubs, and evening institutes. Who would go to a Morris dancing class if the only hope were that it would lead to greater expertise in Morris dancing? Indeed, is not the whole world a vast house of assignation of which the filing system has been lost? These clubs were merely places where men could talk, drink, and dance together. It was the last pastime that so inflamed the imaginations of journalists, but though the foam dripped from their lips onto their typewriters as they worked, the word "homosexual," by the constant use of which modern periodicals seek to make it known that they are serious-minded, was never written down for all the world to see. Even Lesbians, generally thought to be not so sinful because they were less illegal, were not mentioned in so few words.

Policeman: There were also present women—of a certain class.

Magistrate (rubs his hands): Prostitutes?

Policeman (in a lower voice): Of another class.

Magistrate (after a long indrawn breath): Oh! I see.

In spite of their tameness, all these clubs for homosexuals were raided sooner or later, and the cases that followed enlivened the pages of the *News of the World* and the *People.*

The scandal of this kind that I remember best, because a commercial artist whom I knew was involved, concerned the Caravan Club. Proceedings lasted for a fortnight, at the end of which my friend, though sentenced to two weeks' imprisonment, was released on the grounds that he had suffered enough in the police court. The proprietor, a certain Mr. Neave, was clapped in for months. It is indicative of the oversimplified view of homosexuality that was still current that my friend took the trouble to persuade a young woman of his acquaintance to fluff out her hair and state in the witness box that she was his fiancée. This was supposed to make his visit to the club seem to have been a misguided sightseeing escapade. A present-day magistrate would merely think that the existence of the lady made matters worse.

I went to two or three of these clubs in my more optimistic days and observed that every year they grew more respectable or, at least, more restrained. Even in the beginning, when they were slightly sordid, I never felt at home. The management feared that my arrival and departure might draw the unwelcome attention of officials. This I understood, but it was with pained bewilderment that I came to see that even among the clientele my arrival caused a hush, clamorous with resentment.

I was beginning to meet a greater number and a greater variety of homosexuals and having to face the fact that, almost without exception, they did not like me.

Those who camped in private and watched their step in public felt that my not doing either was an indirectly expressed criticism of both these activities. They were right.

Though the strongest resist the temptation, all human beings who suffer from any deficiency, real or imagined, are under compulsion to draw attention to it. To their doing this I could hardly object since I was the living example of this obsession. But about camp, with its strong element of self-mockery, there seemed to me to be something undignified—even hypocritical. At its worst, it is a joke made by someone who acts in a certain way for laughs about a less fortunate person who makes the same gestures unconsciously. When I lived in Maida Vale in the flat of an invoice clerk, if I came into the kitchen and found him washing his socks, he could not have refrained from uttering some such phrase as "A woman's work is never done." I longed to cry out, "You are washing your socks because they are dirty. The situation needs no comment." I never did. I needed the room.

Even those who did not feel that I was secretly judging them were angry with me for presenting to the world, by whose good opinion they set great store, a brand image of homosexuality that was outrageously effeminate. This was resented chiefly by those who were effeminate but did not think of themselves as outrageous. Their objection was part of a much more widespread hostility to my putting forward any propaganda about the subject at all. Homosexuals generally did not look forward with pleasure to living in a world where the facts about their abnormality would be common knowledge and where even the least sophisticated people would learn to think of it as a possible explanation for any odd behavior. An American actor expressed to me the view that obviously gay boys were "spoiling it for the rest." I was dumbfounded by this remark, as to me "it" was not a pitch but an illness. It was as though he had said that consumptives who coughed ruined for others all the fun of tuberculosis.

Publicity is annoying to some homosexuals because they enjoy living incognito. This allows them to practice a hoax upon society and particularly upon its women, and with whom they carry on teasing flirtations. This masquerade seemed not merely unpleasant because it was contemptuous of the girls involved, but ultimately incomprehensible since the admiration or respect or love aroused were really for some other man of the same name. Possibly this perpetual confidence trick satisfied the hatred these men felt for the outer world.

One fact became inescapable. Homosexuals were ashamed. They resented not being in the mainstream of life. The feeling varied from irritation to the anguish of irrevocable exile. It had little to do with God or the neighbors or the police. It was private and irremediable.

Finding that homosexuals didn't like me was harder to bear than the hostility of normal people. To the latter reaction I had become accustomed long ago. There was even a sense in which I welcomed the animosity of the public. It seemed to demonstrate the necessity of my continuing to hammer away at them. The coldness with which I was received by my fellow guests at small gatherings of the faithless was wounding in the extreme. I felt it amounted to ingratitude, as I thought of my life as a burnt offering laid on the altar of their freedom. I could not see that this was but a contributory cause of their unfriendliness. If people speak badly of those who have done them a favor for which they have asked, what will be the attitude of those who find themselves in receipt of a sacrifice for which they have loudly proclaimed they have no use? This was a question that I never asked myself. I merely accepted an ostracism made complete by the fact that, owing to increasing police vigilance, the proprietors of even the wickedest cafés would no longer let me in. I looked increasingly for friendship among normal people. I put their tolerance to the utmost test not, as I imagined, by causing them to risk being involved in some wonderful scandal, but by never talking for long about anything but the social problems of my kind.

Among those who now began to shoulder this burden was the wife of the unspellable Czech who had been brought to my room in Pimlico. She was an artist's model and dressed in accordance with the rigid dress laws of the time. She wore a vermilion polo-neck sweater, curtain-ring earrings, and a black beret balanced at the ultimate degree of obliquity. Her days were spent working in the art schools and her evenings complaining of her husband who, in her absence, pawned her gramophone.

They were a lively pair, who lived in Warwick Avenue. To them I introduced my art school friend. At the weekend we often sat in the Czechs' basement flat talking of sex and eating a kind of sea wrack produced by putting everything that guests brought into a huge saucepan that stood over the eternal flame of the studio stove. When no one brought anything, there remained the residual slime of past ages of prosperity. This we consumed with relish.

In this and many other ways Mrs. Czech introduced into my life a new "continental" flavor. I had no way of knowing (and no intention of trying to find out) if foreigners were really more lax than the English in sexual matters, so I had at least to affect to believe her when she told me that in Paris—and, she implied, in all the glittering capitals in Europe—homosexuals, so far from being objects of ridicule, were hardly noticed at all. She could not see why I did not either live flagrantly abroad or discreetly at home. She was sure the English would never abandon their condemnatory attitude toward me in particular and sex in general.

With all the other unfortunate people whom I had embroiled in endless screaming matches on this subject, there had at least been one point of agreement—that homosexuality was of the greatest importance. Mrs. Czech merely thought of it as a minor, slightly curious fact of life. This disturbed my essential puritanism.

Every opportunity for pleasure that was offered to me automatically carried with it an almost equally strong desire to do without it. I might give way to either impulse, but the presence of the two contrary wishes was what gave zest to both.

In 1653, when God took a turn for the worse, the gusto with which the English took to a life of self-restraint undoubtedly contained an element of debauchery. If we don't suffer, how shall we know that we live?

One evening, while Mrs. Czech was giving voice to her broad-minded views and I was shaking my thin-lipped head, I had interrupted her for a moment while I went to the kitchen for a cup. As I passed through to the other room of the flat, I came upon Mr. Czech and the art student clasped in a passionate embrace. Here were forces of permissiveness that not even Mrs. Czech would have condoned. But Mr. Cromwell is not mocked. Soon the man in this sordid tableau was to go mad and the woman to become a nun.

I did not utter a word on seeing them nor did my feet falter, but I was shaken by the revelation of two people, whom until now I had regarded only as reflections of my own existence, in violent relation to each other. For the first time I was forced to admit that other people existed. It was not a discovery that I welcomed.

Chapter 12

During this period of my life—between the ages of twenty-four, when I started on what I imagined to be my career, and thirty, by which time I had abandoned this folly—my mother complained that my wanderings filled a whole address book, and her address books were not small. I did not have a restless temperament but I selected my lodgings on a fallacious principle. In my secret heart—or, to avoid exaggeration, in my secret space—I still thought of myself as living for others. My choice of a room was never dictated by taste or convenience. I gravitated only toward the greatest opportunity for putting myself at the mercy of other people and moved into a succession of places let to me by friends, and in some instances by mere acquaintances, who wished to lighten the burden of their rent but had no accommodation that they would have dared to offer to a stranger. When the discomfort and sometimes the downright degradation became too much for me, I moved on to fresh pits and pendulums new.

If I mention that I addressed even my closest friends as Mr. This and Mrs. That, it may be easy to guess how hard it would have been for me to reach any degree of intimacy with my own personality. I never called the various components of my character by their first names. Although it had been such a relief to live on my own in Denbigh Street, I changed my address eleven times before I finally gave up trying to disguise from myself my deep-seated indifference to the fate of others, settled into a room by myself, and admitted that solitude was one of my essential needs.

The fact that I wanted to be alone did not mean that I disliked people. I liked my friends and I adored strangers. I have been accused of flirting with everybody, but my intention was not to arouse sexually. It was merely to entertain. Even a minimal remark about the rain provoked me to say, "The weather's been nationalized." If invited to the house of a friend I was cozy, but should I find there people I had not met before, I plunged into a complete cabaret turn. I did not know that a reputation for wit is earned not by making jokes but by laughing at the pleasantries of others.

It was this mistaken idea that to win people I must dazzle them that made it essential for me to live alone. From time to time I had to stagger into my dressing room.

I left my six shillings attic in Clerkenwell to share a room in Maida Vale with a disused actor. He slept in the only bed and I stayed awake bent like a jackknife on the sofa. After a while he started to bring strange men back with him in the middle of the night. In the morning, I frequently discovered that these were people who only a few nights previously had been trying to ravish me with one hand and rip off my wristwatch with the other in Edgware Road. I was as embarrassed as Cardinal Wolsey at finding myself naked in the presence of my enemies. Also I had found my own sex life unpleasant enough. I had no intention of becoming a witness to anyone else's. I moved on to Lynhope Street, where my stay was marked by only one incident. It was here that I was first visited by the police.

My Irish friend had disappeared some time back, but the Scotsman and the girl, who had finally come out in his favor, still kept in touch with me. My chief function in their lives was, when either of them was in jail, to keep them in touch with each other without the prison governor being apprised of any address but mine. This was how the police managed to establish a connection between them and me, and (probably when the young man failed to report to his probation officer) they called on me to ask for his address. I did not give it to them. I held the opinion that however low a man sinks he never reaches the level of the police. I and many of the thieves, prostitutes, and other social outcasts who were my friends resorted to some very dodgy expedients in order to stay alive, but only the police habitually groveled for their wages in the excrement of the world. The rest of us, however clumsily, however over hastily, reached out toward life and love. Only the police trafficked exclusively in darkness and death. "If you go on like this," my visitor warned me, "you will be charged with harboring undesirables." I pointed out that if my Scottish friend had been undesirable I might not have bothered. The interview came to an abrupt end.

Shortly after this I moved again.

At one moment I was sharing two rooms with the art student and at another I was the lodger of Mrs. Czech.

Tired of taking off her clothes for so many for so little, she had become a nightclub hostess and required a lodger to help pay the expense of a W1 address. This had to be someone who would not complain of the disturbance caused by her occasionally heaving semi-conscious men up the stairs in the middle of the night. For a life of this kind she was totally unsuited. She was not merely shy but innately respectable. It was therefore not long before she required yet another lodger. There were so few wolves at the door. I recommended that we should offer the last available room to the daughter of a clergyman whom my sister knew. This girl stole whatever money was left in the house, and finally revealed to Mrs. Czech the secret that I had managed to keep for so long—that Mr. Czech was living in open sin with the art student on Tower Hill. When questioned as to why she had done this, the clergyman's daughter said she was Mrs. Czech's friend.

Against all odds, this story had a happy ending. Mrs. Czech divorced her gramophone-pawning husband and married an habitué of the establishment where she worked. When they went to live in splendor outside London, my mother and I visited them and my lifelong admiration for men of action was increased a hundredfold. During our stay, I became aware of the terrible price they have to pay in their declining years. The new husband had been a born leader of men in some outpost of our not-yet-fallen empire. In retirement he found himself without inner resources of any kind. All the morning he wandered from room to room murmuring, "When will we be having lunch, my love?" and throughout the afternoon he asked if it was teatime. He did not partake of either meal, preferring to sit at the table sipping whisky while we ate. His inquiries were made only because he longed for some assurance that, though all else was now inert, time was still moving.

I had attended Mrs. Czech's divorce breakfast but at her second wedding, which took place after a dignified interval, I was not present. I felt that this would not have befitted my station in life. By that time I had moved to Chelsea.

Here, in a mixed-with-water way, I lived the bed-sitting room existence, whose oddities Rodney Ackland used to flaunt before the amazed eyes of matinée audiences. I entered a boarding house as a foundation member almost before the paint on the backcloth was dry. It was run by actors and soon filled up with stock characters—an actress (tempestuous), a fashion artist (brittle), an American girl in search of experience (bewildered)—and we all ran in and out of each other's rooms making tea and talking about our futures. After a while this mixture was enriched by a touch of social realism. A colored gentleman was added. The announcement of his arrival was made with a flourish to the inner circle as we sat in the basement awaiting our scrambled-egg supper.

Landlord: I want you all to know that there is a coal-black Negro living at the top of the house.

Lodger: Oh dear! And there's no lock on my door.

Landlord: In that case, Mrs. Thomas, you will have to think of some other method of preventing his escape.

This was the first house I had ever lived in, including those of my childhood, which seemed to be home. As far as possible the outer world was excluded. Any real people who did succeed in crawling past the screening devices merely murmured to themselves, if they met me in the hall, "That illusion again," and went upstairs to take two aspirins. All the same I could not have said that I was part of a "Chelsea" life. I knew only one bearded artist and only one model. I never went to a bohemian party and I never got drunk.

For about twenty years I lived in a state of intoxication with my own existence and, perhaps for that very reason, excess of alcohol was one of the extremes to which I felt no urge to fly. I asked many people why they drank so much but never received an explanation that I fully understood. It was the tales of their escapades while under the influence of drink that brought me nearest to comprehending their need for it. It seemed to give them a few hours of freedom from rules which, during the rest of their lives, they reluctantly obeyed. If this was true, then in the example of my life lay a cure for drunkenness, though it was hardly an answer which Harley Street would have approved. The prophylactic is, never to conform at all.

It was while I lived in Chelsea that I became a freelance artist. Most of my nights were spent not in sinning but in executing the work that it had taken all day to wrest from the astonished fingers of manufacturers and publishers. When not busy in this way, if I went out at all, it was to visit friends.

One of these was Mr. Cross, whose life was a recipe for success. Never before and seldom since had I witnessed such indefatigability and such singleness of purpose. He wrote and he wrote and he wrote. "I want," he exclaimed in an accent that you could have cut with a sword, "to have behind me a great body of worrrrrrk." He was twenty-two at the time. Even had I known that all this apparently fruitless effort would one day lead to his ruling the worlds of radio and television, I could not have followed his example. Industry of that intensity is composed only in part of energy. This I possessed. The rest is optimism, which I lacked.

Before my life became one long holiday, I was given a last vacation with pay. A few days of this I decided to spend in Portsmouth, which was in those days the Mecca of the homosexual world.

I could not do anything so brazen as openly to set out for the south coast in a spirit of hilarious research. Because the venture was motivated by sexual curiosity I had to arrange to be edged into it by quite innocent forces. I leaned forward so that fate could see me and waited. Soon an acceptable pretext fell into my lap.

The parson's daughter who had nearly wrecked my Czech friend's life was a student of drama (in so many ways), and through her I had already met a lot more embryonic actresses. They were kind enough to provide me with countless free seats for cultural plays from which I learned, if nothing else, that culture was not for me. Some years before I had given up reading. Now I was ready to give up theater-going (unless it was free). I started to shed the monstrous aesthetic affectation of my youth so as to make room for the monstrous philistine postures of middle age, but it was still some years before I was bold enough to decline an invitation to *Hamlet* on the grounds that I already knew who won. Long after I had ceased to befriend the parson's daughter, I continued to see another drama student with whom she had once shared a room. This girl wanted to take a band of strolling—even meandering—players to the Isle of Wight to play Shakespeare's works in the open air. This scheme entered her head presumably because nature abhors a vacuum and also because every summer her mother ran a boarding house in Shanklin where she may have hoped her troupe could obtain food and lodging when all else failed. I was told about this project because my help was needed. The proposition was that I should lend her ten pounds and she would arrange for me to stay for a week free of charge in her mother's house.

I acquiesced in this on the grounds that the most anyone would expect from a holiday was a change of agony. It also enabled—nay, compelled—me to pass through Portsmouth.

Chapter 13

Like Florrie Forde, I and most of the homosexuals whom I knew best wanted "something in a uniform." Any national dress or occupational outfit may be sexually stimulating, and there are as many kinks as there are kinds of costume. Uniforms appeal to devotees of the fearless man of action. They also pander to the Cophetua complex so prevalent among homosexuals. When any of my friends mentioned that he had met a "divine" sailor he never meant an officer. Women seem to feel differently about these things. They prefer airmen, by which they always mean the higher ranks. I used to sit in the window seat in a King's Road café discussing these matters with a certain Mrs. Gardner. Not long afterward, she met Neville Heath. I should have guessed that she was a born murderee. She used to wear a leopardette coat.

When I was young the word "soldier" meant one of the red-coated guardsmen who strutted up and down Knightsbridge in the evenings. These men were willing to go for "a walk in the park" for as little as half-a-crown. This appeared to be what Berwick Street would call a desperate bargain at a never-again price but, had I accepted the offer, I have no doubt that I should have been beaten to a pulp with or without benefit of sex.

Sailors never asked for money but, on the contrary, had large sums of money to spend in short spasms of shore leave. They also never turned nasty. Perhaps the act of running away to sea was an abandonment of accepted convention and, after a sojourn in strange ports, they returned with their outlook and possibly their anus broadened.

The fabulous generosity in their natures was an irresistible lure—especially when combined with the tightness of their uniforms, whose crowning aphrodisiac feature was the fly-flap of their trousers. More than one of my friends has swayed about in ecstasy describing the pleasures of undoing this quaint sartorial device.

All that is ended now. Naval uniforms have been altered. With a vertical instead of horizontal opening to their trousers, sailors can walk their shoes to the uppers without a single stranger asking them for a light. They can linger even in Piccadilly without ever being offered a pint of beer. I was already long past the age when I knew or hoped to know any members of any of the forces before this happened, so I cannot say whether it was with a groan that the sea gave up its trousers. Among my friends there was certainly a day of mourning. As someone remarked, when told the new atom bombs would explode without a bang, "they can't leave anything alone."

Today a visit to Portsmouth would not be worth the train fare, but in the summer of 1937 the whole town was like a vast carnival with, as its main attraction, a continuous performance of *H.M.S. Pinafore.* As most of the men were in uniform and the girls wore shorts and bras in the street, it seemed that everyone was in fancy dress. This much I saw from the taxi window while I was being driven toward the hotel which the driver had chosen. "It'll be the best—for *you,*" he said. He may simply have meant that it was one where I stood a good chance of being let in. Having been refused admittance to many restaurants and even a few cinemas, I had wondered whether I would meet with any trouble of this kind, but none occurred. With a poker face I thanked the young man who carried my luggage upstairs for both pieces of information when he explained where the gentlemen's and a moment later where the ladies' lavatories were.

When I had unpacked it was about six o'clock in the evening. I decided to lie down for about half an hour to rally my forces. I overdid the relaxing rituals and fell asleep. I got up the instant that I awoke but, by the time I had clapped on as much makeup as the forces of gravity would allow, it was night.

Outside the hotel I paused for a second, not knowing which way to go. A second was long enough. I was instantly surrounded by sailors. I explained that I wished to walk along the seafront and they offered to show me the way. From then on our progress was like a production number in a Hollywood musical. The chorus was continually on the increase as my guides called out to their friends who, even if they had been going in the opposite direction, turned back to join us. When we arrived at the sea front as many of us as could sat on one of the seats while others perched on the railings. The beach was strewn with lovers, and even a few couples sleeping with their children and their luggage beside them. The distinction between indoors and outdoors, which in England is usually so marked, was temporarily suspended in a hot gauzy trance.

The sailors told me how to recognize the north star and explained various quaint items of nautical lore. I expressed suitable amazement, addressing my remarks to the sea. I quickly found that if I spoke directly to any one of my companions he blushed and the others hit him till he fell off the seat. There was a great deal of laughing and flopping about, but the conversation never fell below the level of the risqué. There were no threats, no insults—and very little personal interrogation. The only question I remember being asked was one that was always cropping up in those days, "Do you know Fred Barnes?" A few years later this became

"Did you ever meet Fred Barnes?" for he had committed suicide.

After a while, when it became obvious that there was going to be speech but no action, without becoming angry the sailors began two by two to drift away until I was left with two castaways—older men who had once been in the navy or possibly merely wished they had. These walked back with me to the hotel, which turned out to be shut. I was surprised, having imagined in my Monte Carlo dream that all seaside hotels were open all night. To my companions this was one last huge joke. They took me to a place where we would be able to sit around until daybreak. This too was shut. My escorts banged on the doors until, with a rattling of chains and a creaking of hinges as though we were about to enter a dungeon, we were admitted to a huge canteen full of down-and-outs. The proprietor had hair so red that the pigmentation had flowed out into every visible inch of his skin and even into the pinks of his eyes, as the color of flowering cherry trees stains their leaves.

The place we entered was just like the dining hall at school except that there was a large tea urn on a counter that ran along one end of the room. We ate as much as we could, to make it worth the redskin's while to have undone all those bolts. Then we settled down to innumerable cups of tea. Our chatter and our laughter awoke other inmates. They lifted their heads out of their plates and crossed the room to join us in yet more rounds of teas. When I judged that it must be daylight in the streets, I crept back to my hotel. I had been speaking off and on (but chiefly on) for about eight hours. I slept until the following evening.

I never saw Portsmouth by day.

When, the morning after that, I sat in the early train back to London, I tried to recall what adventure, what romance, I had expected this visit to offer me but, as though I had seen the movie after reading the book, reality had now obscured the dream. I had beheld a miracle. That was the first, last, and only time that I ever sat in a crowd of people whose attention I really desired without once feeling that I was in danger.

For this reason all the quality of that evening, and all the evenings like it that never came, remained with me for many years until I no longer felt the need for this kind of relationship with this kind of person—until my desires had changed and my whole nature had coarsened in a way that on that night in Portsmouth I would have thought impossible.

Chapter 14

At that period of my life the average length of my tenancy of any one room was about four months, so I would have described myself as having lived in Chelsea for a long time. I was there just over a year. Toward the end of my stay it transpired that I had only imagined that I was among friends. When I had already given notice, I was accused by one of my landlords of stealing money from the room of another tenant. After a day or two the lost purse was found but no apology was offered. I was then accused of having put it back. Of the two indictments the latter was by far the more annoying. I have never had much respect for the law, including the law of property (though, until St. Genet set his famous example, I had never thought of boasting about this), but I was very indignant that my enemies should suddenly pretend to think me likely to give way to remorse. They had constantly exclaimed that I was ruthless. This last epithet, although it was intended as an insult, I had always covertly regarded as praise. Gestures of atonement sickened me. Unless it was by accident that I caused harm to somebody, I never apologized. Pardon, sought or granted, was to me a fatuous social flourish. It was a further infliction of cruelty on a victim, forcing upon him who already had some ill to bear the humiliating chore of uttering a few words of feigned forgiveness.

I no longer inhaled a permanent atmosphere of disapproval, but suspicion, once aroused, automatically fell on me. (I do not think that, to this day, things have changed much in this respect.) Also it was only when I was already leaving that people's true feelings emerged in the same way that, in the street, the whistles and the catcalls began not when I was approaching but when I had already passed by.

I took up residence in a mews in Belgravia as the lodger of a teacher of ballet. She had rented a huge barn of a place with a view to sleeping in it by night and giving lessons there by day.

Living in this mews placed us at the bottom of a deep ravine formed by the five-story houses of the rich. From the top back windows of these mansions, the last members of the dying race of domestic servants looked down—but not in mercy. When I first moved into my room I had no curtains and later, when these were provided, I seldom drew them. This was a difficult operation necessitating a climb onto my desk since even the bottoms of the windows were above my head. What could be seen of my room was the bed. On this there was usually somebody lying. Since there was only one chair in the room—an upright wooden one that I used when sitting at my drawing board—there was nowhere else for my friends to relax. I soon received my second visit from the police. This time there were two of them—a detective-inspector and a younger man with no speaking part who merely stood by the door as though he half expected he'd have to prevent me rushing hatless into the street. The inspector explained that he had called because of complaints lodged by the neighbors that they could see into my room. What they saw they didn't like. It is said that when Mae West was told that Americans complained of the suggestiveness of her radio program, she drawled, "They could've turned it off." My sentiments were the same, but my aplomb was not. With downcast eyes and scarlet cheeks, I promised that in future I would be careful what I did. This seemed to be an insufficient answer, for the policeman then shouted, "Things go on in this house for which the penalty is seven years' imprisonment." This was the first time that the laws regarding private indecency had ever been brandished before me. I remained calm and a few minutes later he left. As he did so he told me his name twice, as though, if I ever decided to give myself up, he expected me to send for him. As soon as my visitors had left, I telephoned all those friends who might not wish to call at an establishment that was being watched by the police. I started with a man, fairly highly placed in one of the ministries, with whom, after many years of happy celibacy, I was having a dismal affair. His terror of disgrace was such that he never visited me in daylight. He was careful to telephone a few minutes before his arrival to make sure that no one—not even the ballet teacher—was on the premises.

All liaisons between homosexuals are conducted as though they were between a chorus girl and a bishop. In some cases both parties think they are bishops. I realized I was a chorus girl and quite happily knew men for as long as seventeen years without knowing their surnames or their addresses. Anyone who allowed himself to become my friend was doing me a favor. I always tried to make it clear that I was aware of at least some of the penalties that went with knowing me. Before a relationship had gone very far, I usually explained that, in difficult circumstances, I did not expect to be acknowledged. I only ever knew one woman who did not treat this remark as an attempt to put the loyalty of my friends to the utmost test. One day, as I was walking wickedly up Rathbone Place, I saw her coming innocently down accompanied by an anti-hooligan whom I guessed to be a client of the firm for which she worked. Talking airily in millions she passed within a foot of me without either of us glancing in the direction of the other. Neither of us mentioned the incident subsequently but, from that moment onward, with that woman I felt absolutely free.

There were others, however, whose very fear seemed to urge them to defy the world. Once I was invited to the house of a movie writer with the words: "Mrs. Smith will be here with her two children. She comes from Pinner. I can't imagine what she'll make of you but still . . ." When I remarked that it would surely be better if I came on a different day, my suggestion was swept aside as though I was being morbidly sensitive. At the great confrontation, as I stretched out to this woman a hand weighed down with coral and turquoise, my host said to her, "You can touch him. He's quite real." Until that moment, she had been doing all right. She had doubtless thought, "I'll ask my husband about this when I get home" and then made her mind a complete blank. As soon as the remark about me was uttered, she was visibly stricken with embarrassment. So was I. At one time Crisp's First Law would have stated that those who most fear disgrace invariably behave outlandishly. Now I see that I mistook the cause for the effect. It is those who, for some unknown reason, have no idea how they will behave in a social emergency who quite naturally dread the world's censure.

On this principle the man from the ministry continued to visit me and, on one occasion when I was clambering about on the furniture, said that he couldn't think why I bothered to draw the curtains. I took no notice of this foolhardiness. As it happened, the threats of the police never came to anything. I was not arrested for many years and, when I was, the circumstances were different.

While I lived in Belgravia, two new ways of supplementing my fitful income from commercial art presented themselves. The first of these was writing, at which so far I had never had the least success. The Blandford Press, for whom I had often designed a book jacket or laid out an advertisement in one of their magazines, suggested that I should write a book about window dressing. I had never thought of doing this because I knew nothing about the subject. The publishers did not think that this was any handicap, so I flung myself upon the project with all my half-starved weight and quickly wrote thirty thousand words. I had only one idea to put forward—that, in any visual field, maximum interest lies at the point of maximum contrast. After several shaky years the book sold its edition. This only proves once more that people will pay to read what they already know. I made sixty pounds but, though I have written one book and a few articles since, I cannot say that my hope that writing might become a second career was ever fulfilled.

The other profession in at the door of which I desperately thrust my lacquered toe was tap dancing. My landlady did not want pupils who wished to learn other forms of dancing than ballet to be turned away for lack of a fully equipped staff of experts. This was another subject of which I was totally ignorant, though this weakness never came to light. Only one student with tap dancing in mind ever turned up and she was a beginner. I taught her by keeping one tap ahead at each lesson. The occupants of the workshop below had to endure a noise overhead like an African hailstorm beating on a tin roof while I hastily practiced what I had just been taught before my pupil arrived to learn it. The steps were not made any easier for either of us by the clearly audible curses from below. To those poor workmen peace only came with the outbreak of war.

When war was declared I went out and bought two pounds of henna.

Chapter 15

If any astrologers have read this far, they will now wave their star-tipped wands over their heads and jump up and down with glee until their pointed hats fall askew on their silvery locks. I was born under Capricorn and am logical to the point of idiocy. Having learned with such difficulty to go about the streets amid catcalls, raspberries, and flying stones as though nothing unpleasant had happened, I decided to make use of this capacity for feigned indifference and treat all signs of hostility with contempt, even now that they had transcended the personal and were on a national scale. Apart from getting in a good supply of cosmetics, I made up my mind to ignore the war as completely as I could.

I never bought newspapers, for fear that people might think that I liked what went on in the world, and I had long ago given up listening to the radio the moment that I realized that it was always going to be jolly without ever being witty. Therefore the news of Hitler's move into Poland was brought to me by a new Irishman who often called on me to beg for half-crowns, which I liked, and to bring me in exchange stolen silver spoons, which I loathed. While he was still with me the air was filled with a fluctuating wailing sound. "What's that?" I asked. "Oh, they're just trying something out," my friend replied. Thus the first air-raid warning came and went.

One thing the war compelled me to do was to

change my address twice more in a frantic search for cheaper and ever-cheaper rooms. All work had ceased for me. The money that I had in hand dwindled fast. But, though I now sank socially from Belgravia to Fulham and later Chelsea, there was a sense in which these moves were for the better. The ballet teacher had virtually given me the furniture that she had bought for my room while I was her lodger. This was a stroke of wonderful good fortune. I would never have been able to spare at one time enough money to furnish a room and I totally lacked the resources of character to arrange for delivery to my home. A great many transactions that involved dealing with strangers were still quite beyond me. Though I had progressed far enough to be able to hail a taxi or even ask a policeman the way, I could not have acquired a passport or opened a bank account. Now, without having to make a fool of myself in any specific way, I had come quite effortlessly by the means to take unfurnished rooms. I took two in rapid succession. The great space famine had not then begun. I was able to look at several possible premises in a single afternoon. The second move I made more or less at random, but the place suited me so perfectly that I have lived there ever since. I had thought once before that I had reached home. Now I really had.

The unfurnished life was different from the furnished in many ways, all of which were improvements. Now for the first time I had life on my own terms. I decided immediately that I would never become a thrall to rituals of domesticity.

In my childhood I had seen these engulf half my mother's life. Sitting on the floor watching her take from a bookcase and dust every single one of the works of Bulwer Lytton, I said, "I shouldn't do all that." She replied, "I know you wouldn't. That's why I must."

Perhaps because of such memories as this, squalor

rapidly became my natural setting. I felt it was only by a series of unfortunate accidents that till now I had always lived in the captivity of hygiene. Nancy Spain had not yet become one of the sages of the air and had therefore not had the opportunity to promulgate her first law—only a fool would make the bed every day—but this was one of the truths that I knew by instinct. As soon as I began the unfurnished life, I practiced sleeping on my back as still as if I were in my coffin. I slid out of bed in the morning like a letter from an envelope. Except for the thickening film of sullied cold cream that as time went by piled up on the pillowslip, no one would have been able to detect that my bed had been occupied. I changed the bed linen once a week. I realized that if I did not, I would one day reach a point of no return beyond which the laundry would refuse to accept my dim gray sheets. This Augustinian state of affairs was acceptable when I slept alone, but it would no longer do once I was not sure that this would always be so. About cleaning the rest of the room I did nothing at all. Except that after a while it became necessary to jump in the air while putting on my trousers so as to avoid trailing them in the dust, I never found that this omission brought in its filthy wake any disadvantages whatsoever. As the years went whizzing by, I was able to formulate a companion law to Miss Spain's. Mine stated that there was no need to do any housework at all. After the first four years the dirt doesn't get any worse. Later, on the Third Program, I was given a chance to deliver this message of hope to a drudging world.

After an absence of fifteen years, Mr. O'Connor, once a hooligan like the rest of us, stood on my doorstep. He wanted me to take part in a program about eccentrics. Ever delicate in these matters, I asked, "What's in it for me?" He assured me that I would be paid and ran back into the street to bring in a "tape" machine. Holding a microphone in front of my face, he said, "Say something about life and death." As I break out into a cold, quicksilver sweat at the mention of one and elevenpence I was amazed to receive later a substantial sum for sitting in my room and talking about myself. If only I could get some of the back pay!

I doubt if my words were heard by many inveterate dusters and sweepers or if the conventual rigors of Women's Hour were subsequently relaxed, but we must not mourn. The measure of a woman's distaste for any part of her life lies not in the loudness of her lamentations (these are only an attempt to buy a martyr's crown at a reduced price) but in her persistent pursuit of that occupation of which she never ceases to complain. Although housewives know deep down that they are doing, if not what they like, at least what they prefer, this does not prevent them from envying the tousled bliss of others. In tones of asperity, the ballet teacher once said to me, "No wonder you have the time and energy to be nice to everybody. You never do any housework."

When I had lived in my room for some fifteen years, and I was feeding a starving outcast, we were called on by a small deputation of guests from a party going on elsewhere in the house. They brought glasses of sherry. As the rest of us sipped and chatted, one visitor sat silent. Through thick horn-rimmed spectacles he gave the scene a panoramic stare. His name was Mr. Pinter. Later he confessed that this was the moment when he first felt that he might write a play.

To the unfurnished life I found I could add a whole new dimension by installing a telephone. This gave me people to nod to not merely up and down King's Road but ranged hundreds deep into the uttermost distance. Even when I had returned to my room defeated by not finding any of my friends in their homes, I could still by telephone pan the suburbs for a few last nuggets of conviviality. This instrument was like a window which gave not only on to the world I knew but also on to one full of strangers. Through it work came to me from publishers I didn't know and bookings at schools I had never heard of. I turned it on as other people switch on the radio. The programs were far more interesting. A pessimist is someone who, if he is in the bath, will not get out to answer the telephone. I was incorrigibly hopeful. I never willingly let the telephone bell ring for fear that I might miss a message from God. The first words I spoke into the receiver used to be "Yes, Lord."

After a while, if you have a telephone of your own and billing in the book, you have appointments with fear. Most of mine were merely tedious—an extension of the treatment I received in the street. Strangers, refusing to give their names, claimed in would-be sexy voices to know me intimately. They sometimes rang me more than once in an hour. Presumably they hoped to make an appointment that they would not keep at some windy street corner miles away. Others only wanted to amuse their friends. These could be heard giggling at the other end of the line. After many years these calls thinned out, but they never ceased altogether. It is hard to imagine what pleasure can be gained from listening to a tired voice repeating over and over again, "What is your name and what do you want?"

Remembering my own disappointment at learning that there was no confederacy among homosexuals, I felt I must try wherever possible to come to the aid of the party. If one of these telephone conversations began with a white-faced voice saying, "I must see you," I always invited whoever was speaking to visit me. I chose a time when I would be at home whether they arrived or not, in case this too was a hoax. I realized that I was placing myself in some danger. Before the stranger was due to appear, I put on my shoes (which I almost never wore indoors), locked my money in a cupboard, put the key in another cupboard, and locked that. Then I was as ready as I could be, although there was still a vulnerable moment when I opened the front door. There might be a whole army of ill-wishers on the other side of it. There never was. Indeed most of the people who visited me in these circumstances seemed more apprehensive than I. One looked as though he would not get up the stairs without a blood transfusion.

As soon as I had led him into my room, I offered him a seat and said gently, "Now. What's your trouble?"

Stranger (almost in a whisper): There's no trouble.

Me: Then why are you here?

Stranger (becoming agitated): I don't know.

Me: You mean you came here for no reason at all.

Stranger (the words bursting from his pallid lips like a cry of anguish): They dared me to!

I rose to my feet and he to his. In all he had only been in the room about three minutes. As I accompanied him down the stairs, I said, "I don't advise you to treat any other eccentric old gentlemen in this way. They might be even more annoyed than I am."

Chapter 16

As the meteoric dust fell invincibly and insatiably on the early Caledonian Market furnishings of my room, I sat and waited for my call-up. Although I now had no work to do it was not hard to fill in the time. While other districts of the trembling city were busy fire-watching, learning first aid, and digging incomprehensible trenches in London squares, Chelsea was occupied exclusively with amateur theatricals. Wearing steel helmets and gas masks, air raid precautionists and auxiliary firemen hastened along King's Road. If asked by anxious civilians what was up they said in tense voices that the pantomime rehearsal had been changed to half past six at the Town Hall. Apart from shows arranged with a jolly laugh by absolute amateurs there were also innumerable productions put on quite seriously by semi-professional actors in dim billiard halls in Notting Hill Gate.

Through a Miss Murison, who later knit her soul more permanently with the theater by marrying Paul Holt, I became connected with one of these ventures. She asked me to write a revue. When I had finished it, I found the idea had been abandoned some time back by her codirectors in favor of a production of *The Scarlet Pimpernel.* As the stage of the theater at which this play was put on was the size of a kitchen table (but not so strongly constructed), the great whirl of the ballroom scene was difficult to manage. Indeed the whole play suffered from its constricted setting. An exiled aristocrat entered through a doorway so narrow that she was compelled to hold down the wide brim of her hat against her ears. When first seen she appeared to be wearing a poke bonnet. A moment later, when she let go of her hat brim, she seemed to have on her head a great flapping bird that was finding it difficult to settle on a moving perch.

This ill-advised production was followed by a work called *Fishing for Shadows.* Acts Two and Three were still being translated while the first part was already in rehearsal. Miss Murison had asked the young man, a Russian, who was doing the play from French into English, for a comedy to "take people's minds off the horrors of war." She had received his word that this was just what *Fishing for Shadows* would do. Almost every page that he handed her contained another suicide. At length Miss Murison felt compelled to seek reassurance by asking, "You did say it was to be a comedy, didn't you?" The young man indignantly replied, "It's as fully as *The Seagull.*" Now that his reputation has reached its full scale we can assume, which no one dared to do at the time, that this was a joke. The translator's name was Peter Ustinov.

Except in the incompetence of their productions neither of these shows was typical of the output of the little theaters of that time, all of which had a more or less homogeneous policy. Before the rise of Joan Littlewood there was a great gulf fixed between the commercial theater and those far-out playhouses that presumptuously described themselves as non-profit-making. They meant "loss-making." There were always more people on the stage than in the auditorium. The West End managements provided patrons with a glimpse of wickedness that never sank lower than adultery sketched in with a kiss before French windows. In Notting Hill Gate producers went in for works whose style can best be described as Venetian kitchen sink. In these the rape, murder, and incest that were one day to become more a part of family entertainment than scenery or footlights stalked the stage clothed—nay, swaddled—in verse more blank than even John Dryden would have dared to write. Some of these poetic dramas went so far that not even highbrow audiences could swallow them. A young man, so dedicated to one of these theaters that he painted the scenery by day and acted in front of it in the evening, described his agonies as he tried to think of some way to prevent the house from bursting into unsuitable mirth at his first line. This was "The Pope's gone mad."

Feeling, as it turned out wrongly, that my innate theatricality must one day pay off, I tried my utmost to attach myself to one of these theaters. After my abortive revue, I wrote an anti-Pirandello play so bad that to this day I cannot see why it was never staged. I also witnessed with conscientious regularity the plays of my friends. Such entertainment as I was able to extort from these visits to the theater came from sitting in the bar drinking a little and talking a lot. Once, I was thus engaged at the Chanticleer with Peter Noble, who in those days was already a well-known writer of theatrical gossip, and also an actor. A woman darted out of the auditorium to hiss at us, "We can't hear a word in there." "Then prop the door open," said Mr. Noble.

A letter requiring my appearance before a medical board reached me in the first April of the war. This was early, for I was already, in fact, thirty years old, but when, some time back, people had called at the mews to ask impertinent questions about my sex and age, I had stated that I was twenty-five. I had not done this because I was eager to denounce a monstrous tyranny but to bring nearer the moment when the problem of how to avoid starvation would be taken out of my hands. Many of my friends were able to find work in camouflage. This seemed an unlikely way for me to earn a living. My function in life was rather to render what was already clear blindingly conspicuous.

In spite of the frantic efforts I had made in so many directions to fortify myself against destitution, in a national emergency it transpired that I was utterly useless. It was almost enthusiastically that I set out for the drill hall in the middle of Kingston to which I had been summoned.

I was fully prepared to march at the head of my men, an occupation in which I had had considerable practice, but the authorities were not having any of that. The moment I stood naked before the first doctor, Harley Street, collapsed. I was surprised. My appearance was at half-mast. I wore no makeup and my hair was hardly more than hooligan length. Many of my friends on seeing me thus would have cried out, "Whatever's happened to you?" but of course my hair was still crimson from having been persistently hennaed for seven years and, though my eyebrows were no longer in Indian file, it was obvious that they had been habitually plucked. These and other manifestations of effeminacy disturbed the board deeply. Even while I was merely having my eyes tested, I was told, "You've dyed your hair. This is a sign of sexual perversion. Do you know what those words mean?" I replied that I did and that I was homosexual. The doctor who had asked the question immediately left me to whisper to one of his accomplices. Within a minute the entire governing body had gone into a spasm of consternation behind a hessian screen leaving the would-be members of the forces to shiver in their nakedness and urinate into an assortment of bottles. After a while a great effort was made by everyone to regain composure and I was passed on to another doctor. He asked me why I had dyed my hair. While I was filling my lungs with air in preparation for delivering one of my favorite speeches of self-justification he shrugged his shoulders and said "I suppose you prefer it red." Having expected some brand of Hippocratic remoteness from my examiners, I could hardly conceal my amazement at their awful humanity. It was as though a chemist were to wink at a customer buying a condom.

From my hair, interest passed to my anus, with which two of the doctors tampered for some time. Their private dreams of what the lives of homosexuals were like must have been very lurid. When I was vertical once more, one of them asked me if I thought I could walk four miles. I, who had stalked the streets for hours, was secretly piqued by this, but from lifelong habit I forbore to show my irritation. I said I thought I could but it was obvious that no amount of humility would now avail. The tide of opinion had turned against me. When I had been sitting alone in another part of the hessian forest for a few minutes, a young man appeared holding at arm's length, as though he were about to read a proclamation, a sheaf of papers which he tore up with a flourish. "You'll never be wanted," he said and thrust at me a smaller piece of paper. This described me as being incapable of being graded in grades A, B, etc., because I suffered from sexual perversion. When the story of my disgrace became one of the contemporary fables of Chelsea, a certain Miss Marshall said, "I don't much care for the expression 'suffering from.' Shouldn't it be 'glorying in'?"

I was totally exempt.

My ministry friend had warned me that I would never be called up. As he had had experience of the First World War, I should have believed him. I had laughed him to scorn. I had assumed that the authorities would realize that, without my hair, the mandarin half of my fingernails, and a few other detachable adornments, I would pass in the gun smoke for an ordinary mortal. I was wrong and had now been given the most bottomless sack of all. I thought of myself as deprived by prejudice of a glorious and convenient death. I had absolutely no visible means of support.

With a slightly annoying air of spirituality many

people have expressed in my hearing the opinion that financial worries, however grave, were never the worst of their troubles. Certainly the two people whom I nagged into describing their nervous breakdowns never mentioned poverty even as a subsidiary reason for their collapse. They named two main causes. One of these was God, from whose territory I had withdrawn my ambassadors at the age of fifteen. It had become obvious that he was never going to do a thing I said. The other problem was love—a word about whose meaning there seemed to be some ambiguity.

Often during this period of my life, to the embarrassment of my hearers, I claimed that my whole existence was love. I meant that I was trying never to close my hand against anyone—even the unlovable (in dealing with whom I was having a great deal of practice). I would have placed at anyone's disposal my meager resources of money or advice or concern. Sometimes I fancied that all the elements of a golden age of universal well-wishing were already known and would become instantly effective when, as with the components of D.D.T., some genius combined them in their right order. I was always delighted with the slightest breakthrough in this field.

There was a restaurant that I frequented because it was so small that by speaking slightly above normal pitch I could fuse the private conversations being carried on at each table into a general discussion. Here, an elderly lady seated at the table nearest to mine nodded her head discreetly in the direction of my soup and said to her companion, "That looks nice. I wonder what it is." I took a spoon from one of the unoccupied places at my table, dipped it into my bowl, and held it to her lips. For a doubting second she telegraphed a helpless glance to her friend and moved her hand to take the spoon from me. Then she leaned forward and, like a child, tasted the soup while I held the spoon. "It's very nice," she said. "We'll have some."

The only thing at that moment that could have brought the golden age nearer would have been if I had been able to make her drink from the spoon I had used.

The idea of love as a universal accessibility was not merely different from other people's. It had nothing to do with it. The consuming desire of most human beings is deliberately to plant their entire life in the hands of some other person. For this purpose they frequently choose someone who doesn't even want the beastly thing. I would describe this method of searching for happiness as immature. "Immaturity" is one more word that requires definition. To men it means the inability to stand on one's own two feet. A woman flings it at anyone who doesn't want to marry her. Here I find myself for once inclined toward the masculine view. I feel that, though no one must ever deny his dependence on others, development of character consists solely in moving toward self-sufficiency.

In adolescence I searched diligently—even dangerously—for some sheet-music kind of love that would fulfill the erotic dreams the literature read to me in my childhood had colored so romantically. In this fantasy I would be the cherished object of some great man's total preoccupation. In return I would become his perfumed slave. Of course I was willing to adopt this attitude of abject prostration only before someone who never asked me to do anything I didn't like. As soon as a man demanded that I modify my scandalous appearance or agree to being passed off as someone's nephew, my love, which was a chronic invalid, died in an instant.

This idea of love I abandoned in my twenties for something which I thought nobler, though really I was merely throwing over Elinor Glyn for Patience Strong.

At one time I imagined my sexual abnormality constituted the whole of my difference from other people; later I decided that the rift was caused by my exalted views on love. Finally I saw that these two causes were interdependent. Universal love goes with masturbation.

In an incorrigible fantasist, auto-eroticism soon ceases to be what it is for most people—an admitted substitute for sexual intercourse. It is sexual intercourse that becomes a substitute—and a poor one—for masturbation. If this is evil then Baden-Powell, instead of urging the male adolescents of the world to take colder and colder baths and make wilder and wilder assumptions about the stuffiness of their mother's views on puberty, should have found some way of warning boy scouts that alienation was the probable result of this habit. I regard this alienated state as good. It grants the intellect some freedom from the body. It saves a person from judging others by the confused standards of male, female, old, young, beautiful, hideous, in a way that can never be achieved by eating vegetables or sitting cross-legged in the middle of California or wearing purple on Wednesdays.

This was the state of mind at which I had now arrived. Though I treated even the slightest variation in my relationships with other people as a fascinating crossword puzzle, the problems that arose were not aggravated by sexual frustration. They caused me concern but not anguish.

I had severed the connection between sex and love. It wasn't the complete solution to the human predicament but it was a help. It enabled me to make the contrary statement to that made by most of my friends. My only serious problems were financial.

The trouble with this state of blessedness was that when money difficulties arose, they seemed total. I did not live simply in order to be solvent but, as soon as I was not, there was nothing in my life that made the ensuing hardships worth bearing.

When a third wave of poverty overwhelmed me, I knew with even greater certitude than when I had lived in Clerkenwell that the only complete solution to my problem was suicide. I never brought it off. I was afraid. A lifetime of never making positive decisions, accepting instead the least of the evils presented to me, had atrophied my will. It was not so much that I longed for death as that I didn't long for life. Emptiness, though, was not a sufficiently definite feeling to lead to a violent act. Instead of sitting in my room and balancing the relative convenience of various ways of ending it all, I ought to have been busy trying to summon up a reasonable amount of despair. Hopelessness was thinly spread like drizzle over my whole outlook. But, in an emergency, I could not find a puddle of despondency deep enough to drown in.

Chapter 17

For several weeks after my rejection by the medical board I lived on borrowed money and, without warning them, crawled around to the houses of my friends at mealtimes. Getting back into a commercial studio turned out to be impossible. Whenever I applied for a job I was careful to explain that I was totally exempt but I was always obliquely accused of being a pacifist. Even when I protested that I was one of the few people who actually liked the war, I still didn't get taken on.

The only money that I can remember earning at this time came from Mr. Hall. Without ever having met me, he telephoned me to ask if I would allow him to paint my portrait. When I asked if he would be willing to pay me he said with frankness, "Only if it's absolutely necessary." It was.

The moment that he opened the door of his studio to me, I recognized him as one of the landmarks of the district. I had often witnessed him in King's Road wearing a huge black hat and a stiff pointed beard with which it would have been possible to scrub the sink. He was the first real artist that I had ever met. I was delighted that he looked so perfectly the part. His home was also the first studio that I had ever entered. I exclude those bed-sittingrooms which are so sparsely furnished and so lavishly unkempt that their occupants feel the only thing to do is call them studios.

My friends—even those that lived in Chelsea—received the news that Mr. Hall was painting me (and might do a picture of me in the nude) with amused contempt mixed here and there with a sickening archness. Some openly suggested that he had proposed this out of sexual curiosity. Even in those days, long before Mary Quant and John Stevens turned the place into a vast boutique for the rich, Chelsea was evidently not, as advertised, the home of the broad-minded. It was merely lousy with people who lacked the nerve or the energy to give positive expression to moral judgment. Indeed, if a bohemian is someone without prejudices and without roots, then what there was of the *vie de bohème* seemed to reside in Mr. Hall.

I was flattered by his interest in me and charmed by his courtesy. He utterly lacked the brutish iconoclasm with which many seek to establish themselves as "characters." His melancholy dignity, however, baffled me. I sometimes thought he would have liked to shed this but couldn't. He answered with candor even such questions as "Why do you paint?" but I never got to know him.

And I tried.

I tried hard, for I wanted to enter the world of which I felt he was a consul, though I knew that I would be an impostor there. I don't hold with art.

The only time I gave a gracious nod in the direction of culture was when surrealism came to London. This movement appealed to me because the pictures executed under its banner were akin to the works to which my mother had directed my attention in childhood. Their especial quality was Victorianism now put into a perverse form. I was only sorry that this was not enhanced by giving the paintings such titles as "The Blight of the World" or "When Did You Last Rape Your Father?"

In spite of this minor disappointment I went to the famous exhibition in the Burlington Galleries, where I found myself an unwitting, though not entirely unwilling, exhibit. In and out of the different rooms glided a certain Mrs. Legge, wearing full evening dress and carrying in her hand an uncooked pork chop. With orange face and vermilion lips I weaved my way past her, clanking with amulets, but, as her face was entirely covered by a hood of roses, I could not see whether she registered fear that I might be a materialization of the surreal world or annoyance that another voluntary worker had got his rota mixed with hers. For a moment one of the dearest wishes of surrealism was fulfilled. The barriers between art and life fell down.

Subsequently cultural trends soon restored and even reinforced them. I came out on the side of reality. I began to feel that art was not merely superfluous but actually insulting to life. Its implication was that the visible world was intolerable unless a bunch of amateurs at the creation business shoved it around. For this reason I never wanted to paint but hoped, to borrow a phrase from the jargon of a later aesthetic movement, that I might become an *objet trouvé* in the world of art. Some of this hostility to culture I may have expressed when talking to Mr. Hall. If I did, it may have formed a part of the barrier between us.

I got to know slightly better a writer who occasionally came and sat with us while Mr. Hall worked at my portrait. I attended a small party at this man's house. One of the guests, who managed to wear his naval uniform as though it were really only fancy dress, sang himself to bits. He shouted, shuddered, hooted, until the sweat poured down his face and his hair fell into his eyes. Among the young, such behavior is now as common as smoking reefers, but at that time it was a startling phenomenon. I enjoyed his performance a little less for fearing that he might have a stroke. I need not have worried. Soon he was carrying on like this several times a night. It was Mr. Melly. He had a genius for getting others to see a joke as he saw it and this won my admiration but, whenever we met in later years, my part in our conversations consisted chiefly in saying "Sh-sh." Mr. Melly had to be obscene to be believed.

In all, Mr. Hall painted three portraits of me. The fees he paid me for sitting for these were very helpful, but I had the misfortune to outlive them. I reached the end of my tether and the tethers of most of my friends. I was rescued by the documentary movie industry.

Chapter 18

I seemed always to be walking along a corridor flanked by doors barred against all knocking, all entreaty. These were interspersed with other doors looking exactly similar but which opened almost before I reached them. I now came to one of these.

While I had been living the furnished life in Chelsea, among the inmates of the house in which I lodged had been the secretary of a film producer. As well as she could she had explained me to her employer. Without seeing one of the dingy letterheads and layouts of advertisements in such papers as the *Fur Times* and the *Cactus Journal* which were pasted into my book of specimens, he had offered me the job of lettering the titles of a number of travelogues he had made in pinkest Petra and other cities of the Near East.

All but one of these had been distributed before the war started. The remaining one was now brought forward by another producer who, when my work for him was finished, distributed me among the poor of the documentary industry. I could hardly keep pace with the work, partly because there was so much of it and partly because the lettering of a film was never commissioned until a few days before the trade show. The movie business had a genius for bringing some kind of chaos out of order.

Of course lettering credits was only another form of commercial art. It required the speed, the high gloss that I had always lacked, but because it was connected with the movies, for me it had glamor. I flailed my limbs so wildly in my efforts to cling on that at one moment I caught hold, by accident, of an art directorship.

I had been called by telephone to the top floor of the building over a Chinese restaurant in Wardour Street. When I arrived I was asked by a man with a delicatessen accent if I would paint the sets of a film that was to go into production there the next day. I had never painted scenery in my life, but I said I would if he would tell me what I was to do. When I turned up the following day, this man was not present, though a great many other people were. None of these seemed to know anyone else or to have the faintest idea what he himself had been hired for. I wandered around the room eavesdropping at various uneasy conversations as though I had gate-crashed a dull party, until I arrived in a corner where one man was asking another, "Well, what's it supposed to look like?" Then he had an idea. "Let's ask that bloke with the funny . . . Oh, here you are," he said as he caught sight of me. Explaining me to the other man, he added, "He's your art director."

"Oh, am I?" I squeaked, delighted but surprised.

With the swiftness of a tropical sunset, assurance faded from the faces of both men. My moment of glory had come and gone.

Working for the movies was the first job I ever wanted to do for reasons other than to show I could. For once, though I was prepared to accept defeat, I did not intend to embrace it. I wanted to be what would now be described as the Saul Bass of British movies and, to this end, I abandoned for a moment my existentialist posture. I applied for and, to my amazement, obtained, a job in Studio Film Laboratories. This was a mistake. I was not able to flit from room to room learning the secret of the celluloid universe. I was confined to the art department where, even if my ineptitude had not almost immediately been unmasked, I do not think I would have lasted long. My presence caused agony to the head of the studio. From lifelong habit I called him "Sir," never noticing that every time I did so he winced. Also, after a few weeks, he became aware that other members of his staff had learned by heart and were starting to use the detestable curlicues with which my discourse was decorated—nay, cluttered—and which later came to be called Crisperanto.

Within nine months I had once again been given the sack. All that I had succeeded in doing was to go out of circulation for long enough for most of my movie connections to forget about me.

Life was a funny thing that happened to me on the way to the grave. I had never thought of my progress—perhaps we had better say my movement—through time as a triumphal march, but at this point I felt that I had stumbled. It is only when looking at an aerial shot taken by memory that I see how little was lost by my failure in the movie industry. If I have any talent at all, it is not for doing but for being. In the humblest way, this I was now given the opportunity to demonstrate.

I became a model.

Chapter 19

In my final week at Studio Film Laboratories, I received a telephone call from the model I had known when I lived in Chelsea the first time around. She implored me to go and pose in Toynbee Hall in her stead. This was not as farfetched an idea as it may sound. The sending of substitutes to art schools is as common among models as the parallel practice is among orchestral musicians.

"I've telephoned everyone," she said. "They're all booked." Then she added in a voice that carried a faint tone of bitterness, "You're always saying it must be nice to be a model. Now's your chance."

As soon as I had put down the telephone receiver, I flew at one of my older pairs of underpants and—with those very same paper shears that had once nearly brought disgrace upon me—cut away everything but the waistband and a small triangle of fabric in front. I had been an art student and knew that in England (though not, I was told, in Germany or any of the Scandinavian countries) male models were never quite naked before a class containing female pupils.

The following evening I arrived in Toynbee Hall for a four-hour evening class. I was eager but a little apprehensive lest I should faint as I had often seen models do. As I stepped onto the "throne," the master said, "I suppose you couldn't hold on to the top of that screen behind you in a kind of crucifixion pose?" I pointed out that I had died after three hours last time.

This idea was abandoned, but I was asked to stand for the whole lesson (with the usual ten-minute breaks every hour). I was glad of this. It made the evening a representative test of my endurance. When at ten o'clock I found myself still conscious, I knew that yet another way of earning a living had been presented to me.

Though being a model was such a great physical strain, there was a sense in which the work was easy to do. It required no aptitude, no education, no references, and no previous experience. You had only to say "I do" and you were stuck with it like marriage. It was also easy work to get. The war was on and I was almost the only roughly male person left with two arms and two legs. I applied to the secretaries of many of the London schools and a few of these gave me work, but it was the suburban and even provincial schools that kept me busy. To these I was recommended first by other models, who were amazingly kind to me, and after a while by the instructors. In a frantic effort to be full-time part-time teachers and so earn colossal temporary wages for forty or more hours a week, they rushed from one county to another snatching up in each the maximum number of hours that the Ministry of Education would allow. Once they discovered I was reliable they took me with them—frequently by car. One of the worst hazards of teaching "life" was the lack of dependability in models. Nowadays big schools employ "battery" models. Their engagement lasts a whole term or even a year. In those days bookings were often given six months in advance and the work was "free-range." It was spread over the term in odd patterns—six Mondays, perhaps, for portrait or every Wednesday of the term for sculpture, depending on the school's curriculum. By the time these scattered dates came around the person engaged for them had often found elsewhere a full-time job that he preferred. There were only a few devotees of the profession. Even in those days someone masquerading as a model was frequently only a typist with romantic ideas, a hooligan in need of funds, or a dancer who hadn't made the grade. In the suburbs, the nonarrival of the model was a disaster. A replacement could not possibly arrive until the middle of the day and by then the students, always on the boil, would have wrecked the place.

Posing was the first job I had ever had in which I understood what I was doing. Always until now I had worked or tried to work to a standard other than my own. In commercial art I had always made an effort to draw things so that others would find them appetizing and worth their money. Even in my book I had attempted to describe ideas so that others would find them interesting. For some artists and writers this may not be difficult. They may have tastes they share with the average consumer or the gentle reader. I had so little in common with real people that someone once said to me, "I think I like things better before you've praised them." In these circumstances it was hardly surprising that my drawings and my writings brought me so little success. I decided to set about the job of modeling in the opposite way—to force upon the students the qualities that I felt life drawing ought to possess.

When I had attended the art school in High Wycombe twelve long dark years before, the hours I had most enjoyed were those spent in the "life" room but, though some of the models had been of a beauty like the sun, hardly any of them had seemed to me to be doing enough. They had stood or sat or lain about like ordinary mortals and not a bit like the figures of Michelangelo. I wanted to change all that. I was an avowed enemy of culture but I admired his work unconditionally.

Of all the paintings from the nude that I ever saw, only his appeared to me to be not merely of living people but of what it is like to be alive. The drawings of Ingres, continually held before the lusterless eyes of students as an example for them to follow, always seemed to me to be seen from outside—to display a lascivious preoccupation with surfaces—with the convexities and concavities of the body. Michelangelo worked from within. He described not the delights of touching or seeing a man but the excitement of being Man. Every stroke he made spoke of the pleasure of exerting, restraining, and putting to the utmost use the divine gravity-resisting machine. His work had the opposite quality to the paintings of Rembrandt, into whose canvases the subjects stumble, broken, conscious of their physical faults and begging the beholder for forgiveness.

I was determined to be as Sistine as hell. It was fully in accord with my endeavor to live in the continuous present from head to foot. Unfortunately I was not naturally equipped to carry out this mission. I was undersized in all respects except for a pigeon chest and a huge head. When stripped, I looked less like "Il David" than a plucked chicken that died of myxomatosis. It could hardly have been otherwise. I had lived most of my life by starving and gorging alternately and had never taken any exercize other than walking the streets. However, I twisted and turned, climbed up the walls of life rooms and rolled on their paint-daubed floors morning, nude, and night for several days a week for six years.

The students were furious.

I had not foreseen this. I had only anticipated hostility from the staff, thinking of teachers as thin, bespectacled, Gothic creatures hysterically concerned for the reputations of their schools. This turned out to be a false image. Art masters were at great pains to distinguish themselves from other pedagogues. Even in those days they were deliberately jolly. When, with time, even teachers of academic subjects began to relax their forbidding posture, art masters found themselves compelled to resort to a rusticity amounting in some cases to oafishness.

Even those who were embarrassed by my antics remained kind. Unhooking me from the picture rail, they would say quietly, "All you have to do is to stand as though you were waiting for a bus." What kind of an injunction was that when, at a bus stop, I looked as though I were on the dais of some life room? One man, working on the Sickert principle, went so far as to assemble a washstand, a cracked basin, and a dim gray towel in the hope of toning me down. As I stepped in among these negligently posed props I asked, "And how do you propose to make me look like home?" The instructor who had gone to all this trouble breathed deeply down his nose. "There you have me," he said.

Aware of this difficulty most teachers simply turned me loose on the class. As I stood *en arabesque* on top of a pillar, Mr. McCullough said, "Now draw that. Wings optional." He was secretly filled with a fiendish glee at seeing his pupils struggle with a subject that not even they could take for granted. My poses were so extreme they could not be held long enough to suit a painting session. I worked chiefly in drawing classes. I preferred them. Drawing is a science; painting is just something for the long winter evenings.

More than anything it was the fact that my contortions made their work more difficult that caused the students to manifest such hostility. When I had first seen the boys in their corduroy trousers and the girls in their Hungarian blouses, I had assumed that I would get on all right with them. It had been many years since I had been in a crowd of young people. I had forgotten or had never really known what they were like.

The young always have the same problem—how to rebel and conform at the same time. They have now solved this by defying their elders and copying one another. The result to grown-ups is that they seem brutish and stuffy at the same time. The fact that I was eccentric did not prejudice them in my favor. I was peculiar in a manner other than theirs, and my naive enthusiasm merely highlighted the fact that I was a generation older than they. I was a senile delinquent: In their eyes an unforgivable sin.

Toward the end of the war art students became very numerous. Perhaps drawing was a pleasant distraction from the bombs before which some people tended to go to pieces. When people broke out, their number did not decrease. The Minister of Education ran down to the water's edge and, as our brave boys disembarked, scattered grants to art schools over their heads like confetti. Some fell on men whose art training had been interrupted by their service with His Majesty's Forces; some reached stockbrokers, stevedores, streetwalkers, and stage managers. Everyone who could availed himself of the Minister's kindness. The chance to study anything without paying fees, even if it is something that can never be the slightest use, must not be allowed to pass by. In this way the Great Art Rush began. Gone were the dignified days when an intending pupil visited the principal by appointment and was advised which classes to attend. Now, on the first day of each session, a mob of would-be students pressed with Klondike intensity against the entrance to every art school in the country, waving their grants above their heads like prospecting claims. At ten o'clock, when the doors opened, the crowds surged up the stairs and sat down wherever they could. If, by some miscalculation, anyone found himself in the lavatory, that was what he studied for that term.

The climate of art was milder than it is now. The enmity felt for me by students remained for the most part unexpressed. I was part-time sacred—a hated demi-god who occasionally became an object of reverence. Once in a while a female student, to show her peers that she could, would make bringing me a cup of tea a pretext for sitting on the corner of the throne and talking.

This sometimes led to trouble.

There are girls who do not like real life. When they hear the harsh belches of its engines approaching along the straight road that leads from childhood, through adolescence, to adultery, they dart into a side turning. When they take their hands away from their eyes, they find themselves in the gallery of the ballet. There they sit for many years feeding their imaginations on those fitful glimpses of a dancer's hand or foot which seats in the upper part of theaters afford. When I was young I too "adored" the ballet. For me its charm was that one of the dancers might break his neck, but what appeals to these girls is the moonlit atmosphere of love and death which the withering hand of truth can never compromise. During the intervals they hold hands, numbed by excessive applause, with the homosexual young man who is bound to be sitting on their right or left. Even the boys, who have no positive intention of deceiving them, are drawn into a relationship damaging to the girls. After a lot of squeaking at the bus stop when the ballet is over, the young men pursue on the way home other interests, which at least yield a morsel of satisfaction. The girls can do nothing but return to their joss-stick-perfumed nunneries. From this position there is no way back. They can only stay where they are until, in middle age, they awaken to the realization that they don't know a single person who isn't queer. Then they move on to the uncharted quicksands of nudism, Yoga, vegetarianism, and other diseases of the soul too terrible to name.

Some of these girls are innocent enough to think that these unreal friendships will lead to true love—a kind of sexual intercourse that will happen to them without their having to take too horribly much notice. Even those who are sufficiently sophisticated to know that this will not be so persist in these relationships. They provide an opportunity to lavish emotion upon a pseudo-man without paying the price that in heterosexual circumstances would be inevitable.

Apart from the young woman who threw herself on the linoleum of my room in Denbigh Street, I met several other girls of this kind. One overtook me in Smith Street in Chelsea and begged me to teach her to paint cats; another wrote me anonymous poetry in care of a café where I used incessantly to sit. The worst case that I ever had to deal with occurred shortly after I became a model.

The day before one Easter holiday, I was standing in the corridor of a vast technical college outside London waiting for my wages. A student with whom I had exchanged a few polite words came up to me to say good-bye. It was her last day. I was still trying to think of something eternal to say when she suddenly seized my hand and kissed it. The moment I had recovered from the shock, I glanced up and down the passage to see if there had been any witnesses to this blurring of my public image. Then I turned to ask the girl what on earth she thought she was doing. She was already running away, as well she might. I later realized that her behavior was the result of having read a book by Mrs. Nijinsky, in which she describes a similar gambit in her merciless pursuit of her husband. On finding this partially reasonable explanation of the event, I regained my polar calm. A week or two later the girl wrote to me asking if we could meet. Foolishly thinking that all I represented to her was a glimpse of the life beautiful, I suggested that, after a Sunday morning class at her old school, I should bring her back with me to London, give her lunch in a hooligans' restaurant, and take her to tea with someone sufficiently untidy to pass for a genius. This scheme was put into action, and all seemed to be going well until we were standing in Holborn amid the usual crowd of hostile witnesses waiting for a bus that would take her home. Then, without even a cry of warning, she flung herself upon me with a weight fit to bring me to the ground and implored me to kiss her. I was very annoyed. Straightening my knees with a great effort, I said sternly, "You had better catch your bus." This she did, but the hideous entanglement did not end there. I received a letter from one of her friends entreating me to continue to see the girl. The implication was that suicide would follow if I refused. I replied explaining that I was homosexual and that, as we now all knew that a beautiful friendship was not all that was expected of me, further meetings would be a complete waste of time. It took several other letters saying the same things more and more unkindly to bring the relationship to an end.

A friend in the forces to whom I described by post this chain of degrading incidents replied, "How could you have been taken in by all that soulmate rubbish?" My sin had not really been naivety but vanity. I had, as always, been reluctant to forgo a single ounce of friendship and had imagined that, by strength of will and the use of an unremittingly antiseptic manner, I could have and hold the situation on my own terms.

Another friend who was told the tale asked me what the girl looked like. When I described her, he said, "But if she had been good-looking and as masculine as you are feminine (if such a thing were possible), would not her advances have been acceptable?" By asking this question he showed me that to him and doubtless to many other people, an effeminate homosexual was simply someone who liked sex but could not face the burdens, responsibilities, and decisions that might crush him if he married a woman. This idea seemed to me totally erroneous. It left out altogether the devouring preoccupation with the male sexual organ which, as soon as his erotic habits are completely formed, becomes the main and finally the only interest in a homosexual's life. The question was put to me quite sincerely by an entirely heterosexual man. This showed me that in normal love the emphasis was not on the sexual organs. The relationship was a clash or a union of personalities laid bare by sexual passion. Between two men it consists of each using the utmost force of his personality to gain access to the sexual organs of the other. Of this situation I was not yet in my own life aware.

Chapter 20

Most of the models I knew I had met very casually while we stood in some secretary's office or waited in the tea queue of a school canteen. We flexed the muscles of our bare feet and pooled the misery of our falling arches and distended veins. There was one whom I met by formal introduction. Just as I was about to begin work in one of the top floor rooms of St. Martin's School, Mr. Hofbauer came and stood at the foot of the throne. He was really the art editor of Ivor Nicholson & Watson, but occasionally he disguised himself as an evening student. He told me that the man posing in the next room wanted to meet me. I went next door where, not in entire forgetfulness but in utter nakedness, this other model and I bowed and shook hands.

When the class was over he suggested that we should visit one of two of the cafés which he frequented in Charlotte Street. If it had not been for this casual invitation, a whole world might forever have remained closed to me. By night, when these places came most vividly to life, no one who had not a pathfinder's badge could have reached them. The blackout made them indistinguishable from the ordinary shops on their right and left. Even if I had known their whereabouts, I would never have dared to enter them alone. Eating under the ferocious scrutiny of strangers gave me indigestion. But once I had been introduced by an habitué and found that my appearance was acceptable there, my whole social life changed.

Until now my evenings had been spent lying down (to recover from the strain of standing for seven hours) or writing to my mother or mending my socks or having a good cry. Suddenly all these activities, which I had regarded as mildly pleasant before, were brutally squeezed into hidden corners of my leisure so that I could devote two or three nights a week to sitting in one or other of the cafés in Charlotte Street. This occupation represented far more than a change of pastime; it marked the discovery of a new self. To go with my public face I now began to construct a public character. I moved from concentrating on individuals to dealing with crowds; but with a difference. In youth my object had been to reform. I now wanted to entertain. Here the reformation had already taken place. I was moving among people to whom my homosexuality was of no consequence whatsoever. I began a whirlwind courtship of an entire district.

In appearance these cafés were just like those from which I had been barred fifteen years before in Old Compton Street. In all other respects they were very different. Many homosexuals were present but there was no element of camp. They were also quite unlike the places which were to spring up fifteen years later where, amid the excruciating discomfort of industrial design and the cacophony of guitarists, people of all ages could be seen teen-aging like mad. They even differed from their contemporary counterparts in Chelsea, which were clean to the point of primness and riddled with an artiness which I now saw to be but a feeble pretense of bohemianism.

In Charlotte Street there was a sound of revelry by night and London's capital had gathered then her beauty and her chivalry and bright the lamps shone on brave women and fair men. There was a marvelous generosity about the way the restaurants were run. The helpings were large, even discounting the portions of drowned cockroaches which were served, at no extra cost, with every dish. The staff was friendly and unhurried to the verge of immobility. So was the clientele: bookies and burglars, actresses and artisans, poets and prostitutes; and there was an entirely new caste brought into being by the war—deserters. These did not merely frequent the cafés. They couldn't leave. In a smoky cellar called "The Low Dive" they stayed for weeks at a time. Ultimately this place was closed by the police. This seemed a foolish move since the deserters there could be taken in the swarm. With this subsection of hooligans I had a special bond, because I had two exemption papers. One had been flung at me by the medical board and said that I suffered from sexual perversion. Another sent to me by the Labor Exchange presumably out of sheer kindness gave no particular reason for my inability to enter the forces. These I could lend to anyone who wished for a few hours to leave his hideout. It was only necessary for the deserter in question to decide whether he preferred the hardships of jail to the disgrace of being Quentin Crisp.

Despite the variety of classes, sexes, nationalities, and callings represented in the cafés of Charlotte Street, there prevailed an effortless acceptance of the other person's identity. There were rows—even fights—but I never heard any cattiness. I was never told any scandal.

From my point of view it was the restaurateurs whose broad-mindedness was most amazing. Whereas in Chelsea eating houses I was on sufferance and was warned not to sit near the window, in Charlotte Street I was not merely accepted without question but was frequently given meals on credit. Occasionally I was even lent money by the proprietor to buy black-market goods that the customers and the staff were perpetually offering for sale.

The only people I ever saw turned out were those who combined fighting too much with eating too little. Even for these exile was never intended to be permanent. When Toni tired of a rowdy group of girls he flicked their bare arms with a wet tea towel. They left without taking offense to return later, with cheerful grins and long sleeves.

I still sometimes dabbled in commercial art—usually by doing book jackets. These were the commissions I liked best. They did not necessitate doing a drawing so large that distant parts of it could only be reached by pinning it on the wall (I never owned an easel). On the other hand, none of the work was so small that it could only be done with the aid of a magnifying glass. Also the amount of lettering involved was seldom great. I learned to handle books so that they fell open at the murder and, even when this did not happen, I was soon able to read through them rather than read them. The narrative evaded me but the style in which it was written told me what kind of reader it was intended for. Once I knew this, designing the cover became simple. If my eye was caught by the words, "Her eyes filled with tears and her bosom rose and fell," it was obvious the book was meant for women (pastel shades, dark-haired heroine with shallow cleavage); if the novel had been written for men it would have said, "Her huge breasts shuddered with emotion in their straitjacket of pink satin" (dark tones, red-haired heroine with deep cleavage). If in three hundred pages there was no mention of breasts at all, the volume must be a documentary (no illustration) or for children (bright colors, mouse-haired heroine with *no* cleavage).

These rules applied at that time because the intentions of publishers toward readers were still honorable. Now that the marketing of all goods, including books, has become a shameless hoax practiced on innocent consumers, the works of M. Zola are packaged to look as though they were by Mr. Spillane. This ruse works because no one would dare to take a book back to a shop because it wasn't as filthy as the cover promised.

Among the firms for whom I most often worked was Messrs. Ivor Nicholson & Watson, whose art editor told me that if I wanted to write something for publication, the time and place were now and here. During the war, though there was a widely advertised paper shortage, publishers would issue any old muck. Even so I thought it prudent not to attempt anything long. I decided to write a mere pamphlet in verse. The idea for this had come to me some time before when a friend had uttered in my hearing a limerick about a kangaroo who offered himself to the zoo. It ended:

But whenever he tried
The committee replied,
"We already have plenty of you."

But the time I next saw my friend I had added a second verse:

If you like you may leave us your name
So that we may go into your claim
And then doubtless you'll hear,
In the course of the year,
An evasive reply to the same.

My friend said that this had now become a slashing indictment of the Ministry of Labor. I rather shakily agreed but, even when elaborated into forty-eight rather clumsy verses of angerless satire, the idea seemed to need something else to make it worth a publisher's while. I decided to try to ensnare Mr. Peake into illustrating it. He was at that time the most fashionable illustrator in England. In spite of this he frequently sat in the Bar-B-Q in Chelsea and was not in the least inaccessible. When talking to him I allowed it to seem that Messrs. Ivor Nicholson & Watson had already commissioned the book and he declared himself willing to illustrate anything that was certain of appearing in print. These words had hardly issued from his lips when I leaped up and ran all the way to Manchester Square to tell the publishers that Mr. Peake was simply dying to illustrate a book I had written. They expressed their interest in anything that Mr. Peake chose to work upon. Running to and fro and making a series of statements that seemed increasingly positive but could never be used against me was much harder work than writing the verses. These only took two afternoons. That was as it should be. It was certainly not the writing but the chicanery that ensured publication.

When the book came out, anxious to know if sales were booming, I crept into Hatchards, where a pile of copies was on display. To my delight there was a man staring at the uppermost of these. This, however, turned out to be Mr. Peake.

I do not think *All This and Bevin Too* can have been a triumph. Although I was immediately commissioned to write (and paid for) another book, the second was never published.

I sank back into oblivion.

I saw myself sinking and would have cried out for help had there been at hand anyone who could have been the slightest use. Coming closely upon my defeat at the hands of the movie industry, this failure to reach the literary big time might have been hard to bear had not my social life at that time been so eventful.

Chapter 21

Into the Cuzco of the layabout civilization came a man who was the size of a barn door and as easily pushed to and fro. The night I first saw him he was badly in want of a meal but, as soon as some supper was placed in front of him, his great shock of white hair fell forward onto the mound of chips on his plate. More than food, he longed for sleep. I took him home with me. Nothing reared its ugly head. The man slept and slept. The next morning when he was leaving, I nodded toward a small bundle of possessions that he had brought with him and said, "You can leave your things there while you're looking for a room."

Three long dark years later they were still there.

At first our association consisted of my meeting him in Toni's or The Scala. To both of these I went at least twice a week. I brought him back to my room if he needed a good night's sleep. Heaven knew where he kipped when he was not with me. After a while, he formed the habit of visiting me every weekend, and my life became a series of Saturdays for which I prepared and Sundays from which I recovered, but I never gave up hope. I never let more than a few hours pass without including in the conversation the words, "When you have a room of your own . . ." and I never gave him a latchkey. I knew that once I had done that I was a lifer. In all other respects my manner was, as one of my friends said, "dedicated." Because I could tell that he had never known a world in which he had the upper hand, I became his slave. When, presumably to normalize our relationship, he suggested a little sex, I concurred. A year or so later, in the middle of a sketchy embrace, he said, "Let's pack this in." I said, "Let's."

Like the heroine of *The Garden of Allah*, I put my love to the utmost test.

It failed.

Shortly before one Easter holiday I told him that it was time I visited my mother for at least a weekend. These words touched his sensibilities. He was deeply devoted to his mother. He gathered up his things and left. As he did so he said, "I don't see what I've done wrong even now."

He had done nothing wrong. He could do none. He was a man without guile. His only fault was that he existed. His parting words would have reproached me till my dying day were it not for the fact that, immediately after the war, I heard that he was married. This was an outcome of which I had despaired. I knew he was Kinsey-queer rather than coot-queer. He merely associated with homosexuals because they bought their love by the pound. He had gravitated toward Charlotte Street because there people were so appallingly equal. I had feared he might never marry because his idea of courtship seemed to be a few neolithic lurches toward the object of his desire. Living with him was the practical part of an examination in the theoretical section of which I had already done badly. In the second half I scored no marks at all.

Having lain alone for thirty-odd years I found that I could not fully relax if I shared my bed with anybody, let alone someone of Barn Door's dimensions. Never get into a narrow double bed with a wide single man. After a while we took it in turns to sleep among the dust on the floor and wake in the morning more or less flock-finished. The routine of my life was altered in areas which I had thought were fixed for all time. We ate at home on Saturday and Sunday evenings. I was compelled to shop—an activity which I had gradually reduced to a minimum so as to avoid the veiled insults which, together with inferior goods, were heaped upon me by salesmen.

In the matter of clothes I was supported entirely by voluntary contributions, like a hospital, and, when introduced to anyone, however interested in other parts of their bodies I might be, I always looked first at their feet to see if these were as small as mine. I hoped their cast-off footwear might be given to me. The trouble with shoes is that they are unalterable. All other clothing I accepted indiscriminately. I could at any time enlist the services of a certain Mrs. Markham, known throughout Soho as the greatest trouser-taperer in the world.

Thus the need to visit men's-wear shops had been almost totally eliminated, but no way had yet come to hand of acquiring secondhand food. I was compelled to buy it new.

If in the future a doctor discovers that certain diseases are indigenous to homosexuality, one of these will be a distended bladder—the result of trying to avoid the risk of arrest automatically incurred by using a public lavatory. The other will be vitamin C deficiency acquired because the staff of vegetable shops are so impertinent that one would suffer almost anything rather than deal with them.

Having put up with Saturday morning's round of humiliations, I was obliged to cook. This I could only do by racial memory. I had never before gone further than to make toast when the bread had become too green to eat raw. Now I found myself clawing away at the carcasses of dead animals until my nails were full of blood and I felt like a mangy old eagle.

Washing up could still be kept to one operation a week if I never tried to pass the fish barrier but ate fish, if at all, only on Sunday evening.

I found that I had become so spinsterish that I was

made neurotic not only by my life of domesticity but by the slightest derangement of my room. I would burst into a fit of weeping if the kettle was not facing due east. My efforts at self-control completely exhausted me, but I knew that if I ever said with the faintest asperity such words as "Oh, do be quiet!" or "Don't put your feet up there!" one or other of us would have to join the Foreign Legion.

Though the situation often got out of hand, my friend was never rebellious, but there were times when the realization swept over him that I was all he'd got. Then he hated me.

I got shingles. My skin hung down over one side of my rib cage like the wallpaper in my room. Yet I was only bearing two-sevenths of the weight that lies for a lifetime on the shoulders of the average married woman. I had to face the fact that as tender comrade, faithful friend, I was a dead loss.

These unpleasant facts about my own character were but grim confirmation of long-held suspicions. What I learned about the rest of the human race through my association with Barn Door was a startling revelation, but I have no doubt that in knowing him I came to know the whole world.

There is no great dark man.

Even under an exterior as rugged as a mountain range, there lurks the same wounded, wincing psyche that cripples the rest of us. Where we are led to think we will find strength, we shall discover force; where we hope for ruthlessness, we shall unearth spite; and when we think we are clinging desperately to a rock, it is falling upon us. Even with a man whose neck is thicker than his head, if we are not careful, we shall be involved in an argument about who most loves whom. The trouble is that, if you find that by mistake you have bitten into a soft center, you can't very well put it back in the box.

A little old lady once said to me, "I have known a

great many men. All of them had to be carried every step of the way."

This was true of my friend. He could hardly stand, let alone totter forward under his burdens. They were no less heavy for being imaginary.

In a heartless hoax practiced upon innocent dragonflies, entomologists laughingly placed the tails in the mouths of some of these creatures. The insects gratefully ate their nether extremities as far up as they could reach. They then died. This was the stage of evolution at which my friend had remained. When I gave him a nail file he used it on his toenails until they sank below the horizon; then he filed his toes. This and other similar happenings at first gave me the idea that he was a divinely rudimentary being. If he was it did not save him from being painfully aware of his unenviable position in society, rendered no better by knowing me. About this he could never make up his mind what to do. Sometimes he walked several yards behind me so as to be able to send me up for the amusement of passers-by; at others he made unprovoked protestations of friendship in the presence of strangers who happened to be sitting at our table in a café. In spite of spending so much time among hooligans he conceived of himself as being poorer and of lower degree than his acquaintances and felt that these handicaps caused him to be alone in the world. I pointed out that he spent his weekends with me, his days with his workmates, and his nights flailing his arms and singing snatches of opera in various cafés crowded to the walls. None of these activities assuaged his feeling of isolation. Its real cause was his inability to take an interest in other people. No one had ever taught him how.

His greatest burden was time. Now for the first time I understood the true purpose of the radio, in the wailing, crooning, stuttering stream of which he bathed himself every waking hour. Its function is not to entertain but to drown the ticking of all clocks. Having, myself, spent so many happy hours alone, frequently doing nothing but breathing, I was bewildered to discover that for my friend spare time was an imposition. If one event, say Sunday lunch, ended before another such as the movies could begin, he became distraught. He cleaned his shoes—yea, though they were already like crimson glass. He put a new flint in his lighter, and he twiddled the whistling, creaking, cracking knobs of our crotchety wireless set but, though he spent his days picking and shoveling, the one thing he never did was to sit and dream. In this respect I would have been tempted to say that he was ill did I not know that health consists of having the same diseases as one's neighbors.

Chapter 22

There had to be another war. The sadness of the First World War and the sweetness of songs like "There's a Long, Long Trail" were qualities memory had bestowed on experiences that at the time were colorless. While I lived through them, if I noticed anything except the men in uniform, it was a slight lack of variety in the food. My prep-schoolmaster once told the class I was in that it was part of the air-raid generation. I tried to look deprived but I had no clear notion of how to act out the distinction his words gave us.

Perhaps it was because the First World War had left me so unmoved that I did not take the second one very seriously. When news reached me in 1940 that London was burning I was sitting in a cottage outside Basingstoke with a pregnant actress. I had nothing to lose but my airbrush and my typewriter but, explaining that I ought to spread my brooding pinions over these, I rushed home. The truth was that I couldn't bear to miss the great drama of my time.

Back in the city I noticed at once that, though some of the buildings had been ruined, most of the people had been improved. Everyone talked to everyone—even to me. The golden age had temporarily arrived.

Even before this, my position in society had undergone a change for reasons over which I had no control. The women of London had gone butch. At all ages and on every social level, they had taken to uniforms—or near-uniforms. They wore jackets, trousers, and sensible shoes. I could now buy easily the footwear that I had always favored—black lace-up shoes with firm, medium heels. I became indistinguishable from a woman.

Once, as I stood at a bus stop, a policeman accused me of this. After looking me up and down for nearly a minute he asked me what I was doing.

Me: I'm waiting for a bus.

Policeman: You're dressed as a woman.

Me (amazed): I'm wearing trousers.

Policeman: Women wear trousers.

Me: Are you blaming me because everybody else is so eccentric?

Policeman (louder): You're dressed as a woman and you'd better catch a bus quick or there will be trouble. People don't like that sort of thing (pointing at my flyless trousers and my high-heeled shoes).

The policeman was right. People did not like that sort of thing and could now add patriotism to their other less easily named reasons for hating me. It was only superficially and only by day that strangers were friendly. Throughout the war I was at times in very unpleasant situations. The difficulty was to pass from a place where I could be clearly seen into the blackout without being followed. I did not always manage this.

As I was standing in an Underground train on my way to Tottenham Court Road station, the nearest stop to Fitzrovia, some men left their seats and came to have a closer look at me. They stood around discussing my private life in public voices. Then one of them put his hand on the front of my trousers and said, "Yes, he has got something there. It is a man."

At Holborn station I waited until the doors of the train were about to shut. Then I darted out onto the platform, but one of the men must have managed to wedge his foot in between the closing doors. As I ran up the escalator, I could hear feet pounding the stairs behind me. I should not have gone out into the street. It placed me, when I turned around, in a position where my pursuers could see me better than I could see them. This time they hit me with a weapon of some kind or hammered my face against the wall or else I fell very heavily as I lost consciousness. Certainly the damage was worse than usual. As soon as I came to, I stood up to avoid being trampled on by accident and, as usual in such situations, counted my fingernails and felt my teeth with my tongue. They were all present and correct but my face was bleeding. Holding my handkerchief to my nose, I began to walk home. I couldn't go back into the Underground station. I had no idea what I looked like.

After an evening class in Willesden I was returning to real life by bus. From the top front seat I saw an Australian soldier standing in the queue at Notting Hill Gate. Even in the blackout I recognized his road-sweeper's hat. As the bus moved forward again, using the darkened window before me as a mirror, I noticed that this man had seated himself immediately behind me. A moment later I felt his hand solemnly placed on my head. I sat motionless, never taking my eyes from the window. Presently I saw his reflection take from its pocket a comb. At this point I guessed that whatever was going to happen would not involve violence. For the rest of the journey to Hyde Park Corner, the soldier sat quietly and combed my hair. I do not think he can have been drunk. He could understand the architecture of my coiffure which baffled many total abstainers.

Australia must be a strange country. It is the home of the kangaroo, the duck-billed platypus, and the hair-comber. Sometimes when I told this tale in Toni's someone would say, "Can't have had any idea you were really a man!" On other occasions the comment was, "Must have known you weren't a woman."

The blackout was almost never really black. One night, when London was filled with a dense fog, I remember that it became necessary for me to creep along with outstretched hands feeling brickwork, railings, and passers-by in an effort to keep my bearings. The rest of the time, even in winter, I did not have to diminish my pace or even watch the ground at my feet. I never fell down and seldom crashed into anything.

On one of these twilit nights I was sweeping along Ebury Street when a tall bearded silhouette passed me by. I could not put up with that so I stopped. The stranger retraced his steps to where I stood. "Who are you?" I asked, and he replied, "I am Angus McBean. Who are you?" I hurriedly explained that I was nobody but added, as an extenuating circumstance, that I knew plenty of people to whom his name was sacred. There and then he said he would photograph me. When I told him that I never paid for anything he did not withdraw his offer. A few evenings later he took about a dozen pictures of me in three-quarters of an hour.

Even if we had not met in Ebury Street, I feel that we would have met somewhere sooner or later. Though it was something that he did every day of his life, Mr. McBean longed to take photographs as fervently as I desired to be photographed. He worked very quickly and methodically, his instructions as clear as lenses. "Lick your lower lip and let it hang" and, the moment before the camera clicked, "Pull your ears back." When I asked him what portrait photography was all about he said, "It's simple. They want to be beautiful." To this end, even on great beauties, every surface that was at half moon—that was passing from light to dark—was retouched from the texture of an orange to the smoothness of an apple. With some of his sitters everything was retouched but their titles. One woman, while he was deciding what on earth to do with her, snatched up in both hands the swags of superfluous flesh that encumbered her jawbones and said, "You do understand, don't you, that all this is not part of the essential me."

Perhaps the best exposition of his technique is contained in this story. Dandy Nichols, the cockney comedienne, when I mentioned Mr. McBean's name, said, "I must go to Angus and have some mugs done." Later I asked him if a certain Miss Nichols had visited his studio to "have some mugs done." "I saw that was what she had come for," he replied, "but I did cups and saucers."

Of the pictures he took of me, my friends said, "I see you can go down to history as a famous beauty whatever you happen to look like."

The recipe for success that I had seen in the life of Mr. Cross I now witnessed again in the boundless energy of Mr. McBean. At eleven at night when I was departing, he was just beginning to make props, mount prints, and construct surreal backgrounds for actresses to lie on, lie under, sit in, or poke their heads through.

In obedience to that force in my nature that drove me long ago to pass from admitting that I was homosexual to protesting the fact, my slightly British determination to ignore the hazards of wartime London soon became a desire to embrace disaster. It was fear that was the lure. All other emotions I had to work up artificially. I could never be sure whether I felt them or only wished that I did. When I was afraid I knew the sensation was genuine. As soon as the bombardment of London began I felt totally engaged. When the ground began to shake and the sky became pink with doom I could hardly stay at home. I ceased to go out only when it was necessary and started to search London for my own true bomb.

Among the places which could be used as a pretext for crossing the city in an air raid was the flat in Russell Court that my art student friend shared with the Czech. I visited her unmercifully until, one day, she telephoned me to implore me not to come as the Czech seemed to be on the fringe of a nervous breakdown.

I should have foreseen this but I did not. In the

company I kept a man would have to behave very oddly indeed before his friends would call in a doctor. We all attributed the Czech's eccentricity to his nationality.

After a while he took to standing all night with his back to the wall, his gaze fixed on the door in case *they* should come in. His girlfriend could not do otherwise than commit him to a mental hospital.

The war did not cause his madness. It aggravated it by pressing on the soft wall of a hopelessly unrealistic personality. In order to enjoy the war it was essential to be tough—and lucky.

For most of 1940 London by night was like one of those dimly lit parties that their hosts hope are slightly wicked. In a cozy gloom young men and women strolled arm in arm along Piccadilly murmuring, "It's not as bad tonight as last night, is it?" Policemen allowed themselves a certain skittishness. "Don't care, huh?" they cried as I passed them sheltering in doorways. Taxi drivers unbent so far as to take one part of the way home free of charge. As soon as bombs started to fall, the city became like a paved double bed. Voices whispered suggestively to you as you walked along; hands reached out if you stood still and in dimly lit trains people carried on as they had once behaved only in taxis. I was only becoming aware that railway carriages were the playgrounds of exhibitionists now that I spent so many hours a week traveling to and from art schools in the Home Counties. I was surprised at the frequency with which I found myself sitting opposite some man who between stations decided to try to win fame, like Mr. Mercator, for his projection. The insult implied in these offers of instant sex no longer troubled me. I was worried because I knew so well that what seemed to be starting out as a frolic might easily turn into something quite different. I realized too that if any unpleasantness occurred, so far from being able to enlist anyone's sympathy, I should be considered to have caused it. Neither distaste nor apprehension must be displayed at such a moment. As I hope all compendiums for young ladies tell their readers, it is best to adopt a completely matter-of-fact air and, feigning a yawn, to say, "Oh, put it away."

Outside railway trains, overtures made possible by the blackout—though hardly delicate—were at least a little more romantic.

Once, when I emerged from Leicester Square Underground station, the outline of the buildings on the opposite side of the road looked so unfamiliar that I thought I must have taken the wrong exit. When I asked an invisible passerby where I was, he kissed me on the lips, told me I was in Newport Street, and walked on.

By heterosexuals the life after death is imagined as a world of light, where there is no parting. If there is a heaven for homosexuals, which doesn't seem very likely, it will be very poorly lit and full of people they can feel pretty confident they will never have to meet again. It is only partly because they are ashamed of themselves and wish to remain unrecognized that this environment seems so desirable. The chief reason is that it makes possible contacts of astounding physical intimacy without the intervention of personality. To either partner, the other is a phallus garlanded with fantasies, chiefly of masculinity. The homosexual world is a world of spinsters. Most homosexuals over the age of twenty-five will play, on the physical level, an active, passive, or unspecified role with the same or a different partner from night to night or even from hour to hour, but emotionally they search perpetually for a real man who desires passionately (as opposed to making do with) another man. This being, if he exists, is so rare that one might as well enter a monastery on reaching puberty. The less drastic alternative is to live a real sex life in a dream world. This can best be done in the dark with strangers.

Playgrounds where these circumstances obtain are not easy to find. When discovered they are frequented first by the few, later by the many, and finally by the police. At one time the towpath at Putney was such a dreamland, but it became so well known that the police took to driving motor launches along that part of the river and suddenly shining searchlights on its southern bank. When this happened everyone who was not already in that position flung himself flat on the ground.

As this riverside brothel declined in popularity Whitstone Pond on Hampstead Heath became all the rage. More foliage abounded there. This lent a certain sylvan charm and some useful escape routes. Now there is a certain cinema in London where it is said that all the films shown have a "Q" certificate (no normal person may be admitted to any part of this program unless accompanied by a homosexual). It hardly matters what films are exhibited. War films are the type most frequently shown: their soundtracks help to conceal the noise of creaking seat springs. Movies which have extensive snow scenes are avoided as these cast too much light back into the auditorium. During the war, however, this cinema was almost empty and the riverbank at Putney became a desert. The whole of London was one long towpath, one vast movie house.

I had always shunned these homosexual playgrounds; less from purity than vanity. I did not want a liaison in conditions which might tend to obliterate my individuality. On this subject the last word must go to a Canadian actress who said, "If the fuss is not about ourselves, then what the hell?"

Then suddenly, into the feast of love and death that St. Adolf had set before the palates of the English—parched these long dark twenty-five years—Mr. Roosevelt began, with Olympian hands, to shower the American forces. This brand-new army of (no) occupation flowed through the streets of London like cream on strawberries, like melted butter over green peas. Labeled "with love from Uncle Sam" and packaged in uniforms so tight that in them their owners could fight for nothing but their honor, these "bundles for Britain" leaned against the lamp posts of Shaftesbury Avenue or lolled on the steps of thin-lipped statues of dead English statesmen. As they sat in the cafés or stood in the pubs, their bodies bulged through every straining khaki fiber toward our feverish hands. Their voices were like warm milk, their skins as flawless as expensive India rubber, and their eyes as beautiful as glass. Above all it was the liberality of their natures that was so marvelous. Never in the history of sex was so much offered to so many by so few. At the first gesture of acceptance from a stranger, words of love began to ooze from their lips, sexuality from their bodies, and pound notes from their pockets like juice from a peeled peach.

The obliquity of the English was something to which I had been accustomed from childhood. My father was a living—well, an example of it. Taught by him I had walked all my life in the excruciating armor of self-restraint. I was, therefore, never more than mildly surprised at the hedging antics of strangers who followed me in the street. They would sometimes walk behind me for half an hour, quickening their pace if I hurried, slackening it if I dawdled, and crossing over the road when I did, as though we were playing Follow-my-leader. If, to avoid any further waste of their time, I turned and politely explained that I was a dead loss, they would snort with indignation and say, "I don't know what you mean." It was the directness of the Americans that astonished me. Apparently from the 49th parallel to the Gulf of Mexico face-saving is unknown. These young men walked, not behind, but beside you, and at once began a conversation with some such words as "You and me's interested in the same things, I guess." If you wanted, like Madam Butterfly, "a little bit to tease them" and said "But I'm interested in the life of the spirit," they replied, "Me too." If they were rejected without equivocation, they accepted the fact good-naturedly. Even when it was obvious that they had mistaken me for a woman, they allowed themselves to be enlightened with no display of disgust.

American: Can I walk you home, ma'am?

Me: You think I'm a woman, don't you?

American: You waggle your fanny like a woman.

Me: Oh, I should ignore that.

American: I'm trying to, but it's not that easy.

Conversations such as this told me that I was by nature American. To the rest of the world happiness was a suspiciously regarded by-product of some other pursuit (preferably noble). Americans and homosexuals sought it for its own sake. The Portuguese explorers of old set out across the Atlantic Ocean in search of the Islands of the Blessed. They were not mocked. If the golden age flourishes anywhere it is in the United States.

By the time the last Americans had vanished into thin Englishmen I was nearly forty.

While the G.I.s were still around, I lived almost every moment that I spent out of doors in a state of exhilaration. It was my nature to deploy my forces in breadth, so at first I was content to know many soldiers superficially, but after a while I decided to change my strategy to one of depth and concentrate on a single individual. You can't have your cake and not eat it.

Never before had a physical relationship been presented to me so completely without stint and without overtones.

Sex is generally processed in one of three shades. It may be crude, which leads to the numbing repetition of the shortest words for the longest things, or naughty, involving one or both or all parties in dressing up, or it may be poetic. This was the tint favored by me in my youth—it transforms the facts of life into an ego-boosting device. Americans serve it plain but, sad to say, about the physical practice of homosexual intercourse there tends to be something contrived. This robs the act of its function as a means of communication. The two participants will never be of one flesh. When I was moaning about this to a Lesbian friend, she drew in her elbows and, with her face contorted in a grimace of disgust, asked, "Who wants to be of one flesh with anybody?" I think that initially most homosexuals do. To outsiders the idea that between a man and a woman the sex act can be natural, unnamed, inevitable, and lead to total oneness gives normality the radiance of the Holy Grail. Only a lifetime of receiving the confidences of unhappily married middle-aged women brought me to the realization that in time, even for heterosexuals, sex is reduced to an indoor sport. This was consoling. It is nice to be in the same boat as one's betters, especially if it is sinking.

For the practical level of human contact I was now prepared and I was happy but, of course, no more so than if I had met someone who could do a Ximenes crossword or play chess at my shaky standard. I learned to like my American but would never have put his interests before those of my lifelong friends and he would not have expected me to. I was always pleased to see him but would have left him with no more than a sigh for a steady income, a job in the movie industry, or a man who weighed twice as much. I could not have said that I loved him. When he ceased to call on me, I had no idea whether he had gone to heaven or to New York—but, then, to me they were the same place.

When the Spartans burst into Troy, the women of the city hid themselves in conspicuous places and screamed if they were not observed. Similar antics were now performed by English girls. This I recognized was mere coyness in the face of a frontal attack, but I could not help noticing that, among my friend, my adoration for Americans was not wholeheartedly shared.

The behavior of those who wished to be thought highbrow bordered on discourtesy. One night as I was sitting in the Wheatsheaf, an American soldier leaned with both hands on the table in front of me and asked, "Are you by any chance a celebrity?" With downcast eyes I explained that I was not but that I would introduce him to some. Rising and leaving the nonentities with whom I had been sitting snorting behind me, I led the culture-seeker to Nina Hamnett, explaining that she had known Modigliani. She was leaning her laughing torso against the bar. "Miss Hamnett," I said, "allow me to present an American who wishes to meet a celebrity." I then started on a list of her claims to fame as though she were a public monument and I a tourists' guide. "Is he going to buy me a drink?" she said. This he promptly did but she remained obviously displeased with both of us. I found this hard to understand. All she was now being asked to do was make like a genius for a few minutes. It took a lot more coaxing from me and a lot more drink from the soldier to persuade her to do this. In the end our persistence was rewarded. She told us one of her best stories.

A friend of hers sent a statue of a nude boy that she had modeled in black wax to an art gallery in Derby. Black wax is soft and, before you could say "sex," the figure had been robbed of what some would consider the most important part of its anatomy. When this vandalism came to the notice of Miss Hamnett's friend she complained to the municipal body that she considered responsible. They replied that the loss sustained by the statue came under the heading of fair wear and tear.

I secretly preferred the cafés of Charlotte Street to its public houses and, on the days when I had no work at all to do, would gladly have drunk pale-gray coffees from midday to midnight if I could have found people to listen when I spoke; but life in that part of the world was tidal. At six o'clock every evening the nomadic tribes moved south to the Wheatsheaf, the Marquis of

Granby, and the Bricklayers Arms. The northern regions became depopulated.

Drink and the world drinks with you; eat and you eat alone. I regretted the truth of this maxim because the life of pubs is never as gay as the life of cafés. As at a party so in the Wheatsheaf; unless I arrived within an hour of opening time, I found the deadening effect of alcohol had begun to work on everyone present. Some had become sleepy; some had become surly; and Mr. Tambimuttu had become Spanish and was dancing it off. Conversation did not flow with the drink; it drowned in it. This did not produce silence, for some drinkers erroneously imagined that they had become wiser and wittier and consequently spoke louder than usual.

These pubs, these cafés, and the space between them were Fitzrovia—that kingdom afterward to be described so well by Roland Camberton in a novel called *Scamp* and later still by Maclaren-Ross in his memoirs. As though we had some foreknowledge that we were living literature, we all set to work to be cameos. We tried with significant gestures and memorable phrases to give good value for the welcome that I at any rate was so surprised to find that we received.

What was required was a bizarre idiom that was completely consistent within itself. Of all the natives of Fitzrovia only one person really had this qualification. The suit she was calling was fallen grandeur and in it she never missed a trick.

A day came when this woman found in a dustbin in Bond Street a backless bead frock. No sooner had she seen it than she longed to wear it. As she did not at that time live anywhere in particular, it was difficult to think of a place sufficiently secluded for trying it on. She chose the churchyard in Flitcroft Street and sat among the dead to wait for nightfall. When it was barely dusk her eagerness had overcome her prudence. She started her impromptu striptease performance. A crowd collected large enough to attract the attention of the police and she was led away.

The next morning when the magistrate asked her what she had been doing, with a gently mocking laugh at the uncouthness of the question she replied, "What any woman would be doing at that hour. Changing for dinner."

Though we never stopped trying, none of us ever achieved such high style as this, but converting one's life into a form of public entertainment turned out to be less difficult than I had imagined.

I had feared that I might run out of quips, gags, anecdotes, and epigrams and, on the way back to London from Watford, Willesden, or Woolwich, worked assiduously on my material. This was effort wasted. If the aesthetic posture of my youth had not forced me to show the utmost contempt for the music halls, I might long ago have learned that what audiences most want to hear is what they already know, so that even newcomers may know that the lines are stale and may enjoy the idiocy forced upon the comedian by his profession. It is only to remarks that were not funny even in the first instance that a performer must endeavor to give some kind of sparkle. In the last resort he, himself, must laugh.

With practice it became easier to deck out my discourse with these tricks than not, and soon what had once been my café technique became my only manner of speaking. In middle age I found that I had gone beyond my original aim of purging my speech of the dross of sincerity. I had robbed it of all meaning whatsoever. I became like a stopped clock. I was right about once every twelve years, but what good was that when everyone had ceased to look at my face? To people who knew me well, listening to me became almost unbearable. In some houses I was only welcome if I undertook not to utter the same catchphrases more than twice in any one evening. I tried to stay within bounds, but really there was nothing for others to do but listen, act as stooges, or leave.

Among those who often came to Toni's and had sufficient vitality to wade into the torrent of my volubility was a certain Mr. MacQueen. The moment that he learned that I was a lettering artist, he hired me, though when he uttered the words he had not even formed a company. All he had was a tiny house on Campden Hill on which the paint was not yet dry and a headful of ideas in an equally unusable state. He proposed to start a firm that would build exhibition stands, decorate showrooms, and construct display units. I don't really hold with exhibitions unless they are of myself, but I graciously accepted the wages he paid me. I also helped him engage other members of the staff. This frequently entailed interviewing art students and looking at drawings of myself curled around window poles. It was while I was in Mr. MacQueen's employ that I was arrested.

Chapter 23

This was an eventuality that I and my enemies had expected ever since the far-off days when I had first been questioned by the police. A young man called Bermondsey Lizzie had once said, "You'll get years one of these days, girl, but you'll tell them everything, won't you?—when you come up for trial, I mean. I'll never forgive you if you don't."

Being in a display firm is like working for the movie industry. When you are not coping with a crisis you are wondering how on earth to fill in your time. During one of these lulls I was given a day off. I decided to spend this buying a pair of shoes. This was always a difficult and dangerous mission for me. If I wanted to use the longest words for the shortest thing I would say that I was a passive foot fetishist. My feet were smaller than an ordinary mortal's and I wanted everyone to know this. As time went by I wore shorter and shorter shoes, not because the length of my feet decreased but because the amount of discomfort I could bear became greater. Finally I was able to endure footwear that was hardly visible to the naked eye. For me, as for Hans Andersen's little mermaid, every step was agony, but as she had finally been rewarded by dancing with a prince, I never gave up. Almost as uncomfortable as wearing the shoes was buying them. Both I and the shop assistant needed all the fortitude we could summon. I would describe the shoes I had in mind and ask for a size four. The salesman or woman (according to what sex the management had decided I was) would measure my foot and bring me a shoe that fitted me perfectly. This immediately aroused my suspicion. When I ripped it off and looked at the sole, I found it to be a six. Moving down the scale in semitones, I would try on successive sizes until my toes were folded inside the shoe like the leaves of an artichoke. Then I would say, "Now lift me up." If I could stand in them, those were the shoes I bought. Tottering into the street, I screamed for a taxi. To this day my feet are two misshapen plinths of twisted bone.

Since I knew what an ordeal awaited me once I had entered a shoe shop, I did not do so lightly. I scrutinized the goods in the window until I was sure what I wanted was inside. This was what I was doing on the fatal afternoon. I had already systematically searched all the likely windows in Oxford Street and was just starting on Charing Cross Road when I was stopped by two policemen disguised as human beings. They demanded to see my exemption papers. As always I showed them the one that said that I suffered from sexual perversion. When my inquisitors had retrieved their eyebrows from the roots of their hair, they gave me back this by now rather grubby document and I moved on.

Outside the Hippodrome Theater I met by chance a certain part-time hooligan called Mr. Palmer. I slapped on to his plate his ration of eternal wisdom for the day and turned into Coventry Street. Almost immediately I was stopped a second time by the same two men. "Just a moment, you," they said. "We are taking you in for soliciting."

I marched before them following the instructions they muttered to me from behind. These led to Savile Row police station where I was searched by one man while others stood around saying, "Mind how you go." I was not stripped, but my pockets were emptied and I was sufficiently unzipped for it to be seen that I was not wearing women's underclothes. Then I was asked if I minded having my fingerprints taken. I replied that it couldn't matter less. To this day, my prints lie in the files of Scotland Yard and just beyond them there are ten little squiggles that I expect Edgar Lustgarten sits up nights pondering over. They are the marks of my fingernails, which it had not been possible to keep out of the ink.

The police did not start to be really irritating until the question arose of finding someone to go bail for me. This was necessary so that I could by telephone distribute my most immediate bookings in the schools among the various models and warn Mr. MacQueen that I would not be at work the next day or possibly for six months to come. If all this had not been necessary, I would quite contentedly have spent the night in the police station. I can sleep anywhere. I offered to supply a list of names, addresses, and telephone numbers and the money for making the calls so that someone might quickly be found who was free to come to Savile Row. This they would not allow me to do. "Just give us one name," they said stubbornly. So I gave the ballet teacher, on whom they called several times without finding her in. At about ten at night they asked me for the name of another person and I gave them that of the man who had written the kangaroo limerick. Fortunately he arrived almost immediately. I dashed through the blacked-out streets of London, first to Mr. Palmer. He was the young man to whom I had been seen speaking in the street during the afternoon. I asked him (if he could get time off from work) to come to court the following morning and say that he knew me. Then I went on to Toni's to tell the world in case anyone was interested in seeing foul play. Finally I reached home and made countless telephone calls, some offering speaking parts to friends of long standing who could act as character witnesses, and others to people who might like to appear as crowd artists. The next day, dressed in black so as to maintain the great tradition, I set out with my entourage for Bow Street.

As soon as I stepped into the courtroom, I was assailed by two contrary feelings. The first was that here was the long-awaited, fully involving situation to which I could summon all my capacity for survival. The second was that I might fall on the floor in a dead faint and that it might be just as well if I did.

In the days when I knew the Irish and the Scottish boys, I was often in police courts to act as a chorus to them or their friends and to cry "Woe unto Ilium" if an unfair verdict was given, but as soon as I, myself, was on trial, I found that I knew nothing of the judicial ritual. I had not, for instance, remembered that the magistrate sits in a state of patient trance while the case against you is conducted by his clerk.

I marveled at the benignity of the magistrate, who himself instructed me in the procedure of the court, and I was appalled by his clerk's bitchiness. He played the whole scene for laughs, turning slowly toward the public, with his hands in the air like George Sanders uttering his best lines. These included, "You are a male person, I presume." This total abandonment of dignity reminded me of the collapse of Harley Street at my medical examination four years earlier.

The police behaved in the perfectly conventional way that I remembered well. They rattled off their evidence as though it were the litany. They said that between the hours of this and that, they had observed the accused stopping and speaking to various people who had looked horrified and torn themselves away. At one moment they included in this great work of fiction a touch of realism. They mentioned the young man with whom I had talked outside the Hippodrome.

When the police had completed their evidence, the magistrate asked me if I would prefer to reply from the dock or go into the witness box where I would have to take the oath. I chose the latter, not because I hoped to gain anything from invoking the aid of You-Know-Who but because it would raise me to a higher vantage point and, like posing on a rostrum in an art school, lend me a spurious nobility. It also meant that I did not have my back to the audience for the whole of my big scene, which I had decided to play dead straight like Imogen in *Cymbeline*.

I forbore to state that the two policemen who had arrested me were inveterate liars. I humbly put forward the opinion that they had drawn mistaken conclusions from what they saw and that their error had been prompted by their having read my exemption paper which described me as homosexual. This they had not mentioned in their evidence. I also suggested that they might have misinterpreted my appearance. I said that I dressed and lived in such a way that the whole world could see that I was homosexual but that this set me apart from the rest of humanity rather than making it easy for me to form contacts with it. Who, I asked the magistrate, could possibly hope to solicit anybody in broad daylight in a crowded London street looking as I did?

At this point, I was later told by one of my friends who was sitting in the court, a stranger whispered, "They can't do nothing with 'im. He can't 'elp 'isself. You can see that."

This we all agreed marked the dawn of a new day.

Various kind people gave evidence as to the irreproachability of my character and, to my relief, Mr. Palmer went into the witness box to declare that he had spoken to me the previous afternoon because he knew me. He was nervous, but he spoke clearly and without hesitation. That he had secret reserves of courage I did not at that time know. I only discovered that ten years later when, at about the age of thirty-two, he committed suicide. Everyone who spoke on my behalf was asked by the magistrate's clerk if he knew that I was homosexual and replied that he did. This question was in each case followed immediately by the words, uttered in a voice hoarse with incredulity, "And yet you describe him as respectable?" All said, "Yes."

When the magistrate tired of this recital of my praises he said that the evidence against me was insufficient to convict me. I was dismissed. He meant that the evidence was a lie. If it had been true, it could have caused the downfall of an archbishop.

Everyone who was present at my trial or who was told about it later was amazed at my acquittal. One friend, fearing the worst, had advised me to try to have my case postponed while I engaged the services of a lawyer. This would incidentally have brought up one of the nastier points of the law. If I did this and then lost my case, I must take it for granted that my sentence would be heavier. In other words Justice revenges herself not only on those who commit crimes but also on those who take up her time. I decided against seeking legal aid not because I feared that my time in jail might be prolonged but because my case did not seem to require the help of "my learned friend." There were no subtle legal points to be argued. Unless the accused produces an alibi there never can be evidence of a person not speaking to strangers. I felt that if I clearly protested my innocence it should be effective. I also feared that a lawyer might deliberately blur the issue of my being homosexual on the quite logical ground that it was not the point. Whether it was relevant or not, my one desire was to state in a court of law that I was homosexual and as stainless as Sheffield steel. This was a distinction that, ten years earlier, would have been very difficult to make, but this magistrate at least had seen that this might be so.

The police, as usual, merely wanted a conviction. They thought that their case simply could not go wrong once I had been seen in court. This scramble to gain promotion by securing a large number of arrests is an unpleasant part of the police system, but I could not say that, either in this case in particular or throughout my life generally, the police have treated me badly. What made me feel so unremittingly hostile toward them was their facetiousness and the insulting manner displayed by a group of people who should at all costs remain neutral.

When they arrested me they could only be accused of stating a little more than they could prove. They followed a known homosexual who stopped several times (possibly pretending) to look in shop windows. Whenever I stopped a small crowd collected. I don't remember the details of that afternoon, but it would be safe to assume that a few remarks were made to me or at me. Unless constables were standing between me and whoever was speaking they would not be able to say for certain whether I replied or not. Their crime was that they swore I had and implied that I had spoken first. I could swear that I did not speak first to anyone because I never did. I could be fairly certain that I did not answer at all because remarks uttered by strangers, unless they are made in an American accent, always contained a veiled or a naked insult. So I was technically not guilty and, at the time, felt appropriately outraged. Yet if there are degrees of innocence, I would not now claim to have won first class honors. My thoughts on this subject are vague because I am not sure what the laws against soliciting are framed to prevent. If soliciting is a crime because it is a nuisance to those who do not wish to be importuned, then not only I but most homosexuals are guiltless. Very few men would dare to annoy strangers by detaining them against their will or even continuing to speak to them if the slightest irritation were evinced. Is soliciting criminal because it is the first step in the procedure of prostitution? This can less be taken for granted in a homosexual context than in any other. Many men make overtures to others without any thought of receiving or parting with money.

Of all these charges I would claim to be not guilty, but how innocent am I?

I do not solicit for immoral purposes because it would be unfeminine—and risky—but perhaps my very existence is a form of importuning. I no longer ask strange men for money because I do not think I would get it but, if it were offered to me, I would not feel ashamed to take it. In the last analysis I cannot say that I have ever refrained from taking any course of action on the ground that it was wrong or illegal or immoral.

Chapter 24

When the trial was over I went back for about a year to work for the display expert. He had sent a note to the court expressing his confidence in me and he continued to employ me as though nothing disgraceful had happened. The police were not equally magnanimous. They began systematically to make sure that I was barred from the public houses of Fitzrovia—finally, to everyone's amazement, even from the Wheatsheaf. My friends protested hotly to the landlord. He coolly pointed out that he could not have a license and me. In the past four years he had observed so much eccentricity that my presence made very little difference, but the police had accused him of running "a funny kind of place" and, when he had said, "How funny?" they had pointed to me. I was compelled to take the veil of abstinence, which suited me quite well, but I also had to relinquish half my audience, which did not. At first I complained volubly at this narrowing of my kingdom, but gradually snorts gave place to tears as I realized that this was but part of a gradual lessening of scope to which time was just starting to subject me.

Peace broke out.

On that terrible evening, as I was weaving my way through the West End with a prolonged "grand chain" movement as though I were doing the lancers with the whole world, my name was called. I heard it above the shouting, laughing, singing, that went on all that night. Turning, I saw in a doorway the man who had put up with my airs and graces all those long, horrible months in Baron's Court when I had first come to London fourteen years earlier.

I paused questioningly in front of him. He said, "You look terrible."

The horrors of peace were many.

Death-made-easy vanished overnight and soon love-made-easy, personified by the American soldiers, also disappeared. At a Christmas party in one of the rooms in our house a woman entered and embraced me. Over her shoulder I saw, hesitating in the doorway, a G.I. The woman said brightly, "I brought him for you. He's a bit small but they're getting difficult to find. Come in, Ricky."

But not only did love and death become rationed. Even mere friendship grew scarce. Londoners started to regret their indiscriminate expansiveness. People do when some moment of shared danger is past. Emotions that had been displayed had now to be lived down; confidences had been uttered which must now be gainsaid. I, who had once been a landmark more cheerful-looking and more bombproof than St. Paul's Cathedral, had ceased to be a talisman. I had become a loathsome reminder of the unfairness of fate. I was still living while the young, the brave, and the beautiful were dead.

All these external changes came at a bad time for me, when they could add their weight to other unwelcome alterations that were taking place within.

I was growing old.

My friends were delighted and did not resist the temptation occasionally to nudge me toward the grave with a straight talk. A teacher of languages called Lamb Chop came further out into the open than most others. He said, "You are dyeing your hair in order to seem younger." This was untrue. I had started to use henna when I was twenty-four, but as my life was one long journey toward self-assessment, I felt I must always give consideration to the opinions of me held by other people, however malicious I might secretly think them. Since I had adopted my chi-chi appearance partly as propaganda, if the message became confused, I must alter it. I set about forcing red out and forcing blue in. This would continue my original purpose of showing that my hair was dyed but would allow it to be seen that, underneath the tinting, I was gray-haired.

The moment that I had decided upon this course of action—long before I had begun to put it into practice on my fortieth birthday in 1948—my entire body went into revolt. My face became blistered with a crimson rash. It irritated so much that the effort not to claw myself to pieces was totally exhausting. As soon as the red marks began to appear the only thing to do was to go home and lie down in the dark—preferably in a draft. After a day or two the redness would begin to subside and the places where it had been to dry and harden into white scales. Within five days the skin of my face had fallen to the ground with a clatter, leaving the surface beneath as good as new. Then the whole process would begin again. This illness continued for a whole summer. It was said by my friends to be caused by an allergy. If so it was an allergy to middle age. I never recovered. Forever after I could only keep the disfigurement quiescent if I was awash with cortisone and pickled with antihistamine.

During a shaky transition state which lasted for about six months, I passed from doubtful youth to unmistakable middle age. I became one of the stately homos of England. This was the result in me of entering my blue period. On others the effect was equally marked. For many years after the war I was never badly savaged by members of the public nor even directly insulted by them. This was not because anyone had seen the light. Abatement in the hostility of one's enemies must never be thought to signify that they have been won over. It only means that one has ceased to constitute a threat. The attitude toward me of strangers waned from fear to brutish contempt. Without my scarlet hair I was like a Westerner without a gun.

I was growing old.

A day came when, on leaving the café that was fashionable with hooligans at the time, I saw that it was raining. During the war a flood would not have deterred me from proceeding on foot. Now I took the weather to be a sign and that evening I traveled home by bus, resolving to do this from then on.

As I took a seat on the upper deck, a stranger said, "Too wet even for you?"

A year or two after this, I was made aware that I was not only a characteristic of the night life of London but that my name had become an international rate of exchange.

As he wandered through the streets of New York, a friend of mine saw ahead of him a man whom he felt certain must be English. His clothes were consciously ill-fitting. Hoping that a conversation with this stranger might assuage his homesickness, my friend overtook him and asked the way to Grand Central Station. They began to talk airily of this and that. After a few sentences, a look of suspicion o'erspread the stranger's features.

Stranger: You're a foreigner?

My Friend: I'm afraid I'm only English.

Stranger: From London?

My Friend: Yes.

Stranger: Do you by any chance know someone called Quentin Crisp?

My Friend (positively delighted): I do indeed.

Stranger: I thought somehow you didn't really want to know the way to Grand Central Station.

I once saw a documentary movie in which fishermen cut out the heart of a dogfish and threw it on the deck. There it beat, *diminuendo sostenuto*, for eight hours.

This was how, once the war ended, I went on posing in the art schools. During the next three years the zest leaked out of even this occupation which had once represented total fulfillment. There seemed to be no new schools within reach to go to, no new positions to try out that could be held for long enough for students to draw them. I became aware that being a model was a profession at which, after the first year or two, I could not get better. I was bound to get worse. Even the physical agony became monotonous. Boredom, which I now saw was my industrial disease, set in.

I was growing old. My accumulating discontent with posing was really only part of my general state of mind.

It was as though I had been climbing a hill in expectation of finding on the other side a landscape utterly different from the one through which I had passed. Now I was at the summit. I could see that what stretched ahead was exactly the same as what lay behind. For an introvert his environment is himself and can never be subject to startling or unforeseen change. My failures to win true love, to stay in the movie industry, to write books that anyone would publish, were not a series of unconnected accidents to which I was prone because of my exposed position in society. They were the expression of my character—the built-in concomitant of a morbid nature to which dreams were more vivid than reality. The infinitesimally small success that I had known had been achieved inevitably in terms of being rather than of doing. I had gained what I had aimed for when I first got control of my own life. But in middle age physical well-being faded. Money, fame, wisdom, which are the booby prizes of the elderly, I had never been able to win. My preoccupation with happiness had been total.

I would not yet have described myself as miserable, but I was deflated. I realized that the future was past. Whatever I could hope to do or say or be, I had done and said and been. This state of affairs occurred prematurely because I had subjected a shallow and horribly articulate personality to a lifetime of unflagging scrutiny. Even a marriage with oneself may not last forever.

Until I was forty it had never dawned on me that I was not immortal. I had once said to the Czech's true love, "I can never get it into my head that I shall one day die." She replied, "Neither can I, but I practice like mad." I now started to do the same. It was harder for me than for her. Being of a shy and very modest nature, she had been largely content to observe life without disturbing it. My very existence was such that I never had, and never wanted, the opportunity to see people as they would be in my absence. Everything changed the moment I arrived.

While getting on, at differing rates of progress, with our practice, what we both needed was some way of filling in time between now and the grave. She became a Catholic and almost immediately went into a convent.

I took to sex. It became a time-filler and ceased to be the pursuit of an ideal.

After about seven years of working in a French prison, the nun returned for one last glimpse of the past. In an upper room in Chelsea, she described to the ballet teacher, the Czech, another of her obsolete true loves, and me what her life was now like. She said, "The trouble with human nature is that you're stuck with it." She summed up with these words, "Every hour has been agony, but I could not have done otherwise."

I was finding it much the same with sex except that for the ennobling influence of anguish I was substituting the degrading effects of discomfort and exhaustion. Sex was not one of my A-level subjects. It is only a mirage, floating in shimmering mockery before the bulging eyes of middle-aged men as they stumble with little whimpers toward the double bed, that somewhere there is a person or a position that will evoke from them sensations of which they dimly dream they are capable. In fact, you can only snatch from sex what your nervous system can stand.

In theory, the pursuit of strangers divested of the needless convolutions of romance—the indulgence in chance encounters stripped of the clash of personalities—leads to unfettered self-gratification. In practice it leads rapidly to monotony and, for homosexuals, to danger and expense. Now that I looked so much older, though the treatment I received out of doors was less cruel, indoors I was used much more shoddily. In my own room no one ever actually demanded money with menaces, but the hard-luck stories with which I was regaled became shameless. When on one occasion I explained apologetically to someone I had known for fifteen years that at that particular moment I was not able to give him any money, he stole my gold watch. This did not deter him from telephoning me a few weeks later, obviously expecting a cozy chat about old times. So much is robbing queers a matter of routine with such men that it was quite a while before he realized that I did not wish to continue our association.

Even if one treasures like pressed flowers these sacred moments of defilement one cannot for long put off the monotony of sex for sex's sake. Staring at the front of people's trousers is, after a time, even less rewarding than gazing into their eyes. As the appeal of any pastime weakens, the habit of it strengthens. I found that it required a continuous effort of will to keep in mind that what was needed to make sex tolerable was not more of it but less.

At least my daylight hours had to be occupied with other thoughts. I had to earn my living and, if I was going to escape from modeling, I would be compelled to return to some kind of employment in which what was left of my brain was used. I went into the art department of a publishing house. This was the first and only job I ever got by answering a newspaper advertisement. I was amazed that my application was successful. So, I think, were my employers.

I sat at a desk and handled a pen and ink or a brush and poster paint. Except in this, my new occupation was utterly unlike being in any other kind of studio. The pace was that of an Antonioni film; the atmosphere, as undisturbed as a St. James's Street club. However lowly your station in life, the treatment you received even from directors was as courteous as a minuet. Doors were held open for you though you were only a speck on the horizon, and you were addressed as "Mr." however angry your interlocutor might be. Most remarkable of all, nobody was ever given the sack. Even had a member of the staff arrived tottering drunk, I am sure he would have been scooped into a taxi, readdressed home, and reported to be ill.

Finding it impossible to take any further interest in myself because I had exhausted all the potentialities of my character, I decided, since I was suddenly surrounded by new people in a new setting, that I would try to devote some attention to them. It wasn't easy.

The art editor noticed this. He asked, "What do you hold with—apart from yourself?" I racked my brains, but I couldn't think of a thing.

The last medium-sized organization that I had worked in had been the film laboratories. There I had seldom been into any other room than the art department and, as I was there only a few months, I never understood the workings of the firm at all. In the publishing house I stayed longer and observed a little more. My first discovery was that, though everybody's feelings were masked by impeccable politeness, each department was slightly afraid of all the others. Quite a lot of time was spent not so much in remedying errors as in disguising them from the scrutiny of neighbors. In the outer world I had been made a fool of for so long and accused of sins so scarlet that admitting to some slight mistake such as having spelled a word incorrectly was like boasting. If anyone had asked me where I felt most at home I could have replied, "In the wrong." In the publishing house the pleasures of indiscriminate confession were denied me. I was made conscious that, however unworthily, I was a member of a regiment whose honor was brightened or tarnished by my individual conduct.

The one common bond that united all departments and in moments of danger overcame all uneasiness was the same old hostility toward the ruling caste. When a note was included in everyone's pay packet asking him in future to be more punctual, there was no outcry. That would have been too ungentlemanly. There was a prolonged reverberation of affront. One man uttered the words, "I wouldn't mind arriving at the right time, if *they* did." It was difficult to imagine how anyone could hear himself utter a sentence beginning with the words, "I wouldn't mind arriving at the right time . . ." without laughing, but the complaint was serious. Apparently, even in an organization run like a rest home for retired gentlefolk, the inmates felt themselves to be enduring the humiliations of slavery. To me the job was like going into retreat before facing the rigors of real life again. I luxuriated in my retirement for two and a half years. By that time, by hooligan standards, I was rich. It was my policy never to spend more than half my wages so as not to have to work for more than half my days on earth. At home the drawers where I kept unanswered letters were so full of pound notes that they fell out into the dust whenever I went in search of somebody's address.

When I announced that I was leaving the publishing house, the first words uttered by my immediate boss were, "You swine." I think he was chiefly perturbed by the prospect of having to interview new prospective artists. I was hardly a loss to the department. In my room at home I could gladly sit for hours wrapped in a filthy dressing gown and filthier daydreams about myself, but I became restless when I had nothing to occupy me in other people's time. I was always clamoring for work. The moment I was given anything to do, I couldn't wait to get it finished. The other members of the staff adopted the ruse of filling in the hours by doing the work well. This device never occurred to me. Even when I saw from their example the endless time-consuming possibilities of attention to detail, I could not bring myself to try it. I greatly admired meticulousness, but the capacity for it is part of an entirely different temperament from mine. There are strange people in this world who build galleons in bottles for fun. If I had ever attempted a feat of this nature, before the first spar was in place I would have been bleeding with knife wounds, sticky with gum, and blind with fury.

When the day was fixed for my departure, I received a present from the members of the firm who knew me best. I thanked them with unfeigned amazement. These were the people who had suffered most from the annoyance of having me sitting on the corners of their desks screaming with laughter when I could find nothing better to do. I had been teasingly asked if I intended to go around to every department and shake hands with the entire firm. I had said that I did not but that I would like to see the boss himself before I left. This idea was received with a certain amount of mild mockery. I was still bowing my head before this when a message arrived saying that the boss would like to see me. I wanted to thank him for being so long-suffering. As I stepped into his office, he said, "I just wanted to say how tolerant I think you've been."

I left work partly in order not to be doing it and partly because I wanted to write a novel. Until now I had never had the time. I had never been able to collect enough money to live for a year without a job. Now this was possible, and at the outset of this period of affluence I was introduced to a publisher who, while we were sitting in what he called "one of my tatty teashops," suggested that I should write a book. I almost took a taxi home to begin. Six months later I was rushing in the other direction to deliver my typescript to his office.

There are three reasons for becoming a writer. The first is that you need the money; the second, that you have something to say that you think the world should know; and the third is that you can't think what to do with the long winter evenings. I expect the liveliest books are written from a combination of all three motives. I had only the financial one and that may have been part of the cause of my failure. The publisher didn't like the book.

This was a cause for mourning but hardly for amazement. I am not really equipped to write a novel. As E. M. Forster says, novelists presuppose a world of people interested in human relationships. My trouble was not merely that I was uninterested in them. I didn't think they existed. I tried to write without the literary convention of love and, in the words of one publisher's reader, to succeed in doing this would require genius or at least style. Another comment was that the story was a satire without anger.

I now know that if you describe things as better than they are, you are considered to be romantic; if you describe things as worse than they are, you will be called a realist; and if you describe things exactly as they are, you will be thought of as a satirist. This was the only sense in which my book contained any satire. Every incident depicted had taken place in or on the fringe of my own existence; every line of dialogue had been spoken in my hearing. As there were no sympathetic characters in real life, there were none in my book. Only the pattern of events was invented. If I wrote without anger, this was natural enough, for before an author can write indignantly about the way things are, he must feel that somebody deserved better. The simplest comment on my book came from the ballet teacher. She said "I wish you hadn't made every line funny. It's so depressing."

Of course the most obvious explanation for my total lack of success was that I was a bad writer. This idea I did not entertain for a moment. I continued for months to nag all my friends who had any connection, however slender, with the book racket, into promoting the sale of the book. Finally, when even Fred Urquhart, darting about London with my typescript under his arm, could not produce favorable results, I began to lose interest. There was no actual moment when I decided that further effort was useless. For months the pathetic parcel of greatness continued to lie around in my room waiting to be sent somewhere else. It was removed from the bed at night, from the seat of the armchair during the day, and flung from the desk when there was any drawing to be done. Then the failure of the whole venture became overshadowed by a far greater mistake that at first I did not even know I had made.

Chapter 25

After being rejected by many religious orders, in some instances because she wasn't rich and in others because she couldn't sing, the Czech's true love finally found a convent that would admit her. She made a request that for some time I had been secretly dreading. She asked me to go occasionally, when she had left the world, to visit the Czech in the mental hospital into which he had been clapped.

About eight times a year for about eight years I made reluctantly the journey that she had undertaken without complaint every Sunday for so long. Added to her special difficulties with traveling was the burden of reproaches with which the patient loaded her for having placed him in captivity. When he was not blaming her, he was demanding that she produce proof that she was herself and not an impostor cunningly got up by *them* to look like her. In spite of the gloomy and sometimes hostile reception that she came to know awaited her, she made this weekly excursion without fail, even in snowy weather which sometimes caused her to fall more than once in a few yards.

When I took over her duty, I was relieved to find I was met with no reproaches and was never asked to prove that I was myself. (Who else could I be?) By that time he had become merely a "funny old gentleman." He wore a monocle and decorated his discourse with quaint flourishes of style and quotations from French, Latin, and other languages, for he was riddled with Penguin scholarship. He was no trouble. We sat and talked in a room whose floor was so polished that even the sane could hardly stand upright and which was full of inmates and their relatives. We were careful not to look out of the window because among the laurel bushes that luxuriated in the grounds men were in the habit of exposing themselves to the visitors—a sight which tended to interrupt my train of conversation. We drank tea. He purchased three cups, explaining, "The place is an absolute madhouse."

I tried to perform gladly the chore that had been bequeathed to me, but the trouble was that I was stuck with a two-hour journey there, two hours of gibberish, and a two-hour journey back in loving mummery of a woman who, being a nun, was as if already dead. The man I was visiting I had never liked even when he was normal. It was distressing to find that, in the midst of his wild mental derangement, his character had remained as unpleasant as before. Even in circumstances where everybody's personality appeared to an outsider to have been reduced to a cipher, he was still snobbish beyond the wildest dreams of the Mitfords, sentimental, and oozing with sly, circuitous jokes about sex. However, I was mindful of the fact that soon I too, unless I was very lucky, would reside in an institution which I would doubtless find so boring that even the sight of those who despised me would seem welcome.

Then one day I received from the hospital a letter written partly in Olde Englyshe to warn me that the Czech would be coming to see me. I was surprised, but when I had thought about it, slightly relieved. An outing would constitute a greater diversion for him than a visit in the surroundings that he hated, and I would be spared the long journey out of London and back.

I rejoiced too soon. His arrival was to make greater demands on our thinly spread friendship than I had dreamed possible.

He had hardly been in my room for two minutes before he kissed me. At first I thought that if I remained calm—bordering on benign—what I took to be a squall of sex would subside and serenity would be restored. I was wrong. The situation got worse. It became obvious that this was a climax in our relationship for which the Czech had been waiting for some time. From amazement at the freakishness of this encounter I rapidly passed to the opposite point of view. The whole thing was pathetically inevitable. This was the measure of his loneliness; I was the limit of his degradation. Though I was somewhat confused as to whether or not I was carrying to their logical conclusion the nun's instructions, I felt that I could not do otherwise than try to comply with the wishes of her former lover. If I could not say that I was morally shocked, if I could not claim that I had anything to lose, then it was the least that I could do.

His hair and his whole body were covered with cod-liver oil. He explained that if, taken internally, it was salubrious, then it must likewise be good for the skin. Also, as I saw for myself, it turned his hair gold. This he felt made him look younger and more desirable. Until this moment it had always puzzled me that fish did not bother with propinquity but, instead, conducted the business of procreation by remote control. I understood them now.

In return for my compliance, though it was less than wholehearted, the Czech used to bring me tributes of molten chocolate and ruined meat pies which he had somehow obtained from the institution. Once he took the trouble to carry to my room a suitcase full of fallen apples heavy with maggots that spent the afternoon crawling sensually over the bedcover. At first I tried to act kind of cute on receiving these presents. I said, "Oh, but you shouldn't have . . ." and I meant it. Even in depravity I lacked stamina and, though his visits thinned out during the course of the ensuing years, my amenability thinned faster. I found myself, at the age of fifty and more, fleeing like a crotchety nymph before a satyr of seventy.

As I look back on this whole episode, I am assailed once again with the feeling that overtakes me whenever I think of anyone that I have known well. I didn't do enough.

Chapter 26

By the early nineteen-fifties, when I was writing my book, the inhabitants of Fitzrovia had come a long way, all of it downhill, from the happy time. Toni had succeeded in offending somebody (and he must have sat up all night to think how to do that) and his clientele had left in favor of a café called the Alexandria. This place was Toni's mixed with water, as Toni's had been the Low Dive mixed with water.

The Low Dive had set a standard that now only middle-aged hooligans could remember and to which they looked back as Mrs. Lot at Sodom. It had been a paperbacked Café Royal, opened, I imagine, especially for outsiders because of its unique location in a dim alleyway in Soho. No sunlight, not even a hated breath of fresh air, ever reached its door or those grime-caked gratings that only a house agent could have called windows.

The whole *vie de bohème* was passing without hope or warning. It is a way of life that has two formidable enemies—time and marriage. Even hooligans marry, though they know that marriage is for a little while. It is alimony that is forever.

There was a shop in Old Compton Street whose proprietors served tea and coffee with one hand and foreign newspapers with the other. Here I saw the entire cycle from hope to despair acted out before my very eyes in the course of two years. As I sat drinking cup after cup of pale-gray tea some girl that I didn't know from Eve would flop down beside me and engage me in conversation. After a while, with any luck, she would let slip some such words as "Do you still do Gravesend?" Then I would know that she had been a student there. She would tell me she had won a scholarship to the Slade or the Academy. On her next visit to "The French" she would be accompanied by a pot-bellied giant with a kitchen-tablecloth shirt and a face that was no more than a clearing in the jungle. After that there seemed only time for another round of teas before she would return with a baby in arms. With it she would sit far back in the café so as not to be questioned about her private life by any policewoman who happened to be passing.

There was no such thing as a hooliganette.

The rest was silence. When next the man was seen it was not in a café but in a public house. He was alone. The girl had been sold into slavery and the child, once hailed as the youngest layabout in the world, was living with its grandparents in Upper Norwood.

This would count as a story with a happy ending. In some cases all souls were lost. The man also went to live in Upper Norwood.

The other enemy of the *vie de bohème* was old age. Hooliganism requires considerable stamina and a degree of adaptability that a lot of people lose with the passing of the years. The monasteries of Bohemia demand more of their brotherhood than some are prepared to give. The daily routine of back-breaking idleness proves too much for certain novices. The self-inflicted orgies that are the inevitable punishment for the slightest deviation into the bourgeois way of life are more than their frail flesh can stand. Many discover to their shame that they have scruples; they have roots and, greatest disadvantage of all, they have hope. The fathers superior of the order do not try to influence their children in Satan; they merely shake their heads in sorrow. They know that the apostate must work out his own damnation.

Even I, though I felt no attraction toward respectability, began to lose some of my enthusiasm for vagabondage. I took a permanent job again in another display outfit. I was introduced to its director by a female inmate of the house where I lived. She was the firm's secretary, though her manner seemed hardly subdued enough for such a position. She was the richest and noisiest girl in the world.

In spite of the fact that she could have bought St. James's Palace (and frequently threatened to), as soon as she heard about our house she longed to live in it. There she felt she would be free.

The place already had the reputation of being a home for incorrigibles. I had taken my room while the landlady was away running a hostel for foreign sailors in Portsmouth where, toward the end of the war, she was almost the only thing left standing. When she came back to London, she accepted me as one of the hazards of her dedication to humanity. Her house was the last in England which was run for the benefit of the tenants. Although this is the age of amateur landladies, some of whom were hooligans in their day, all but my landlady gradually sold out to the other side. They defiled their lips with such phrases as "Lowering the tone of the neighborhood" and "Depreciation of property." They broke their vows of squalor and changed their role from party-giver to light sleeper.

With the help of time and Mr. Wilson I became what Mr. Rachman would have called a "stat," but there is no doubt that I would have been evicted somehow by anyone who was not the patron saint of hooligans.

It was once discovered by the few who went out to work that there was a strange man sleeping night after night in an armchair stored under the stairs. When they informed my landlady, she was appalled. "Oh," she gasped, "he must be so cold. Couldn't one of you lend him a blanket?"

In these circumstances it required real talent to get turned out, but the display secretary succeeded. In the little back room behind mine, she fought with a boxer dog and its owner until the neighbors ran up the walls and the blood ran down with a gurgling sound. I went permanently into half-mourning when she left. She was a true friend. She used to drive me, squeaking with delight, through the streets of London at eighty-five miles an hour. I was one of her favorite passengers because I was among the happy few who, so far from trying to restrain her rashness, urged her on to greater feats of daring.

As we roared down an avenue of red lights one day, two nuns stepped off the pavement in front of us. "Get them," I cried. St. Theresa longed to hear the clock strike because every hour was one hour nearer the grave. Since her time there must have been some fresh arrangement. As we swerved toward them, the nuns leaped back on to the path like two huge black crows.

My friend's car was built so that its occupants lay rather than sat with their heads almost on a level with the curb. It was wide enough for two narrow people but there were often three of us in it. On these occasions I was in the middle, partially reclining on the other passenger's fair ripening breast. Every time the driver changed gear she nearly changed my sex. "You should worry," she snapped.

The firm of which this girl was, for a while, the secretary was somewhat unconventional. It dealt chiefly in counter display units—stands, trays, containers, which manufacturers employ a special man to cajole or, in the last resort, bully the concessionaires into using in their shops. Everyone hates these labor-creating devices. The travelers are embarrassed at having to distribute them; the retailers resent having to devote time to erecting them. As soon as the manufacturer's man has got back into his car, the shopkeeper flings the display unit into a dim corner of his stock room. The traveler knows this and complains to the board of directors because he knows that what is needed is not a means of bringing the manufacturer's name to public notice but some way of using up excess profits without having to resort to the embarrassing extreme of giving the money to someone who might need it.

The makers of point-of-sale units provide one of the largest and most satisfactory sources of income for the inhabitants of Soho. These gadgets have to be hand-painted and packed. The work can be done at odd times and in odd clothing; it requires no skill and no employment cards. It calls for great concentration of energy for short spaces of time. Squares seem to resent this. Real life, husbands, and children make it difficult for them ever to work day and night with only a few hours' sleep taken on work benches.

To muster a force of hooligans it is only necessary to know the name of one. Like the inhabitants of the Village of the Damned, information given to one is simultaneously understood by all. The trouble is that outsiders almost never have telephone numbers, often do not have addresses, and occasionally do not have names. That I had all three sometimes made me an object of suspicion in Soho.

Still eyes look coldly upon me;
Cold voices whisper and say,
"He is crazed with the spell of Suburbia.
They have stolen his wits away. . . ."

The monotony of painting display units did not worry me. If I had ever had a soul it had been destroyed long ago. What I expected from any kind of work had changed with the years. I no longer did it to show that I could, as though being employed were a dazzling virtue that I might flaunt before my detractors. I merely wanted a sitting-down job that would yield a change of agony from posing. I was not grieved to find myself engaged in a pursuit that could only lead to more of the same thing. The time for having a career was far behind me.

Without a murmur I painted the faces of four thousand dolls.

Then my boss offered to take me into the firm as a fulltime member of her staff of one. I accepted gladly, though for me no job could ever be more than a seaside romance with respectability.

My duties as a permanent employee were different from the free-lance work. I made cocoa and washed up the cups; I added up my wages and subtracted my income tax. I typed letters and filed the replies; I answered the telephone and learned how odd my voice sounded to other people. A telephone conversation with an unknown woman client with a baritone voice ended in her saying, "Your voice is very deep. It's almost as low as mine and I'm frequently taken for a man—over the phone, I mean."

After that, I tried to round out my voice and pitch it lower. I never found a way of eliminating its jangling quality as of a ruined piano that I noticed when I later heard myself speak on a tape recorder. Almost immediately I began to be offered appointments with fear over the telephone. These were less sinister than the calls I received at home. Receptionists of other firms, who had originally dialed our number in error, rang a second time from a switchboard on which other people were listening.

The only work directly connected with display that I ever attempted was to think up and draw a picture of—or sometimes merely to act out—gimmicks (preferably with some mechanical movement to them). A subcontractor, once he had understood my mime, could make these in wire or wood or what you will. My far more essential function was to keep the peace between my employer and the outer world. This was no light task. She was never polite to people unless they had more money than she. I pointed out that this behavior was founded on a vanishing myth. The working classes, whom she thought she was addressing, had long since been replaced by the striking classes.

Strangely enough, to her employee she was extremely kind. As soon as we were alone in the office, which was frequently for days on end, we drank a mixture of Canadian whisky and Coca-Cola and played Scrabble. I played all games seriously—even nastily. They provided an enclosed world whose triumphs compensated me somewhat for a lifetime of defeat elsewhere.

Another interest that we were able to share was watching from the office window the girls leaning against the walls of the street below. We measured the amount of time they were out of sight with the men they had picked up. Including getting into her flat and returning from it to the street, one woman was sometimes away for only seven minutes. In the midst of such preoccupations as these some subcontractor's vanman would appear in the doorway and I would be seized with a spasm of industry. Flinging off my shoes and socks, I would start to run up and down the stairs with boxes under my arm. This activity, which sometimes went on for more than two hours, was so strenuous that I tore my calf muscle from the Achilles tendon. The van was in the street and the office was on the second floor and as many as two hundred and fifty boxes had to be transferred from one to the other before someone came along to tell us that the lorry would have to move on.

When this happened, if the policeman looked inexperienced, I would clasp my hands under my chin and say, "Oh, officer. Have I done the wrong thing again?" This sometimes had the desired effect. A dazed, almost a bruised look would creep over the face of the young man and he would walk away hardly knowing where he was going.

After four years of these antics I left. If you traffic in ideas on however low a level, four years is a long time. I have yet to meet a commercial artist or a copywriter with a marble clock, but an accountant, if he told you he had been with one firm a long time, might mean twenty-four years. It was as well that I left when I did for, about six months after my departure, the firm collapsed. Now the building that housed it has been removed—carefully, like a slice of cake. Weeds grow where once I stood.

While I was still in this display job, I used, after office hours, to pose in evening classes, go to the movies, or sit in cafés and pubs. During the past ten years, the ban on me had slowly lifted like a mist. Visibility was now so good in the Coach and Horses that a man was asked to leave because he persistently made fun of me. When this happened I knew for sure that Soho had become a reservation for hooligans. We could at last walk majestically in our natural setting, observed but no longer shot at by the safaris that still loved to penetrate this exotic land.

Chapter 27

Into the Coach there sometimes came a young woman whom I knew well, but only from having seen her so often in the neighboring cafés. During a silence that must have been caused by my having to pause for breath, she said, "Why don't you come and talk to our lot?" Something about this question and in particular about the words "our lot" warned me that she might be a social worker. I instinctively recoiled, though no opportunity to speak uninterrupted could be allowed to pass without investigation. I began to question her. "They're raving," I said, and she agreed. It transpired that she spent much of her spare time organizing entertainment for the patients of a day hospital for mental cases. I told her that I would talk to anyone who couldn't get away but that I never spoke for long about anything but myself. "That wouldn't do," she said. "It would be therapeutic." I thought this objection closed the subject.

A few days later she informed me that she had spoken to the doctors with whom she worked and that they had given permission for me to tell all. So, one Sunday afternoon, weighed down with notes, I went to her hospital and spoke and spoke and spoke.

The snags that I had feared did not crop up. I did not lose my voice and, as we were all sitting cozily in a recreation room and not, as I had feared, in a vast lecture hall, I think I am right in supposing that I could be heard. I found that even "giving a talk" had its own technique and that I was reading my notes instead of addressing my audience. However, the doctor in charge was polite enough to appear satisfied. He was chiefly glad that what I had said had provoked my hearers to question me and to converse with one another.

The conversation that followed my talk was sad. It was all in psychological terminology. Even patients who had difficulty in arranging their thought in any kind of order at all knew all the long words—all the delusive alibis. This was what always seemed to me wrong with psychology. It did not stop at ridding the misfit of his feeling of shame; it went further and gave him a vocabulary with which to glorify himself. Why should anyone bother whether he steals or not, once he need not say, "I'm dishonest," but can claim to be a kleptomaniac?

The final nail was hammered into the coffin of psychology when a friend of mine, whose tears had trickled down to his toes for several weeks, sought the aid of a psychiatrist. He explained his problem and was told that it was nonsense to assert that one man could fall in love with another. All that was needed to set matters right was for my friend to find some nice girl and flop into bed with her. I was interested to know whether this advice was accepted.

Me: Whatever did you do then?

My friend: I rang up Mrs. X and she said, "Very well, dear."

Me: And are you redeemed?

My friend: It's the same.

Me: Well. Well. Then everything's all right now?

My friend (his tears beginning to flow afresh): It's not. It's more confusing than ever.

A fortnight after my visit to the hospital, I too went to see a psychologist. He had gone to the same institution the following week and been told about my visit. I was surprised that his first question was "Is there anything you would like to ask me?" He was obviously equally bewildered when I said there was not.

The interview was very short. He told me that he was preparing (yet another) survey of homosexuals and, indeed, of all the minorities he could think of. Twenty years earlier I would have thought this such a noble undertaking. Now I tried not to sigh. As I rose to leave him, the psychologist said in a faintly irritable tone, "I think it's a pity you dress the way you do but still . . ." I was taken aback by this remark. We seemed to be reading once again that paragraph which used to occur in all books about sexual abnormality and which began, "There is no need to waste time considering that small group of men who dress and act in an effeminate manner. . . ."

Men whose bedroom habits differ markedly from those of their friends have troubles. They touch a spot where no survey can reach but, if these same people feel no compulsion to wear the clothes of the opposite sex or to teeter awkwardly along the vanishing demarcation line between men and women, they have no "minority" problem whatsoever. In a time outworn, when God was alive and words like "decency" and "purity" were used seriously, people objected on moral grounds to associating with men they even suspected of being queer. Now that morality is finished and social convenience is the only criterion of behavior, it is only obviously effeminate men who are ostracized. It is universally agreed that men are neither heterosexual nor homosexual; they are just sexual.

Of my visit to the day hospital for the insane the ballet teacher asked for what possible purpose it had been arranged. Before I was able to reply, another friend began to say, "Well, Quentin has a problem of adjusting himself to society and he . . ." This sentence was never finished. The ballet teacher expostulated, "I don't agree. Quentin does exactly as he pleases. The rest of us have to adapt ourselves to him."

This remark seemed to me to outline a great dilemma. Almost all the psychological ills that a man can suffer spring from self-doubt. Once this is removed, his troubles vanish, but if anyone really came to believe that he was wise, witty, kind, and beautiful, think what troubles his friends would have!

A friend of mine used to come, weighed down with tales of stony-hearted landladies, to the office of the display firm where my boss, temporarily abandoning her rule, fed him with cocoa and allowed him to sleep in her flat on coverlets of leopardette. This was touching, but it was obviously not a permanent solution to his plight. I telephoned a hooligan and his wife who ruled a boarding house in the north of London. They took him in. Thus it became possible to visit my friend and his landlords for the price of one bus fare. Feeling that this was a bargain, I took to going to Crouch End quite often.

One summer's day we were all sitting in a heap in a garden full of broken bicycles and ruined sink baths. My hostess's two children clambered all over her as though she were a playground fixture. Suddenly she declared she couldn't go on living in this way much longer. I had told her, even when she was pregnant, that she had taken the veil for at least seventeen years, with no time off for good conduct. I was distressed to hear her already complaining. Her oldest child was barely three. I asked if she could think of any possible escape route. She said that she needed a huge sum of money. When I questioned her as to how she hoped to come by this, she pointed to a paragraph in one of the culture papers which announced a television-play contest.

Once again, and once again fruitlessly as it turned out, I roused myself. I jumped up and down, swung on the trees, stood on upturned sink baths and declaimed in an all-out effort to bring to life before her very eyes a science-fiction musical ("Take me; make me your flying sorceress") with which I told her that she could easily win any competition. Hitching up her sunsuit she rushed indoors and typed a letter to the paper in question to ask for a list of rules for the contest.

When I next visited her, she had received a reply from Granada Television informing her that three plays were required. I ran all the way home and searched under the bed where no human eye had looked for eighteen years and there found two plays, dusty in more senses than one. All the inmates of the Crouch End house were compromised into condensing, retyping, and generally warming up these unappetizing leftovers while I searched Soho for a South American guitarist who would write some science-fiction music. The entire combined efforts of all these geniuses were a total loss even though the scripts were accompanied by a covering letter which said, "Granada shall live again."

Just as I was sinking uncomfortably back into oblivion, I received a telephone message from the guitarist saying that he had begun yet another musical. I was on the brink of crying, "Oh, no!" when I realized that I could not fairly do this. If he had so generously written the music for my words, I must now write the words for his music. He explained to me that he wanted a simple boy-meets-girl story with lyrics. This I felt was quite beyond my capabilities. I did not know any boys who met girls. I persuaded him to settle for a "horror" musical ("Ev'ry little monster wantster"). This play was great fun to write and my association with the composer was without disagreements of any kind. He didn't understand the jokes and I didn't understand the music. I never understood music. It all seemed to me to be the maximum amount of noise conveying the minimum amount of information.

I think of these failures as happy disasters. Unlike the writing of my novel, which took me away from people and used up time in which I could have been speaking, the plays contained built-in success of a small kind. I was able continually to show off before my collaborator. Indeed a large part of our time was spent jumping up and down and exclaiming at each other's greatness. Also failure no longer depressed me deeply. Each unsuccessful attempt to win fame brought me nearer to the time when triumph would be useless even if it came. I had gradually become more or less immune to feeling of every kind and to disappointment in particular. I had been hit in the same place too often. I also had by now learned that the way to deal with unpleasant events was to tell everyone about them. Words had become a salve with which to heal the wounds inflicted on me by experience.

When the war ended and it dawned on me that never again was I likely to play a leading role in the streets of London, I started to live a rich, full life by proxy. I took to the movies. This was an admission of weakness—dearer but less embarrassing than evening classes. All culture—even popular forms of it—was in my eyes a sin. To point out that works of art were beautiful did not justify their creators. Pearls were beautiful, but only diseased oysters had them. The enjoyment of works of art seemed to me even more damnable than the fabrication of them, since there could never be any money in it. Moreover, to read a novel or see a play was to drink life through a straw—to smoke it through a filter tip. If we were not afraid of blackening our teeth or riddling our lungs with cancer—if we were a dauntless race of men with strong digestions—we would be able to devour life without the aid of these overcivilized devices.

To minimize my guilt in going to the pictures—to call this wanton pursuit of an effete pleasure by another name—I needed movie companions as drunkards need drinking companions. If I entered a cinema alone, God might plunge his arm through the roof of the auditorium booming in a stereophonic voice, "And you, Crisp, what are you doing here?" I would never have dared to reply, "I'm just enjoying myself, Lord." I remembered too well what happened to Mr. and Mrs. Adam. A commissionaire with a flaming sword came and asked them to leave. If, however, I could gesticulate toward a friend and shrug my shoulders, I might be thought to have performed an act of self-sacrifice. This would at least divide my shame by two. The trouble was that good movie-goers were hard to come by even though I was willing to pay.

I had just started to feel the pull of the expanding universe. The life that starts in the heart of London gradually drifts outward. As my friends became older, many of them married and moved out of Soho into the suburbs, where their failure would be less apparent. If their unions were cursed and children were born to them, they went even farther. By the time I was forty-five, I found that almost all my older friends had gone, if not like Henry Vaughan's into a world of light, at least on to the North Circular Road. I had to nag strangers into coming to the cinema with me. This was hard work, for the strangers who were willing to talk to me in cafés were hooligans and hooligans do not like entertainment. They will talk and they will drink, in their weaker moments they will even eat, but they will not go to a theater or read a book or see a film.

Even so I managed to go to the pictures—and never alone—on an average once a week for many years; sometimes I went three times in three consecutive days and, very occasionally, twice in one day, thus spending seven hours out of twenty-four in the "forgetting chamber." Real life became for me like a series of those jarring moments when the screen goes blinding white, the jagged edge of a torn strip of film flicks one's eyeballs, and there is a flash of incomprehensible numerals lying on their sides (like a message in code from Hades) before the dream begins again.

I gladly saw almost any film unless it was English. My taste in movies had changed very little since the far-off days when, in the Black Cat, I and my friends had acted out to each other the stories of the various pictures we had seen. I was still a devotee of the divine woman.

In my lifetime she changed her name three times, calling herself first Brigitte Helm, later Greta Garbo, and finally Marlene Dietrich. I thought about her a great deal, wore her clothes, said her Sphinxlike lines, and ruled her kingdom. I came to the conclusion that beauty was not a girl but an Aryan face seen through Semitic eyes. This was what gave her that tragic and remote quality. If what the Wandering Jew (who might by now have changed his name to Fritz Lang) most longed for was unbearable pleasure indefinitely prolonged, then he had to invent for himself a woman who was both beautiful and unattainable.

We have come a long degrading way from Miss Helm to Mlle. Bardot. The fault lies not in our movie stars but in ourselves. Those beauties of the last generation symbolized hopeless love. Now it is too late for tears. What modern young man has the time to play a guitar under his true love's window or the energy to climb up the ivy into her room? In bed he is embracing the bomb. Someone had to invent espresso sex, and to serve each cup of this tasteless beverage there had to be a mechanical doll whose only recommendation was her infinite availability. The woman who came to embody this ideal to the full was Marilyn Monroe. Her directors persuaded her to flaunt her astonishing sexual equipment before us with the touching defenselessness of a retarded child. She was what the modern young man most desires in life—a mistress who could be won without being wooed. She was the football pool of love.

This was no kind of diet for anyone brought up on Rider Haggard. Nevertheless, I continued to linger in the one-and-ninepennies on the principle that any film is at least better than real life. In the absence of stars, I began to concentrate on the stories. I became disturbed by their curious morality. It seemed that to scriptwriters sex was sacred and money was damned. Over and over again I saw heroines forgiven—even praised—for the most dubious behavior if they could claim that their object had been sexual fulfillment. To me this seemed not merely a flimsy excuse but a circumstance that only increased the crime. My views on this subject were expressed once and for all by a char hired by a friend of mine. She was unaware that she had begun to live in a street of shame. The cleaner knew not only what sins were committed but who was committing them, and her comments were an education to my friend. The most enlightening day of all was when the char dragged her by the sleeve to the front window and said of a figure disappearing around the corner of the street, "Quick, madam. Look at that one. Girls that do it for money are bad enough but *she* does it to oblige." This was a moral standpoint that no filmmaker would ever have understood.

When movie ethics became too confusing for me I ceased to bother about them and turned my attention to the technique of film construction. Before long, even this interest was snatched from me by the modern passion for the haphazard—for the abandonment of style. When Antonioni ascended the celluloid throne, pictures became as boring as being alive.

After almost twenty years in the twilit zone, I came blinking back into the light of day.

Chapter 28

I would never have embarked even upon such a cozy disaster as writing a "horror" musical if the opportunity had not presented itself when I had nothing profitable to do. I left the display job in November and there was just time to write *Carry On, Hearse!* or *The Thing and I* before the start of what the schools mockingly call "Spring" term. I was going back to posing not because I still preferred it to all other ways of earning a living but because there was nothing else for me to do.

Only four years had gone by since I had last been a full-time model, but I was shocked to find how much worse the situation had become. During the war things had been somewhat haphazard. Now students enrolled for chaos. Work had almost ceased. The young people wandered through the corridors in droves, shouting, cursing, singing, necking.

The amount of life drawing available to them had increased, but their interest in it dwindled and had in some cases vanished altogether. Although these young people took almost no notice whatsoever of what went on in the outer world, they did go to the galleries, and in them they no longer saw any paintings of naked girls flopping about on piles of cushions. No nudes was good news. This change in aesthetic fashion meant that they could produce a large number of pictures with very little study. The sudden arrival of a model in the life room signified a temporary return to a pursuit that was old-fashioned, unprofitable, and difficult.

One art school in Kent was, I felt, a kind of cultural Borstal. While working there, out of the corner of my eye I perceived two students lying one on top of the other on a long wooden box which had been pushed into a corner of the life room. The art master saw the look of horror that o'erspread my withered features and followed the line of my gaze to its cause. Standing over the entangled couple, he waited, thinking that the very proximity of so much contempt would chill their ardor. This proved a vain hope. He was compelled to stoop and, plunging his hand into the matted hair of the girl, to pry her face from that of her lover. There was a sound like tearing sticking plaster from a painful wound. I thought the young man would say, "The woman thou gavest me, tempted me . . ." but no! From eyes dull with debauchery, sunk in faces glistening with saliva, the two pupils gave their teacher a sullen stare. Then, very slowly, they got up and returned to their easels.

If being treated with indifference was now the daily lot of most models, it was obvious that open contempt would be shown to me. I was a natural target and my heroic postures on the throne now seemed more ludicrously outmoded than ever. In some schools the mounting hostility led to insults about my appearance and my private life being hurled at me by students sitting on the window ledges to watch me arrive and depart.

I found it depressing that this kind of behavior should still prevail. On so many levels, the age of tolerance was in full bloom. The Utopia dreamed of by me and the friends of my youth was here. Anyone could do or say or wear anything without being arrested—almost without public disapproval. This applied particularly to men's wear about which, when I was young, everyone had been so sensitive. A factor no one had foreseen had come to the aid of the party. The population of England now contained more men than women. Therefore masculine plumage had become more colorful. Also Mr. Bronowski's arrow of time, which, he assures us, always points in the direction of diminishing difference, had struck at the heart of our civilization. The distinction between the sexes was reduced to the point where it would have been difficult to tell the boys from the girls if the clothes of the young men had not become so sexually revealing. Indeed their trousers could go no further—or, should it be, no nearer—unless they adopted a Plantagenet style, wore tights, and carried their pride and joy in a specially tailored sack tied with two smart bows.

All these strange manifestations do not prove that more copulation is going on in the world than formerly but that sex, as an idea—as a topic of conversation—is enjoying a freedom never before known and what can be spoken of soon comes to be condoned. If you asked the man in the modern street for his opinion of homosexuality, he would probably reply, "I've nothing against queers myself but I wouldn't like one of them to marry my father."

In Neuilly-sur-Seine there is an apartment house in the hall of which this notice is pinned up: "In this establishment windowboxes are strictly forbidden. Will each tenant therefore make sure that his are firmly fixed to the windowsills." It is odd that this admonition should have been issued in France. It seems to typify a particularly English mode of thought and one that currently applies to the national attitude toward homosexuality. The law remained the same as it was before Brigid Brophy was born, but public opinion had moved on. This "windowbox" morality was offensive to legalists and logicians, but to homosexuals it was easily acceptable. As a member of the Law Reform Society said, in tones trembling with reproach, "It's you—the people concerned—that are so hopelessly indifferent."

This is true. The fundamental predicament of homosexuals is one that no amount of legislation can improve. Even the argument that the repeal of the laws against private indecency will lessen opportunities for blackmail is founded on a misunderstanding. No one in his right senses will attempt to blackmail anyone to the police. The realization of the threat would merely lead to both parties being clapped into a dungeon. Blackmail operates by the threat to reveal facts of which a man is ashamed to those whose good opinion he prizes. This is hardly ever likely to be the C.I.D. It may easily be the victim's mother or wife or employer. To rob blackmail of its potency, it would be necessary to remove the homosexual's feeling of shame. This no power on earth can do. From this feeling of inadequacy and exile I was not immune. The only difference between me and other outsiders was that I cried aloud for pardon. Almost every living being seems to feel that if all were known he would be admired, and even I was never able to rid myself of the idea that if all were known I would be forgiven.

At least a step in this direction was taken when it was at last understood that human beings respond to almost any erotic stimulus. It was only while people still felt that God was watching them that they directed their impulses exclusively toward certain parts of certain people. In everybody the anus is at least as capable of sexual excitement as the lips. Sex acts are now termed masculine and others feminine only to keep the subject tidy.

In my own life a mystery still lingers. It seems that, as a child, I was particularly susceptible to anal stimulus and that my repeated "accidents" were the result of my unwillingness to forgo the pleasure of retaining my feces until it was too late. It would be unreasonable to think that at that age I deliberately adopted an effeminate exterior in the hope that this would one day introduce me to other ways of obtaining the same satisfaction. On the other hand, it is difficult not to presume some connection.

All the intimate subjects which were now being discussed so loudly in such public places had been known on higher levels for a long time, but the knowledge had only recently seeped down to places where it made a difference to the general attitude toward kinkiness. As Brophy's First Law says, it is not the simple statement of facts that ushers in freedom; it is the constant repetition of them that has this liberating effect. Tolerance is the result not of enlightenment, but of boredom.

The sad truth remains, however, that adolescents must have something to scorn at least as much as they feel themselves to be scorned. "Queer-baiting" has not vanished. It has fallen into the hands of younger and younger boys. Quite recently I was asked for money and, when I feigned not to have heard, was kicked in the groin and threatened with worse by six children young enough to demand half fares when they scrambled onto the bus that I had boarded to escape them. This incident was not a boyish prank. The leaders of the gang knew all the wounding words and were sufficiently worldly to threaten to tell the police that I had tampered with them in Trafalgar Square.

If all the praise that I had ever received seemed no more than my due, it follows that all the rough treatment that I underwent appeared undeserved. Only by a great effort at detachment could I see that to other people my appearance, which had once provoked them to indignation because it represented sin, now aggravated them because it had become the overemphatic statement of a tired axiom. To the younger generation to whom the words "good and evil," "innocence and guilt" have lost all meaning, it was no longer my wickedness that annoyed them; it was my pomposity—my insistence on taking the blame for something on which judgment was no longer passed. Also, by an unlucky chance, the symbols which I had adopted forty years earlier to express my sexual type had become the uniform of all young people. By wearing bright colors and growing my hair long I had by mistake become the oldest teenager in the business. It was irritating for the men to see me converting their attire to my own ends. I inadvertently gave the impression of trying to gate-crash a King's Road party for people two generations younger than I. I was not merely a stopped clock; I was a stopped grandfather clock. Before this criticism I was defenseless. It was much too late for me to rejoin the human race I had left in childhood. I would have had no idea how to go on in the presence of real people as their equal. If I had originally been a member of their club, I had certainly never paid my dues and, as Macbeth would have said, "I was in tinsel stepped in so far that, should I wade no more, returning were as tedious as go o'er."

Chapter 29

For the first three years after I returned to posing I did not take any of the drawbacks involved very seriously. I expected them—indeed, the whole world—to end at any moment.

When the war threw me over, I took up with the atom bomb. We were to be married in the spring of 1963. Take heart, I said to myself, all may yet be lost. *Time* Magazine, which cannot be contradicted except by its own subsequent issues, promised that something called the "missile gap" would then be at its widest. They said that when this happened, the enemy would strike. They and I were unduly optimistic.

That was years ago. If the bomb comes now it will be too late. I shall embrace radioactivity only in the resigned spirit in which Laetitia agreed to marry the Egoist—partly to round off the story and partly to save the bomb's good name.

Recently I have inclined toward the view that there should not be this undignified element of hazard about the date of a person's demise. There ought to be a Ministry of Death, though, in Orwellian terminology, it would be named the Ministry of Heaven. This august body of men, all preferably under thirty years of age, would deal with the chore of exterminating old people. Before everything else they would have to agree upon a time limit (say, sixty) to live beyond which would be an offense (punishable with life?). Then the ministry would have to make sure that, six months before his sixtieth birthday, every living being received a notice offering postdated congratulations and advising him which town hall he would be required to visit on the happy occasion. A week before his birthday he would receive a final notice and then, at the glorious hour, unless he preferred to walk there on his own two feet, the van would call to take him to oblivion. In America this vehicle would be painted to look like a fiery chariot, but in England it would be plain blue with the words "Ministry of Death, Kensington Branch" discreetly lettered on its side. For the first few years after such a law was passed there might occasionally be undignified scenes, but in Britain individual liberty is so often curtailed for the common good. Order would soon prevail. Everyone would come to see that the idea was basically good. It would eliminate the dreary effort put by most middle-aged people into trying to set up circumstances conducive to a tolerable old age which, in many cases, never comes. Above all, the creation of this new government body would end the racially suicidal practice of limiting the number of young people in the world by the use of contraceptives. It would substitute a decrease in the heaps of old men and women cluttering up the planet. To this law there would be no exception on grounds of lack of hardship and no extensions of time, but some people might wish to avail themselves of the ministry's services at an earlier date than that prescribed. They would be allowed to make two applications, separated in time by an interval of at least six months, so that the authorities might review their financial status and make sure that public facilities were not being used for the purpose of avoiding payment of private debts. This would also permit applicants to change their mind if their first application had been made in a fine, careless anguish.

Like any other new political measure, the Laws of Death would come trailing crowds of snoopers, fixers, and black marketeers peddling contraband old age at exorbitant prices; if food rationing worked in spite of the inhuman element, so would the controlled apportioning of days.

If the government does not soon adopt some such plan as I have outlined, I shall have to put into action a more personal scheme for limiting my span of years. I shall commit a murder. This is something that for a long time I have wanted to do. It is a natural extension of the desire to hit strangers in the street or to answer them back. It would have been impossible to get through the kind of life that I have known without accumulating a vast unused stockpile of rage. Retaliation, though, was a luxury I could never afford. On the physical level I was too feeble. On any other I was not rich enough. I never dared be rude to anyone. I never knew that I might not need him later. Long after fantasies of sexual excess had ceased to torment me, my imagination was inflamed by lurid daydreams of having my revenge on the world. Whenever people read in the papers that someone has purchased a machine gun and mowed down a whole neighborhood, they invariably say, "I wonder what brought that on." They even make some such remark when the subject is an American Negro. To me the motive is self-evident. Mass murderers are simply people who have had ENOUGH.

Wishing to go out in a blaze of ignominy, I shall limit my activities to killing a policeman. If I am not arrested for the first murder, I shall try a second. It will be like a game of musical chairs.

In the meantime I continued to pose in the art schools—chiefly in the recreational classes. As I sank into old age I was more often given portrait sittings. This was not because my face had crumbled any less than my figure. It was in an even worse state of repair. My teeth became such that my dentist said, "It's not your teeth that are decaying. It's you." As my character coarsened, my features thickened. On the other hand my hair thinned. A receding hairline can be thought to add to the face an undeserved look of nobility, but when you are noble all the way to the crown of your head, you're in trouble. However, certain Slade-type students can paint a tragic greatness into eyes that hang like an impending avalanche over the cheekbones. Nothing for which the life beautiful has a name can be read into a pot belly.

Professionally it is considered a comedown to work in portrait classes, but at least head sittings were less exacting than other kinds. I did them with what grace and gratitude I could. My lust for martyrdom had vanished long ago.

I had never been legally married to real life. Between the ages of twenty-two and forty I had merely conducted an uneasy and illicit liaison with it. In taking up modeling once more, it transpired that I had gone home to mother culture once too often. I made a desperate effort to get another full-time job, but now, not only my odd appearance but also my age were against me. All doors were shut. I fell back into the oubliette of art. In its Havisham twilight I was grimly at home. About me there was something of the dusty elaboration of her mouse-nibbled wedding cake. So here, propped up on some rickety Victorian chair, I sat silent and, I hope, apparently resigned—an ashy clinker from the long dead fires of Bohemia . . .

Ironically, long after the shouting and the tumult had died, a feature writer from the London office of the *Scotsman* telephoned. He suggested that he should write an article about me. I agreed, and a very urbane gentleman with no kilt and no accent came to question me. "They've got the idea that you're the most famous model in the world—up there," he said.

Me: In heaven?

Scotsman: No. In Edinburgh.

Me: Pity.

Scotsman: Is there any justification for this opinion?

Sadly I explained that, as far as I knew, the conditions in which anyone could be a famous model had vanished long ago. Those few of us who were still in the racket had dwindled into naked Civil Servants.

* * *

What happened? What went wrong?

This is the question that, from a throat parched by brick dust, I ask the rescue party as they lean for a moment's rest on their Reform Bills and their Acts of Parliament. When they see me tottering toward them, they find it difficult not to recoil. I am the survivor they hoped they would not find—something too broken to be restored to active life but not quite ready for decent burial. My lips still move.

I have learned, though I never mastered it, the modern manner. I know that on no account must I point a moral or trace a pattern through my past. I clearly see that my life was only an imprudent dash between the cradle and the tomb across open country and under fire. Yet I find it hard to take a prolonged look back and not attempt to excuse results by rearranging causes. Though intelligence is powerless to modify character, it is a dab hand at finding euphemisms for its weaknesses. D. H. Lawrence said that it was not living life that mattered but watching it being lived. I would say that it was not watching life that mattered but explaining what you saw.

Some years ago, in a New York house the windows of which were never opened, two brothers lived. One of them became blind and partially paralyzed. Toward the end of his life he never went out at all; the other left the house briefly to buy food and newspapers with which, after a while, the rooms were piled so high that the place was transformed into a network of canyons from one strategic point to another. To keep out intruders every inch of this labyrinth was mined with booby traps. One day one of these was set off by accident. When, months later, the corpses of the brothers were found, one of them was still sitting up in bed waiting for the other. The second lay only a few yards away, pinned by tons of newsprint to the floor. Even before he was quite dead, the rats had begun to gnaw at his body.

In a sense this was the way I lived, this the fate that overtook me. The place where no harm can come is the place where nothing at all can come. Here I stood. By constituting myself the one among the many I had provoked the worst behavior in others. With this I felt compelled to deal politely. This wrought no change whatever in the character of my enemies but caused the total disintegration of my own. In the end the habit of taking no notice diminished my perception to the point where I became impervious to influence of any kind and therefore to all change except decay. I grew boring to my friends and, which was worse, to myself. I wanted nothing except to get into my coffin without getting into debt.

But, when I ask myself what went wrong, what do I feel that I missed?

Love?

No one has ever been in love with me even faintly—even for half an hour, or if they have, it was a well-kept secret. Yet I can write this sentence with nothing more than a feeling of wounded vanity. I experience no keen sense of loss because I, myself, was never in love with anyone and do not clearly know what the expression means.

Fame?

If fame is merely to be known by a large number of people whom one does not oneself know, then I was famous or at least notorious for many years. The most that I can say is that some by-products of this state of affairs were amusing.

Power was what I craved most ravenously, though not because I felt I merited it. If I had had what I deserved in life I would have starved long ago. I wanted dominion over others in order to redress the balance. A lifetime of being constantly at the mercy of others left me, even though mercy was undoubtedly shown, crushed and seething with a lust for tyranny. No one forced me into the role of a victim. Indeed many of my friends tried to lead me out of it, but the wall-to-wall puritanism of my early years made me excruciatingly conscious of the "sin" of homosexuality. I had no alternative use for my passion for showy extremes but to make with it a Carnaby Street hair shirt.

All this at the last I dimly saw, but an autobiography is an obituary in serial form with the last installment missing. We think we write definitively of those parts of our nature that are dead and therefore beyond change, but that which writes is still changing—still in doubt. Even a monotonously undeviating path of self-examination does not necessarily lead to a mountain of self-knowledge. I stumble toward my grave confused and hurt and hungry. . . .

HOW TO BECOME A VIRGIN

Contents

The Beginning

I am not a drop-out; I was never in.

I have not spent my life hacking my way through the constraints of a bourgeois existence. I was always free – appallingly free.

For my first fifty years I was like someone standing alone in a landscape which led to infinite possibilities in all directions but in which there was an arena surrounded by an insurmountable wall. Over this floated shouts and cheers provoked by an Olympiad from which I keenly felt my exclusion both as spectator and player. In England this perpetual tournament has no name; Americans call it 'the big time'.

These games are incapable of sharper definition than this because their rules are rearranged by each person who goes on to the field and the rewards of victory are not entirely measurable – not wholly of this world.

If you beat your head against this high wall or, indeed, against any wall, after a while it will crumble but such a course of action requires at least a positive temperament. This, if I ever had it, I lost in childhood. At a time when my two brothers aspired to be splendid icons of manliness such as firemen or ships' captains, all I wanted was to be a chronic invalid. For this vocation I had a certain flair. Unfortunately my parents decided that, as a career, it would prove too expensive. Now I could obtain a grant but then I was forced to strike out of my heart all hope of becoming a kinky Mrs Browning. Even so, nothing that has happened to me since that unhappy time has been the result of healthy, vigorous action on my part. I have always proceeded cautiously. However, even if you only lean limply against a wall and you happen to live a very long time, gradually it will begin to give way.

In my case, this process took more than half a century.

My journey from the outer suburbs almost to the heart of the city of happiness came about only partly as a result of my own feeble persistence. It was chiefly caused by a fragile chain of lucky events and by the inexplicable kindness of a series of people who knew me only slightly and one another not at all.

This entire volume is an extension of that list of acknowledgements that in other books occupies but a single paragraph.

One

By the time this century had reached its middle sixties and I had attained my middle fifties, the wages of art school models had risen so steeply that the difficulty they presented was no longer how to live on them, it had become how to deserve them. In trying to solve this problem, the students were little help. Nothing could persuade them to suggest some difficult, dangerous pose that might rouse them from their permanent lethargy. To them life drawing was merely an arduous chore in which there was no money; they clearly wished I was not there.

One day when I was working in Loughton College of Further Education, the 'life' master was able to prevent only one of his pupils from escaping. 'Well,' he exclaimed, turning towards her and beaming broadly, 'the entire day, the whole room and all of Mr Crisp are yours.' Folding her arms across her sullen breasts, the girl replied with the weary question, 'Why is it always up to me?'

In some ways the decline in popularity of life drawing was a secret blessing. My physical stamina was declining so drastically that, even if enthusiasm for my efforts had been evinced, I could no longer have sustained wildly heroic poses all day and every day. To conceal this fact I took to posing intermittently. In the end this would have made my declining years extremely impecunious but, for a while, I preferred this way of life; it allowed me more spare time which I put to good use by indulging in my only hobby – doing nothing.

For this innocent pastime I have always been severely criticized. When I was a child, my mother and my sister used to sit each side of a threadbare fire busily sewing or writing letters. I lay motionless on the hearth rug between them. At least once an hour one of them, with an irritable sigh, would ask, 'Why don't you get something to do?' I always replied, 'Why should I?'

Later in life, when strangers asked me what I did with my spare time and I told them I did nothing, they too instantly became agitated. To them even the most fatuous alternatives to idleness seemed preferable.

'But you don't really do nothing, do you?'

'Yes.'

'But you read.'

'Books are for writing, not for reading.'

'Well then, you write.'

'Not if I can possibly get out of it.'

'Don't you listen to the radio?'

'Listening to the radio is like holding a conversation with someone who is wearing dark glasses.'

'Then you watch television.'

'Seldom and never to kill time.'

'But you can't just do NOTHING.'

With my back to the wall I concede that I breathe and I blink. At this point my inquisitor's fury usually explodes over me like a hand grenade.

I can't deny that secretly my pathological indolence had begun to cause even me a little anxiety. I was faced with the problem which will continue to confront all elderly people until such time as the government undertakes to decide when its senior citizens shall die. The night was coming and I increasingly felt the need for a tin box full of coins lurking under the bed but, at the same time, my earning capacity was on the wane. Not only my physical strength but my resourcefulness and my optimism were gone.

By now it was years since I had applied anywhere for a specific job and decades since I had written anything and sent it unsolicited to an editor. My efforts to deal with my predicament were generalized: I leaned permanently forward so that fate could see me and I tried never to say no to anything. My chief weakness was my life-long lack of specific ambition. If a man demands a lot from fate, he will probably receive something; if he wants but little, he will almost certainly get nothing. In the long run, in spite of everything, I have been very lucky. I asked for bread and was given a stone. It turned out to be precious.

Two

One afternoon, wrapped in a filthy dressing gown and seated by my asthmatic gas fire, I was staring aimlessly at my feet which were sitting in the chair opposite me when the front door bell rang. No one was expected but I took this sign from the outer world calmly. By this time I had lived in the same room so long that I knew perhaps a hundred and fifty people any of whom might call on me without warning. On this occasion my visitor was Mr O'Connor. This I did find mildly surprising because I had not seen him for about fifteen years.

In the happy far-off time when I knew him best, Philip O'Connor was a full-time hooligan. He sat all day in layabout cafés and stood half the night in the public houses of Fitzrovia spouting improvised doggerel to friends and strangers alike without hoping or even wishing to be understood. That stage of his development was evidently past. Looking back on this incident I think he must by now have written *The Memoirs of a Public Baby* and that the instant fame that this book had brought him had introduced him to the BBC's Third

Programme. He now worked for it. This had changed him.

He looked the same as before. Disraeli ringlets still hung over a brow not merely pallid but incandescent with moral decay. His eyes were still as bright as those of a sex maniac and his smile as mirthless as the hilarity of a skull. It was his personality that was different. He now wanted to get things done – an ambition absolutely forbidden in the southern confines of Bohemia which he used to frequent.

After feverishly walking up and down my room for a while, he suddenly asked if he might bring in his tape recorder. When I gave permission, he rushed downstairs returning a minute later with a contraption as big as a gas meter. (It must have been in his car – another sign of redemption from hooliganism.) As soon as he was sure that the black magic box was working, he thrust a microphone towards my astonished lips and said, 'Say something about life and death.' If I am ever told that this method of conducting an interview succeeds with other people I shall be amazed. It suited me perfectly. Compensating for the breadth of the subject by the shallowness of my views, I spoke and I spoke and I spoke. Only when the machine seemed out of breath did I stop. Mr O'Connor appeared satisfied with what had been said and left almost immediately.

I set little store by this episode. In the good old days Charlotte Street was full of people who were nearly on the stage or were just about to write a play. It seemed at the time so unlikely that anyone who had once been an habitué of that twilit land could ever in fact establish a working relationship with the real world or even with the BBC. I was wrong.

Mr O'Connor returned to my room a few days later with his boss and, when I had added a few peroratory phrases, my contribution to the programme was considered complete.

I never heard what I had said to the world because I do not listen to radio broadcasts. I cannot even say if my words were generally well received but I know that at least one person listened because, long after the entire incident was closed, I was told that a publisher had said that I ought to write a book. One's acquaintances are forever saying this even if one only makes one joke a year. The words are intended as a vague compliment rather than as specific encouragement but, if anyone in the book trade makes the remark, it must be taken seriously. Secretly I was annoyed that I had not been told of this comment sooner.

The publisher in question was called William Kimber. I was informed that he published any number of books by disused colonels and the memoirs of a lot of extinct district nurses. We had never met but I made so bold as to telephone him. He bravely admitted that the words he was rumoured to have uttered had indeed fallen from his unguarded lips. Furthermore, he promised that, if I would write a two-thousand-word synopsis of my autobiography, he would read it (or possibly cause it to be read). He would then tell me whether or not he could offer me a contract.

Even a little of my life proved too much for Mr Kimber. He wrote me a very courteous letter praising my frankness but added that he feared that, if he published a book founded on the incidents I had described, he would be bombarded from all directions with libel suits. I cannot imagine why he thought this. Though I am relentlessly outspoken about myself, I am unlikely to be indiscreet concerning others. Indeed, I seldom mention them. In any case, if I were to say that, on some specific occasion, I had popped into a dark corner with the Duke of Birmingham, a compositor could easily have set the name as 'B.rm.ngh.m' and kept the reader guessing.

I had expected Mr Kimber's reaction but being accustomed to sorrow is not the same as suffering in silence.

Late in my career as a model, I began to find the competition for employment in the London schools too fierce. I took to working in the home counties. There the college to which I went most frequently was Maidstone. I travelled thither in a railway carriage stuffed to the brim with art masters.

To them I told my tale of woe. Nothing shortens a journey so pleasantly as an account of misfortunes at which the hearer is permitted to laugh. One member of my audience was a man who, I am told, now rules Maidstone but who was then only a hireling. Even so he wielded considerable power being married to Thames and Hudson. 'Kimber!' he exclaimed, when I had come to the end of my story. 'I think you can do better than that. I have my spies,' he added, 'and I will put them out.' He must have done so at once. Within a few days I was introduced to my first literary agent, a Catholic Texan married to a Protestant Irishwoman living in Putney. He submitted what I had written for Mr Kimber, together with photographs taken of me some thirty years earlier, to Messrs Jonathan Cape and in no time at all I was given a contract and £100.

I nearly fainted.

By the time the book came out I had received, I think, about £300. After that, on the English hardback edition, my royalties never amounted to much. I imagine that, when advance payments to authors are being fixed, the publisher's accountants go into a dim corner of the office, their fingers tap their thumbs rapidly and their pale lips move as they calculate exactly what the writer's earnings will be on the edition they intend to print. This is the sum offered.

I had wanted my autobiography to be called *My Reign in Hell*. I was convinced that, after turning the first few pages, readers would agree that I had closely followed Mr Lucifer's example by refusing to serve in Heaven (respectable society). This title was rejected and, from a few random ideas, *The Naked Civil Servant* was chosen. The name was suggested by an incident described towards the end of the book. A feature writer contributing to a paper called *The Scotsman* came to interview me. During our conversation or rather my monologue, while I was drawing breath he managed to ask if I was a famous model. I explained that, by that time, there was no such thing. The relationship between artists and their models had ceased to be a cause of prurient speculation not because newspapers and their readers had become any more clean-minded but for the simpler reason that painters no longer worked from the nude. Models now work only in the schools, they are engaged by the term and their wages ultimately come from the Minister of Education. They are just like civil servants except that during office hours they wear no clothes.

This title was a mistake. Almost everywhere I go, audiences ask me to explain it and, if I do not, bewilderment in the minds of book buyers gives place to fatal misunderstanding.

A friend told me that, while she was visiting her mother in Lewes, the first object that caught her eye as she entered the chintzy living-room was my book lying on a table. 'Whatever made you get that?' my friend gasped. In a calm, slightly supercilious tone her mother replied, 'I don't know what you're making such a fuss about; you know I've always been interested in the civil service.'

Before my autobiography was published I had written three books on various subjects and one longer work of fiction called *Love Made Easy*. This had been rejected – rightly as it later transpired. When, twenty-five years after it was completed, it was very kindly published by Duckworth it received bad notices even in New Zealand.

The difference between all these previous efforts to earn a living by writing and my life story was its scandal value.

The young, led to victory by the Beatles, had inherited the earth about ten years before my book was ready for publication. Their wealth has given teenagers throughout the world the power to set fashions not only in what to wear and how to dance but also in what to say. Since children always wish to talk about what their parents never mention, sex became a subject of open, nay, incessant discussion. When inevitably as a theme for table talk heterosexuality was worn threadbare, it was supplanted by homosexuality which became all the rage. The fact that the laws concerning it were in process of being changed gave this particular pastime an added topicality.

If to be a man of destiny is to arrive at a point in history when the only gift you have to offer has suddenly become relevant, then in this tiny and purely social way that is what for the moment I became.

When my book was as nearly complete as I could make it, my publisher gave me the hand of an editress in literary marriage. She was a beautiful woman whose eyes, whether she was redeeming my ungainly prose or merely shopping in Fulham Road, forever held an expression of dismayed surprise. Naturally I cannot say if she wore this look before she encountered me. She was infinitely patient, never making the slightest emendation to my typescript without consulting me, always explaining why an alteration would be for the better. If I interpret her correctly, she was advising me to make my sentences short. She was saying that, if they were in the right order, conjunctions would seldom be necessary. Then, on the rare occasion when a connecting word was used, it would be endowed with a special dramatic power of its own. I do not mean that she told me all this at any one meeting. It is what I deduce from the nature of the improvements that she urged me to make. Some years later I told her that I now write by the Miller method. I think she said, 'Come off it,' which no editress should ever say. If she happens to read this book and finds it to be full of grammatical errors no doubt her look of dismay will be intensified.

In spite of all the care lavished upon my book, it could not be described as a wild success. The reviews of it were at best kind; at worst they were, as I am sure most authors find, contradictory. One said that it was full of self-pity; someone else remarked upon its freedom from precisely this emotion. One critic was delighted by the aphorisms with which the pages were riddled; the *Times Literary Supplement* deplored the arch and jaunty style in which the story was told.

I never reject criticism on the fatuous grounds that it is prompted by unworthy motives or that to care about it is in some way beneath me. I hold that the very purpose of existence is to reconcile the glowing opinion we hold of ourselves with the appalling things that other people think about us. This book is therefore written in a minimum risk style with which I hope to offend nobody. I am aware that this does not guarantee that I shall please everybody.

Ultimately I believe that, with a hideous struggle, the hardback edition of *The Naked Civil Servant* sold out its edition of about three thousand, five hundred copies. The failure or success of the book was, however, not the point. What mattered was that another chunk of the wall against which I had for so long been leaning had given way.

Through the aperture thus created, I could now see a tantalizing corner of the arena that I longed to enter.

About a month after my autobiography was published, I was interviewed on television for the first time.

Three

To celebrate the fact that, in a parochial way, an inhabitant of the kingdom of Bohemia was beginning to make good, a hooligans' party was given. The idea for this feast was put forward by someone who during the war had himself been an habitué of the Charlotte Street cafés but who was now redeemed, firstly by marriage and secondly by having become a barrister. The arrangements for this occasion were thrust into the astonished hands of a young woman who though known to both of us had never truly been a hooliganette. It was a thoroughly embarrassing assignment that she had been given because all the guests had to be asked for money – ten shillings, I think. She implored me to supply her with a list of subscribers but I could think of no one that I would have the nerve to suggest should pay for the mere privilege of eating with me. In spite of my lack of co-operation she managed by charm and persistence to muster enough diners to enable her to hire what the Bible would call an upper room. It was in Schmidt's restaurant. Though this establishment was in the middle of Charlotte Street it presented to the world a face so cold and, worse, so clean that I do not think any of my friends had ever ventured into it before.

The party was a lively but rather awkward gathering of people whom I knew intimately, slightly or not at all. Among them was a man well-dressed and well-behaved beyond the demands of the situation. When he left the other guests asked one another in awe-struck tones, 'Who was the visitor from the outer world?'

In fact he was a televisionary who, on leaving, promised to 'see what he could do for me'. A few weeks later it was at his command that I was summoned at the dead of night to the BBC studios in Shepherd's Bush.

I found myself in the cast of a programme called *Late Night Line-Up* whose other members were a monk and Fanny Craddock. I took to her immediately because of the degree of animation that she infuses into her public appearances and, indeed, into her entire life. After the show was over and we were all sitting in the drinking room waiting for taxis to take us home, someone approached her and said, 'It's over, Fanny. It's finished.' She laughed. She had been speaking just as fast and as vigorously as when the cameras were watching her. Eagerness to please devoid of sycophancy is a characteristic I greatly admire.

While I was waiting to go into the cage with the interviewer, I was questioned three times as to whether or not I was nervous. After twice saying no I asked, 'What have I got to lose?' 'Quite right,' said my interrogator. 'Just the right attitude.' If I had been afraid, the repeated question would have turned me into a nervous wreck.

At this first interview the words 'What have I got to lose?' were uttered almost in self-defence but they exactly expressed my attitude towards the occasion. I had only negative goals. I wanted not to start every sentence with 'Well' or 'Er'. I wished to survive whatever was said to me without displaying embarrassment or shock. I need not have worried. The questions were very bland. Most of them concerned the oddities of my appearance and of my domestic routine.

As the years have flown by, the questions have remained much the same. It is the answers that have changed, not in content but in manner. I no longer regard television interviews as ordeals that must be endured without flinching. They have become welcome opportunities for presenting myself and my ideas to the world – mini-parties which I enjoy and through which I try to offer entertainment to others. I could almost say that they have become a way of life.

Within weeks of the publication of *The Naked Civil Servant* I found myself being asked to speak to small gatherings of people. They were of various denominations. Sometimes they were literary aspirants. To these I repeated that books are for writing – not for reading. To be more explicit I explained that no one who intends to take up writing as a career should read any work that lies in the category in which his own efforts would be placed. If he disobeys this rule, he will almost certainly feel that he must write literature instead of trying to say what he means. Even though he may not attempt patches of deathless prose, he will become preoccupied with grammar and syntax far more complicated than he would ever use when speaking. This is now quite unnecessary. Since the invention of Frank Norman, writing has at last ceased to be a middle-class accomplishment. It has become an activity as universal as sex and almost as exhausting.

When not with embryonic authors, I was invited to universities or art schools. There I explained that education is a mistake. Cluttering one's skull with facts about any subject other than oneself I hold to be a waste of time. All general knowledge can be discovered in the nearest public library and even these hushed and apparently harmless establishments should be visited with caution. Being well-informed is but a stone's throw from being boring and stones will be thrown.

In seats of learning on whatever social level audiences are often livelier than elsewhere. While I was talking to the inmates of East Ham Polytechnic one young man abruptly stumbled out of the room. He returned a few minutes later with the explanation that he had found it prudent to stand in the corridor for a while to cool his rage. 'You're lucky,' he warned me, 'I've got a terrible temper and I nearly clobbered you.' What had so incensed him was my statement that artists should disregard social issues. East Ham is a fully committed region.

Inevitably the audiences that I was most often asked to amuse were members of the Campaign for

Homosexual Equality or other kindred organizations. If I spoke to Lesbian societies, no men were ever present. Perhaps like a masonic lodge in reverse they occasionally held a gentlemen's night but I never attended one. Their policy at that time seemed to be gently isolationist. To give an example: at a mixed gathering in Croydon, a girl said, 'I suppose I shouldn't ask you this but why do the boys keep on at us to come to their meetings? I can't see any point.' I gave a non-committal reply to conceal my surprise at this question. Traditionally, in the heterosexual world, it is the men who will not attend any social occasion unless it holds carnal possibilities. That is what makes them so hard to get along with. I was sorry to be made aware that girls were now adopting this bleak way of thinking.

As the years went by, matters worsened. Lesbian attitudes towards gay men passed from indifference to hostility and upon any manifestation of effeminacy they began to pour open contempt. It was regarded not so much as sinful or repulsive as politically ineffectual. One of the surest ways of making yourself and other people notice your masculinity (whether you are in fact a man or not) is to talk incessantly about politics or money. This is what the majority of Lesbians had decided to do. Their 'cause' became almost synonymous with Women's Liberation. The partial merging of these two factions was almost inevitable. Not many liberationists would say that they demanded the right to make love with partners of whatever sex they chose but many Lesbians would certainly state that they wished for a life in which they could enter without question all masculine territory including that of sharing and possibly shouldering the financial burdens of living with a woman. There is on the other hand a species of gay man which finds the practical worries of life intimidating. Such a person likes the society of girls because he hopes that with them conversation will be less worldly, less political, less mercenary. For this reason there were usually a few women at gatherings arranged by male homosexuals. Their presence made functions look well attended and their subscriptions swelled party funds. None of the boys seemed threatened by them.

If I were asked to describe the difference between the sexes in the gay world, I would say that the men wanted to be amused; the girls sought vindication.

In the late sixties it seemed to me that these meetings were mostly genuinely social. If they were political, they were not stridently so. If, secretly, they were vast shopping centres, they never exuded that atmosphere both crude and furtive which makes frequenting gay public houses such a daunting prospect.

Once, while I was in Bristol helping to declare it a gay city, the convener of the event said, 'This is gay week – and I mean GAY. I know that the place is full of gay bars and that many of you stand in them night after night but you never speak to anyone, you never seem to be enjoying yourselves.' That young man had all my sympathy.

From the beginning, the Campaign for Homosexual Equality was as fundamentally political as the word 'campaign' implies but it also catered for the human needs of its members. Trips along the Thames, musical evenings, even a CHE fair were arranged. Perhaps because my sister was the wife of a country parson, I was quite accustomed to such activities and I was never contemptuous of their parochial element. I was also aware that, if there had been such an organization when I was young, I would have been a founder member. If there had been in existence any building in London where the very thing that made it impossible for me to feel at ease with other groups of men would have been taken for granted, I would have been on the doorstep before the place was opened.

In the early days, whether speaking to men, women or a mixture of the two, I always assumed that my function was to entertain but I did occasionally issue warnings. One of these was against forming an exile's view of reality. It was, I thought, likely to be as wide of the mark as Mr Browning's idea of an English April. Just because full-time homosexuals are on the outside of certain experiences – just because they stand with their cold noses pressed against the window pane gazing through it at the carpet-slipper set-up – they should not suppose that everything by the fireside is permanent, peaceful. The terrible truth is that the people on the inside are trying to get out.

At all these events I was indulgently received and very courteously treated. Someone always fetched me, fed me and transported me back to Beaufort Street when the evening ended. The Campaign was poor and so was I. A fee of about £5 was most acceptable and these transactions had about them a pleasant amateurishness. Inevitably, as my hold on the reins of my band-wagon tightened, this passed.

I am writing of a time when I was both working as a model and giving these small talks. Between them these two professions earned me a living but I was aware that I ought to be turning my new situation to better account. I was still not in the arena – not even in a ringside seat. All my friends tried to help but no fringe benefits seemed to dangle from the fact of my having written a book. My agent came to the rescue.

He was not content with trafficking in the work of others, he also wished to write. Like a nurse ministering to the sick in a plague of words, it was only to be expected that eventually he himself would succumb to the disease. The theme that he chose as the subject for his own book was style – not of writing but of living. He showed me a list of chapter headings, a plan of campaign and so on and asked me what I thought of them. I replied that they displayed masterly powers of organization but added that, as a way of convincing a publisher that a book was actually in the process of being written, they were a dead loss. I suggested that what was needed was a tin suitcase stuffed to bursting with typescript. My agent agreed and solicited my help. The longer I contemplated the subject he had selected, the more opinions I found

I had. I wrote and I wrote and I wrote. When the gold – well, the yellow metal – was sifted from the dross of my discourse, there appeared to be very little that would enrich the publisher to whom it was to be presented. Though I was most handsomely rewarded for my useless assistance, I felt somehow let down. I had the nerve to borrow back the work for which I had already been paid and take it to Messrs Jonathan Cape whence it was returned as quickly as if we had been playing badminton. I embraced my oldest friend defeat and went on as though nothing unpleasant had happened. My agent fled to Texas.

My unloved typescript lay among the fluff under my bed until I received a visit from an actress who had divorced the stage and married a member of the legendary Woolf family. As she reclined amidst the dust of my room, she asked wistfully, 'Don't you ever write anything that Cecil could publish?'

I dived under the bed and brought out my thoughts on style, now a greyish-yellow in colour. 'If he doesn't want them,' I said with a bitter laugh, 'throw them away.' This statement I later regretted. When I asked for the return of my work, I inadvertently brought into effect Proust's First Law. Love does not cause jealousy; it is jealousy that engenders love. The moment it was implied that I had found a use for my typescript, Mr Woolf's indifference vanished. He decided to publish a book on style.

The recall of my literary effort was not a ruse. I wanted it because I thought it might be of interest to Mr Mitchell, the famous maker of television documentaries.

Looked at from the front, a television screen is a small space in which personalities and events jostle one another for a brief moment of glory or, at least, of public attention. Seen from behind it is an arid waste in which, like farmers in a dust bowl, broadcasters and producers dig for something – anything – on which to feed their bleating flocks. If somewhere there is a woman who has made the largest patchwork quilt in the world, immediately this is known documentary interest in her will become keen – nay, desperate. 'Get her,' snarls the director. 'She's in the Antarctic,' his secretary quietly explains. 'Get her,' her employer repeats louder than before. The indefatigable needlewoman is snatched by helicopter from the ice floes, her air fare to New York is paid, she is placed in an expensive hotel. The next day she murmurs a few shy words into a microphone and is returned to the everlasting snows. Only God and Mr Bernstein know the cost of such an escapade.

When not even this much material is to hand, a programme is made about Soho.

For this reason I was not altogether surprised when, walking innocently along Old Compton Street, I was waylaid by an acquaintance with the question, 'Do you want to be in a thing about Soho?'

'Another?'

'Yes, another.'

I remembered with how little enthusiasm I had occasionally watched these programmes. They are invariably mixtures of interviews with bemused Italian caterers, insults from beery Bohemians and the confessions of bored prostitutes. Even so, I nodded. If we wish to be totally free from blame for our anonymity, we must never say no to anything.

So much later that I had quite forgotten the few words exchanged in the street, a minor televisionary whom I had never met telephoned me to remind me of them. I agreed to meet him in the As-You-Like-It Coffee Bar in Monmouth Street. This was positively the last of the layabout cafés – those marvellous places where you could sit through lunch and tea and supper without ordering anything more than one cup of coffee. I chose this venue so that, if the appointment was not kept, it would not in any way disturb my way of life. It was an establishment where several times a week, either accompanied or alone, I sat for hours eating lotus petals.

As it happened I was not betrayed. The stranger fed me with tea and questions about the difference between Soho now and what it had been like when I was young. I explained that the district had gone down terribly. You used to be able to get your throat cut on a really big scale but now the entire region was riddled with nothing better than dim basements where girls take off their clothes for money. I pointed out that, as a test of the closeness of your relationship with the world, sex could never be a patch on being murdered. (That's when someone really does risk his life for you.) My inquisitor seemed dazed rather than enlightened by what I said but he must have regaled his employers with a favourable account of our meeting because, after another interval of several weeks, he telephoned me again.

This time he wished me to go immediately to a public house in Greek Street. There, half an hour later, I found the televisionary, two members of a pop group called The Strawbs and Mr Mitchell whose genius for television documentaries was explained to me. He wore a suit and seemed slightly ill at ease. To offset this, he was very friendly and bought innumerable drinks for all of us. At that time I formed no positive opinion of him whatsoever. This I later learned is the minimal impression that he aims to create at all times. He was the first to leave the party saying, 'We must meet again some time,' which everyone knows is English for good-bye. I was therefore astonished when, within a few days, he visited my room in Chelsea. During the next few weeks several conversations between us took place either at my home or his which was temporarily in London. To me our discussions did not seem particularly purposeful but they must have been to him for a day finally came when he said, 'I think we'll make it all in this room.'

'Make what?' I asked.

'The film.'

'About Soho?'

'It won't be about Soho.'

'Then what will it be about?'

'You.'

Early in October of 1968 a production team of

six marched on Beaufort Street. So small is my room that the sound equipment and the two men who claimed to understand it were compelled to spend all their working hours in the bathroom. The girl who lived in the back room on my floor couldn't go to the gent's for a week. Not only was the routine of the house disrupted, the whole street was disturbed by a generator which chugged away happily outside the front door until the neighbours complained. Sheets of pink acetate were fixed over the windows of my room and for four days as though lit by the dawn of a new Doris day, I walked about, sat in my chair or rolled on my bed droning on about eternal things. The resulting abundance of material I am happy to tell you was rendered down until it lasted only half an hour and was shown on Granada Television at the end of the following year. This programme was well received except by the *Daily Express* and even that paper savaged me rather than the makers of the film.

The public curiosity aroused caused an unknown woman working for Granada to telephone me.

'They keep asking who you are,' she complained.

'Who indeed?' said I.

'Apparently there's some book that you've written.'

I admitted that I was the author of a meagre number of books and mentioned that the latest of these was called *The Naked Civil Servant*. She seemed content with this information and I heard no more from her. Evidently, as far as she was concerned, the mystery was solved. For me it merely deepened.

I had no difficulty in understanding why, from the television company's point of view, no mention of the book must be made during the programme. Had it been, the entire project might then have seemed to be an advertisement for which the wrong people were being paid. Worse, my ingrained eccentricities might have appeared to be assumed for the purpose of boosting book sales. What I found strange was that, when the papers mentioned the time at which the documentary was being shown, they made no reference to the book, and in no advertisement for the book was anything said to connect me with the film. My bewilderment mounted to downright astonishment when I learned that the publishing house and the television company concerned were as one on this matter.

You cannot turn your toes towards Golden Square without being asked of any programme you have made, 'Will it be part of a series?' I have no idea whether Mr Mitchell was asked to make other films similar to mine after it turned out to be a mild success or whether, before he began, he already thought of it as one of several such features. The final result was that the film about me was shown twice, first by itself and later as the first of six documentaries about old men looking back on their lives.

After all these events I came to know the Mitchells personally. They proposed that another film should be made, this time not about my habits but my opinions. It was to help with this project that I asked Mr Woolf to return my book about style.

When this second documentary did not materialize I was disappointed. It seemed that fate had thrust me back into limbo or, at least, not drawn me forward. I did not dream that one day, beautifully made though it was, Mr Mitchell's film, in terms of publicity, would seem no more than a trailer for the television version of *The Naked Civil Servant*.

I still hold Mr and Mrs Mitchell in the highest regard and we write to each other at Christmas time but it has become doubtful that we will ever make another television programme together. In a small way I now live the 'show biz' life which to Mr Mitchell is like cock-crow to a vampire. The word 'actor' causes him to fling his arm across his eyes and fall back against the nearest wall.

Four

Immediately after the publication of my autobiography in 1968, I had begun to receive telephone calls from part or total strangers at the rate of one a week and about twice as many letters. When I asked a friend if she had ever written to anyone she didn't know, she replied, 'Of course I have. You're far more likely to find you have something in common with someone whose work you admire than with a man who merely happens to have married your sister.' I bowed my head before the invincible logic of this observation but I have never corresponded with a total stranger in all my long, dark life. I wouldn't dare. This may be why I regarded the communications I received with such amazement.

I once said that I liked my friends but that I was simply mad about strangers. This is still true but during the past twelve years my attitude towards people whom I do not know has changed. If possible, their reaction to me has become even more extreme and, consequently, mine to them has grown more cautious. The letters that now rained down upon me usually came from women. This was natural enough. Men say they have no time to write letters but they rise at dawn to jog, watch television until midnight and even neglect their own best interests to pursue activities they enjoy. We must therefore conclude that they do not like correspondence that does not begin 'Your esteemed favour to hand . . .' While at that time the spoken messages to me were polite, interested, amused, the written ones were often sad. They began, 'You won't remember me but . . . ' or 'You don't know me but . . .' These words were preceded by a few kind phrases of eulogy about my life or my book – payment in advance for the sympathy about to be solicited.

What followed was usually a vague cry for help. The burden that was too great to bear was life itself – a feeling that, from my youth, I understood so well. My attention was being engaged not because it was thought that I possessed any specific knowledge but because it was known that I would never be shocked or bored or feel tempted to tell anyone to pull herself together. On the few occasions when these appeals came to me not by post but through the telephone, I realized that my main function was to listen.

I hold that words are the salve with which we heal the wounds inflicted on us by our actions. If an unpleasant incident is described often enough, its sharp edges become bevelled. Moreover, if a problem is stated with sufficient accuracy, the solution has already been formulated. I merely waited, almost in silence, for this to happen. Occasionally strangers asked me for practical advice: 'Shall I leave my husband?' or 'Shall I tell my parents that I'm gay?' The first remedy that I suggested was to do nothing. To young men who felt that their homosexuality was a social handicap, I recommended that they should neither confirm nor deny it. If asked to amplify this statement, I said, 'Don't become involved in a dialogue which might lead anyone to suppose that you are likely to marry someone of the opposite sex with whom you have been to the movies twice; on the other hand there is no need to waltz down to breakfast with the words "Guess what?"'

Unfortunately I have found no way of keeping out of these exchanges, whether written or spoken, an element of condescension. A grandparent-grandchild relationship, that is not entirely due to my age, inevitably sets in.

Since leaving home I have never had any problems other than financial. I have not been deeply involved with anyone. In the house where to this day I have a room, there once lived a woman whose lust for rows and reconciliations to some extent involved the lives of all the inmates. When we realized that her recantations were nothing but a means of not paying the usual price for speaking one's mind, we came to despise her apologies more than her rages. Even I did not quite succeed in avoiding either but I tried. My desire was never to win this woman's good opinion but always to have a quiet life. When threatened, my wish is to disengage myself – so that not even a fragment of my life resides in someone else's. Therefore, when anyone presents me with human problems, I have no similar experience to offer in exchange. If any of my unknown correspondents has felt deflated by this, I here ask forgiveness. It would be heartless to say that I enjoy hearing about the misfortunes of others but it is true that I profit by becoming acquainted with them. It brings me a little nearer to understanding people. If they are grateful for my sympathy, I am glad of their confidence.

These encounters of the fourth kind were just beginning to abate when Mr Mitchell's documentary about me was shown on Granada Television. After it, the letters continued their gradual decline in numbers but the telephone calls became more frequent and their character became more hostile, or perhaps it would be truer to say they became more contemptuous. Evidently letter-writers are a restrained race while televiewers are a violent people.

I imagine that the nuisance calls came chiefly from girls working on switchboards. Such conversations would be useless without an audience who could hear both ends. Besides, it was often possible to detect a certain hollowness not only in the content of these dialogues but also in their sound and, once in a while, another voice than that of the original caller would interrupt a long silence with the question, 'Is he still on the line?' When this happened, I replied that I was, but suggested that, as none of us had come up with anything very witty, it might be as well to ring off.

Some calls sought merely to inconvenience me. A girl would pose as an employee of some well-known television company and would ask me to go, say, to Euston Station to be photographed. I replied that she must communicate with my agent.

'We don't work through agents.'

'Then I fear that we cannot come to a satisfactory arrangement.'

'We'll make it worth your while.'

'You're very kind.'

'Then will you do it?'

'No.'

At other times an effort was made to embarrass me socially. A young woman would say that she was giving a party. I would wish her every success.

'Will you come?'

'No, thank you.'

'There will be lots of lovely boys.'

'How nice!'

'Then won't you come?'

'No, thank you.'

This kind of discourse frequently continued for several minutes.

I could have understood these feeble attempts at entrapment if the programme that provoked them had left my homosexuality vague. If a viewer merely suspected my guilty secret, she might regard it as a triumph of perspicacity if she could trick me into giving some sign that her suspicions were correct. As my sin was never in any doubt, what could anyone gain even if I expressed ludicrous eagerness to attend a kinky orgy?

I have often been asked why I am so patient with these unseen enemies. The cause is partly habit. I was the youngest child and consequently was the butt of mockery and abuse almost from birth. The only member of my family who did not heap ridicule upon me was my father and that was because he never spoke. I would have died of exhaustion if I had tried to combat the treatment I received; instead I feigned not to be angry. The only method known to me by which one can survive one's emotions is to feign not to have them.

It works. I am now almost entirely free from indignation. I can't remember the last time I 'answered back'.

Other-cheekism is not only a way of purifying the soul, it is also part of every weak person's survival kit. If I had tried to defend myself in any of the street incidents of which in my youth I was the victim, I might easily have been killed. I seem now to be in less physical danger than formerly but even when dealing with verbal harassment the principle is the same. If, as soon as the hostility of a stranger reaches me through the telephone, I were to put the receiver back on its cradle, my tormentor would ring again and again. If I shouted at him, he would goad me with redoubled savagery.

I also remind myself that if I, however gently, have insisted on preserving my personal freedom I must never try to curtail the liberty of others – even when it takes the form of baiting a complete stranger.

When teasing calls came from men, they were seldom openly hostile. They tended to be pseudo-subtle. A voice like that of a monitor lizard would announce itself as Nigel or Basil or any other name thought to be slightly precious and would claim to have met me in Hyde Park or Piccadilly Circus. As I have not tried to pick anybody up for fifty years nor even made myself conspicuously available for thirty, I was always certain that these statements were a flimsy hoax. I merely declined politely whatever invitation was offered. Very occasionally these assignatory calls were genuine in the sense that, though my caller could hardly long to know me, he might wish to find out certain things about himself and might feel that in me he had found someone who, without either giggling or being contemptuous, would assist his self-knowledge.

'You're Quentin Crisp,' the voice would say.

I would reply that I was.

'You've written a book or been on a telly programme about homosexuality?'

'Ye-es.'

'Well I've never done anything like that but I've wanted to.'

'Thousands have.'

'It's a question of getting someone to do it to me [or for me or with me].'

'I'm afraid that I can't help you but I hope you find someone who will.'

Sometimes I made so bold as to suggest that Nigel or Basil sought someone nearer his own age and whom he actually liked. Here again I wanted to show that I was not disgusted. I felt mean in refusing to become involved in these proposed experiments. I hate to think that there is anyone in the world who never fulfils his fantasies because of mere shyness but I could not be sure that the situation was what it seemed. I was afraid. I am an old man of feeble physique. It would be foolish of me to place myself in a room with a stranger so odd, so obviously peculiar, that none of his friends had ever made the slightest attempt to help him overcome his self-doubt.

And how did such people think of me? Did they envisage me in rimless glasses and a white coat, standing at the top of the stairs and saying, 'Next, please'?

Sometimes I persuaded callers to pass through the social equivalent of the metal detector used at airports. I made an appointment in the not so immediate future. The introduction of a time-lag eliminated all the jokey customers and nearly all the kinky ones but once a youth kept one of these delayed assignations. He was about twenty years of age, tall, slim and with blond hair faintly gilded by artificial means. He talked for about an hour. That was how long it took to reach the subject of sadomasochism. I explained that I had been lucky – that, even in my youth when my poverty was at its bleakest, I had not been forced to take part in painful situations of the kind to which he was referring. I gave no sign that I knew we had now reached the heart of our discourse nor did he but he left soon after my disclaimer.

I was amazed that anyone so presentable had found no way of stirring into his relationships with his friends a little at a time of his favourite flavouring.

When, many years later, Mr Mackie's television play about me was shown to the world, these telephone calls passed from tittering contempt to growling hatred. For the first time direct threats upon my life were screamed at me from invisible lips: 'You're queer. I'll kill you.' I could only ask if the speaker wanted an appointment. It was not possible to take these menaces seriously. I regarded them as no more real than the offers of rape that are forever being made to girls with foreign surnames listed in English telephone books. I have no doubt that England is bristling with people sincerely longing for my death and, when they can tolerate my existence no further, presumably they will jump without warning from behind a tree in the street where I live.

It was also noticeable that, with the passage of time, harassment was starting to come from younger and younger boys. Once a schoolmaster whom I have known for many years was visiting with me. I placed him by the telephone so that he could act as a taster for the poison dripping from the ear piece. On that day we received several hostile calls in the course of a few hours. They required no replies; they were merely a spate of filthy words. My friend judged them to be from boys no more than twelve-years-old.

And why do I not have my name removed from the telephone book? I gave up being a model in the art schools in June of '78 so I can no longer claim that the telephone represents money but the answer was never as simple as that. The first objection to becoming 'ex-directory' is that it looks as though you think you are somebody. The second reason for not doing so is that it would be ages before the gesture took effect. It would be a year at least before the A-D section without my name in it was published and even then all the old copies would not instantly be swept from the face of London. Furthermore, my number would still be engraved upon the stony heart of every schoolboy in England. He will forget only when the notion of sex ceases to torment him. Finally, and more important than all other objections, is the feeling that, if your number is no longer in circulation, like Electra, you have shut the windows of your house forever. From that terrible moment onwards, you will never see the outer world again; you will be stuck with your friends.

In spite of all that my persecutors can do or say to me, I still want the world. What else is there?

The most unusual threat to my life came from a woman. She was in no way inimical. In fact killing me was to be an act of mercy.

Shortly before I departed for America the second time, I received a flattering letter from the north of England. Later the writer telephoned me to say that she was coming to London to show artwork of some kind to a prospective buyer and would like to weave into her itinerary a visit to my room. I agreed. This woman, neither old nor young, turned out to be of neat appearance and, during the entire time that she spent with me, she neither did nor said anything the least bit peculiar. Nevertheless, several days after our meeting, I found, wedged between the door of my room and its frame, a piece of paper informing me that a police inspector from the local station wished to see me urgently. Within half an hour of my telephoning him, he and one of his accomplices were in my room.

Times have changed. The last occasion on which the law had invaded my privacy occurred during the war. Since then it had never paid me a visit and had seldom questioned me in the street. I do not deny that in the past it treated me better than it might have done and this is not my opinion alone. When someone showed the teleplay of my life to a police officer, his first words were, 'Can't be true.' Asked how he was so sure of this, the man replied, 'He'd have been arrested on the first day.' I myself have often wondered why it took so long for anyone to get around to 'taking me in for questioning', considering that I used to waltz along the streets of the West End totally unaware that they were infested with plainclothes coppers. Though they did not arrest me until 1943, they knew that I was in a weak position and constantly threatened me for their own and one another's amusement. Their condescension towards me on these occasions will never fade from my mind. Even now I could never wittingly become acquainted with a policeman; nor would I, except under torture, betray anyone to the authorities. Life is so hard for poor little crooks at the best of times.

I imagine that these opinions which I hold so intensely are, in a milder form, fairly common. As a former police chief has himself said, 'If the police were popular there would be something wrong somewhere.'

On this occasion I tried to give no hint of any of

these feelings and invited the men to sit down. For their part, though they could not prevent their invasion from being sinister, their manner of questioning me was in no way aggressive.

The inspector informed me that he had that morning received a letter from my female visitor. He showed me a copy of it which had been typed out on a long strip of paper in such a way as to keep exactly the same number of words on each line as were in the original manuscript. It looked like a printer's galley for a poem by e. e. cummings and, when read aloud, it made as little sense. The writer explained who and what she was, stating also that she was a Lesbian. She described her visit to my room and her reactions to the occasion. She had apparently been overwhelmed by the spectacle of my loneliness. It was to put an end to this that she proposed to kill me and then, so as to leave no loose ends, to do away with herself.

While my visitors questioned me, I tried to think what on earth could have provoked this deeply emotional response in a total stranger. If living alone was mentioned, I am sure that I uttered no cries of anguish. It is a subject that either from the stage or on equal terms I have discussed with many people and I have always explained that I prefer to live by myself so that I may have time and space to recharge my batteries before my next onslaught upon the world. By the time I met this woman my life had in fact become unexpectedly satisfactory. I doubt that I complained about anything.

I suggested to the police that they should ignore the letter as I intended to do. This they said would be improper. I had no idea that I was making an improper suggestion to a constable. It seems that for one human being to threaten the life of another is an offence. It is only because such menaces are usually delivered verbally leaving behind no usable evidence that cases of this nature seldom come to court. The inspector told me that he felt compelled to communicate the following day with the constabulary in the town where the letter-writer lived. I made no effort to dissuade him from doing this. It was obviously what the woman most desired in life, otherwise she would have carried out her bizzare plan without any advance publicity. Perhaps she was kinky for policewomen. What happened to her I have no idea.

Now that England has become so easy to live in, now that no one who resides here need work or suffer any other curtailment of liberty, it is difficult not to despise someone who goes to such lengths as I have just described in order to draw attention to herself. The ruse seemed specially obnoxious in that it involved someone else (for whom, incidentally, sycophantic admiration had been expressed) in the degrading experience of a visit from the police. Yet even an incident as unpleasant as this was not a total loss; it shed a murky ray of light on a particular area of human experience.

If male homosexuality is, as some people seem to think, a way of enjoying sex without the unpleasantness of involvement, then may not Lesbianism be the opposite, may it not spring from a dread of emotional isolation? Certain women may, almost from birth, be made aware by their home life that companionship between the sexes is, to say the least, unlikely. This realization could cause them to gravitate towards the exclusively feminine world where, if a girl is lucky, she may find a partner who is willing, even eager, to spend twenty-four hours a day with her – someone who will sit on the edge of the bath and watch her washing her hair. Though I am now over seventy, I still receive messages, sent in the kindest spirit, willing on me the horrors of eternal love. These friendly wishes always come from Lesbians. Sometimes I ask one of these women how she imagines I could remain wise, witty and beautiful from dawn till dusk and beyond. She never tells me. My question, which is absolutely sincere, is evaded by the use of platitudes. It is explained that all relationships require a little give and take. This is untrue. Any partnership demands that we give and give and give and at the last, as we flop into our graves exhausted, we are told that we didn't give enough. Everyone knows this but so great was my prospective murderess's fear of isolation that she could not conceive of my living alone as a way of being content.

Occasionally mysterious telephone calls have been intended to seduce me not into mere folly but into crime.

One evening, when the telephone bell rang and I laid my eager ear to the keyhole of the world, I heard the sound of laughter and more than one voice speaking in an unknown tongue. After a moment, this babble sorted itself out and one man with a broken or perhaps only chipped accent took over the conversation. He told me that he had just arrived in England from Norway where he claimed that the story of my life had recently been shown on television. The programme in question had not been shown there but I did not contradict him; it would not have befitted my station in life. Then a small sexless voice interrupted this dialogue to explain that its name was Jasper. Another lie, I said to myself. No one since my godfather has been called by that name and he was so unbalanced by the burden that he took to wearing a monocle.

During the next afternoon the front door bell rang. Ah, another person, I thought rubbing my hands together with glee. I was wrong. On the doorstep there was only half a person – a child of less than eight who suffered from some hideous disease which caused him to blink compulsively. Once again he announced that he was Jasper. 'Semi-precious,' I snorted. 'I knew there would be something wrong.' I looked over the child's head into the street. Slavering white-slavers were nowhere to be seen. There was no way of returning this baggage to its sender. I was dressed in nothing but socks and a dressing-gown. Pointing to these, I excused myself from inviting Jasper into the house and shut the door on him.

If this incident was a clumsy attempt at entrapment by the police, I suppose we must try to find it in our hearts to praise their ingenuity. If it was the work of a civilian, we are forced to conclude that Norway is full of people who, to put to some feeble test a homosexual person whom they do not know, will subject children to embarrassment, unpleasantness, terror and even the possibility of a fate worse than life.

The notion, evidently universally held in Norway and not unknown elsewhere, that all homosexuals are sexually interested in small boys, is without foundation. The number of gay men who molest or wish to molest small boys is no greater than the number of sad heterosexuals who want to interfere with little girls. Of those homosexuals who do harbour these desires, none is obvious or camp for the simple reason that only effeminate men look for liaisons in which they can indulge their helplessness, their frailty. Translated into physical terms, the deepest sexual longings of this type of man are mainly for passive sodomy and in this context the equipment of children is inadequate. My guess, but of this I admit that I have no proof, is that child molesters go to work on children of either sex with no preference whatsoever.

It may be hard to believe but glimpses of the human soul have been revealed to me even more revolting than what psychologists will one day call the Norwegian psychosis.

I once received a telephone call from a strange man who said that he held a letter with my name on the envelope but which had arrived at the house in Hampstead where my agent formerly lived.

'Are you with him now?' I asked eagerly. The thief replied that he was not. Somewhat bewildered I thanked him for telephoning me and humbly asked him to forward my property to me.

When, after about three weeks, this had not been done, I journeyed all the way to Hampstead to the house where I had so often called on my agent. As always I found the street door open and went up to the top flat. A woman came to the door with a towel wrapped round her head. I apologized for troubling her at what was obviously an inopportune moment and explained why I had called. 'Your letter's not here,' she said. 'It's in Streatham.' She offered no reason why this should be so nor did she evince any shame that she had taken it upon herself to distribute among the poor something that did not belong to her. On the other hand there was no sniggering and no hostility was manifested. She even offered to telephone the address in the deep south of London to which she had so inexplicably taken my property. Her accomplice there said that he did not have my letter – that it was in his flatmate's room.

Tentatively I asked if I might take away with me the number she had just dialled. This she gave me without hesitation. Then, holding the towel about her head, she walked down several flights of stairs with me. I found this mixture of courtesy and diabolical cruelty in her nature absolutely baffling. When we reached street level, she said, 'We opened the envelope.' Again there seemed to be no hint as to whether this statement was a boast or a confession. 'What did my correspondent say?' I asked, trying to match her calmness though by now I was in agony. The young woman could not remember in detail but she recalled that the letter had come from Greece and that it was about the possibility of translating *The Naked Civil Servant* into Greek. I now at least knew that whatever the actual message was, it came from a Mr Valamvanos who a long time ago had proposed this idea.

When I reached home, I telephoned Streatham. The missing young man had returned. He read to me what my Mediterranean friend had written. I thanked him and asked that my letter be forwarded to me. It was agreed that this should be done and, in about three weeks' time, I finally received it with a Notting Hill postmark. Like their accomplice in Hampstead, the culprits in Streatham also offered no explanation – certainly no apology.

Until this bizarre incident occurred, I would have said that there were three ways of dealing with mail which arrives in your house but is addressed to someone no longer living there. You can ignore the beastly stuff forever: you can repost it with the sad word 'Unknown' written across the envelope; or, if your life is exceptionally dull, you might try reading it and then throwing it away.

Now I know that there are other ways of coping with communications that do not belong to you. You can hand them round like chocolates among your friends.

I did not feel that the men in this case had behaved any worse than such people usually do. Their natures were obviously too complex for them simply to reseal the envelope and despatch it to my address which has been in the telephone book since before either of them was born but at least they had felt that I ought not to be altogether cut off from my friend abroad. Their delay in ultimately reposting my letter may have been due to their regarding this gesture as a mere formality. They had already acquainted me with the contents and had been patient enough to spell out to me the address from which they came.

The girl's behaviour is another matter. Many years ago, when I read *Les Liaisons Dangereuses*, it seemed to me that the antics of the principal characters were nonsense – that no one would spend all that time and ingenuity on ruining the life of another human being. When I gave utterance to this criticism, someone pointed out to me that, at the time when this book was written, the aristocracy of France had absolutely nothing with which to fill its days except a little amusing evil. I now realize that, even in the busy modern world, there are those among us who take up sadism like skate-boarding. The fact that the girl in Hampstead opened my letter meant that almost certainly she knew who I was. This being so, she must have been aware of my circumstances – that I live on the fringe of destitution. Nevertheless she deliberately withheld from me information that might have led to my receiving money for translation rights. This young woman was not ill-favoured; presumably she could have found other pleasurable ways of filling in time between now and the grave and yet she chose to weave this diabolical plot against me.

In the end, the Greek offer was not accepted. As Miss Hampstead hoped, my penury continued but for different reasons. In my opinion this in no way mitigates her sin.

I have dealt so far chiefly with the remote and the hostile communications that I have received from the outer world. There is a connection between them. It is less embarrassing, less dangerous, to abuse someone from a distance. My face-to-face encounters with strangers in recent times have improved dramatically – nay, they have reversed their nature. I have passed from being an outcast to being almost universally acceptable with such speed that I have had no time to experience ordinary life. I am never with people; they are in my presence. I never take part in conversations; I am subjected to interviews. This has happened because television is a redemptive medium. If any reader of this book is in the grip of some habit of which he is deeply ashamed, I advise him not to give way to it in secret but to do it on television. No one will pass him by with averted gaze on the other side of the street. People will cross the road at the risk of losing their own lives in order to say, 'We saw you on the telly.'

The Thames rendering of my life story was, quite rightly, a saga of human depravity. It offered to the viewers visual proof of what previously had only been suspected, feared or, possibly, hoped. This did indeed cause certain people to despise me even more deeply than before but in the eyes of others I gradually started to become sanctified.

Five

That my book was made into a television play was a miracle or rather a series of tiny miracles in which I played only the most passive part. These events began as far back as 1970.

While I was hard at work writing my book about life-style or sitting by the fire wishing I were hard at work, I received a message from Messrs Jonathan Cape. They wished to know if the movie rights in *The Naked Civil Servant* were for sale. I thought the question must be a joke. When told that the enquiry came from a Mr Haggarty, my amazement and amusement increased a hundredfold. In the long chain of men and women by whose kindness I have been handed through the crowd, nearer and nearer to the front of it like someone who has fainted at the boat race, this man is the totally inexplicable link.

During the war Mr Haggarty was an airman but his feet were surprisingly often on the ground of Fitzrovia where he enjoyed the status of an honorary hooligan. He was kinky for tall girls, which took up a lot of his time but occasionally, perhaps from exhaustion, he sat at the same tables in the same cafés as the rest of us. Towards the end of the war he disappeared. Possibly he went to fight somebody. Coming down to earth again when peace broke out, he landed in the documentary film industry. While thus employed, he overtook me one day as I was walking innocently along a turning out of Wardour Street. I told him that I was writing a book which was in part about the making of short movies. 'Will it', he suggested, 'be called *Nobody Ordered Crisps*?'

Twenty years later, when I telephoned him to ask if his enquiry about my life story was serious, he assured me that it was. Into this conversation he introduced the fair name of Philip Mackie. Though I now listen eagerly to every word of his wonderful television plays, I must admit with downcast eyes and cheeks scarlet with shame that at that time I had never heard of him. He lives in Buckingham Street and, when negotiations and options and contracts and all that rubbish were settled, it was in his flat there that the three of us used to meet.

For some time we talked airily about my sex life – a subject of which I almost never tire – but in the end I could not help pausing to ask Mr Haggarty what he stood to gain from the project under discussion.

'Is Mr Mackie going to produce this movie and are you going to write it?' I asked. To my utter bewilderment the answer was no.

'I'm casting my bread upon the waters,' Mr Haggarty explained and added, 'you've heard of people doing that.'

Indeed, I had. For a life-time I had been standing on the river bank with a bent pin trying to fish some of it out, but to this day some of my puzzlement about Mr Haggarty remains. Years later I designed the programme cover of a play by him which was performed in a dried-up fish pond in a dim basement in Leicester Square. It hardly seemed an adequate reward to offer someone who had altered the whole course of my life.

Within four years of the televising of *The Naked Civil Servant*, I, for whom until then a journey to Ealing amounted to an awfully big adventure, had visited Canada, Australia and the United States. I had also met dozens of people so far above me in wealth, social standing and achievement that they seemed to have come from another planet. I am constantly asked if I now meet more interesting people than formerly. I never let the question pass. To me everyone is interesting who will talk about himself but, when I said this in Toronto, I was laughed to scorn by one of the city's drama critics. I have therefore since then revised this statement. I now claim that everyone is interesting who will tell the truth about himself.

Although these changes were spectacular, there is a sense in which they were superficial; they altered my engagement calendar but not my soul. This was in the nature of things. Events and personalities did not begin to crowd in on me until I was sixty-six and inner development was no longer possible. Perhaps it was an outward sign of this internal stagnation that I in no way expanded my home life. I continued to live in my small, dusty room, to drink Complan and to wear other people's cast-off clothes. Even out of doors my manner changed only in that I no longer stalked through the streets scorning people before they had a chance to scorn me. Instead, like all who have appeared on television, I now wore at all times an expression of fatuous affability. This was in my case seasoned with a pinch of apprehension. Even today, when my name is called from a doorway, from a van or from the scaffolding round some building, I am never certain that, if I turn to acknowledge the greeting, I may not be spattered with a fusillade of abuse.

Philip Mackie, though white-haired, remains bouncy, amazingly young and eager to know everything you are willing to tell him. His scenario was written from a perusal of my autobiography and at least six hours of taped conversation with me during which he sat with the book open on his thigh, his finger on the page and his bright blue eyes on whatever passage interested him. When I was shown the script that had been composed from all this interrogation, I was disappointed. The result seemed curiously undigested, unresolved. One afternoon he had asked me what my father looked like. I had replied, 'Like Lewis Stone.' Accordingly the scenario contained the stage instruction 'Enter Quentin's father looking like Lewis Stone.' I had imagined that my jumbled speech would be translated into deathless prose. It was not until I saw the television play itself that I realized what common sense should have told me at once. Mr Mackie had simply wasted no time on anything that could not be used on the screen. I now saw that writing for a visual medium is in a kind of shorthand.

In spite of what world authorities have since judged to be the excellence of his work, Mr Mackie was compelled to run hatless through the streets of London for four long, dark years trying to raise sufficient funds to make a movie of his script.

In a voice so faint that I could not be thought to be about to make an offer, I once asked how much money was required. 'Three-quarters of a million dollars?' I hazarded, my lips trembling with the effort needed to utter such daring numerals. 'Wouldn't be nearly enough,' Mr Mackie replied coolly. 'They would have to be pounds.' Secretly I would have thought that Elizabeth Taylor could have been persuaded to act the part of me for a fee as large as that but I said nothing. Finance was never one of my strong subjects.

There was apparently a moment when an unnamed tycoon offered to produce the necessary cash if Danny La Rue could be induced to play the lead. I was delighted with this idea. 'Could it not', I asked, 'be made into a musical?' My proposal was laughed to scorn and the search for unconditional backing went blindly on. Seven years were to pass before my suggestion was taken seriously.

After a few months I forgot about the entire project and went back to the humble task of completing my book about style. It was finished, I think, in 1972 but this too turned out to be a bomb with a very long fuse. It did not see the light of day for another three years. Sad to say by that time its publisher and my actress friend had become estranged. We never all jumped up and down together.

During the past twelve crowded years, assistance has been given to me from so many and such diverse sources that it is not always possible for me to tell my tale chronologically. Occasionally I am forced to work in chain stitch, dragging forward into the present threads from the past.

When my agent fled to Texas, he left the matter of his correspondence in the hands of a Hungarian of 1956 vintage who lived in the flat above him and with whom he had become friendly. Some letters – ones, for instance, that said 'I love you, I love you' – the Texan wished to receive in America. Others, of lesser interest or none, he hoped could be answered or ignored without any decision from him. Into this latter category fell cheques for seven shillings and sixpence which represented my dwindling royalties on *The Naked Civil Servant*.

So it came about that I began to receive telephone calls and letters from my ex-agent's friend and, after a while, an invitation to visit him. These two men knew one another only because they were vertical neighbours and I met the second only because he agreed to deal with the letters of the first. This is but another instance of how tenuous has been the connection between the people and events that have furthered my progress.

At our first or second meeting, the Hungarian

said, 'I will be your agent.' For years we had no written agreement whatsoever. Those years would have been lean indeed if his wife had not fed me and had he not twisted and turned in a frenzied effort to find magazines and newspapers to which I could contribute quips, puns, anecdotes and perverse expressions of opinion.

In the summer of 1975 an afternoon came when, in a dreamy voice, my new agent told me that he had found himself with some money to spare and was thinking of putting on a play – presumably as the quickest way of getting rid of it. The theatre on which he finally settled for this venture was a room behind the King's Head in Islington. How to fill the evenings had already been decided but there were still the lunch-time opening hours to be occupied – if possible, profitably.

'I thought you could go on then,' he said. I was amazed.

'With what object, my good man?' I enquired.

'You could talk to people.'

'What about?'

'Doesn't really matter,' my agent replied. 'You needn't say the same thing each day.' Then he went to Spain.

Thus it was that, alone and totally unprepared, I tottered into the profession of public speaking.

At this point the already bewildering cast of this book is augmented by Mr Jackson. In the telephone book he is billed as being in personal management but I think he sits in a tower overlooking the centre of London like a ranger perched above the tree tops of a spruce forest in

Canada. Instead of watching for suspicious wisps of smoke, Mr Jackson waits to see if the lights go out in any West End theatre. The moment they do, he is there offering to fill whatever gap has occurred. It was he who presented me at the King's Head and, incidentally, he who provided me with a daily glass of whisky which has ever since been a feature of my stage appearances.

The drama upon which my agent had decided to lavish his superfluous wealth was called *Madame de Sade*. Though written by a Japanese gentleman called Mr Mishima about a Frenchwoman, it was constructed upon Greek lines. No action took place on stage; the audience was informed what had happened or was warned what was about to happen but always elsewhere.

The play failed. Not even the magnificent presence of Miss Chasen, striding up and down in thigh boots and brandishing a whip as long as Upper Street, was enough to satisfy modern English appetites. Nowadays people wish to see such a fascinating weapon used, preferably on the person sitting next to them.

Earlier in the day at the same venue, I too was fighting a losing battle. I frequently found myself haranguing a multitude of three people. When, after three weeks, the evening performances ceased, I asked if I might be spared further humiliation.

The subject upon which I had decided to lavish my rhetorical deficiencies was 'Life Style'. It served two purposes simultaneously. Firstly, it provided me with a vague framework within which I was able to talk to audiences about their own foibles which I was sure they would find more amusing than mine. Secondly, it was a suitable topic to illustrate, upon which, while writing the book, I had accumulated a number of anecdotes which I could use to dramatize my discourse.

Although my stay at the King's Head could loosely be called a disaster, I learned a great deal from it. For me it would never be easier to say different things on different days. I hardly vary my parrot cries in real life; on the stage I would never be able to find sufficient material. My experience of the world has been too limited, my understanding of that experience too shallow. Moreover I discovered that, while uttering one sentence, it was necessary to have a clear idea of what the next one would be so that I could concentrate not on what was to come but on the sounds already in my mouth. I found that I needed to pay great attention to their pitch, their volume and even to the length of the silences between them. This newly acquired knowledge did not later prevent the gay newspapers of New York from saying that I recited passages from my books not very well and in a whining voice but matters would, I am sure, have been even worse if my entire performance had been an improvisation.

I cannot claim that, if I had known early in life how my declining years were to be spent, I would at any time have enrolled my name for classes in voice production. I would never have had either the nerve or the money. When I was at my preparatory school my teachers subjected my corrected cockney accent to limp ridicule and that was all the help I was given. How I wish now that they had tried to increase my vocal range or volume or both! As they did not I stagger on, flaunting my defects where I cannot conceal them.

Although using material from *How To Have a Life Style* on stage was a godsend, it also proved to be a trap. Working even loosely from something already written seduced me not only into quoting the same jokes from the same pages each day but also into arriving by the same number of paces at the same position on the platform to deliver them. I knew that such behaviour was unforgivable but seemed unable to resist it. The audience was probably unaware of what I was doing but there was a young man employed to sit by the door and prevent latecomers from creeping in without paying. It was when I passed him that I bowed my head in shame. I found out later that this was unnecessary. He was an actor and inured to the embarrassment of witnessing feigned spontaneity. To offset this old-fashioned element of slickness, I tried to roughen the edges of the show with various cute tricks. I marched straight out of the street on to the platform and paced up and down it until given a sign that it was time to begin but, in spite of all these ruses, a certain staginess gradually seeped into the situation.

In real life I was moving stealthily towards respectability but, in theatrical terms, I was losing my innocence with alarming rapidity considering that I was surprised to find myself on the stage at all. This reaction, however, was not shared by others. When I announced to my friends that I had gone into the public speaking racket, they only sighed. 'When', they asked, 'did you ever do anything else?'

Six

The television rights in *The Naked Civil Servant* were sold for £350. When audiences appear to imagine that my financial status has recently been altered out of all recognition, I mention this sum; I like to hear them gasp. All the same this is not a hard-luck story. During my entire working life, never, over a long period, did I earn more than £12 a week. That £350 meant a great deal to me and I am grateful for a deal which was so conscientiously, so scrupulously, transacted, although it took over four years to complete.

I do not remember exactly how I received the news that Thames Television had bought Mr Mackie's script but I do recall that, when it was arranged that I should meet the director of the play, I was taken all the way to Teddington by taxi. At that time I had had so little experience of television that I was amazed by the extravagance of this method of transport. At Teddington Studios, besides Mr Gold, the director, I was introduced to Mr Hurt who was soon to become my representative on earth. He said, 'I have no intention of merely giving a vaudeville imitation of Mr

Crisp.' I was somewhat relieved by this remark.

This occasion, social, pleasant, informal, was in fact the turning point of the tide against which I had been swimming for more than sixty years. I was on my way back to becoming a virgin. More than that, after a lifetime of condemnation for my sexual deviation, that very fact was to be used to present me to the world as being of interest for human reasons that transcended my sin.

Very kindly, so that I might earn money under the heading of technical advice, I was allowed on to four of the locations where the film was being photographed. First I saw the scene where the child dances in front of the mirror. This seemed difficult to get just right because to my surprise the boy looked not at his reflection but at the director. Later in the day I was taken to Richmond where John Hurt's club membership card was torn up. On other occasions I also witnessed the meeting in the café and the art class. Only in this last place did I offer advice. I feared that Mr Hurt might not know what an operatic business posing can become if you fling yourself into it. I needn't have bothered; he himself was an art student in a time gone by.

I could not get used to the intensity with which the entire team cared whether the production was like my life or not. I had supposed that all that was needed was for some such person as I once was to be seen surviving some such events as I once experienced. I should have known that, if you show the members of an art department a real person, they go mad. They have spent so many long hours peering at faded group photographs in which the third schoolboy from the left is rumoured to be some famous politician. Now, at last, their subject was appallingly distinct. They could work at something that would yield demonstrable proof of their skills. They took pictures of me from above, from below, from the left and from the right. They even took me to a shop in Burlington Street so that the wig-maker there would be able to reconstruct the architecture of my hair. At one time or another during his performance, Mr Hurt wore five wigs in order to pass from innocence (a rich mouse colour) through depravity (scarlet) to senility (discreet mauve).

People often ask me if I worked with Mr Hurt before he began to play the part of me. It is difficult to imagine what any such sessions would have been like but we do not have to try. I met him only twice before he began to make the teleplay – once, as described, at Teddington and a second time when he and his true love invited me to dinner at their home in Flask Walk. I mentioned the difficulty an actor might have in playing a victim of fate because, in an extremely competitive profession, he must in real life cultivate every ounce of aggression of which his nature is capable in order to stay in work. He disagreed and he should know. In *10 Rillington Place* he portrayed Christopher Evans, the all-time victim. Never during the evening did I say (nor would I have dared to say) that my host might try doing this or that while acting *The Naked Civil Servant*, yet when I finally saw the teleplay, I noticed that he had included in his characterization all sorts of tiny details. He had mastered the Red Indian's walk and, as he drifted along the streets of London, he held his fingers straight rather than slightly curved as ordinary mortals do.

When Mr Mackie told me that he had found someone to play the part of me he added, 'I've never seen anyone so willing to play a part.' I suggested that if you were to show anyone in the entertainment business a book in which almost every paragraph begins with the word 'I' he will be anxious to play the lead in it, but I now think that in Mr Mackie's portrait of me John Hurt saw some special opportunity. If he was led to do this by instincts, they did not betray him. He won an award.

When you meet him in real life, Mr Hurt seems shorter than I and he is actually much slighter. He looks pale, frail and very tired. The naturally drooping eyelids, together with having his eyebrows plucked from underneath by the make-up department, gave him on the screen the scornful look that in earlier life I was so often accused of wearing.

John Osborne, whom I once met at a party, suddenly turned on me with the words, 'You've made sure that young man never gets another good part.' In fact the reverse was true. Since making *The Naked Civil Servant* Hurt has hardly ever been out of work. For this reason, and because my own life has recently become more occupied than I ever thought it would be, it is unlikely that I shall ever know him well but I shall always be grateful to him for the immense tact with which he presented me to the world. It is easy to imitate other people and especially easy to imitate me. The whole production might at any moment have become a scream but because of him this was avoided. In any situation, however bizarre, he never saw himself as the camp scarecrow that I seem to other people to be. Instead, he worked from within to reveal me as the helpless victim of a misguided dream.

I saw *The Naked Civil Servant* when it was shown to the press before it was televised. At least I saw almost all of it. The car sent to take me to the Thames Studios in Euston Road was late. I could easily have travelled by bus and been punctual but already I was becoming accustomed to the crazy luxury of the media. I was very worried upon that occasion because I knew that, immediately the film was over, I would be questioned by the critics – and journalists don't want answers, they want jokes. The best that I could manage was to say that the television presentation of my life was better than the real thing because it was so much shorter.

When the play was flashed before the unsuspecting eyes of the public, I saw it with some friends. In a calmer mood by then, I tried to judge it purely as entertainment. This was not easy because it was the kind of programme that, had I been in no way personally involved, I would never have watched in a million years. I have long since ceased to be interested in homosexuality as a subject; there just doesn't seem anything left to say about it. In spite of this I was well aware of what an excellent play had been produced. The unresolved quality that I thought I had perceived in Mr Mackie's script had completely evaporated. The narrative moved slowly but relentlessly forward. Even the captions, which when they were first proposed I could not take seriously, seemed wholly integrated into the mode of telling the story.

I have been asked if there was any detail in which the play differed from my actual past. The question has recurred so often that, after a while, because my whole nature revolts against saying nothing, I searched for some point of deviation however trivial. At length I dredged up the fact at one moment in the play Mr Hurt tells one of his persecutors to sod off. Not only would I never have used such a word (which would have sounded far more unladylike then than now) but no one as habitually acquiescent as I would have risked this gesture of defiance in a situation so obviously dangerous. I made this observation in Mr Hurt's presence. He delighted me by protesting that he had said the words very nicely.

The day after *The Naked Civil Servant* was shown to the public I was interviewed by Mavis Nicholson, the darling of afternoon television. I had been looked over beforehand so the event did not come as a great surprise, nor did Mrs Nicholson. I had often watched her questioning minor celebrities and thought her just like home but prettier. The interview that I remembered best was the one during which she sat between two very discreet homosexual men and asked them if it was true that men find it difficult to form lasting emotional relationships. They gave the conventional reply that in society there are so many bonds that keep heterosexual couples together and so many forces that drive gay men apart. I regretted that neither interviewee had said that he was glad that, owing to his temperament and his position in society, he was free forever from the damp, dark prison of eternal love. I must have written these words somewhere because, when we met, Mrs Nicholson quoted them.

I regarded my meeting with Mrs Nicholson before the public interview as an opportunity to set her mind at rest. It is always the interviewer who has more to lose than the interviewee. The latter can say what he likes so long as he does not expect ever to appear on television again. The interrogator, on the other hand, is the employee of a vast corporation with a carefully guarded public image and, if by some awful chance something treasonable or blasphemous is said, he may be held responsible.

Mrs Nicholson said that she did not know what questions to ask me. I assured her that I would not be shocked or embarrassed by anything that she might say and that in my replies I would never use the shortest words for the longest things.

Our interview turned out to be one of the best I have ever had and the highest point of it came when by mistake I allowed the word 'camp' to fall from my lips. 'Do you think your little friends will understand the word?' I asked, nodding towards the world beyond the camera. Mrs Nicholson leaned forward to give the lens a searching look. 'I should think so,' she said in a slightly cynical voice.

In my first interview on *Late Night Line-Up*, I

had only wanted my replies to be heard, understood and, by a miracle, believed. By the time this second programme was promised I wanted more than that. I wished to add what I am to what I said. To some extent I desired to have the situation on my own terms. Mrs Nicholson never tried to prevent this from happening; indeed she aided and abetted me.

I had taken to watching other people being interviewed – not in order to hear what they had to say but in the hope of discovering techniques for dealing with the special hazards of this highly artificial form of self-presentation. What is needed is some way of talking intimately with the interviewer while acknowledging that we are both on display. If, for instance, I am asked whether or not I like writing books, I cannot pass my hand across my brow and say that my genius is a great burden to me. I am in the presence of millions of people some of whom may get up at four every morning to milk cows while I rise at ten and sit by the fire making a few unusable notes.

Although I never questioned him about it, I imagine that when, worn out with trudging the unrelenting pavements of Wardour Street, Mr Mackie at length accepted Thames Television's offer, he may have felt that he was settling for less than his original dream of seeing his scenario made into a real film.

Certainly I, though glad of any outcome to his heroic persistence, was slightly deflated because I am so mad about the movies.

Since then I have changed my mind.

Financially there can be no comparison. If *The Naked Civil Servant* had become a picture, I need never have stepped out of bed again but, in other respects, television has advantages that movies lack. If a film has a homosexual theme, it is heavily advertised as such. In consequence it is seen only by gay people and liberals wishing to be observed going into and coming out of the cinema where it is being shown. On television I reached a more mixed audience.

Books and plays are diversions about which most of us exercise some decision even if our selection is based on totally misleading publicity. The movies are in a twilit zone. A woman may save up time and money to spend on a film of which she has very definite expectations or she may flop into the nearest cinema to fill in time between the end of a shopping orgy and the beginning of a train journey back to Chorley Wood. Television is even lower down the scale of human choice. We nearly always see it by default.

In my mind's ear I hear a housewife calling from the kitchen to her husband in the living-room.

'What's on now, luv?'

'The queers.'

'What's on the other side?'

'The news.'

'Oh Gawd. As you were.'

In some such circumstances as these, my life story was unfurled before the eyes of people who until that moment had never given a serious thought to the subject of homosexuality.

I have pondered deeply the difference between

the public reaction to Granada's documentary and to the play shown by Thames Television. The telephone calls provoked by the former were contemptuous or hostile; by the latter, mixed. The letters that I received after the first were negligible; those that followed the second were kind, sometimes laudatory. The manner of strangers encountered in the street subsequent to the first programme was uneasy; after the second it was a subtle blend of curiosity and forgiveness.

Some people have attributed these differences to the passage of time between 1969 and 1975 but there has been very little profound change in morals since the war. While my book was in the process of being published, amendments were being made to the law concerning homosexuality and someone said to me, 'They'll make a lot of difference to you.' This remark was kindly intended but absurd. No one has ever pointed the finger of scorn at me and cried, 'Look at him, he's illegal.' If anything the piratical element in my predicament was an advantage. It appealed to all outsiders who, for quite different reasons, despised the conventions. The English hated me for being effeminate and, in a country where women are still to some extent despised, this attitude has not altered.

The gradual and very slight change that we have witnessed during the past thirty years has occurred because more and more power has passed into the hands of the young or, to be more accurate, a louder and louder voice has begun to issue from their lips. Teenagers have always been interested in gaining more sexual freedom than their parents wished them to have and have never been keen on acquiring the social leverage that their elders constantly recommend. Now they can say so. In other words, we have not moved into a permissive society: the young are just as stuffy in their own way as adults. We are merely stuck with an outspoken society.

Since neither I in the documentary nor Mr Hurt in the teleplay flashed you-know-what before the cameras and since neither of us uttered obscenities we might both by modern standards be considered old-fashioned – even pre-war. In this respect the two programmes were therefore equal and, since in the first my sins were only discussed and in the second they were acted out, the latter, at least in the eyes of older viewers, must have seemed the more immoral of the two yet the reaction to it was more benign.

I think the answer lies largely with the press. Critics will, I am sure, agree that they have no power to change minds that are already made up but they can reorientate the ditherers. When one journalist went so far as to say that the Thames programme justified the existence of television, she made it legitimate for even the most refined taste to have enjoyed itself and when Clive James (of all people) said that the protagonist in *The Naked Civil Servant* appeared to be 'some kind of a hero', amusement was nudged in the direction of condonation.

I cannot deny that I was surprised at the unqualified praise lavished upon the teleplay. I had feared that one or two critics at least would point out the degree of depravity in my life story. In fact no mention was made of this. I was pleased that no opprobrium had fallen on the makers of the programme and my pleasure turned to delight when I found that some of the glory properly meant for the play itself was descending like golden rain upon me. The redemptive element in television was beginning to work in my favour.

It is also true that the sheer bulk of critical opinion and therefore of general discussion caused my existence to impinge upon even the most sluggish consciousness. As my agent said, 'You must accept the fact that you will become part of the fantasies of total strangers.'

The teleplay in which I had appeared for about a minute and a half came to be called my programme. This was not because my presence was in any way dramatically effective but because, from being constantly photographed, my image became recognizable – as unchanging as a stuffed bird, though not as silent – an object of ridicule to schoolboys and of curiosity to taxi drivers.

At first this latter reaction was a source of wonderment to me but, after a little reflection, I saw that it was natural – even inevitable. If you have driving skills and you don't like people, you find a job as a long-distance lorry driver. On those seemingly interminable nocturnal hauls you need speak to no one and meet no one except hitch-hikers whom you ravish and whose used bodies you fling like empty Yorkie wrappers into the hedges. If, however, you do like people, you acquire a taxi. Whom then will you meet? The rich, the famous and the desperate.

Bit by bit, a taxi at a time, I was becoming the almost acceptable face of homosexuality.

When the laws of England were being changed, market research into homosexuality was carried out. Nothing significant emerged from these enquiries but this. When asked what they would expect a gay man to look like, housewives replied, 'Oh, you know – actorish, effeminate, inclined to wear bright colours.' (Now they would merely say 'someone like Quentin'.) If, on the other hand, they had already admitted to knowing a homosexual man and were asked what he was like, they usually answered, 'Just like everyone else.'

Superficially the present fashion among gay men for normalizing their clothes and their mannerisms is a relief to the rest of the world. Socially it makes dealing with them less embarrassing but, deep down, this subdued public image makes heterosexuals uneasy. If gay men look like everyone else, then they may be anywhere – everywhere. How much safer to be able to see one coming from a mile away! It gives you time to make up your mind what to do – call the police, lock up the kids, scream with laughter or duck. This, of course, is what I told the whole world as far back as 1931 but then it paid no heed because, at that time, it did not realize that there were any queers other than the ones that could be spotted. Now that intimations of a large hidden minority have come to light, meeting an obvious pansy is almost a relief.

I do not merely infer that public attitudes towards me have softened. I have proof.

Recently I was standing at a bus stop in Shepherd's Bush when a lorry drew up on the opposite side of the street. The driver climbed slowly down from his cabin on to the ground, crossed the road and said, 'You're Quentin Crisp.' When I falteringly admitted that I was, he added, 'I get the hang of it now.' He meant that he had come to see homosexuality on my terms – as a desire to live as though one were a member of the opposite sex.

It is, of course, precisely this easily digested image, camp, ineffectual, slightly silly and, worst of all, almost indifferent to sex, that the gay community finds so distasteful. Aversion to it is so strong that *Gay News* expressed the opinion that it would have been better for 'The Cause' if *The Naked Civil Servant* had been published posthumously – a literary way of saying, 'Drop dead'.

It was not, however, the book that caused the rift between me and the great body of homosexuality.

While my identity remained in the form of written words, the Gay Movement (as distinct from gay people) accepted and to some extent welcomed it. The fact that a book in part about my sex life had been published at all was considered to be a tiny triumph for the cause even if my image did lack the aggression requisite for an era when protest was developing into a fad and the voice of minorities was becoming everywhere so shrill. As very slowly I moved from the written to the spoken word – as I ceased to be an idea and became an icon – certain attributes of my nature, which before could only have been inferred, became obvious. My struggle to ingratiate myself with the majorites grew to be horribly apparent.

I once went to address all the homosexuals in Westminster – not in the Houses of Parliament but in a public house called the Westminster Arms. During the meeting someone said to me, 'You used to be the Martin Luther King of the Movement. What are these Uncle Tom sentiments you now express?'

Never, even with a jolly laugh, would I have dared to compare myself with Mr King. Any endeavour to do so would not merely be presumptuous, it would be pointless. I was never militant. As I explained to the gentleman who asked me the question, if, in that far-off time, I sat on a bus next to a stranger and he ostentatiously moved away from me, I said, 'If you like, I will get out at the next stop but even people like me cannot walk everywhere.'

Public interest was beginning to be focussed on me just when the new image of gayness (by no means the same thing as gaiety) was being advertised. Homosexuals had not only modified their appearance, they were forever popping up on television to explain that they were really quite ordinary. In my opinion this ploy will never work. Except in the state of Illinois, ordinary people do not go about claiming – nay, boasting – that they are hum-drum. The declaration is chiefly interesting because it is the reverse of a previous posture.

In a time gone by, homosexuals, when challenged, used to rattle off a list of names of writers whom history claimed were gay. They seemed to derive self-assurance from a supposed kinship even though they, themselves, never wrote a word – not even home.

When I was young most men who indulged in any sort of sexual deviation went about their business – especially their monkey business – discreetly. The people who proclaimed their difference from the rest of the world did so, like me, because they had no real choice. Any other course of action would have demanded a life-time of perpetual self-watchfulness, as opposed to self-regard. Our brazenness was the solution to a personality problem rather than an explicitly sexual one.

This is difficult for young people nowadays to understand because sexual freedom has become more important than identity. Indeed it has superseded it. The modern philosophy states, 'I ejaculate therefore I am.' Those who now protest and demonstrate and march most persistently are often those with the least clearly marked personalities. Like cells in an organism, it takes thousands of teenagers to make up a single identity. They feel that it will be through numbers rather than willpower that they will at last become a force of which society must take some notice. The trouble with this method of trying to gain more liberty is that those who adopt it, instead of bowing to the laws of the community in general, must conform to the narrower and even less rewarding constraints of their chosen regiment.

There is a restaurant in New York in which there is not a woman to be seen. At any one time the place contains about forty men all of whom are between the ages of eighteen and twenty-eight, or wish they were. All are wearing tractor boots, pre-ruined jeans, kitchen tablecloth shirts, and little scrubby moustaches. The only way in which an intruder can tell that he has not accidentally stumbled into the canteen of a building site is because everybody looks so clean. These young men *look* marvellous but, if we are speaking of personal liberty, they have taken a step forward only in that they have entered a more fashionable ghetto.

In England the craze for uniformity has passed into the realm of parody; manliness has given place to cruelty. (They were never so very far apart.) In Earl's Court there is an establishment where the entire clientele is dressed like the Wild One in black leather decorated with chains. Almost everyone present has remembered to carry a crash helmet but no one mentions that he has arrived at his destination by bus. Even as a sexual visiting card this gear is often totally misleading. In an encounter of the fourth kind, half these boys would turn out to be in search of nothing more bizarre than a little friendly sensuality.

I do not think that any of these antics is sinful. I complain only that they all confuse an issue that is already surrounded by misconceptions. I have never expressed the opinion that what modern homosexuals want they do not deserve. Whatever tricks they get up to I wish them well. I am also aware that what they demand they demand for others as well as for themselves. Thus an element of altruism is added to the call for justice. I have only tried to make two points. One is that, if anyone submerges his individuality in a group for the sake of gaining political acknowledgement of his mere sexual needs, he may find that he has thrown away the larger part of his personal freedom. I also fear that the ultimate outcome of too much militancy shown by any minority may not be what is hoped. This stridency creates panic in the majority and brings about a fierce confrontation between the gay people and the sad people. This can only re-open that hideous chasm between them that time and boredom were just beginning so conveniently to fill in.

When I was working in Newhaven, a psychiatrist invited me to spend a day at his home. I had a wonderful time but, at the outset, was worried by the fact that, as he drove through the town, all his spare attention was given to pointing out which bars were gay or had been gay, which restaurants were straight though run by homosexuals and so on. I know that psychiatrists must deal in what is not in what might be, but I was disturbed by the kind of glee with which he surveyed the ugly rift between two warring factions. I longed to ask my host if he was not yearning for the day when he would be able to frequent a bar simply because it was near or warm or quiet. It seems to me that the Kinsey Report counts for nothing if we have not learned that the answer to the question 'Are you queer?' is no longer the desperate cry 'I am, I am', but merely a polite 'Not today, thank you.' My host's imagination seemed to dwell with alarming intensity upon the rituals of that sex-sodden monastery which, even when I was young, I hated. I would not then and I will not now accept the notion that, if someone has not been propositioned by eleven o'clock on Friday night, his week has been wasted.

I urgently feel that, if gay people want to be happy, they must vacate their secret world, they must stop frightening not only the horses but also their riders. They must recognize that it is in the very nature of integration that you cannot fight for it. You can only wait. Mr Lustgarten, who practically invented crime, has pointed out that it is not the law that changes public opinion, it is public opinion which very gradually modifies the law. If homosexuals prematurely bring about the passing of a law for which society is not ready, they will earn its hatred. Anyone who demands acceptance places himself in the same position as a girl who asks, 'Do you really love me?' Every mature woman knows where that gets her. It is more than forty years now since I presumed to think that I represented homosexuality. Since then I have come to realize that I represent nothing grander than my puny self. This does not mean that I have in any way connived at the hostility of the gay world. Especially in New York I was sorry to find that I had made enemies. If this saddens me less now than formerly, it may be because I have recently acquired more friends among heterosexuals. On the stage in America I was often asked how the gay scene in New York compares with that of London. It was a question I couldn't answer because I'm never there. My journey has not taken me deeper and deeper into the jungle but mercifully out into the common light of day.

I will not be nudged into a quarrel with the human race. Now that we've finally met, I love it.

Seven

The difference between my life before and after *The Naked Civil Servant* was broadcast became most clearly visible at the King's Head. When I returned there in the spring of 1976, the little huddle of embarrassed friends sitting at one table had become a crowd so numerous that some members of the audience were obliged to lean against the back wall of the room for an hour holding empty beer glasses and the plates on which their pork pies had stood.

Lunch-time theatre-goers in public houses are not only drinkers whose feet are killing them and who want to sit down anywhere at almost any price, people gather from far and wide and even from high and low. On one occasion, Mrs Churchill brought Lady Diana Cooper who looked magnificent in a huge black hat, as though she were in mourning for Ascot.

As far as I know the phenomenon of lunch-time theatre has never been explained. During the war it was justified by the fact that many people were reluctant to go out in the evening. They either found the black-out too confusing or the aerial bombardment too frightening. Now that these adverse conditions no longer prevail, why has such an obviously inconvenient form of entertainment returned?

Undoubtedly it is part of the general de-glamorization of show business. It accords with the modern notion that anyone can entertain. Get yourself a guitar and you'll be a pop star in no time. But in fact, theatre in a very confined space is acknowledged by professionals to present its own particular difficulties. There can be no anxious glances into the wings to see what on earth has delayed your leading man; there must be no nervous trembling of the hands except for dramatic purposes; no perspiration must appear on the brow. The entire audience is so close that details like these can easily be seen. Actors only do this work because they must. Employment is so hard to find that they will adapt themselves to whatever conditions are imposed upon them. In lunch-time theatre they will force themselves to act with the same attention to detail that they would display before the television cameras.

Lunch-time entertainment is welcomed by impresarios as well as by starving actors. It provides as many showcases as Burlington Arcade and at half the price. It is a place where a protégée can be seen performing in a properly-lighted area before an audience that has paid to see her. For all concerned this is at least a fairer test of histrionic ability than sitting in a producer's office crying, 'Woe unto Ilium'.

All these advantages to individuals who are in or

on the periphery of show business do not, however, explain why real people attend these events. It must be very inconvenient for a girl to fling the cover over her typewriter and dash through the streets snatching up a sandwich en route like a Polish lancer displaying his horsemanship. Nevertheless I know that women in full employment came to hear me. On one occasion a girl started to leave before the end. When I implored her not to go – even offering to say the opposite if she would stay – she replied in a mournful voice, 'I have to go back to work.' It seems strange that, for such a fragment of diversion, anyone would risk incurring her boss's displeasure with her unpunctuality and start an afternoon's drudgery wracked by indigestion and with a heart pounding from having run all the way along Upper Street, yet some people have not found the price too great.

Perhaps there is no mystery. Possibly lunch-time theatre is merely blindly following a fashion set by the Edinburgh Festival. There entertainment starts at half-past eleven in the morning and covers every available horizontal surface (of which there are not many in Scotland's capital). This welter of frivolity in the grimmest city on earth was something of which at that time I had barely heard. Soon I was to experience it.

I have been to the Edinburgh Festival three times. The last time, I took part in the inaugural parade and sat in a coach beside a famous Scottish actress called Miss McArthur. Crowds lined the streets, leaned out of every available window and even climbed the trees along our route. As Miss McArthur smiled, bowed to right and left and waved, she said to me, 'We'll never work for a bigger audience than this.' She was right. I enjoyed myself enormously but, looking back, I think the year I liked the Festival most was my first in 1976 when everything about it was new to me.

That summer the city was ruled by Miss Greer. She was there to explain to the world the various events. She is very tall and quite formidable, an effect that she offsets by weaving into her public image an element of self-doubt. While she interviewed me sitting on a bench in some public gardens, she brushed the front of her dress and said to the technicians, 'I've got marmalade on my skirt.' This small gesture I took to be a manifestation of what Mr Tennyson called, 'craven fears of being great.'

I was working for a group of students from Bristol University. I occupied a room in one of the two huge flats which they had rented. Early one morning, Miss Greer visited us. The television crew that accompanied her everywhere woke up the students and told them to look as though they were asleep. When the sea of horizontal bodies had been photographed, we all sat round the kitchen table for a cornflakes session. I think the young people were required to be helpless waifs far from home. This is one of my favourite roles but the students seemed reluctant to co-operate. Perhaps they feared that their parents would watch the programme and that thereafter the hall would be knee deep in a snow of anxious letters. During this visit, Miss Greer was taken on a tour of inspection of the various rooms. When she beheld the dilapidated state of my hair brush, her heart was touched and she bought me a new one. Years later, she said to me, 'The way the press went on you would have thought it was of solid gold.' To me, of course, it *was* solid gold.

Every fringe theatre in Edinburgh is full because, out of loyalty to the profession, all the actors who are not on their own stages are in the auditoria of their colleagues. The Heriot-Watt theatre where I worked was no exception. On my very first day, when I asked the audience if it had understood and, furthermore, believed me, a man sitting right at the back of the house complained that I had not, as he had hoped, conducted a serious existential discussion. I apologized and explained that he must not imagine that, because I was smiling, I did not at any time say what I did not mean. Seated beside this gentleman was his wife or worse. She asked if she could not have a life style which included her children. I pointed out that the trouble with children was that they were not returnable. When the audience seemed to find this remark amusing, the unknown orator deflected his rage from me to the people around him. 'You're sycophants!' he cried but his enemies were not to be cowed. For the first time I then realized the truth of a statement made in her autobiography by Miss Bergman, that people come to the theatre hoping, longing to be entertained; they want performers to succeed. They certainly do not come primarily to be informed.

Now that I have had more experience of public speaking, I know that I should have invited the heckler down on to the stage. We could have had a debate which would have enlivened the afternoon miraculously. At the time I only waited feebly for the storm to pass.

During that first week in Edinburgh, I was summoned back to London by Thames Television so that I might appear on a programme with Mr Hurt and Mrs Whitehouse. The umpire was Mr Cavett. After the show, when we were in the drinking room, he said that, if I ever went to the States, he would invite me on to his own programme. Such a possibility seemed very remote then.

I admire Mrs Whitehouse though I do not suppose that my adulation is something that the lady seeks. She knows exactly what she is doing. Just as Miss Greer uses self-doubt to soften her personality so Mrs Whitehouse adds to her puritanical image a pinch of sensuality. On the evening when I met her she was wearing a brick red suit, she had curly hair and her slightly pouting lips were painted a pale orange. These adornments that ran counter to the public's idea of her would lose her a few marks were she being judged as a stylist but, as the adjuncts of an evangelist, they work in her favour. If she wore dull clothes, had thin lips and scraped her hair back from her brow, the world would say, 'Look at her. No wonder she's against sex.' She has seen to it that this sort of comment shall not be made. She is watchful not only of what she looks like but also of what she says. When asked if she found *The Naked Civil Servant* shocking, she replied that she did not and added that she thought the programme had been sympathetically made and that she had learned a great deal from it. Mrs Whitehouse never puts a foot wrong.

Going to Edinburgh was not my first visit to Scotland. I had already been for a day a night and a day to St Andrews to talk to the university students.

There is no railway station at St Andrews. When they built the famous golf course, they removed all hope of reaching it. Instead I arrived at a place called Leuchars. Standing on the station platform I found myself in a typically Hitchcockian setting. All around me the land was as flat as Texas and no matter where I looked I saw no sign of human life. If the sinister crop-sprayer flies overhead, I thought, I shall have no sugar canes among which to hide. Fortunately some students came to meet me with a car. Immediately I found them more relaxed than their equivalents in England. The reason for this had already been explained to me by Mr Coren who then ruled the university but who now rules *Punch*. 'The young of St Andrews never march,' he told me. 'There are only two streets to march along and they never carry banners because the wind is too strong.'

St Andrews is built on the very edge of the world – not by the sea but overhanging it. The whole town bristles with cannon emplacements, is riddled with dungeons and encrusted with ruins. The traditional English view of the Scots must have been based on the landscape. In fact the inhabitants not only of St Andrews but of everywhere that I have been in Scotland are communicative, laughter-loving and indulgent with foreigners to the verge of folly.

On my way back to real life, I was shown the beauties of Edinburgh by a friend of mine who rules Waverley Station. He is devoted to antiquity. Pointing with a Charlie's Aunt umbrella to a row of houses the colour of atomic ash, he said, 'Modern 1820s stuff.' To me the greatest delight of that hilarious sight-seeing tour was the river. The Leith has mossy banks, is canopied by tall trees, bejewelled with emerald green subaqueous ferns and runs laughing through the forbidden city.

Arriving back in London I reckoned that I had travelled for over eighteen hours in order to speak for two but it had all been worth it.

Eight

Once, during a childhood holiday, an aeroplane landed in a field behind whatever seaside resort my parents had chosen for that year. As soon as the inevitable crowd had collected, a tout started to sell five-shilling tickets for a short air trip. My sister and I queued up, were whisked round a few neighbouring fields for about five minutes and were then returned to earth. As so often happens if I recall any childhood experience, I remember trying to feel the appropriate emotion. I wanted to be afraid or, at least, amazed, as the wind rushed past my ears and the world dipped beneath me. I did not succeed.

More than fifty years were to pass before I again travelled by air. This time it was to make my mad dash from Scotland to London and back for my brief meeting with Mr Cavett. This journey was a little more exciting. Flying machines, I discovered, had become heavier and, when they leave the ground, it is possible by an effort of identification, to share with them their struggle to gain altitude. I found air travel to be a mode of transport that I enjoyed, so, when invited to go to Belfast, I had no qualms. Once you've done one festival, I thought, you've done them all. I was wrong. Going by plane to Ireland is a slightly different experience. The amount of time spent in the sky is about the same as when you visit Scotland but the number of hours occupied by wandering round the airport is greater. I think that there is only one plane making the Belfast run. If it hasn't returned, you wait. If you haven't any crossword puzzles to do, you can always spend the time being searched so thoroughly that you are even required to take off your hat and you may have everything you are carrying taken from you – even your umbrella. 'What', I asked, 'could I do with that which would be considered immoral or subversive?' I received no reply.

The Festival of Northern Ireland relies heavily on that one vehicle shuttling to and from England. If it doesn't arrive on time, programmes have to be altered or even cancelled. I was two hours late but that hardly mattered as I was not due to perform until the early evening. I was met by an organizer and taken into the city by a circuitous route. The driver explained that it was prettier than the more direct route. I dutifully admired the scenery but I knew that what she meant was that on this route we were less likely to be questioned.

My arrival, like that of any British person, was regarded as a gesture of affirmation – almost as a message of hope. The organizers of the festival were very concerned that I should be treated well. Even so, once in Belfast, there was hardly time to eat. Every moment until my first performance was taken up with interviews. The press was not hostile but the questions it put to me were less bland than they had been in Edinburgh. I was asked if it worried me that people might come to see me out of mere curiosity. In fact that is the reason why I am watched by audiences anywhere – to see how anyone so wicked can still move and speak – but I replied that the spirit in which the public arrived was less crucial than its mood when it left.

The weather was more predictable than the interviews. It rained. The sky was incessantly wracked by dark, swiftly moving clouds like the tattered flags of a defeated rabble.

All this I had expected. My first real shock was finding that the façades of both the television stations were ironclad like the sides of battleships. Once, presumably, they were resplendent with wide glass doors, a few marble steps and a long enquiry desk. Now there was an opening no wider than the front door of an ordinary house. When this was unlocked I saw almost immediately behind it another door. In between the two there was just room for me, my escort and the janitor. If we had shot him, the second door would not have been opened. Except that the small space was not filled with water, it was like the Davis device of a submarine. I realized then how great was the city's terror of inflammatory propaganda. If any unauthorized person could have reached the microphones to say that the pope was infallible and that the city had fallen, panic would have set in. In London we would know that it was Mr Welles having us on but there the effect would be disastrous.

My audience on my first evening consisted almost entirely of women. They were very attentive but were made uneasy by almost everything I said – even though I remembered not to mention You-Know-Who or the pope. When someone complained that she couldn't possibly do any of the things I recommended because she had to hurry home to cook a meal for her husband and three sons, I said, 'Leave them.' The whole room gasped. An English audience would only have smiled. It is difficult for us to comprehend that the people of Northern Ireland are ruled by a regime that is less concerned with morality than with religious doctrine. Their sectarianism is so divisive that, if you say you are an atheist, they ask, 'But is it the God of the Catholics or the God of the Protestants in whom you do not believe?' Apart from their religious beliefs, the poor, in Ireland, as everywhere else, seem chiefly concerned with living to the next day. It is the rich who are worried about the fair name of their country. At a posh party I attended, before I had uttered a word someone had protested, 'Things are not as bad as they are made out to be.' The terrible truth is that there is a sense in which the troubles are not bad enough. Life can go on indefinitely absorbing a few more pointless deaths every day. No major decision is forced upon anyone and, if it were, what would it be? When you ask the young people there what they want, they reply, 'To be left alone.' They have no desire to be annexed by Holy Ireland nor do they wish to be part of England. They want to be the inhabitants of Northern Ireland. Perhaps the solution to the whole problem would be to give the place an entirely new, non-inflammable name.

On the evening when I was not working, I was taken to a banquet given by the city's gay population. They are angry and no wonder. They have to bear the shame of being part of the British Empire while reaping none of the benefits of its genial depravity but even there, as in so many places on earth, the quarrel is less with the law than with the police. You might think that the constabulary of Ulster had enough to do just staying alive but no. It finds time to chivvy the gay men incessantly. One young man had been held in a police station for hours 'on suspicion'. No complainant had come forward to state that he had been corrupted; no time or place had been specified when or where the crime was supposed to have occurred. I would say that, by any standards, this procedure would be classed as harassment.

I had gone to Northern Ireland not exactly to be shot but certainly in the hope of being shot at. I was beginning to realize that, though some may have publicity thrust upon them, I was someone who must achieve it. I jumped up and down in front of the soldiers but they ran away.

Because of the various festivals, I was starting, in a very small way, to travel. I had never envied people who went abroad. I knew that the experiences that they described as so pleasurable would for me be uncomfortable or might lead to humiliation. My relationship with the English was dodgy enough. With the inhabitants of a foreign country it might be downright frightening. Those of my friends who took their holidays outside Britain, usually went to France. They either spoke tourist French without any apparent feeling of degradation or they were content to wave their arms and offer less which, in Paris, is practically a full-time occupation. The ostensible object of these vacations was either sight-seeing or, if they were spent on the Mediterranean coast, sun-bathing. The first of these pastimes tires me; the second makes me positively ill. The real purpose of these holidays abroad was to air a sophisticated preference for a continental way of life which, to the English before the Common Market opened, represented culture or art – two more causes of fatigue and nausea. Abroad, in those days I felt, had nothing to offer me.

Now at the festivals I saw that foreign countries need not be irritating regions where I would be compelled to sit around wondering what people were saying about me. If carefully selected they could be new worlds to conquer or, at least, new worlds to con. I also discovered that the appalling anxieties attendant upon getting from one country to the next could be delegated to others.

Within two years of my first timid departures from England, I was in a situation where these conditions were nearly always fulfilled.

Among the men who interviewed me in Northern Ireland was a Mr Rafferty. When I returned to England after my first visit to New York, we met again. This time, on the Mohammed principle, he came to Britain for the purpose of preparing a radio programme on the invasion of privacy. He wished to start this project with me because he judged that my opinions on the subject would be the most extreme.

He was right. What is privacy for if not for invading?

By now, I am happy to say, I have no private life. I want none. Like most people who are not quintuplets, I started out with one but, a little at a time, I have divested myself of it as a traveller abandons superfluous luggage when he sees that the night is coming and his destination is still a long way off. I quite understand Miss Loren's indignation at being photographed in church at a funeral, I only doubt that I would experience the same reaction as she. Inevitably I would find myself trying to mourn more picturesquely.

This kind of response to public notice is part of my attempt at the unification of my personality. I avoid using the word integrity because there is nothing particularly moral about this endeavour, it is merely something I wish to accomplish. I am saddened when anyone does not recognize that this is my aim.

Occasionally after a performance, I receive a letter from a member of the audience asking me to interpret in terms personal to her some general statement that I have made during the show (and there are many). This I do gladly but my answer often provokes another letter complaining, 'But these are the responses that you would make from the stage.' This comment makes it appallingly obvious that my correspondent has supposed that what I said in the theatre I did not mean. While it is true that I seek to entertain with every word I utter, I am never insincere. Indeed, if there is any enjoyment in *An Evening with Quentin Crisp*, it seems to me to lie in the fact that I am saying exactly what I think and that my ideas strike the audience as bizarre. A discrepancy of modes of thought is at the heart of one kind of humour. For me every performance is a small essay in self-revelation. At the end of it, whoever is seated in front of me knows me as well as people whom I have met on and off throughout the years. On occasion someone will say slightly contemptuously, 'Yes. You know all these people but are they really your friends?' I do not grade my acquaintances in order of intimacy. The ones I see most are usually those who live nearest or who make the most insistent demands. If being in love involves laying bare one's body and soul to one person, then I am in love with the world and my whole life is a slow and often interrupted wooing of the human race.

I am seen and heard therefore I am. The more often and the more clearly I am seen and heard, the more fully I feel that I am alive.

Should these sentiments reveal me to be a shallow character, I accept the criticism without a murmur.

People repeatedly warn me that, if I am not careful, I shall start to believe my own publicity. It is my opinion that I must believe it. Any other attitude would be deceitful. It would imply that lesser mortals might be dazzled by the flak with which public figures are surrounded but that we are sitting at the heart of it indifferent or, worse, cynically amused by a hoax being practised in our name upon an innocent public. We must either insist that what is printed on the dust jackets of our books or in our programme notes be reduced to human proportions or we must continually strive to become what our public relations experts claim that we are.

To be identified with our publicity is simply yet another way of merging our outward and inward selves.

Nine

Before I could justifiably be taken any further abroad, I had to consolidate my position in England. This process began in Hampstead.

There is a large hospital in the north of London called New End. (To which particular extremity of the human frame renewal is promised has never been revealed.) In a small side street running downhill beside this building stands a tiny theatre. It looks like a Protestant church in a Swiss village but it was once the hospital's mortuary. It has now been christened the New End Theatre. Thus, in my opinion, an opportunity was lost; it should have been named the Mortuary Theatre. There, night after night, a different person, preferably a celebrity, should have been placed supine under a sheet on a marble slab in the middle of the floor waiting to be asked questions, scalpel-sharp, by the audience.

At the New End I was not to give lunch-time performances and my agent decided that in an eight o'clock show, audiences must be given more. I saw the logic of this decision. However wonderful certain midday plays may be, there is no doubt that at that informal hour, people will accept a lower standard.

An evening at the theatre is an outing – a treat. A man chooses a day and books in advance which gives him time to practise looking eager. He washes and finds a girl to accompany him so as to spread the load of guilt that attends all wanton pursuit of pleasure. After such elaborate preparations an hour's entertainment will not do. As a way of extending the show to fill a whole evening, my agent hit on the idea of having me tell the audience just before the interval that it would be given pieces of paper on which it could write questions. These, in the second half of the evening, I would endeavour to answer. The programme was now divided into two more or less equal parts and lasted in all about two-and-a-quarter hours. This scheme worked like magic. It is very difficult for an amateur like me to cajole strangers into asking questions. I do not possess that ample lovability which enabled comedians to persuade music-hall audiences to sing and it must be remembered that what I was asking would put a greater strain on people's nerves. You sing in chorus: asking questions is a solo performance. The anonymity of the written word made everybody bolder – even me. I was replying to a sea of faces not to one threatening or defenceless individual. Even on a bad night when only two or three slips of paper were handed to me after the interval, audiences realized from the answers that I gave that whatever the question I would take it seriously and treat it with sympathy. Finding that no one had to be profound or witty made everybody bolder. They talked; sometimes they even shouted each other down.

This device of the written questions was not only useful to anyone in the theatre who wished to communicate with me, it also helped me to make a long overdue connection with the world.

Someone once said to me, 'I wonder what your material would be like if delivered by a real actor.' Somewhat shaken I asked what the question meant. I was told that it was obvious that everything I said was written on the inside of my skull and that I was merely reading it. I know that I have never quite eliminated this monotonous element from the first half of the show because even in America a critic said the same thing in a milder form. He remarked that he preferred the second half of the programme because then the colour returned to my voice. From answering the questions, at first blandly but in later shows as though I were speaking to one person, I am gradually learning to address a whole group of listeners as though it was one person. This I take to be part of the performer's craft.

While I was in Hampstead, I was asked no hostile questions but I did receive one amusing but angry letter. A married woman with children wrote to tell me that I was an idol with feet of clay up to my armpits. She was incensed because I had said that marriage and motherhood were impediments to style. I replied apologizing for having annoyed her. On stage or off, it is occasionally my intention to tease but never to offend. She forgave me.

Not long after I had left the New End Theatre, it was sold. In an interview with the press its owner stated that my two weeks there were the only time she had ever made money. It is only fair to say that this happy though short-lived result was not due to any superiority of my performances over others given at the New End. It happened solely because I required no expenditure of time or cash on rehearsals, scenery or direction.

Except at festivals, this two-part format is the one in which my programme has remained ever since.

You know when you have succeeded in the eyes of other actors: they send you telegrams. This did not happen to me until I went to the Duke of York's Theatre. It is in what is called the West End, that ill-defined area of London which includes Shaftesbury Avenue, the Strand and a few dim streets between. Towards this mysterious region the tired eyes of provincial leading ladies are forever turned as the three sisters looked towards Moscow. I took my graduation to St Martin's Lane calmly not because I am by nature blasé but because I am not an actor. Dearly as I would love to see the process of movie-making from the inside, it is obvious that I could only lend my gracious presence to a film as certain other notorious characters have done. I could never play a part. Who could I pretend to be? Nevertheless many of my friends very kindly decided to treat my arrival in the West End as the ascent of a theatrical Mount Everest.

In reality I was a stop-gap.

A thriller had been playing at the Duke of

York's Theatre which, although it had been running only a few weeks and in spite of the presence of Miss Phillips in the cast, had failed so utterly that the management had decided to take it off. While I was totally on the outside of show business, I never gave a thought to the magnitude of a disaster of this kind. Apparently even a small theatre in London costs £2,500 a week empty. Running a group of them must be like letting rooms on a desperate scale. Managements never know when a part of their kingdom may suddenly become vacant. When this happens, a mad dash must instantly be made to find something – anything – that will in some measure lighten the terrible financial burden. This was the situation that brought me face to face with Brian Rix. After all those bedroom farces at the Whitehall Theatre I hardly recognized him with his trousers up.

In his watch-tower, Mr Jackson noticed that the lights had gone out at the southern end of St Martin's Lane. Immediately he rushed me to the scene of the accident. Mr Rix agreed to see me, the reason again being that my act required so little preparation. Even my lighting arrangements only took a few minutes to settle. If it had been necessary, I could have gone on the stage the evening of the day we met.

'How many people a day did you speak to in Edinburgh?' Mr Rix asked as we stood in the empty theatre.

'About two hundred and fifty,' I replied.

Mr Rix seemed relieved. 'What's the first thing that you say to them?'

I explained that I used to tell the audience that I was about to deliver a straight talk from a bent speaker but that someone had objected to this opening on the ground that it gave homosexuality a bad name.

'What do you say now?'

'I say that I have been forbidden to say that this is a straight talk from a bent speaker.'

I got the job.

Once again mere chance had come to my aid and placed me in what might at least be called the fourth division of the game I longed to play. I was being assisted not merely by the particular misfortune that had befallen Mr Rix but in a general way by the decade in which this had occurred. Before the invention of the Edinburgh Festival with its fringe down to its toes, I would never have been allowed into any theatre to do nothing but stand before a paying audience and say what I thought.

The Duke of York's is what an actor would call a small theatre but to me it was big. I could no longer chat. I was compelled in some measure to declaim.

If such a thing is possible, I was becoming more theatrical.

After my initial performance in the West End, I and half the audience went to a party given by Olga Deterding, as far as I know, my only millionairess. We assembled in her penthouse at the corner of Clarges Street and Piccadilly. I had been introduced to her some months before and so was less surprised than some of my acquaintances by the opulent jokiness of our hostess's home.

The main room contained a dummy man appearing perpetually to be urinating in a corner, a stuffed sheep, innumerable science fiction burglar alarms and a sports commentator's clock on which tenths of seconds ran by like demi-semi-quavers. The apartment was large but part of the ceiling was so low that one evening I saw a very tall man charge through the room with his head bent forward like that of a Spanish bull until he came to an area where he could stand upright.

Through this oddly appointed space, from the roof above to the floor below, ran a spiral staircase. I never ventured upwards but frequently went downwards because that was where the food was served. I once spent an evening with Miss Deterding when there was only one other guest. A magazine, which I think was called *People*, had asked her to write something for it. She had decided on me as her subject. Since she did not need the fee, she must have decided to do this purely for my sake. I do not think this article was ever completed but she interviewed me absolutely seriously and covered a lot of sheets of paper with notes. On all the other occasions when I was with her the place was full of guests – chiefly Indian princesses of spectacular beauty.

It is always possible for anyone to judge the financial status of his host by the distance of the table tops and chair seats from the floor. The higher the income bracket, the lower the furniture.

In Miss Deterding's home all horizontal surfaces were well below the knee.

The rooms looked neither carefully planned nor haphazard. It was as though the décor were the result of a system of taste to which the key had been lost. I have no idea whether or not Miss Deterding's places of abode in other capital cities were like the one in London but if she felt herself to be represented by the look of the apartment in Clarges Street, it is impossible to tell what she wanted the world to think of her. In a way this was appropriate. She was a veiled character – a restless woman who often gave the impression that people were on the verge of irritating her. To me she was unfailingly kind though I was never given the faintest idea why.

One of her problems was that she seemed to think of the press as a door through which she might enter a world even wider than the one she already occupied. She was strangely reluctant to be photographed but constantly invited journalists to her home although she seldom liked what was written about her. For that she could not be blamed. Fleet Street frequently made her out to be an absolute fool. Once a paper printed the story that she had written to the Queen to make sure that a party she, Miss Deterding, was giving would not clash with some royal occasion. She could not shrug off her resentment at being made to seem so unsophisticated. My fingers will not type the words 'her money became a burden to her' but I do think that her wealth was like a lazy servant – better than nothing but a source of unremitting annoyance because it never fulfilled her most urgent needs. Certain people seemed to treat her badly simply because she was rich. At one gathering a guest arrived with five of his friends none of whom Miss Deterding knew. When she protested, his reply was, 'You can afford it.' The poor escape such rudeness as this.

It is bad enough to suspect that you are loved for your wealth alone; to discover that, because of it, you are openly despised is too much.

I cannot say that I ever expected to become a close friend of Miss Deterding but when she died I was sorry.

When I was transferred to the Ambassador's Theatre, another change overtook the show. Because of the shape of the auditorium there, it was decided that I should arrive on stage from the wings. I was being seduced by fate into observing the normal traditions of the theatre. As I stood behind the backdrop waiting to go on, inevitably I started to rev up my engine. I shut my eyes so that when I opened them on stage they would be wet and dark. I held my hands high above my head so that when they were first seen they would be pale and the veins would be countersunk. Most important of all, I started to breathe deeply. At every inhalation I lowered my diaphragm until it almost touched my pelvic bone. I have no idea if real actors go in for these antics, I merely found myself practising them. The body of the performance changed little: only the beginning and the end were altered; they became less naturalistic. Originally, just as I had begun by asking the doorman if it was time to start, so I concluded by looking at my watch and saying we should stop. In other words at first everything was done to lower the expectations of audiences. Now I was trying to live up to what they had a right to see.

For my increased theatricality I was to pay a terrible price.

While I only worked in festivals or at lunch-time my humble station in life saved me from the sansculottes of the profession. As soon as I appeared in St Martin's Lane, a deputation from Equity, waving its tattered banners, marched on the Duke of York's Theatre to ask the management why it was employing someone who was not a member of the union. Mr Rix, never completely at a loss, explained that I was not acting – that I was very sincere. This argument was thought to be specious so now, in one small respect, I am like the great Maxine Sullivan. At a public meeting in New York, I once heard her say, 'I know I am an actor because I have an Equity card.'

One night at the Duke of York's Theatre one of the questions asked was, 'Can't you prevent the audience from laughing too soon? I'm a little hard of hearing.' Until that moment I had tried to say every sentence as though it were a joke in itself and, at the same time, the prelude to another, bigger joke. I did this because I never knew when people were going to laugh. It now dawned on me, though dimly, that it was up to me to decide when laughter was permitted. I remembered having heard actors talk of controlling the audience and now presumed that it was of this problem that they were speaking.

A day was soon to come when I seemed to be about to learn the answer to this conundrum. Instead I learned something better.

A friend told me that Elaine Stritch wished to meet me. At the time she was rolling about on her bed in the London Clinic. As she could hardly escape, I telephoned and asked if she would like a visit from me. She said she would.

In real life, if you can call the London Clinic real life, Miss Stritch is much milder than when on television she is bringing the immaculate Mr Sinden to heel. Her voice is less of a growl and the corners of her mouth are less sharp. Though in no way coy, she is very feminine.

I realized that our meeting was the opportunity that might never come again to ask an undeniable expert what was meant by this to me mysterious notion of audience control. 'Don't bother with any of that, honey,' she said. 'Just get 'em to like you.'

Since that unforgettable afternoon, I have tried to make what historians will one day call 'Stritch's First Law' the guiding principle of my life.

I can't say that I have always succeeded.

While I was in the West End, I received an even angrier letter of complaint than the one sent to me by the Hampstead housewife. A man who ruled an orchestra in Brighton or, perhaps, Bournemouth wrote to say that he did not consider a lot of philosophizing based on shaky premises was entertainment. I replied at once with an apology and a cheque for the price of admission that he so bitterly regretted having paid. Unlike the Hampstead lady, he did not acknowledge my effort to make amends.

Speaking more generally, I could not help becoming aware how deeply disappointed in the show were certain members of London's gay community. They could not get it into their heads that I am not someone who hires halls throughout the land in order to deliver a manifesto. I myself am hired by Mr Rix or others to bring people into the theatre by whatever means I can. I never mention homosexuality unless, in the second half of the programme, I am asked about it. Even then I do not dwell on the subject because I fear that it may not be one that many members of the audience wish to discuss. In thinking this I am justified. Once a woman asked me a question about Lesbianism. I replied; she replied; I replied. At that point a man's voice cried out, 'Can't we move on to something of more general interest?'

During an interval at one theatre, while as usual I was autographing books in the auditorium, a young man bounced forward and in an accusatory tone said, 'You're reading from a script.' When I denied this, he barked, 'Yes, you are.' I modified my negative by explaining that though at that time there had never been a speech written down, tested for length and then memorized, I was making use of a certain amount of the text of *How to Have a Life Style* – one of the books that I was at that very moment signing. My accuser was dissatisfied with this reply.

'There are a lot of gay people here tonight,' he

said, 'and we're waiting for you to tell the audience you're gay.'

I was unable to suppress my amusement. 'How could that possibly be necessary?' I asked. 'What do you think brings people here except that I am the subject of *The Naked Civil Servant*?'

'All the same, that's what we want,' the young man persisted. I suggested that he should write down a question that would elicit from me my guilty secret.

When I unfolded what I took to be his question, it said, 'Are you an active or a passive homosexual or are you just acting?' I replied that if by acting he meant pretending to be somebody else, then acting I was not. I further explained that by temperament I was a passive human being but that, if the writer of the question was curious about my sexual techniques, he could rest assured that in a very long lifetime I had probably done everything that he could imagine. It is my secret opinion that even among heterosexuals, in a prolonged relationship both (or all) parties try all the permutations of which their nervous systems and the limitations of their anatomies are capable. To my mind all attempts to relate sexual habits to temperament are doomed. Secretly I could not help reflecting sadly on the fact that now, when at last the straight people of the world are willing to drop the subject of my long dead sex life, gay people cannot leave it alone.

All in all I worked for seven weeks in one part or another of the Cooney Marsh empire. When I left, the stage door-keeper said, 'You will come back, won't you? You could be a one man *Mouse Trap.*' In spite of my indifference to the venues that I work in, this experience apparently changed me. After it, somebody commented, 'You've – um – er – expanded.'

One of the rewards of performing in a more central locality was that such wonderful people came round to my dressing-room after the show.

One such was Harold Pinter. I was introduced to him more than ten years ago. Someone who then lived in the same house as I and who had known Mr Pinter before there was such a person sent him a copy of my autobiography drawing his attention to the page on which his fair name was mentioned. This led to a visit from Mr Pinter to our house to meet old friends whom he had known when he was a touring actor. At that time I was making feeble efforts to become state-owned with the help of the Arts Council. Mr Pinter offered to recommend me for a grant. Some time later he invited me to a party in the days when he still lived in Hanover Terrace and I mean terrace. That is to say that it is impossible to reach the door of Number Seven without going back to Number One and walking along the piazza. While I stood in front of the playwright's house, before I could ring the bell, the mottled glass door was opened by a man in a white coat. I was dazzled by the splendour of the way in which successful dramatists live. If, as critics at that time asserted, playwrights were preoccupied with their kitchen sinks, they must have been of solid gold. At that party, half the guests seemed to be actresses and the other half their agents. In the room where all these illustrious people foregathered, I noticed that a copy of my book had been left with kindly negligence on a table where all might see it.

Because he is so dark, his eyes not emphasized but in some way hidden by his glasses, and because he introduces into his real-life dialogue the same long silences that are employed in his plays, Mr Pinter presents to the world a brooding, almost stern aspect. With few facial movements and no gestures of the hands, he gives an impression of stillness and great density of character. It is possible to imagine situations in which he would be absolutely, even unreasonably, implacable but to me, he has always been more than polite. He has been actively kind – motivated, I think, by a muted chivalry towards the weak.

After hearing me at the Duke of York's Theatre, Mr Pinter took Lady Antonia Fraser, two other guests and me to supper. When someone remarked that at last the world seemed to have accepted me, our host added 'And about time too.' With the minimum of direct praise, which can only embarrass, he remembers always to convey to those about him that he is on their side.

Another remark, which I now weave into the show whenever possible, was made on that evening. I was asked what I had thought of my first fleeting glimpse of New York. I explained that the only possible sorrow that an Englishman could feel about such a visit was the realization that the British could live on the food thrown away every dawn in that city. Antonia Fraser's suggestion was:

'They give you doggy bags. What we need now is a doggy Concorde.'

On another evening, when a famous actress accompanied by a friend arrived in my dressing-room, it was stuffed with strange art students. I was compelled to apologize for not offering introductions; I couldn't remember any of their names. The students said, 'I am Mary, I am Tom,' and so on. The new visitor replied, 'I am Claire and this is Philip' – an example to my mind of true graciousness. They were Miss Bloom and Mr Roth.

When my reign at the Ambassador's Theatre ended, I would have been at a loose end had it not been for the proprietor of that very café where a few years ago I had met the man from Granada Television who had introduced me to Mr Mitchell. This establishment was christened the As-You-Like-It coffee bar but as none of its habitués had the stamina to utter seven words in a row, it came to be called 'The As'.

Unlike his customers, the man who ran the place was blessed with boundless energy and unquenchable optimism and he was mad about the theatre. From time to time he would leave a hooligan in charge of the premises and rush with a taxi full of tea, coffee and sandwiches to various stage doors. This operation required split-second timing. If the tea arrived too soon, it might cool before the player who had ordered it left the stage; if it arrived late, he might not have time to sip it before his next cue. All the habitués of the café knew that they must neither move nor speak while the food and drink was being packed by the owner whose lips could be seen moving silently as he memorized what was for whom. The absence of speech and the staccato movements made these occasions like silent films. For me, as for many, visiting The As was a leisure occupation. I never minded waiting to pay my bill until the proprietor returned from the Adelphi or the Vaudeville. I welcomed delays as I had only gone to the place to pass the time.

When not flying round the West End like a blue bottle in a third-class railway carriage or ministering to his part-time residents, the owner telephoned various producers and casting directors to recommend unknown singers and dancers. Of these aspirants he spoke in terms so glowing as to be a source of entertainment to the diners who listened shamelessly to these conversations and occasionally tried to take part in them.

This indefatigable gentleman trafficked in souls with exactly the same eagerness that he lavished upon the sale of food. Tea was delicious, Florentine biscuits were divine and when he spoke over the telephone about any of his protégés, they sang like Caruso and, as dancers, were Mr Astaire's only rivals. Little did I guess that I would one day be on this sumptuous menu. With what hyperboles he recommended me to provincial theatre owners I dared not think but he seemed to have little difficulty in finding engagements for me and in the most unlikely places – Bury St Edmunds, Chipping Norton, Mold. When not out of England, I happily worked for him.

Ten

The first finger that beckoned me across the Atlantic was not American but Canadian. A woman's voice spoke to me over the telephone.

'Will you come to Toronto?' she asked coolly.

'When?'

'Well, now, actually.'

'For how long?'

'Just for the day.'

If until that moment, I had only suspected that the world had gone mad, the notion now became a certainty. In fact I was still employed by several art schools and could not leave at once. I went a fortnight later and stayed a day and a half. The journey was my first long-distance flight. It is impossible not to regard the cloudscape below you as the surface of the earth. You are not aware of any motion and feel that you are standing in a disused lighthouse surveying a snowbound planet, long since bereft of human habitation, making its last meaningless, million-year dash towards the sun.

Inside the plane a cosier atmosphere prevails. The staff of British Airways has been schooled in more than mere airworthiness. The stewards address you by your name and, if you seem reluctant to eat or uncertain what to choose, with twinkling eyes and seductive smiles, they act out the various delicacies on their trolleys. Because I was such a novice, I could not help contrasting their treatment of me with that inflicted on me by the slaves of British Rail.

In other respects, I found air travel less exciting than the movies had led me to expect. No one became hysterical, no one near me was handcuffed to anyone else and I couldn't glance nervously at the ice forming on the wings because I couldn't *see* the wings. You eat, you sleep and you go to the movies. You're hardly any better off than on earth.

A tailor would say that the east coast of the new world had been poorly finished off. Coming into Canada it is hard to say at what exact moment you leave the ocean and are flying over land. At first there are below you innumerable capes, inlets, islands and tiny lakes.

Toronto is very beautiful. Its skyscrapers are honey-coloured which, as they are mostly banks, is appropriate. They seem almost to rise out of the lake and are lit horizontally by a light emanating from the water. In the middle of the city is a secular minaret which I was told was the highest free-standing structure in the world. I did not ascend it; the lifts were loaded with tourists because the day I was there was Columbus Day. This I thought was an apt coincidence because my sense of wonder at the new world compels me to go on about it as though no one had ever been there except me and Chris.

Many of the buildings in Toronto are made of identity parade glass. I hope that from the inside of these edifices you can see out. From without all I saw was a reflection of myself standing at a window with the words 'Toronto Hotel' written backwards above my head. On my first evening I had difficulty in forcing myself to stand near the window because of its immense distance from the street below.

The main purpose of my visit to Canada was to be seen and heard talking about *The Naked Civil Servant* which had recently been shown there.

It had been solicitously decided that I could not travel three thousand miles and be interviewed on the same day. In fact I could have done so without any feeling whatsoever of exhaustion. There is no such thing as jet-lag – especially if you are journeying from east to west. All the plane has to do is to go up into the air and, like Nijinsky, pause there a little; Canada will come by presently.

Appropriately the man sent to meet me when I arrived in the new world was called Mr Dvorak. In a purring limousine he escorted me to the hotel from which he promised to collect me the following evening.

Before I had fully unpacked, I received a telephone call from the Toronto office of my paperback publisher. It was the caller's intention to whisk me the following morning in and out of various radio stations. My arrival twenty-four hours early had not been in vain.

A year before, I would have been amazed at this proposal: now I remained calm. I had learned in the meantime the difference between hardback and paperback publishing.

Hardback publishers are not seriously in the business of selling their wares; they are content with laying them at the reader's feet. Any more energetic practice might seem ungentlemanly. At parties in the last few years I have met men in the trade who could be bullied into agreeing with this statement so long as their names were never mentioned in this connection. They admit that there are no junior employees in their offices whose function day after day is to read the papers in the hope of finding that one of the firm's authors is dead, has been sent to prison or done anything else to merit a reprint. To laymen it is obvious that televiewers love to see writers in alpaca suits sitting on swivel chairs and talking about their sex lives provided that these divine beings do not make the mistake of rabbiting on about their dreary books. Inside the business no one can bring himself to accept that writing is not a literary career but a personality racket. Many English writers are relieved to know that their actual bodies will never be used as sales adjuncts. It might have been difficult, for instance, to persuade E. M. Forster to run round Bedford Square in a funny hat. As for me, I've got the hat – all I ask is, 'Which way do I go?'

For this reason I had been bewildered when I discovered that Cape had no intention of dipping its toe – much less plunging head first – into the tide of publicity that flowed first from Granada's and then from Thames's television programmes about me: there were to be no more printings of my autobiography in its original format. Since that terrible time, Duckworth has been kind enough to bring out a different hardback version solely in order to attract more recent reviews while Fontana, which may be another floor, another room or merely another desk in Collins, published a wonderful cheap – or, at least, cheaper – edition. They are, moreover, pleased to make use of the element of vulgarity in my nature. For this purpose they have a press office in which at least one person is constantly at work. Day and night, like a lighthouse, her gaze ransacks the ocean of human activity in search of an island (a mere rock will do) on which a bookstall can be set up. In England, wherever I went to speak to the multitude, she was willing, nay eager, to pay my fare and feed me. I was delighted to find that, though she organized these book-signing sessions with great efficiency, ruled provincial book sellers firmly and commanded area representatives to meet our trains as though we were ambassadors, she was never shrill. She remained forever silky.

As with London so with Toronto. In Canada, because of the whirlwind nature of my visit, I was taken to four small radio stations in one day. These brief interviews were much as I had expected but I had not imagined that Canadian men would be such a self-indulgent shape. There is no national face above the forty-ninth parallel but there is a typical figure. In spite of all that ice-hockey that we see on English television, I do not think much exercise is taken by the average Torontan.

Between these appointments, we managed to wedge in several large meals and a visit to a paper called the *Body Politic*. This periodical is the gay voice of Toronto. As its name implies, it is more militant than, say, *Gay News* but it is determined rather than strident. The issue of the paper I was shown espoused the cause of a man who had been dismissed from his job on the explicit grounds that he was homosexual. He was a horse trainer. It is difficult to imagine what goes on in the minds of some heterosexuals.

The *Body Politic* is run by very young people – several men and a girl. They occupy a warehouse situated beyond the business and shopping areas of the city. We went up to the editorial office in a lift like the one which Miss Dietrich fell to the bottom of in Pittsburgh. The room where we talked was large and airy – possibly difficult to heat in winter but the staff is dauntless. I was given a cup of tea and questioned about my private life. I apologized for my lack of aggression. I think it saddened them but they remained unfailingly polite.

After this interview some of those with whom I had been speaking accompanied me through the streets in search of lunch. They noticed without surprise that a few passers-by stared at me but expressed amazement that I paid no attention to any of the 'pretty boys' that wandered past us. I can only express a counter-surprise. My life has, in recent times, become literally an open book. Everyone who is interested in me at all knows that in earlier years I spent a great deal of time trying to qualify as a pretty boy. Surely they must be able to guess that, because of this, I am horribly aware how self-regarding, feeble and generally not worth the money this particular species can be.

When I left Canada, I did not immediately return to England. I went to New York. Entering the United States I proferred my passport for the very first time in my life. A gigantic airport official examined it thoroughly before giving it back to me. When I thanked him and turned to go, he bent down and, in a very quiet voice, said, 'Is it nice to be vindicated at last?'

My spies are everywhere.

When, a year afterwards, I did the one-man show in Newhaven, Washington and New York, I again went to Toronto. During my later, longer visit, my impression of the city was different though not necessarily any more accurate. Mr Muggeridge, whose voice was made for expressing bland contempt, says that I live a 'show biz' life and shall never see places as they really are. He is absolutely right. The second time round everything seemed less frighteningly grand. I do not wish to imply that, during one short year, the glory of Canada had faded. All that happened was that I inhabited a slightly cheaper part of town. I do not think I even so much as walked past the Toronto Hotel where I had spent two nights of deep-piled opulence nor did I catch even a glimpse of that strange edifice that claimed to be of unparalleled height. I stayed at the Waldorf-Astoria which, contrary to what its hyphenated name might lead guests to suppose, was quite unpretentious and in no way intimidating even to someone as pathologically terrified of hotel staff as I am.

I appeared at the Workshop Theatre to which I travelled by taxi but only to show that I could. If compelled by fate to traverse the distance on foot, the journey took less than a quarter of an hour so I saw little of the city. As always, when not in my hotel room or on stage, I made sorties to various television and radio stations. Canadians are very conscious of the power of publicity. In fourteen days I was interviewed twenty-one times. In between these professional activities, I just managed visits to my two spies in Canada.

One of these was the woman who, in England twenty long, dark years before, had ruled the display firm where I had painted the faces of four thousand dolls. Now, in quieter mood, she runs a curiosity shop for cat worshippers. I am happy to say that the place harbours no actual animals but it is full of feline fetishes – cards, calendars, knick-knacks.

The other spy is the woman to whom, when she lived in Crouch End, we tried to bring notoriety by writing television plays in her name. She has now abandoned her quest for fame and settled for mere happiness. One of her daughters took me to see a dancing class. The hunger for culture is far less self-wounding in Canada than in Australia but it is present nonetheless. When I asked this girl if she was a pupil at the school, she replied that she was not – that she was a member of a ballet company. This seemed to be an improvement until I learned that she received no wages. I was saddened by hearing this. To an outsider, Canada looks physically so open, so full of light and spiritually so free from deviousness or pretence but even there there seems to be a certain amount of double thinking and therefore perhaps, though I personally saw none, of double dealing. The fact that young people donate their energies and their talents so eagerly is no argument for accepting them without payment. No art should be subsidized either by governments or, worse, by its practitioners.

Now that I habitually travel distances so much greater than formerly I would have dared or could have afforded, I am often reunited with people whom I have not seen for huge stretches of time. The changes that the years have wrought in them are consequently more obvious. So far these confrontations with the past have always given me pleasure. My friends usually seem to have grown calmer. This is a development that I applaud but, as a devotee of relativity, I must constantly remind myself that, if this is the alteration I see in them, they must find me more feverish – a suspicion recently turned into conviction by a letter received from a friend in France. It contained this warning: 'Try not to start wanting things.' It would appear that the asceticism for which I have had a life-long reputation was prompted by circumstantial necessity rather than innate spirituality. I doubt that I shall ever want things, but, now that I am free, there is no limit to my appetite for events and people.

Eleven

For weeks there were rumours that, like other wrongdoers before me, I would be sent to Australia. I tried not to hear them. Thus I did not know that this mad scheme had become a certainty until I was sitting at a lunch table opposite a Mr Cook – perhaps a descendant of that seafaring gentleman who discovered the place. In his native land he is called an entrepreneur. This I found strange. Even in England, twelve thousand miles from that proverbially no-nonsense continent, the word sounds a trifle fancy but impresario is not much better and the American word promoter carries with it a faint suspicion of chicanery. But what's in a name? He had chosen a profession in pursuit of which he travelled all over the world in search of entertainment that he could transplant in the Antipodes. While he was in America on one of these foraging sorties, he spoke with the Mr Taylor who later brought Mr Brynner in *The King and I* to England. Mr Taylor had seen me at the Duke of York's Theatre and advised Mr Cook to do the same. What chance had caused these two gentlemen to meet I never asked.

By this time I accepted that fate was my agent.

All the same, when I saw that a visit to Australia was irrevocable, I was very frightened. I explained that I had never spoken to more than seven hundred people at any one time and that even that number had proved too many. Mr Cook said that I need have no fear – that I would be wired for sound. I pointed out that Australians despise the English nation in general and would find me particularly revolting. Mr Cook said that a theatre audience was the same the whole world over and that, if I'd managed all right here, I would have no trouble there. Every objection that I raised was overruled, every doubt silenced. During this dialogue the enigmatic Mr Taylor arrived and remarked that my act would have to be made more elegant. He also suggested that its contents should be altered slightly to appeal to Australian tastes. I bowed my head assuming that he was an authority on that distant world of which I knew nothing. It transpired later that he had never been near the place.

In spite of all this reassurance, all this friendly advice, I still had secret misgivings. I was right.

The Australian tour was a disaster.

Even so, it might have been worse had not my agent succeeded in bamboozling into coming with me the young woman who had assisted me at the Duke of York's Theatre. She was of high-degree, her father being a baronet or worse, but asked why she worked when she could so easily have stayed in bed all day polishing her coronet, she replied that she needed the money. Nevertheless public relations was an odd career for her to have chosen. It is a ruthless profession whose practitioners are sometimes driven to manipulate their victims while pretending to protect them and in which fulsome praise is forever trembling on the brink of downright untruth. My assistant was a moralist and consequently spent most of her working life in a state of collapse.

She turned out to be the ideal travelling companion. Being so slight as to be hardly visible to the naked eye, she could easily be folded and stowed away in any make of car without the least inconvenience to other passengers. Moreover she not only took up very little space but also demanded almost no attention. As she did not like the real world, she spent most of her time in it asleep. Miraculously being frail turned out not to be the same thing as being scatter-brained; at least we never arrived at the wrong place on the wrong day.

As we stepped out of the plane in Sydney I reassured my companion that, it being only seven in the morning, we would easily be able to slip into our hotel unnoticed. Never was prophecy more spectacularly unfulfilled. The moment that we wheeled our luggage out of the airport, we found ourselves in a lightning storm of flash bulbs, a thunder clap of interrogation. Even when the car that was taking us to our hotel drew away from the kerb, reporters ran beside it, their lips still moving. Once we were in our rooms, the hubbub that I had assumed would cease became worse. We discovered that a small documentary movie was to be made of our arrival. There were people photographing the people photographing us. It was as though we had come to save the whole continent.

Just as the entire world adores France but has recently come to dislike the French, so, though Australians despise the British, they love England and for a while, at any rate to the press, I became the embodiment of the traditions of my native land although in fact I have always rebelled against them.

What is at the heart of this inordinate passion for Britain? I think I may by accident have hit upon the answer.

Many long, dark years ago, I took a friend to see a movie called *King Kong* (the first time round). During a dramatic episode in which a certain Miss Wray lay gibbering across Mr Kong's wrist, my companion, in a voice shrill with irritation, cried out, 'I can't think what he sees in her.' I suggested that it might be her littleness that was her attraction. Perhaps it is a similar discrepancy of sizes that binds Australia to England.

In the ten weeks that I worked for Mr Cook, I went to Orange, to Newcastle and, except for Darwin, to every capital city in his kingdom. Some of these towns I visited more than once, going there first to say that I was going there and later to do the show. In all that time I was embroiled in only one hostile interview. This was with a man and woman who were quite unable to take their minds off what I looked like. As I was leaving, the man assayed a mild send-up by remarking that, if I wished to add a few small touches to my appearance, the make-up department would be only too willing to help. In the theatre I was compelled to read no more than a dozen questions calculated to embarrass me. The word 'poof' was only used once – at least in my hearing.

Most of the questions asked by the professional interviewers were self-deprecating. One reporter kept saying, 'We're so far from everywhere, aren't we?' I pointed out that Sydney is no further from New York than New York from Sydney. 'Well, no,' the lady grudgingly admitted.

'Nobody,' I remarked, 'is sitting by his window in America sighing because he is so far from Australia.'

'Exactly. That's just what I mean.'

'Then,' I suggested, 'remoteness is in the heart.' The young woman wrote these observations down but she didn't look as though she believed me.

Another often repeated question was, 'Australia is a cultural desert, don't you think?' This statement was wasted on me. If I ever use the word 'culture', it is to describe television programmes so boring they cannot be classed as entertainment.

Australians are a nation of Madam Butterflies. They are forever standing on the shore watching for that wisp of Heaven-knows-what that will appear on the horizon one fine day.

But why? They lack nothing. The streets beneath their feet are paved with opals. The air about them sparkles like diamonds. The atmosphere is so clear that the roofs of their houses are always as red as the day they were tiled; the walls as white as when they were first painted.

Strangers kept saying that it was a pity that we had arrived in winter but, in fact, every day that we were there was warmer than an English May. This appearance of eternal summer was reinforced by the look of the trees most of which are evergreen. Those that are look not as though their foliage had sprung spontaneously from their boughs but rather as if it had been flung on to their branches from a distance – wet. Those that are not evergreen display scarlet flowers the size of table mats.

Partly because of this halcyon weather, all Australian cities are holiday resorts. On their free days, the natives take off their socks and shoes and walk down to the sea's edge. If you tried that in London, you would feel very ill by the time you got there.

Furthermore, in Australia there seems to be no poverty. The trains are empty but the aeroplanes are full – chiefly of men carrying their board meeting suits in plastic bags. Occasionally in Sydney I saw sun-burnt old men who looked as though they were left over cold from a gold rush but there were no beggars, no street bands, no little old ladies slumped in doorways under several overcoats. Except for the black swans of Perth, there were very few even of nature's born cadgers, the birds.

I constantly tried to reassure my interviewers; I seldom succeeded. It is possible that Australians are self-deprecatory out of politeness. They may well feel that it would be graceless to flaunt their ocean-to-ocean prosperity before the hollow eyes of travellers from a dying star.

My tour of the Antipodes failed not because of any hostility from my audiences. No empty beer cans were thrown on to the stage. I foundered (and this we had not in our arrogance thought possible) on their indifference. When I strolled about the streets or went into the shops of King's Cross, the district of Sydney in which our hotel was situated, my presence seemed to be taken completely for granted.

In Melbourne the reaction was the same. I stood in the entrance to a cinema waiting for a taxi while near at hand two young men discussed whether they had or had not seen me on television a few days earlier. When they decided that they had, one of them approached and shook my hand. After the usual exchange of pleasantries, he said, 'So you're homosexual. Big deal.' I did not think these words were meant to discomfit me but rather that they were a comment on the folly of the sex-obsessed world. The same cool attitude was expressed even in Brisbane which, in other parts of Australia, is the butt of jokes similar to those that in England are heaped upon Wigan. One evening I was standing in my hotel room looking down on to one of those doll's-house churches that nestle among the skyscrapers of Brisbane when the telephone bell rang. My caller explained that he was attending a school in which his class had been told to write an essay about the television documentary programme showing my arrival in Australia. This piece of information by itself astounded me. In England no teacher would set his pupils such an inflammatory subject unless he were more interested in publicity than in a steady job. More amazing, however, than the shadowy figure of this broad-minded master was the very real student. Apparently without any prompting from his elders, he had nagged his sister into driving him into town so that he might embellish his thesis with details gathered first-hand from me. He was fourteen at the oldest yet Mr Darwin setting out in *The Beagle* cannot have had to summon up more scientific detachment than this child.

I realized instantly that I must not figure in a fifth-form essay beginning, 'When I talked with Mr Crisp in his hotel bedroom . . .' I therefore asked my visitor to accompany me to my dressing-room at the theatre where I was to perform in an hour's time. Backstage I answered all the young man's questions, without, I hope, saying anything that, if quoted, would alarm his father or his headmaster.

Even so our conversation was by no means bland. 'My friends say that you're a slob,' the boy remarked with no apparent hostility. He had noticed that my shirt was held together with a safety pin. Had he known it, this was a good night. Sometimes I seem to be dressed in chain mail.

This young man seemed critical but in no way hysterical or angry. He appeared interested in me but not unduly curious about my sex life. How different was this urbane attitude from the mixture of rudeness and cowardice that marks the behaviour of English schoolboys who on railway platforms call my name but, when I turn towards them, scamper into the nearest waiting room!

The sophistication of Australia was so complete that it did more than set the people free to come and see me; they felt sufficiently liberated to stay away.

The blame for the disasters in one's life must always fall upon oneself. I should have protested longer or louder that I could not fill a large theatre in Australia or anywhere else. I should have forced Mr Cook to believe me. There is a sense in which I betrayed him but, in spite of the staggering financial loss that he must have sustained on my account, he remained unfailingly courteous. I hope that for my part I made it clear how grateful I was for the opportunity he gave me to visit this strange continent – sparse but wealthy, barbaric but modern, self-effacing but friendly.

I felt my shame less keenly than I might have done because, to me, all performances elsewhere in the world are but dress rehearsals for America.

America

Until I went to St Andrews University in 1975, I had never left England. Before 1977 I had never been outside the British Isles. Now, only two crowded years later, I have been to every region of the earth where Crisperanto is understood except South Africa which I have never visited because I reckon they are in enough trouble there already.

Even so, I am not an experienced traveller. I never shall be because I so seldom make long voyages alone. The harrowing complexities of airports are usually faced by other people on my behalf. The person who most often shoulders this burden is my agent. When I go to the United States he makes the trip partly on his own account, seeing America as a bookshelf three thousand miles wide, but mostly he does so for my sake. I am very grateful. Being my companion in a strange land demands a certain moral fortitude. Wherever we go, people say, looking him slowly up and down, 'Ah yes. You're Quentin's personal manager.' It might mean anything but he remains calm and explains that he is a literary agent – not only mine but that of many other writers.

Occasionally some of my acquaintances sneer at the fact that, like little old ladies of the 1890s, I seem to need a travelling companion. They are rattled by my fecklessness or, more likely, by the condonation that my passivity receives from my employers. 'Do you like having your mind made up for you by others?' they snort. 'Don't you care that you are being treated like a dog, told when to sit and when to follow at your master's heels?' I remain unperturbed by their indignation. The treatment upon which they spit their scorn is not something I merely accept; I connive at it. It ensures that I am never to blame. To anyone whom the world has for so long tried to make feel ashamed this is a great relief. When I was a child my ineptitude was a burden to my parents and my teachers. They could not see that it was a greater burden to me. I wondered wanly if I would ever discover how to do anything well. At long last I have learned something even better – how not to do anything at all.

This pampered mode of travel serves not only my own purpose but also that of anyone who employs me. One evening during a week in Washington so unsuccessful that it quite put me off wanting to be President, I was taken by my sponsor to supper at the Watergate, no less. During the meal I said, 'But the going on the stage and the signing of the books are a pretext, are they not? Really I'm in the smiling and nodding racket.' Without a moment's hesitation he agreed that I was.

This being so, it is my duty when in the outer world never to appear worried about trying to decipher what an airport public address system is saying, never to be seen in tears because I have lost my ticket. No one must ever be provoked into saying that he saw me somewhere but that I looked so distraught that he didn't dare to speak to me. To this end I not only never travel alone, I have even abandoned my life-long habit of scorning strangers before they have had a chance to scorn me. Now, in public, like everyone else who has been on television, I wear perpetually an expression of fatuous affability.

There is a sense in which, however far I go, I shall never be a traveller at all. I shall never return home with a parrot in a cage and fantastic tales of what foreign people and places look like. It is in the very nature of my situation that I traverse the world not to see but to be seen.

My visit to America was given a curious overture.

A day came when, seeking new screens to conquer, Thames Television bought seven consecutive evenings of New York viewing time. Among the items shown was *The Naked Civil Servant*. I trust it was exhibited on a channel that required no sponsorship. I cannot imagine any manufacturer being willing to advertise his product during that tale of degradation unless the copy were to say, 'If you don't eat up your shredded wheat, you'll end up like Quentin Crisp.'

Whether or not this wild gamble turned out to be profitable for Thames I have no idea but it certainly made a difference to me. It foreshadowed the moment when my dream of America became a reality. From the moment that I heard what had happened, I never for long took my eyes from the western horizon.

For many months no invitation to visit the States was received but an American came to see me. This man was Mr Lindsay, the former mayor of New York – a position, in my estimation, only just south of God. I remembered from the invasion of Britain by GIs during the war that all Americans are good-looking. Even so I was amazed by Mr Lindsay's appearance. He is what television would call a new, improved Mr Niven.

He arrived in Beaufort Street at the head of his men – a producer whose nerves were worn down to their stumps by lack of sleep, an Italian cameraman and a lighting expert who only longed for glasses of Guinness.

Mr Lindsay and I were placed so close together that we must have looked like old time radio crooners sharing a microphone. The cameraman trudged through a heap of dirty sheets lying in the corner of my room presumably in the hope of getting far enough away from us to show that we were not embracing. My home affords so little space that, throughout the interview, he was compelled to balance his camera on his sagging collar bone. I could not help wondering if we would be seen in heaving close-up like the windscreen shots in a car chase.

I was too astonished by the entire incident to remember much of my conversation with my visitor but I do recall that he asked me if I was planning to go to the States. My reply was another question: 'What about my sin?' To reassure me, my interviewer waltzed casually through a catalogue of names belonging to famous Englishmen who had safely carried their tarnished images across the Atlantic Ocean but a moment later, perhaps fearing that he had offered too much encouragement, he was warning me that I would have to undertake not to overthrow the government by force. I issued a counter-warning but have since learned that no one who is not born in America can be President.

It seemed to me unlikely that this dialogue would ever be heard in New York but I was wrong. My spy for that city has since told me that this interview formed part of a programme called *Good Morning, America*. That means that it was seen by eleven million people with half-closed eyes. My informant also said that Mr Lindsay seemed embarrassed. The camera evidently sees more than the eye. At the time of his visit he seemed to me polite but relaxed, interested but not inquisitive. He personified that effortless sociability that I now know to be the national style of America.

If proof were needed that democracy is alive and well and living in America this entire episode would provide it.

Mr White says that an Englishman is unhappy until he has explained America; I would say that he might feel guilty if he did not praise it.

Though, at a first glance, New York is less beautiful than Toronto – less airy, less golden – to me it was more exciting because it is the city of my dreams. The moment I caught sight of it, I wanted it and stretched my arms through the car window towards the skyscrapers like a child beholding a Christmas tree. Every street along which we drove brought back the memory of some long dead movie seen when life was dreary and only the world of celluloid was rich and full. Every person on the sidewalks reminded me of the soldiers who invaded London during the happy time.

On this first visit we were the guests of Mr Bennett. This was as it should be. He is the very spirit of the place – a jumping-up-and-down man of limitless hospitality who is wild about the entertainment industry. He arranged for us to live for two-and-a-half days in a splendour to which it would be ruinous to become accustomed. In a hotel suite large enough to house a Catholic family, I was given a bed in which four people could have slept without ever being introduced. Everything in America is on wide screen.

Mr Bennett is the very model of a modern millionaire; that is to say that he dresses for all occasions like a college student. Thus attired he took me, on my last evening in New York, through various theatres of the Schubert group. There, since he invented *A Chorus Line*, he is obviously sacred. The manager of one of these houses walked solemnly before us like a mace-bearer to shoo away any ushers or ticket collectors who might mistakenly have dared to address us. Of all the snippets of entertainment that I sampled in this way the one that impressed me most was my glimpse of Mr Borge. Except that he occasionally plays a few notes on the piano, he does less on stage than I do but to so much more effect.

Finally my host took me to Sardi's. His mode of living is like that of Nature herself; he leaves a wide margin for the unexpected. Though there were only four invited guests, we sat at a table large enough for a board meeting. Within seconds this turned out to have been a wise stratagem. We were joined for a few seconds each by a series of diners from other parts of the room. Among other celebrities I was introduced to Mr von Sydow. He did not look God-ridden; he has a pink face, corn-gold hair and a handshake that could force you to your knees. Either in Mr Bergman's picture or in Sardi's, he was acting.

One man who visited our table became highly excited when he saw me. 'Oh,' he cried glancing rapidly from me to Mr Bennett and back again, 'is there going to be a collaboration of some kind?' Mr Bennett explained that this was a secret. From somewhere a quiet voice murmured, 'Then why are you in Sardi's?'

Throughout the meal – throughout every meal – because of all this darting to and fro, the waiters never enjoy a clear run from the tables to the kitchen. With their trays held high above their heads, they move, stop, start again like six o'clock traffic on Brooklyn Bridge except that there are no tantrums and no collisions.

In Sardi's there is more waving, more squeaking, more embracing than anywhere else on earth. An English restaurateur would find some way of putting a thin-lipped stop to all this hectic conviviality. If he did not, his staff would leave.

This is the very heart of the difference between the British and the American way of life. The English actually want their jobs to be boring so that they can strike. They wish their friends to be dull so that they need not feel inferior to them. New Yorkers, on the other hand, strenuously resist all tendencies to reduce people and events to their lowest common factor. Many years before I ever dreamed that I would one day visit the United States, a friend wrote to me saying, 'Over here everyone is rich and everyone is handsome.'

This is true but it is not all. My correspondent omitted to add that everyone is eager. This is to me by far the most important attribute of Americans. They want to speak, they want to listen and they will endure quite a lot of inconvenience to prevent the colour from being drained out of experience. They like people to be unusual in any way they know how. Even being foreign will do. Visiting Englishmen they adopt as pets and coo at them as though they were budgies that can nearly speak American. For the same reason they worship actors who, to civilians, are the very icons of that instant success the notion of which even the most down-trodden waif never wholly relinquishes. If a man who was once a farm boy becomes a senator, people are quietly pleased but the metamorphosis has been a lengthy, even a daunting process and no one is still around who can vividly describe those early straw-nibbling years. If, however, someone is in a soap advertisement one year and the next is playing the lead in a technicolor, wide-screen first feature, everyone – even little children – can bear witness to the miracle. In the shrivelled hearts of the English such an event, if it ever occurred, would arouse only envy but in America it would inspire hope.

On the morning of my departure from New York Mr Bennett, who had become aware of my infatuation with his native land, came to thc hotel and presented me with a large American flag. All the way back to Heathrow I wore it as though it were my college scarf. Perhaps this was an act of treason. If accused, I would have pleaded invincible ignorance.

Had I died on the way home, I should have been extremely put out at the time but later, looking down from my cloud, I would have been content.

The purpose of that first visit to the Islands of the Blessed was so that Mr Bennett might cast an eye over me and my agent. He wished to buy the stage rights of *The Naked Civil Servant*. In the end, for reasons that were veiled from me, an option on my autobiography was sold to Mr Elkins, an impresario so famous that a book called *The Producer* has been written about him. When, the following year, I again crossed the Atlantic, it was in order that I might begin to work for him. The nearest I can come to describing the nature of this new employment is to mention I once said that of any event my agent would demand to know if there was any money in it but Mr Elkins would merely ask, 'How often will my name be mentioned?' With this prognosis they both agreed.

I have recently been involved in such a whirlwind courtship of the universe that I cannot now remember whether I initially met my American employer before or after my first visit to New York. I seem to have become aware of his existence gradually from oblique murmurs issuing from my agent's lips.

Like Mr Cook who took me to Australia, Mr Elkins was once an actor. When I asked him why he had become an impresario, he said that it was the only thing that he knew how to do. From this we may infer that promotion is where actors go when they die. I asked the question because indirectly I was learning what an uneasy, even hazardous, profession being an entrepreneur can become. He has to be in possession of the money, the script, the leading actor and the right theatre all on the same day.

Impresarios are frequently asked by televisionaries when some scheme or other first occurred to them. They look at the toe-cap of one expensive shoe and murmur dreamily, 'I got the basic idea in 1946.' I used to think that replies such as this were a joke. I now know they can be only too true.

It is not easy to say whether Mr Elkins enjoys going to the theatre, likes the company of stage people or is fascinated by the complexities of show business. Even if he adores all these aspects of his profession, it still does not explain why he was so keen to own *The Naked Civil Servant*. Perhaps the answer is simply that whatever he wants he wants absolutely. When I first met him he seemed to wish to make my life story into a straight play for presentation in London. Later, to my great relief, the project turned into a musical to be staged on Broadway. I remember saying that I wanted whatever he wanted. His reply was, 'In that case we shall never quarrel.' We never did but, in case I appear to be seeking praise for being self-effacing, I must add that, as my agent once pointed out, I can only afford to be so nice because he's so nasty.

That I always accepted Mr Elkins' judgement does not mean that I understood him. On the contrary, to this day he mystifies me. He is a small man whose energy is out of all proportion to his bulk like something dangerous in nuclear physics and he is made restless by ambition as another man might be wracked by indigestion. Nevertheless, in a life so peripatetic that half of it is spent in the sky, he is a family man constantly getting married, begetting children and being visited by his relatives.

His appearance is as extreme as his nature. His hair is white but his eyes are black. As if this did not make them startling enough, he opens them by lowering his lower lid rather than raising his upper lid and keeps them so wide open that he looks perpetually astonished by the enormity of his commitments.

In contrast with him his newest wife is calm and unusually gentle. Perhaps she is the heart of the hurricane.

Once I had become involved in show business, however peripherally, a question arose which I couldn't help asking myself (since I dared not interrogate the people concerned).

Why do rich men put their money into theatrical ventures?

They cannot possibly be interested in becoming even richer. If that were their aim, they would invest their spare cash in oil or automobiles or, indeed, almost anything rather than the stage.

Speaking in very general terms, I think the answer has to be that 'angels' are interested in girls. I know that, on a rainy night, a woman can be pressed into service for a few pence but, in those circumstances, a man's power over the opposite sex is seldom witnessed by his rivals. This may vitiate the sense of triumph. If, however, he allows it to be known that he finances plays, then, wherever he goes in public, all women within a radius of half a mile will creep a little closer to him and, with elaborate unconcern, will present him with their noble profiles or worse. With no effort on his part, Mr Midas can thus surround himself with girls, all of them daring, some of them beautiful and a few with talent – if anyone cares. Furthermore, at any moment (and there must be many) when the conversation in his club becomes boring, a man in these circumstances can glance at his digital watch and sigh, 'I'm afraid I simply must run along and see how my latest show is doing.' As he rises from his ragged leather chair, all eyes will turn enviously towards him, all hearts will silently ask the palpitating question, 'Does he really know Miss Christie and, if so, how well?' If wealth is thus devoted to the strengthening of an image of masculine desirability rather than squandered on Inland Revenue – that old whore who will do anything for money – few of us would think it had been unwisely spent.

Although I never met any of them, I presume it was with these strange men that Mr Elkins so feverishly dealt.

The smiling and nodding racket has many branches. Chief among these is to be interviewed by televisionaries or on radio programmes. For this purpose I went whizzing round the United States – to Boston, to Chicago (where, to my surprise, there was not a glimpse of Edward G. Robinson) and so on. Mr Warhol's first law states that it is possible to be famous for being famous. A corollary of this axiom is that you can often be interviewed simply because you are so often interviewed.

Of the two media, radio and television, I prefer the latter. Even in real life I tend to act out whatever I am saying. This habit is not only useless if no one can see me, it also lulls me into thinking that I am being more expressive than I am in audible terms. On television I feel free but I rapidly learned to conceal my enthusiasm. The technicians despised me when they realized that I was enjoying myself.

In a small way, being an interviewee is a craft. It certainly requires a technique. It is essential to bear in mind that facial movements are exaggerated by photography. If you roll your eyes, they will step out of your skull and slide across the screen. On the other hand, the microphone bevels the edges of even the most articulate voice. You must therefore keep your features calm while charging your voice with melodramatic emphasis – a little like rubbing your head and patting your stomach at the same time.

While performing this feat, you must try to remain aware which camera is watching you and also calculate how much of you it can see. If I did not think my hands were visible I tried, which isn't easy, not to move them at all. I thought that viewers might be aware that some hidden gesture was being made and might be distracted by trying to guess what it was. Even when you are sure that your hands can be seen, you have to remember to hold every gesture long enough for the camera to turn towards it and tell the world what it has seen. These seemed to me to be the chief purely mechanical problems of being interviewed.

The remaining difficulty lies in becoming aware, before your brief moment in the limelight is half over, what kind of reaction is expected of you. As I crossed the States, I became involved in every possible interpretation of my life, grave, flippant, political, psychological, religious. In the Far West, I came face to face with Mr Snyder. He is in the human document industry so remembered anguish could not be shuffled off with a jolly laugh. With Mr Cavett in New York, I was in the entertainment business. It was with him that I felt most at ease. He is working with and for his conscripted audience in the studio and he sits beside rather than opposite you. He is your straight man (comic as opposed to bent) and he obligingly feeds you questions to which he already knows the punch lines.

If your interrogator seems to have no definite method of conducting the dialogue, it may be necessary to treat the situation like a geography examination. Few of us have enough stamina to study the whole world so we trust to luck. The night before our test, we take our atlas from its shelf, blow the tell-tale dust from the top of it and open it at random. If the pages part at China, that is what we study. Of course, the next day we discover that the main question in our paper concerns France. Our answer begins, 'France is not like China.' Translated into television terms, this means that if you arrive at the studios with a wonderful anecdote about your mother and some ill-briefed clot says, 'How's your father?' you reply, 'Father's worn out coping with my mother who . . .' This would be described by a lawyer as converting public questions to private use.

Another by no means distasteful duty that I felt I owed to Mr Elkins was to be photographed as often as possible. At a party given in honour of Miss Midler at the Waldorf Hotel, I was led across the room to meet her. We shook hands and exchanged a few gracious phrases to give the photographers time to gather round us. Then, standing as close to her as I dared, I turned towards the largest camera and smiled. Very quietly Miss Midler whispered, 'That's right, baby. Do the whole bit.'

I have followed her instructions ever since.

Whenever I become aware that I am being photographed, I give myself over to the occasion as completely as I can. I stand where I am told to stand. I try to look as I am required to look. As I am not paying for the results of all this attention, it seems the least I can do. Although it may be no such thing, I behave as though anyone's desire to take a picture of me is a compliment. Doing this is a politeness exactly parallel with giving my full attention to the kind remarks of strangers. For this reason, though I play up to the camera if I am given time, were I 'snapped' unawares, I would never try to prevent an unflattering or even a ludicrous likeness of me being printed.

I am not feverishly interested in the end product. Given a picture of myself I would accept it though I would not frame it or hang it on the wall. If I am not offered a print, I do not ask for one. This attitude is probably the result of having worked in art schools for so many years. When I first took up that profession, the model's lowly station in life debarred him from walking casually about the 'life' room. I would never have been employed again in any establishment where I had made so bold as to stare critically at the drawings that were being done.

Nowadays there is no reason why models should not survey the paintings of students and even comment upon them. Democracy is here to stay. Nevertheless old-timers seldom take advantage of the new regime. Others apart from me are aware that this is so. A short while ago, just before I gave up posing in art colleges, I was resting between sessions in one room when a model from another class came and scrutinized the work in progress. After she had departed, the art master, in tones of glacial contempt, said, 'The hallmark of an amateur.'

In spite of my indifference to the end product I cannot help being aware that the earth is now passing through the second photographic age.

The first began just before or during the Great War when the box camera, the 'Brownie', brought the taking of snapshots within reach of the middle classes both financially and in terms of expertise. In that distant time, the criterion of a good photograph was simply that all the relevant subject matter was clearly recognizable. There was no nonsense about composition then. In fact, when I was young, photography was considered to be the enemy of art. Somebody once brought disgrace upon himself when he tried to show at the Royal Academy's summer exhibition a picture found by the judges to have been painted over a photographic background. Today, though it might be thought dull, this method of working would in no way be considered immoral. All students are encouraged to learn to use a camera properly firstly because carrying small reproductions of their work is so much less burdensome than carting actual canvases to art galleries and advertising agencies and secondly so as to have something from which to work when the light on a landscape changes or a model drops dead.

Today there is no opposition by art to photography. Cameras and artist's materials are equally aesthetic and equally expensive but both have become the paraphernalia of a game any number can play. Though cameras are now far more sophisticated than formerly, they have passed through the phase when they were difficult to use and emerged into the common light of day almost amateur-proof. It is no longer miraculous to be able to make a visual record of a person or an event. We have moved on to a point at which the design and the lighting of a photograph come under perpetual discussion. Perhaps the notion that aesthetic values are involved helps to justify the financial outlay.

I am only aware how universal the second photographic age has become because I am so often in the line of fire. This does not mean that my appearance has recently improved. It only signifies that I have become more notorious. At best the reason for taking a picture of me is that it can be sold to a newspaper, at worst it is proof that the person shown standing beside me has actually met me.

In a copy of the *Readers Digest*, I once read that the duck-billed platypus must eat twice its own weight in worms every day or it may die. The man who took the excellent picture of me used on the cover of the paperback edition of my autobiography was the platypus of the camera. He seemed to feel compelled daily to consume his own weight in celluloid. Since meeting him I have come to realize that a great many photographers are obsessed with their occupation; they take pictures of everything. Presumably this is partly because once again cameras have become so easily portable.

When I was a model I was bewildered that the

desire to paint overtook people who could have stayed in bed all day but I saw that at least an artist has the pleasure of passing judgement on his environment and, by distortion, ruling or even defeating it. Some would say he could not help doing this. The craze for photography is even more baffling. To invent a critical vision with the aid of a camera is much harder but, having recently stood before a great many photographers, even going as high as Mr Scavullo, I have become dimly aware that they too are converting me to their own use – that deep down I am only a sentence, perhaps a mere comma – in the forever unfinished essay that each of them is writing about the visible world.

It is hardly surprising that, by some means or other, each man is trying to record his personal view of the universe. What is amazing is that nations do the same thing. There are national styles in photography. When, in England, I return at nightfall to my room, I turn on my television set without the sound. While I make my lumpy tea and green toast, I glance from time to time at the screen. When the image is American – even if it is only of a blade of grass – I know this immediately. The outline is clearer, the contrast between light and dark is stronger and the object looks more worth the money. I wonder if American photographers are redeeming my image in the same way.

The first time that I actually went on an American stage and addressed a paying audience was in Newhaven at the smaller of the two Long Wharf Theatres.

Someone had told me that this was where the plays of Mr O'Neill were originally performed. Perhaps because so many of his works have a nautical theme, I imagined that to reach the auditorium, the public would be compelled to walk along a booming wooden verandah beneath dangerously swinging hurricane lamps and that the stalls would smell of dead fish. I now saw that the two theatres and sundry other buildings were welded into a concrete structure that formed one boundary of a huge meat market. On the other side was a Howard Johnson Hotel where I stayed. From the window of my room, while I put on my stage clothes, I could watch people arriving sometimes at my theatre but more often at the larger one where *Journey's End* was being performed. Both the Long Wharf Theatres were run by a small staff of very young people who mercifully displayed the minimum of artiness and who were very friendly. Sometimes they and at other times total strangers took me round Newhaven. Wherever we went, apologies were offered for the provinciality of the environment. Had no one mentioned it, I would never have noticed. There, as everywhere I went in America, I invested everything I saw with the wonder I felt at being there at all.

Newhaven is a university town but, unlike Oxford, not affectedly so. For the most part the colleges are tactfully woven in with the surrounding architecture and the students do not look conspicuously different from real people. I went to Yale on two occasions, once at the invitation of a member of the staff and again because a rogue student asked me. On both days I was far out of my depth but remained precariously afloat on a tide of American courtesy. On my second visit I found myself among the divinity students to whom I was required to explain You-Know-Who. I began to comply with this request in a very shaky voice but soon found that, though my audience was lively, it was not disputatious. In the United States the vocabulary of undergraduates is not ostentatiously polysyllabic nor is their discourse seasoned to choking point with obscure quotations. From this entire escapade I conclude that it is the practice of American universities deliberately but in small doses to expose their inmates to the more bizarre aspects of the outer world. Experience is evidently thought to be more fortifying than mere learning.

At all first nights staged by Mr Elkins, the audience is as much under his control as the actors. The theatre is full of smiling faces, clapping hands. This is part of his method of presentation. He also carries with him on such occasions a file for bevelling the nails of critics. I could not therefore at first be sure how I was being received by America but, as my two weeks in Newhaven wore on, I began to assume a certain reciprocity in my audiences. I am not saying that every word I uttered was given a totally favourable reception but, except by the gay papers, I was seldom savaged.

From Newhaven I went to Washington and New York. There I stayed in the Algonquin Hotel, a deliberately and very charmingly old-fashioned establishment run less for profit than as a shrine sacred to the memory of that far off time when Dorothy Parker was alive and bitching. During my stay there, one of her contemporaries, Mr Connolly, was brought back from the dead to be interviewed in that very room where once stood the round table at which they sat. The first question asked of him was, 'Do you think that conversation is as witty now as it was in the good old days?' He replied, 'Mine is.'

If in the Algonquin I was given a 'good' table at breakfast time, I could be seen by all the guests who came and went in the lobby. By these means democracy was put to the ultimate test. A man came to my table and said, 'I am the congressman from Minnesota.' For a moment I feared that I had done something unconstitutional but he only wished to say a few kind words. I thanked him and he returned to his party at a distant table. If you try to imagine an English cabinet minister walking the entire length of a public place to speak to me, you will instantly see how far we have to go before we become a truly homogenized society.

In the Algonquin people talked to me for free; those who could be bamboozled into paying came to the Players' Theatre. This is situated on the western side of Washington Square, a district that has changed somewhat since the characters in Mr James's novels lived there. In London my engagement there would be comparable to appearing in Dean Street.

As soon as I saw the Players' Theatre, I thought

it the ideal place for me to work. The inside looked as though it had once been a kinky cinema. The auditorium, which held about two hundred and forty people, was long and narrow but I never had the least difficulty in being heard – even when, halfway through the run, my voice clouded over from fatigue. I never succeeded in filling the place but even a handful of people looked adequate and seemed to feel comfortable.

Until I reached New York I had always used whatever stage furniture each theatre could provide. Now the stage manager was asked to buy the required props. I was amazed at the thought that he lavished upon this small chore. For instance, when I remarked that any old chair would do, he said that it must not have a fabric seat, it must be made of something that permitted me to slide hither and thither.

'Well, yes,' I conceded, 'but, apart from that . . . .'

'And it must be so light that you can easily drag it forward or push it back.'

'That's true but . . . '

'And it must have arms that you can lean against.'

He even bought a few ferns to make the occasion look like a Dickensian celebrity lecture.

In New York, our engagement began not with a bang but a whimper. We embarked on a series of previews to invited audiences. The purpose of these was partly to acclimatize New Yorkers to me but mostly to familiarize me, before the critics could get at me, with the shortened version of the show which Mr Elkins had translated into

American. During my first few evenings, if anything distracted my concentration while I was on stage, my lips automatically moved back into the sentences that they had become accustomed to uttering during the past three years. By the time the night of the critics had fallen, I was used to the new edition of the show.

The critics were amazingly kind to me.

Americans boast that they are a violent people and politically they are. They have killed twice as many politicians as we have murdered kings but, in the world of the theatre, both critics and audiences have velvet paws. Not even Mr Barnes denied that I was offering entertainment. Almost everybody's attitude was softened by the fact that I am a foreigner – nay, an outcast, an old man and alone. Guessing this to be so, it became difficult not to exploit my disadvantages. I stood forever on the brink of flirting with my audiences instead of performing for them. In theatrical terms this was a sin; socially it seemed to be a virtue or, to say the least, useful.

During my run at the Players' Theatre many events occurred that were surprising and some that were positively hilarious. One night, when I had been on stage for about twenty minutes, the lights began to flicker and some thumping noises issued from the wings. (Really I should say wing; it was only possible to reach the stage from one side.) Then suddenly the lights were extinguished altogether. I asked the electrician, who was lurking behind a curtain, if there just might be something wrong and he admitted that the electrical system was being rebellious. Someone in the audience suggested that we should go on as though nothing unpleasant had happened. I agreed to do this but at this moment the emergency lighting was switched on giving the place a Waterloo Station look and the owner of the building walked down the aisle to announce that the theatre was on fire. In a soothing voice he suggested that we should all leave. The mildness of his manner worked a miracle. There was no panic. Sitting on the stage, I watched everyone leave quietly as though a church service had just ended.

Almost at once an engine arrived with five firemen. Like an illustration to one of Gulliver's travels, helmeted and armed with iron pikes, these benign giants stomped on to the tiny stage. They wore boots that would have carried them through a flood.

Where two or three firemen are gathered together, there will be photographers also. Never asleep at his post, the stage manager instantly saw this occasion as an opportunity for a little publicity. He asked the Titans if they would be willing to have their picture taken with me. I have been told that the Fire Department has raised strong objections to the notion of employing known homosexuals but the invaders complied with the stage manager's request at once. The resulting picture could not be used for publicity purposes because the least suggestion that the theatre was unsafe would have been fatal but it was printed in a magazine called *Where It's At*. In brilliant lighting and holding a glass as though I were about to propose a toast, I stand before these shadowy Titans grouped in heroic postures. By a knowing eye it can just be seen that they are sending me up but so gently that together we form one of the funniest tableaux in which I have ever been involved. Every time that I look at this photograph I am surprised afresh to observe that there is a fire face. These men look more alike than most brothers. All have round, handsome faces decorated with mini-walrus moustaches and tiny laughing eyes.

Soon after this comic turn, another slighter but more enigmatic incident occurred. Someone in the audience asked if I thought that Jesus had style. I had often been questioned about You-Know-Who but very seldom interrogated about his son. As always before I talk about any religious issue, I said, 'Would anyone prefer that I did not answer this query? I wouldn't like to give offence.' Someone shouted, 'Why stop now?' so I explained that, in my opinion, the style resided either in Mr Nazareth or his biographers. This remark led me into quoting the passage from the New Testament about the woman at the well. As I began to say, 'He that drinketh of this water shall thirst again . . . ' the house seemed not only to grow quieter but also colder. This change of temperature was not lost on the stage manager. He later decided that, although it was permissible for me to express my ideas about religion in general, I must never again quote from the Scriptures. Perhaps the audience was shocked to find that anyone so wicked knew the Bible so well.

I was at the Players' Theatre for eleven weeks. By that time it was recognized by the experts that no amount of advertising could keep the show going any longer. I returned to England.

There my feeble efforts to entertain a small number of well-wishers in a tiny theatre on a dim side street in an unfashionable part of New York were described as a Broadway triumph. It has always surprised me to find that anyone at all accepts without question what the newspapers say: I was positively astonished to discover that apparently even journalists believe the outrageous statements of other pressmen.

It was impossible to define what Mr Elkins had expected not merely of my appearance in MacDougal Street but of the entire American venture. As an impresario he almost certainly succumbs from time to time to what Mr Miller calls 'the dreams that come with the territory', but in some respects he is a realist. While I was in Australia, he was in communication with Mr Cook and from him learned that no amount of publicity could inflate my poor market value to any great degree. He also knew that, in a sense, the larger the audience the less satisfying the show was bound to become because it depends on its chattiness. All the same he may secretly have hoped that we could fill a small theatre indefinitely.

In financial terms it is probable that he thought of me as a walking, talking tax loss.

What the people who came to hear me took away from the performance I have no idea. One night, during the interval, a member of the audience came up on to the stage and sat for a while in the other chair. 'What can I say?' she asked. 'What can I give you?' Before I could make out a list, she had taken from round her neck a gold chain. This she placed in my lap. What folly! What wonderful folly! Gestures of generosity such as this, the letters, the hospitality that were showered upon me have made me examine very carefully the almost mystical relationship between the solo performer and American audiences. The enigma certainly does not originate in me. I offer the world nothing but my availability – myself. The mystery must therefore spring from the United States. New York is that Aaronic rock which, if you strike it in the hope of unleashing a miracle, will reward you with a perpetual flow of love.

If I ask myself what I originally wanted from a visit to America, I can now give no reply. The fulfilment has outstripped the expectation.

When not on stage, not being interviewed by straight television or the gay press, I was being lavishly entertained – sometimes by people I had met in England, on other occasions by individuals or groups whom I knew little or not at all. These festivities usually took place in the middle of the night after the show. This was largely due to the fact that, although whenever it rains in New York it rains credit cards from heaven, most of the city's inhabitants work. In England regular employment is considered by those who can find it to be a way of winning eternal life on the principle that work tastes so nasty it must be doing you good. To Americans a job is an excuse for going out into the world where at any moment they may encounter success or, at the very worst, true love.

Almost until dawn generosity was lavished upon me as though I were a star. As Mr Auden has said, 'God bless the USA, so large, so friendly and so rich.' I was not only fed until I could hardly stand but transported in purring limousines to the homes of total strangers and returned in the same fashion to my hotel. This was common practice even when my hosts lived outside Manhattan. Just as well. I still spoke no American and have no sense of direction other than downwards. On one occasion I was even taken to and returned from Staten Island. That day it looked like a Christmas card painted by Mr Breughel. The snow was untouched by human foot and from this Tide-white surface sprang astonishingly black trees. Because the terrain is as lumpy as school porridge, my eye was everywhere greeted by a landscape either spread out beneath or towering above it. The world presented itself as artists see it with the very minimum of sky.

The sky is a mistake.

During the day I spent a certain amount of time sitting in my hotel room. Every now and again my solitude was beguilingly interrupted by telephone calls from journalists asking for my views on topics so general that even I was able to express an opinion about them.

'What do you think will happen in 1979?'

'Everything will get worse.'

'Marvellous. Thank you so much. Goodbye.'

In my mind's ear I hear a compositor speaking

on his intercommunications system to his editor.

'Is that you, chief?'

'What is it now, Albert?'

'Well, I've set the piece on Pregnancy after Forty and it doesn't quite come to the bottom of the column. Shall I reset the whole thing in eighteen point?'

'How much space is there left to fill?'

'About half an inch.'

'Don't bother. It'll be cheaper to ring up Quentin.'

When not incongruously posing for the papers as one of the sages of the ages, I watched television.

In England all good television programmes have come across the Atlantic. If the men are running fast and shooting straight, they are Americans. British television tends to be as boring as being alive. Perhaps I should say as boring as life used to be.

However, when you are in New York where so many channels are available, where so many hours of the day and night have to be filled with something, monotony does sometimes flood the screen. Low tide in entertainment begins at midday and continues until about half-past four in the afternoon. In this temporal desert, five or six continuing narratives flourish like cacti on the very minimum of sustenance. They are so alike that, with practice, a viewer could switch from the question in one story to the answer in another. Each episode of each programme begins thus.

'Have you a moment to spare?' (A needless

enquiry: the entire cast has a lifetime to spare.)

'Of course, do sit down.'

'Thank you. I want to talk to you. I'm worried about Marge. I don't think Gerry is right for her.'

'Ah, if only she hadn't left Andy . . .'

Occasionally into this world of middle-brow, middle-class women, men are introduced. They are always as handsome as the sun with eyes the size of chicken's eggs and they have never in their lives taken anything seriously except a mirror. Even so, they too have opinions as to whether or not Gerry is right for Marge.

By the end of every afternoon at least three women are in hospital. They suffer from the effects of self-administered poison, self-administered alcohol or pregnancy administered by someone who isn't right for them. Day after day I sat before one of the Algonquin's television sets waiting for one of the characters on the screen to say, 'Don't you think that perhaps we should stop meddling in the lives of others?'

These words were never spoken.

Although I never ceased to send them up, I did not really mind whiling away the daylight hours with these pageants of domestic anguish. I was seduced by their unreality. The only programmes than see which I would rather do anything – even work – are those which involve real people as opposed to actors. During the most sombre stretches of television when the screen was disfigured with panels, quizzes or the news, I was frequently saved by *New York Magazine*.

To find out if it was feasible for me to work for

such an illustrious magazine, my agent took me to Second Avenue to call on a certain Miss Koenig, who rules the paper's book page. She not only found the idea acceptable but allowed me to write almost anything that came into my head and further indulged me by giving an office tea party for me just before I left America.

I also became involved in a curious subdivision of the profession of book reviewing of which until recently I had never heard. Publishers sent me uncorrected proofs of forthcoming books not exactly for criticism but rather in the hope of cajoling me into making a few favourable comments which could be woven in with other blandishments on the dust-jackets of their first editions.

Aware that I owe a great deal to the world in general and to the United States in particular, I always try to find something nice to say about whatever rubbish I am given to read. I do this partly so as not to find myself inhabiting a jungle infested with angry novelists who might snarl at me if our paths cross and partly because to produce even the slenderest volume costs money and it is therefore sacred. Even when on one occasion I was sent yet another survey on homosexuality, this time so gross that nothing commendatory could be written about it, I tried to turn my disapproval to account. After all there are many quarters where my disapprobation is considered to be praise.

I once heard someone complain that my critiques of books are less about what I have just read than about myself. I was surprised at this remark. I almost always describe a book first as a physical object: I then say something about its contents and the style in which these are presented. It is true that I quite often pause to explain why I hold the opinions to which I have given expression and, on occasion, I throw in an anecdote in which I have played some part. When working for Mr Kington of *Punch*, I do this because he has said that, from any book review, he hopes to learn something about the critic as well as about the work under discussion. When I adopt this procedure elsewhere, I do so because it seems so unlikely that any editor would solicit my ideas on the grounds that I am a literary authority; it seems much more probable that he thinks that his readers may be curious about me as a person.

Books are for writing – not for reading. Nevertheless I gladly peruse anything sent to me for review. I need the money and the fragment of publicity that accrues from signing a few hundred words in a magazine may be helpful. When I ask Mr Carter for permission to live in America forever, it must seem that I am perpetually in work. Though I would prefer to do absolutely nothing at all, I do not dislike composing pieces of prose if they are short. When I come to the end of them, I may, with luck, still be able to remember what I said at the beginning but, if I write a whole book, after a while I am overtaken by the fear that I have begun to state the opposite of what I said at the outset. I am then forced to read my first few chapters over again. I find re-reading even my own deathless prose tedious in the extreme.

The writing of books is much harder than painting even the largest picture because narrative is disposed in time rather than space. For an artist to be able to appreciate the difficulties that beset authors, he would have to imagine designing a mural that continued from one room to another. Then he would be forever running from the end of his frieze to the beginning and back again to make sure that all the details contributed in the right measure to the final effect. This is what a novelist or a biographer is compelled to do every day.

If, by now, you are weeping for me, dry your tears. The book that you hold in your hand or, possibly, have just flung on to the floor is almost certainly the last that I shall ever attempt to write.

Shortly before I left MacDougal Street someone came to my dressing-room (which was really a dance rehearsal room above the stage) and announced that he wished to make a record of the show. I was a little less disbelieving than I might have been because about two years previously I had encountered a Mr Napier-Bell who had in mind a similar but even more outlandish scheme. He wanted me to sing. This proposal I simply could not take seriously at all. My speaking voice has been described by the kinder newspapers as 'tarnished silver'. If this is an apt phrase, then my singing is like rusty tin. It has no resonance, no range, no volume. Furthermore I have no sense of rhythm or melody.

There are two main ways in which a person may find it difficult to keep in tune. He may either be unable to predict what sound will come out of his face or, if two noises have different qualities, such as a piano and the human voice, he may be quite unable to tell whether or not they have the same pitch. I suffer from both these handicaps.

All this I explained to Mr Napier-Bell on the telephone. He insisted on visiting me.

He looked like Mr Redford but without the permanent expression of suppressed contempt. He was most polite but quite determined.

Mr N-B: Everybody can sing – even you.

Me: Tra-la.

Mr N-B: You're quite right; you can't sing but you can speak a lyric.

Me: Like Mr Harrison?

Mr N-B: No. Like Miss Dietrich.

So I started off in the legendary world-weary moan to say that I was falling in love again. A likely story!

I had not uttered more than a few bars when my visitor interrupted me. 'No. That won't do,' he said. 'It's not you.'

For our experiment he had chosen a lyric made famous by Miss Lee, presumably on the principle that we should emulate the best. It was a song of mourning not for lost love but for vanished happiness. Before Mr Napier-Bell left, we had agreed that I need not imitate anyone but should intone this elegy in a voice charged with feigned emotion.

My task-master was infinitely patient. He caused the lyric to be typed out like a poem so that I could learn my lines by heart and he left with me a quaint machine no bigger than a match box on which he showed me how to play the required tune over and over and over. The difference between this elegant gadget and the huge metal box into which I had spoken words for Mr O'Connor told me how much time had passed since then. As the years rush by, people become bigger but mechanical devices get smaller.

When, as nearly as I was ever likely to, I understood what I was meant to do, a day was fixed for making a record.

In a dim basement in Denmark Street, there is a sinister room divided down the middle by a huge glass wall. The two halves of this studio can only communicate through the microphone or by sign language. In one part there is an instrument panel as complicated as that which bewildered Miss Day when she was required to land an air liner aided only by instructions from the control tower. When you hire this demon machine you are allotted a man like a gift in a packet of Shredded Wheat. He and Mr Napier-Bell sat side by side behind this science-fiction object. I went into the other half of the room. There I found nothing but a huge microphone. I stood in front of this wearing earphones through which the now horribly familiar tune assaulted my skull at discotheque level. At a sign from Mr Napier-Bell I took a deep breath. Before I had uttered a sound, I was waving my arms to indicate that we must begin again. I had not realized that every time I breathed the microphone would emit a hoarse growl. I was told this did not matter and we started afresh.

I think I did about four renderings of Miss Lee's song, before I was allowed into the other part of the room to hear one of them. Having no notion of what was expected of me I was neither shocked nor pleased by what I heard until I noticed that in the word 'never' the second syllable was inaudible. When I mentioned this defect, the man who belonged to the machine slowly dragged a switch along a groove then suddenly with the speed of light moved his hand to another switch and back again. With no more fuss than this, the word 'never' was transferred from another sound track on to the one that was considered the least feeble. I know now that a mouse could give an adequate rendering of 'Softly Awakes my Heart' if the technical staff was on her side.

Nothing ever came of the record that Mr Napier-Bell was trying so hard to make. In a way I was sorry. He was so indulgent with me that he deserved some reward. Also I hate being part of any project which is finally a dead loss to someone who has taken an interest in me but I think it is just as well that this particular dream – this particular nightmare – was never translated into fact.

The idea put forward by the man who came to my dressing-room at the Players' Theatre was a little more realistic; he only wanted to record my speaking voice. Like a fire bucket his request was passed along the chain of employees that connected me with Mr Elkins and some days later we received permission to proceed. The stage manager and I rushed straight from MacDougal Street to a nearby recording studio. This differed from the room in Denmark Street in that this time I and the microphone were in a larger room filled with conscripted listeners.

The occasion was an ordeal because, by the time the record was complete, it was well after midnight and I had been speaking for four-and-a-half hours but the evening was made worthwhile by my discovery that in the audience was Miss Comden.

When the record was released in England, to promote it I was whirled round Britain by a member of the staff of EMI. I asked him what the three mysterious letters meant and he replied, 'Every Man for 'Imself'.

Apart from New York, the only other American city in which my theatrical engagement was prolonged was Los Angeles. From the very first morning that I awoke in California, I felt abundantly well. There was a warm film of moist air lying on my face. It was as though I were living in a happy Ireland – if you can imagine anything so far-fetched. We were staying at the Beverley Hills Hotel in a splendour to which sadly I shall never become accustomed; there isn't enough time left.

My agent thought that what few spare hours were allowed to us we should spend by the swimming pool on the grounds that we might never again be where this symbol of luxury was available. I was frightened by the boiling sun and the frying people but I forced myself to be brave. My efforts turned out to be worthwhile. On a modern version of a chaise longue lay a gentleman who was revealed to be a doctor when his name was called by a telephone assistant. The instrument, on a cable of infinite length, was brought to him at once but for a long while he was obviously unable to stem the flood of words that flowed from the other end of the wire and which, try as we might, we could not hear. They evidently formed some patient's cry for help because when at last he could make himself heard, the physician said, 'I'll do my best to get around to you later in the day but we're terribly understaffed here.' He then laid the telephone down beside the pool and sank back into a recumbent posture.

I have one of my spies even in Los Angeles. When I told him where I was staying and invited him to visit me, he confessed to being intimidated by my setting but he summoned up sufficient courage to fetch me in his purring limousine and drive me to his home. Like many householders in this area he lives his entire life in that hazardous moment which occurs in all cartoon films when the victim, fleeing before his pursuers, does not notice that he has run out of land and is treading air over a bottomless abyss. My friend's house juts out horizontally from the side of a valley regardless of the fact that the earth slopes vertiginously downward below it. From his verandah in the sky it is possible with a telescope (which he has) to survey the whole celluloid kingdom. The dinky rurality that characterizes the English countryside is nowhere to be seen. The view looks like a Japanese painting; each range of mountains is green at the top but fades into a yellowish mist behind the next bright row of hills. Never before have I beheld a natural vista so beautifully conventionalized.

Apart from this delightful excursion in my friend's car most of my days were spent on Sunset Boulevard. The palm trees along either side of this legendary thoroughfare are of an astonishing height but their growth has obviously cost them a great effort; they look very tired. Once a year, as with some of the human inhabitants of the neighbourhood, an expert makes his rounds to groom them for continued stardom. Sunset Boulevard leads from the hotel to the television station where I was interviewed by Mr Snyder. To English eyes he appears blindingly handsome but in California his looks count for less because there standards are so high. Great care is taken to present not only him but his entire programme in a glamorous light. When later I saw the one in which I appeared I noticed that even I had been to some extent redeemed.

Though I have glanced fleetingly at so much geographical splendour in recent years, Los Angeles is by far the most idyllic region through which I have ever passed. There it is always summer; there happiness rains down from the sky; there pretty women and awards grow on trees. By the beginning of April the gardens of the rich are choked with roses the size of cabbages. Humming birds pause in the air above you or dart between the trees like microdot Supermen while, twice the size of these tiny creatures, swallowtail butterflies, which in England are as rare as number fourteen buses, do barre work on the edge of your breakfast table. It saddened me to see that, in spite of all this beauty, the word most often printed on the roadside hoardings was 'hypnotist' and on one occasion, 'Hip hypnotist'. It would seem that the inhabitants of this earthly paradise are not content with it. They devote a considerable amount of time and energy to attempting to enrich their environment still further. First they tried religion, then drugs, then meditation and now hypnosis.

All this cut-price transcendentalism does not prevent California from being a startlingly physical state. This becomes most obvious where Los Angeles saunters down to the sea. The region is called Venice. In the distance lies the Pacific. It is a rich swimming-pool blue and despite its terrifying vastness, it tiptoes towards the shore like a woman approaching a sleeping baby but no one ever dips so much as a lacquered toe into it. The sand, on which no child ever plays, is dented with sand pits. These are furnished with large varieties of gymnasium equipment used so continuously and with such vigour that locally there has sprung up a tribe of men who, like women of the 1890s, cannot lay their arms against their sides. This affliction restricted ladies of the Edwardian era because their ball gowns were padded under the arms. In California today it attacks the men because they have so strenuously developed their dorsal muscles. This has been done to acquire the bat's-wing silhouette so greatly to be desired.

While the males of Los Angeles widen their contours by every means possible, the females narrow theirs. New Yorkers talk about what they eat; Californians go into ecstasies over what they refrain from eating.

During our stay in this heaven on earth, we were invited by Mr and Mrs Elkins to a party at their home on Mulholland Drive. This must be the longest street in the world – the address was in five figures. Our hosts' house was made entirely of glass. Of this I approved – it placed them in the availability business too. The guests were either lawyers or actresses. Among the latter was Miss Browne who told me that giving talks to American universities could easily be converted into a way of life. She said that there are so many that by the time you have visited all of them and returned to New York for a good cry, the day has arrived to start out again. By then the students whom you have addressed so far will all have gone out into the world. I regarded this information as most heartening. It suggested a way in which I might meet more people than I had thought possible – and all without paying my fare.

As I was leaving the party, Mrs Elkins put her head into the car for a moment and said, 'I promised you America and you shall have it.'

In a way I did.

The End

Long after *The Naked Civil Servant* had been translated into a television play but before I had ever been abroad, I returned one last time to St Alban's College of Art where I had been employed intermittently for more than thirty years. I was already standing on my piece of tat in one of the 'life' rooms waiting for the housewives' choice class to begin when the first student arrived. She greeted me pleasantly and added, 'So you've come back to us.'

'Yes, madam.'

'You *were* a nine days' wonder, weren't you?'

'Yes, madam.'

In quite a long time this was the most coolly bitchy – the most English – remark that had been flung at me. Malice is in no way redeemed by being true. The past four years have obviously been band-wagon stuff. I never became, nor shall I ever become, entrenched in the public consciousness. I have not been nor shall I ever be written into even the most frivolous history of my epoch. I never worked in the centre ring of the three-ring circus of show business but, with the help of the people mentioned in these pages, I came nearer to the 'big time' than I ever dreamed I would.

I speak of all this at what to many may seem disproportionate length because I have approached the heart of the world from such a galactic perimeter; there have been so many radiation belts to penetrate and I came so totally unarmed. Nay, I can say more. Never in the history of the printed word has so much mileage been squeezed out of one flimsy book.

By the time this last instalment of my life story is published, I shall have returned to the United States. Either the musical based on my autobiography will have been produced or the project will have been abandoned. In either case, when all the public speaking and the public living are over, when the being interviewed on television and the being photographed for the papers are done, I shall make the first important decision that I have made in a long time. I shall timorously approach the immigration authorities of the United States to ask their permission to spend the rest of my life in New York. Even this dramatic change of habitat will alter my mode of being less than some might think. Wherever I am on this earth, I am and shall always be only a resident alien. People are never with me, they are always in my presence. I am never involved in conversation, I am always being interviewed.

If I am allowed to stay in America, if I can scrape together sufficient money to subsist indefinitely in the fizzy air of Manhattan, I must remember that I shall no longer be the recipient of the special attention the island has so far always bestowed upon me. I shall by then have become at least an honorary member of its divine race of denizens. It will then be my turn to dispense unfailing generosity – if not in money, then in some other currency. In other words it will be my duty to acquire and to manifest the typical American virtues.

When I was burbling on in this fashion to a BBC reporter in New York, he asked me if I did not think my attitude disloyal to Britain. I gasped but quickly converted this unsophisticated reaction to a deep breath taken before launching into a eulogy of my native land.

The question deserves a careful answer. Until recent times, on a superficial level, English society has stared at me from beneath raised eyebrows and spoken of me with thin curved lips but I must never deny that fundamentally the mildness of the British temperament, as codified in its minimum risk laws, is what has made it possible for me to survive into old age. For many years, in spite of pathological laziness and conspicuous lack of talent, I have been permitted to earn a living somehow. Now I am kept by the state for which, unlike Mr Othello, I have done no service. In Russia, in China, in Cuba, I would long ago have been shot – or worse.

Britain cherishes her eccentrics and wisely holds that the function of government is to build a walled garden in which anarchy can flourish. The entire island is a home for incorrigibles where the very young, the very old and those, who, from any cause whatsoever, feel ill-equipped to live will be protected. For these reasons, though I make fun of England with every breath I draw, I have never seriously criticized her.

Unfortunately I am living my later years with their time factor reversed. I ought to have crossed the Atlantic in early middle age and should now be coming home to die but thirty years ago my poverty and my general ineffectuality prevented me from attempting a journey so daring. Now, in the winter of my life, I have been carried across the ocean as though on a plate. This astonishing piece of good fortune I must not waste.

Perhaps the wisest course of action for me to adopt will be to lie down on the White House steps and, when the occupant opens the door, to start whimpering those lines engraved round the plinth of the Statue of Liberty: 'Bring me your huddled masses yearning to breathe free . . .'

If ever there was a huddled mass . . .

RESIDENT ALIEN
The New York Diaries

Edited with an Introduction by
Donald Carroll

CONTENTS

1993

1994

INTRODUCTION

Some years ago the American journalist and editor Willie Morris wrote a fine memoir called *North Toward Home* in which he described his motives, and his experiences, in leaving Mississippi to live in New York City. With that precedent in mind, it occurred to me that perhaps these journals should be called *West Toward Home*. Eventually I rejected the idea – just as, thirty years ago, when I was editing Quentin's autobiography, I vetoed the idea of calling it *I Reign in Hell*, preferring instead his alternative title, *The Naked Civil Servant*. With the present volume I decided against *West Toward Home* because Quentin's homing instincts are fixed on people, not places. Indeed, when we first met he confided, 'I don't hold with abroad' – adding, for emphasis, 'I know, for example, the French speak English when our backs are turned.'

So for this most English of Englishmen (whatever he may say) to uproot himself, in his seventies, and move from London to New York required, above all, exceptional courage. This means his move came as no surprise to those of us who know him well, because we know him to be, above all, a man of courage. To dare to be different, in whatever context, takes a certain amount of courage. To *parade* yourself as different, in *every* context, takes an extraordinary amount of courage. To do it wittily is to invite the constant possibility of being lynched.

Yet Quentin has now lived for fifteen years in one of Manhattan's most insalubrious neighbourhoods – the Lower East Side, hard by the Bowery – alongside drug dealers, pimps, derelicts, Hell's Angels and all manner of low life, without ever having been assaulted or even threatened. He has lived all those years with a listed telephone number and yet receives fewer crank calls than the average housewife in Kansas City. And he has only once been stopped by the New York police: they wanted to know how his one-man show was going, and to wish him well with it.

What accounts for this unique exemption from all the menaces and hassles that the rest of us would undoubtedly suffer were we to live as he lives, where he lives? His own explanation, typically, omits any mention of himself: it is entirely due to the friendliness and tolerance of others. Which may be true, but which misses the point. The point is that the friendliness and tolerance his presence inspires is *reflected* friendliness, *mirrored* tolerance. Although he would probably laugh uproariously at the notion, the fact is that it is almost impossible to behave badly in his company.

I know. In 1981 we were sent by our American publishers on a three-week authors' tour of the US to promote our book, *Doing It with Style*. For three weeks we travelled everywhere together, waited in airports together, attended book signings together, appeared on more than sixty radio and television programmes together, spent hours in hotel rooms together, ate every meal together. Now, anyone who has ever been on holiday with friends for three weeks knows that it is the acid test of one's capacity for friendship; likewise, anyone who has ever been on a promotional tour knows that it is the ultimate test of one's ability to remain sane in a landscape of unreality. Yet we survived our ordeal not only with our friendship intact, but with my having been given a master class in courtesy and good manners.

One example will suffice. At the end of a particularly gruelling day, at the end of a gruelling week, we had collapsed in our suite at the Chateau Marmont in Los Angeles when the telephone rang. Quentin answered it and, after covering the handset, whispered the name of someone I most definitely did not wish to speak to. 'Say I'm not here, say I'm dead, say anything,' I growled.

Quentin nodded, and then spoke soothingly into the telephone: 'I'm afraid Mr Carroll can't come to the phone at the moment, but if you are willing to talk to me I will say exactly what he would have said.' The caller was instantly charmed; I was suitably chastened.

On a later occasion in New York – all right, two examples will suffice – we were being approached by a young man all aglow with a terrible earnestness when I suggested that we beat a hasty retreat to avoid the likelihood of being bored unto death. Unmoved, and unmoving, Quentin quietly corrected me: 'No one is boring who is willing to tell the truth about himself.' That was when I realized just what it was that gave him the *sauf-conduit* which to this day allows him to pass unmolested through the dimmest alleyways of the *demi-monde*. It is his willingness, at all times, in all circumstances, to tell the truth – the whole truth – about himself.

Of course if that was all there was to it, I would be writing here about an unfailingly honest and decent old man who richly deserves the solicitude of his neighbours. Instead I am writing about a man admired and celebrated throughout the English-speaking world. What links the two, and incorporates the former into the latter, is, as everybody knows, his coruscating wit – his almost alchemical wizardry in converting seemingly lacklustre truths into lustrous *aperçus*. It is no exaggeration to say that Quentin Crisp could well be the wittiest man alive.

For that very reason, unfortunately but understandably, he is often spoken of as the Oscar Wilde *de nos jours*. The comparison, however well-intentioned, does Quentin a disservice. For Oscar Wilde, wit was a weapon, a duelling sword with which he could take on all comers and defeat them with his swordplay. For Quentin, wit is more a magic wand of revelation – no less rapier-like than Wilde's, no less glinting in the sunlight of retelling, but waved gently rather than brandished. Because Wilde never came to terms with the truth about himself, because he was for ever trying to graft his persona on to his person, he used his wit to score points off those who would challenge him. Quentin, on the other hand, with no secrets to keep from himself or others, no territory to defend, has always used his wit to embrace the world that now, at last, so enthusiastically embraces him. As a result, whereas Wilde was reduced to wallowing in lachrymose self-pity and writing mawkish verse until his lonely death at the age of forty-six, Quentin at the age of eighty-six is still cheerfully holding the door open for latecomers to his party.

Do come in. I promise you a good time.

DONALD CARROLL
London, Spring 1995

I Serve in Heaven

I never had much luck with titles.

The Naked Civil Servant was a terrible title. Everywhere I go, I find myself compelled to explain it – to describe how a feature writer for an obscure paper visited me once in my room in Chelsea to ask me if I was a famous model for artists and I told him that there was no such thing, that by the time I entered that profession, art had become 'non-figurative', that in a time outworn, when they had nothing better to write about, journalists descended on Chelsea and asked some girl, who spent her time in The Pheasantry in a black velvet dress with one shoulder bare, if she slept with Mr John or Mr Epstein or whoever or only sat for him, that now 'life drawing' was only done – and done reluctantly – by students in art schools, and that the model arrived at the same time every day, that he presented his employment card, signed on and off and was frequently paid by a cheque which came from the Minister of Education – that, in other words, being a model had become as humdrum as being a civil servant, except that you had no clothes.

I had wanted to call my life story *I Reign in Hell,* which seemed to me a self-evident title. Mr Milton recounts how Satan (who is my only role model) had said 'better to reign in Hell than serve in Heaven,' which is what I had done – reigned in the exciting hell of Soho instead of serving in the boring heaven of Kensington. Had I been allowed to use that title for my autobiography, these journals would be called *I Serve in Heaven,* for Manhattan has far exceeded my expectation of happiness.

When I arrived in America, with all my worldly goods tied up in a red handkerchief, I was betrayed. In 1980, I had met a man who had said I could stay with him indefinitely when I arrived. I wrote to him from England telling him of the day and almost the hour of my arrival on the other side of the world. He had not replied so I had assumed that he was waiting for me. He was not. Indeed, he did not even open the door of his apartment but made inaudible replies to my announcement of my presence, so I went to my only other friend in America, a man who had constituted himself my 'manager' while I tarried in Manhattan during the previous year. So I lived in unaccustomed and uneasy splendour on 39th Street for the first six weeks of my life in America.

This man and his little friend were part-time saints because I slept in their living room, which curtailed their social life severely, but they never complained, never made me feel unwelcome. But it was a great relief to all concerned when one of my spies found me the room I now occupy on Manhattan's Lower East Side. This is an ideal spot, though guests look round the place uneasily and say, 'Do you *have* to live here?' I reply, 'Yes' – but that is not the whole truth. If I knew that I would die sometime during the next two years, I could live in a palace riddled with standard of living, but unfortunately I don't. I never dreamed that I would live as long as I have. When I was young, everybody said, 'We never thought you'd live through another winter' and that was nice. It made me feel frail, not long for this world, but here I am, a somewhat grisly sight, tottering about the Lower East Side of Manhattan at the age of eighty-six. When I got to America I hoped I would die before my shoes wore out but now my entire wardrobe is threadbare and I am threadbare too.

There is a strange relationship between the system of a country and its people. In England, the people are hostile to a man but the system is compassionate. The very old, the very young and the ill-equipped-to-live will always be looked after. In America everyone is friendly – almost doggie-like – but the system is ruthless. Once you can be pronounced unproductive, you've had it. You will end up living in a cardboard box at the corner of a street where once you occupied a mansion. That is the reason why I live in one room in a rooming house on the same block as a group of Hell's Angels. They have a bad reputation, but they've never murdered me. When I take my washing to the Chinese laundry on First Avenue, I pass between their house and the row of Harleys marshalled outside it. I walk with bowed head to show that I respect their supremacy and they leave me alone.

My mode of living only represents poverty to Americans – not to me. I live here in exactly the same way that I lived in London. I like living in one room and have never known what people do with the room they are not in. The only trouble is the books. I try never to read. Books are for writing, not for reading, but still they pursue you from three sources. Firstly, authors send you the books they have written. I don't think English writers ever do that. It would seem immodest. These you must read for fear that you will meet their authors on the street and they will question you about their work. Then there are the magazines that send you books with a covering note telling how many words to write about them and what you will be paid. Lastly, there are publishers who send you uncorrected proof copies of books they intend to market with a letter that says, 'We are sure you will enjoy this book and hope you will share your enthusiasm with us.' That means: 'Say something nice that we can put on the back of the first edition. Do not expect to be paid.' To these I always reply, 'Please feel free to quote me as saying anything that will promote sales of this excellent work.' Mostly the publishers do just that. One firm quoted the whole line, which I thought was really daring and funny.

In spite of the march of the books across the carpet, there is still room for a chair, a bed, a cooking stove and a refrigerator. What more can you ask? Rents *are* high here. My room in London, where I lived for forty-one years, cost six pounds a week. My room here is seventy-five dollars a week. All this happiness has to be paid for.

* * *

I have always been American in my heart, ever since my mother took me to the pictures (silent). She did this in a spirit of ostentatious condescension. Films, she said, were for servant gels. Anyone with any taste went to the theatre. When I began to gibber with excitement, she warned me that movies were greatly exaggerated – that America was nothing like it was portrayed on the screen. I suspected that she was wrong and that everyone over here was beautiful and everyone was rich.

Though not everyone is rich, everyone *is* beautiful. This is due to the addition of a Mediterranean ingredient. For instance, in the district where I live, Spanish is spoken. The shopkeepers speak American to you but they gibber away in their native tongue to one another. Those who are not Spanish are Greek or Italian. That means that their lips are curly, their nostrils are flared, their eyelids are as thick as pastry. When I was only English, I asked an American soldier if he thought there was an English face. Immediately he said Yes. Then I asked if it looked as though there was not enough material to go round. To this he also agreed. The English have flap lips, papery eyelids, prominent jawbones and Adam's apples. We are an ill-favoured race. I recognize that now that I live here.

A huge man sitting next to me on a bus going up Third Avenue asked me if I lived here permanently. When I said that I did, he remarked, 'It is the place to be if you are of "a different stripe".' There are so many different nationalities, so many different income groups, so many different sexes, that the freaks pass unnoticed. People have always imagined, or pretended to imagine, that I seek to provoke hostile attention. This is rubbish. What I want is to be accepted by other people without bevelling down my individuality to please them – because if I do that, all the attention, all the friendship, all the hospitality that I receive is really for somebody else of the same name. I want love on my own terms.

Here I have it. I was standing on Third Avenue waiting for a bus when a black gentleman walked by. When he noticed me, he said, 'Well, my! You've got it all on today.' And he was laughing.

In London, people stood with their faces six inches from mine and hissed, 'Who do you think you are?' What a stupid question. It must have been obvious that I didn't think I was anybody else.

People are my only pastime. I do not walk about the streets lost in thought about some problem of politics or mathematics or philosophy, so no one interrupts my train of thought by speaking to me. I welcome them. When we say of anyone that he is boring, it is ourselves we are criticizing. We have not made ourselves into that wide, shallow vessel into which a stranger feels he can pour anything. I have said that no one is boring who will tell the truth about himself. Here people tell the truth – or what they perceive as the truth – because they know that nothing they might say will shock or disgust me or cause me to despise them. They tell me their life stories at street corners while waiting for the traffic lights to change, because, like everyone in America who has been on television, I wear in public an expression of fatuous affability.

In other words, I have gone into the fame business. My agent tells me that I can't just 'do' fame, but I can. Every day through the mails I receive what is crudely called junk mail. It consists of invitations to Broadway theatre first nights, to secret screenings of unpopular films, to the openings of galleries exhibiting works of obscure artists and to parties for someone no one has ever heard of in dim basements. I can't go to all of them but I must go to some or they will cease to send them and I shall be cut off from the world. They serve a dual purpose. They keep me in touch with the press – and, if I can live on peanuts and champagne, I need never buy food again. I have learned not to flinch at the flashes from the cameras and to nod when I have not heard what is being said. That is all I need to know.

I never refuse to be photographed. That is no easy thing, as every fifth person in Manhattan is a professional photographer, and I never refuse to answer questions, however trivial they may be. One woman rang me at seven-thirty in the morning and asked me how to prevent her lipstick from smearing. Another wanted me to tell her what to do because she had allowed her hairdresser to cut her hair short and now she had decided that she didn't like it.

When I go on television, I remember that there only one law prevails: the survival of the glibbest. If your interviewer asks the question, 'What is the secret of the universe?', you do not stutter, you do not hesitate, above all you do not say, 'A good question.' You say, with a gracious smile, 'I am happy to tell you there is no secret.' The remark is inane, but you are smiling and your lips are moving. You'll be back.

All this is very tiring but not working is always hard work, and it has its rewards. Your travel expenses and your hotel expenses are taken care of. This does not mean that you see America. You see the airport. You see the hotel. You see the university or lecture hall. That is all, but you went to some delightful metropolis to be seen rather than to see.

I have actually seen – in the sense that I have roamed about the city – Seattle, which is as far west as you can go (except Alaska, which heaven forfend). I have seen Grosse Pointe, a Doris Day district which forms a suburb of Detroit. When you eat in Detroit, the restaurant turns while you dine. When you have reached the pudding, you are over a river called the Detroit River. When I asked my hostess what lay beyond the river, she replied, 'Canada'. So I reckoned that I was as far north as I could go (still not mentioning Alaska). I have also been to the southern extremity of the United States, to Key West. It is a purely holiday island. No one ever works there. It is full of guest-houses, piano bars and restaurants, and everyone wears white. It is a shrine to Mr Hemingway. Every bar shows proudly his photograph with the words, 'Hemingway drank here' – or 'slept here' – or 'fought here' – or 'wrote here'. All these places and many others I have visited with my fare paid both ways and my hotel bill taken care of. I have generally been given, if not the keys of the cities, at least the impression that I am welcome.

I would not go on so much about this aspect of my life if it were not in such contrast with my previous experience. I have been to a lot of places but I have not spent much time away from home because each visit to a distant city is of such short duration. I travel thousands of miles to be away only for three days. As I never travel with any luggage that I cannot carry on to the plane with me, this suits me fine. I do not find air travel tiring because I sleep on planes, following the advice of Miss Eartha Kitt, who said, 'On a plane, never eat, never drink. Sleep.' Thus I do not suffer from jet-lag. It is my guess that people who say they have jet-lag are the people who start to drink before the wretched plane has got its feet off the ground and who arrive at their destination with scarlet faces and crooked hats. They've got gin-lag.

I am met at the airport. It is like being a spy. If no one is there to meet me, I can only return home again for I have no idea where I am going. So far this has never happened. I have also no idea what I am expected to do. On being asked this question, my hosts sometimes say breezily, 'Oh, nothing really. Just enjoy yourself and be there.' Sometimes I am expected to sign books, sometimes to talk to people, answer questions, be photographed. It is very moving – the love that Americans shower upon you, their gratitude for your presence.

In San Francisco, however, the only American city in which I have ever received totally bad notices, the critics could see how overcome I was and made fun of me. I think my reception there was due to an expectation that I was somebody who went about the world hiring spaces in which to deliver a manifesto. When I explained that I myself was hired and that, as far as I knew, my function was to sell theatre seats and that, furthermore, in my opinion, every theatre-goer throughout the world was a middle-class middle-aged woman with a broken heart, the people of San Francisco's love for me died in an instant. In other cities, I have fared better – noticeably in New York and Los Angeles.

It is very stimulating to work in Los Angeles because when you look down into the audience you see that the theatre is full of movie stars. I once signed books there in the interval of my show and when one person placed his book before me I said, 'And what is your name?' 'Roddy,' he replied. I wrote 'Roddy' and he added 'McDowall'. 'You're Roddy McDowall!' I cried in ecstasy. 'You remember me?' he asked, and I certainly did. 'You divorced Lassie,' I said to prove it. I think he must be the most famous person that I have ever met – except Mr Sting. Because I was in a movie with Mr Sting, when I played his laboratory assistant and he was Baron Frankenstein, people imagine that I see him incessantly, whereas I have met him only twice – once when he took me to lunch in a restaurant on West Broadway and told me he was going to write songs about exiles, and again when I was in his videotape of the song about being an Englishman in New York. Then he took me into his apartment, which was a huge place almost entirely bare of furniture, except that in one room I noticed a cot: evidence of Stinglets. I did not comment on this fact, fearing to embarrass him.

Mr Sting is above all polite, courteous. To say that is to seem somewhat condescending, but it is true that I had not expected a 'pop star' to be so gentlemanly. He offered me two tickets to hear him perform at Madison Square Garden, but the idea of getting mixed up with twelve hundred schoolgirls was too daunting. I thanked him but I didn't go. I would like to see him because I am convinced that there is something that he *is* on stage, over and above anything he *does*, for he has such a spellbinding effect on his audience. '. . . and then that wonderful voice', a woman concluded when speaking of him. I would have said that he had a singularly appealing, plaintive, untrained tenor voice. If you describe it as 'wonderful', what word have you left for Mr Pavarotti's singing? 'I think he is one of the best-looking guys around', a young man said to me. Again, without wishing in any way to diminish his greatness, I would have described him as tallish, slimmish, blondish, and with a very *aware* look in the eyes – as opposed to most stars who are self-regarding and do not look out of their faces but turn their eyes inward, like Hamlet's mother but without any of her feelings of misgiving as they contemplate their very souls. In this he was the direct opposite of Mr Warhol, who would turn his face towards you but never look at you, presenting his image to the world like a shield.

I used to try to stampede Mr Warhol into saying something because he had plenty to say, as is indicated by his book *From A to B and Back Again*, but I never could. If I went to a gathering of free-loaders, and standing apart from the others was a man approaching middle age, looking rather ill and saying nothing, that was Mr Warhol. He would say, when he became aware of your proximity, 'We must be photographed.' Those were the only words I ever heard him utter.

There is a whole book to be written about being the one among the many, the way in which your size and luminosity seem to increase as you become the focus of a crowd's attention, and the way in which the crowd sees something, some quality in you that you cannot name simply because you stand alone and above them. It is the lure certain professions carry with them – teaching, preaching, acting, politics. They are all vocations adopted by people who cannot live within their income of praise. The average man casts about for some poor benighted girl who can be persuaded to say, 'Oh, Rodney, you're ripping.' As soon as the words have been uttered he can get on with his life but there are other people who think to themselves, 'All right, *she* says it, but what about all those other people out there? They haven't said a thing.' And they become restless and television makes their fever worse because they can see two people in Patagonia who are talking about some other person and it drives them mad. So they lift themselves up until the whole world can see them. That is the function of the professions of teaching, preaching, acting and politics and it is why the people hungry for acknowledgement adopt them.

Mr Donne was wrong. It is not true that no man is an island. Except in America, every man is an island seeking to establish trade relations across a dark and dangerous sea. In the United States, everybody takes an interest in everybody else. Of course, though this is wonderful, it encourages gossip and everything has to be known about everybody. I can see that if an evangelist is a secret fornicator, this weakens his hold on morality, but if a politician is known to have had an affair with a typist in a past life, how can this possibly have anything to do with his capacity to rule the world? Nay, I will say more. Would you expect a man who has the energy, the imagination, the daring to think that he can rule the world to display some of these qualities in his private life? The answer seems to be No. America was founded by Puritans and this means that no one should set his sights on the White House until he is so old that all the typists he ever employed (in any capacity whatsoever) are dead.

Only acting is untroubled by this dilemma. An actress is expected to behave badly. Tallulah Bankhead's popularity lay in the fact that the English bourgeoisie went to see her to marvel that anyone so wicked could still move and speak. In America the critics panned her every performance but she transcended their notices. She had entered the profession of being to which we all aspire.

With all these considerations in mind, I have been into films. Firstly *The Bride* with Mr Sting. Then *Orlando*, in which I played Elizabeth I. It was the sort of picture that I would never have seen in a thousand years if I had not been in it. I would have termed *Orlando* unabashed festival material but I would have been wrong. It had a sporadic release all over America and, on the streets of the Lower East Side of Manhattan, I was compelled to cope with people walking backward before me, genuflecting and kissing my hand for several weeks after the film's release.

Being in a film is like giving birth. For a few hours after, while the memory of the suffering is clear in your mind, you swear you will never go through such an ordeal again, but when sufficient time has elapsed and the memory has faded, you have another baby or make another film. In the case of filming, it is the money that is the lure. For two weeks of suffering you are paid sufficient wages to live without doing anything in Manhattan for six months. What the lure of childbirth is I cannot imagine. I would have thought that the moment a woman discovers for certain that she is pregnant would be the worst time in her life. She knows she will not go to the movies for seventeen years.

The American people have done so much for me, have restored so fully my self-confidence, that I am constantly twisting and turning in an effort to live up to their expectations of me. Ingrid Bergman said, 'You must go on the stage knowing they want you to succeed.' She meant American audiences. In England the people in the stalls sit back in their chairs with folded arms, saying in their stony hearts, 'We've paid a hell of a lot for these seats. We hope you're going to DO something.' In Manhattan, the audience is leaning forward eagerly, crying, 'Tell us!' You can tell them anything – how to be beautiful, how to be successful, how to be thin, how to be saved. They will listen intently.

As a friend remarked, I decided to come to America at an age when most people decide to go into a nursing home. I wish I could have come here sooner when I had the energy and the optimism to fling myself with more abandonment, more total commitment, into all opportunities for self-promotion that are offered to me, but I couldn't pay my fare. When I say this people laugh nervously as though it were a joke, but it is the ugly truth. I never earned more than twelve pounds a week in my life in England. There it was enough. My old age was taken care of by Mrs Snatcher. When the day came when I could no longer see or hear or walk, she would spread her iron wings over me. But I would have been saving up for three years to spend three hours in Manhattan so I waited until I was invited by Mr Bennett, the darling of the Shubert Theaters, to visit Manhattan.

That is the story of my life: I go where my fare is paid. Because I have lived so long and travelled so far, I have passed from a masculine space to a feminine one but from a feminine time to a masculine era. I use these terms because gender is a preoccupation at this time and in this place. England is a masculine country. It appropriates and owns other countries. America endeavours (unsuccessfully) to soothe and appease other countries, which is a singularly feminine attitude. Nevertheless I have arrived here at a conspicuously masculine time. When I was young, there was a 'woman problem'. All novels were written by women for women about women. My mother read two of these books a week from W.H. Smith's lending library in Sloane Square. Their plots described discreetly but fervently a series of affairs in which the heroine indulged, but the authoress never forgave the heroine's husband for not understanding and appreciating his wife's 'inward and essential virginity'.

In other arts women also ruled. The words 'movie star' referred to women. Valentino was the only actor who could be called a movie star and he was a pseudo-woman. I am not impugning his sexual orientation in saying this but describing his image – withdrawn, mysterious, capricious. All other actors were in support of the female star and, in German films, any numbers of hours were spent on redeeming her appearance from a disfiguring naturalism while the men all looked dreadfully like human beings. Movies were made for a female audience. Now they are made for kids and the stars are men who spend their time smashing everything in sight, which is what all children want to do.

This shift in direction is particularly worrying to me. When I was young a homosexual man was thought to be effeminate. He dressed in women's clothes at every possible moment and adopted an exaggeratedly feminine gait like a model on a catwalk. This tradition has been brought to an abrupt end in America by 'political correctness'. The gay community, because it insists on being equal with real people, has decided that homosexual men are not an inferior race and so parade an egregious masculine image, wearing crew-cut hair, a kitchen tablecloth shirt, pre-ruined jeans, tractor boots and a small moustache, if not a full beard. They mate with other gargoyles of masculinity, scorning or regarding with pitying contempt those of us who cannot rise to such manliness. There is now no quasi-normal, masculine-feminine, satyr-nymph, pursuer-pursued courtship in the gay world – and, come to think of it, none in the real world either where women have decided to be people.

When I was writing *Manners From Heaven,* I read every book about etiquette and good manners that I could find. I was surprised to discover that all such compendia written before the Second World War devoted half their space to the question of how to comport yourself in the presence of 'the ladies'. Now there are no ladies. I mentioned this dearth on a television programme conducted by a female televisionary and she was affronted. 'I don't think we're putting up with that, are we, girls?' she asked of her audience. The girls said 'No'. I reminded them that they had decided to be people. 'Well, we are people,' they replied, still more affronted. I retreated in confusion. If they are people, they can open the damned door themselves.

Courtship happened because women were more precious as well as more frail than mere men. If the world is going to contain no women – only people – it will rapidly become faster, harsher, louder and the only subjects ever discussed will be sport, sex and money. Nevertheless, I have not gone into half-mourning, pending these unpleasant changes. I am laughing (behind my fan) because I shall have left before they are noticeable.

Every person of my age deplores the contemporary scene because deploring is a rich person's hobby. Writers are great deplorers and writers are always rich. They have the spare time to write. Indeed it is the plethora of hours that is their undoing. Poor Mr Wordsworth and Mr Tennyson wandered about the Lake District or sat in their town houses trying to find something – anything – to pontificate about and wrote a lot of rubbish because of this lack of urgency, this absence of engagement. Mr Hemingway and Mr Mailer scribble between other activities, which does nothing for their style but increases the excitement in their writings.

Those who are compelled to work do not deplore the changes that have come to modern life. They welcome fast transport, immediate communication, universal hygiene, modern medicine and the fact that now justice reaches into the smallest pockets of society. But I, who have not worked in many a long year, do not notice these improvements. I am concerned with the high gloss on society, not with its inner machinery. I am a free-loader, a dilettante, a butterfly on the wheel.

And that's putting it nicely.

QUENTIN CRISP
New York, Spring 1995

The Journals

1990

Spring

*

I can no longer indulge in orgies of sloth

I try not to be cultural. To this end, I have declined an invitation from an organization called *Operation Earth* to attend a gala celebration at the Hard Rock Café, although it was to take place at a cosy time in the evening instead of the middle of the night, and I was assured that I would not be asked to do or say anything. I might even have been given a drink and some funny things on sticks to eat. In short, this might have been a very pleasant evening on the peanut circuit, but I felt that for me to take advantage of this generous offer would be hypocritical in the extreme. I almost never watch programmes on the worthy Channel 13, I am totally uninterested in the fate of the sperm whale (what does it expect with a name like that?), and I regard the earth as a courageous global experiment that failed.

I rarely visit art galleries, for two reasons: the first is that there is never anywhere to sit, and the second is that I do not understand art. When people ask me what I've got against pictures, I can only reply, 'What have you got against the wall?'

The exhibition now at the Trabia Gallery is of works by a Mr la Chapelle. They are described as cibachromes. I have no idea what, technically, that word means, but visually they appear to be photographs that started as monochromes and were coloured later. This elevates them into the realm of art since, though photography may be an art, it can only be considered to be Art if the process of reproduction has been manipulated. How these pictures were accomplished is as interesting as what they mean, and, for once, we have here the right to consider their meaning because, in the catalogue, they have titles of a transcendental nature, such as 'The Search for Truth' and 'Victory Over Nature'. Ostensibly, the subject matter is the nude – most often male, and frequently in a state of conflagration like one of Mr Pryor's worst nightmares. However, in spite of their subject matter, none of these works is in the least pornographic.

The occasion seemed to be a success in the sense that the gallery was full to bursting, chiefly of men under the age of thirty-five dressed in black. (One of the guests explained to me that, below Houston Street, black is worn.) For once there were more people present than photographers. Everybody drank a lot of wine and talked animatedly to the people around him, but whether any pictures were sold I have no notion. Some of them cost more than $12,000. As I wandered out into the night, I couldn't help reflecting that I could live with abandonment on that sum for at least two years.

In *The Waste Land*, when Mr Eliot wrote that 'April is the cruellest month' he was thinking about his income taxes. I dealt with this annual problem last week, though my life in England did nothing to prepare me for the ordeal. In Britain, money is not taken very seriously, and banking is a cottage industry. When I lived there, if I darted into the Chelsea branch of Lloyds Bank and said to a teller, 'Is he in?', she would at once reply, 'I'll see.' In spite of my casual manner, she knew that I was referring to the manager; if he was not actually with a customer, he would deal with me at once. In the days when I was embroiled in the serpentine rituals of acquiring a passport, he trimmed my photographs down to the right size with his own penknife on his own desk.

In America I would not expect ever to stand in the august presence of a bank manager – nay, not even if I were a self-confessed millionaire. Here banks are solemn places the size of cathedrals, and they are manned by black ladies of such elegance that their ankles are no wider than other people's wrists. These beautiful creatures start to smile the moment they see me arriving because they know that I will have no idea what I am supposed to be doing. On one occasion I mentioned to one of them my bewilderment at finding that I had two accounts. 'That is correct,' she said. 'You do.' When I asked why, she replied in a sorrowful tone, 'I think you need an accountant.'

I have now acquired one. He is a gentleman of limitless patience who sits like a large hamster in a nest of papers. I have never actually seen him chew up the more troublesome documents and store them in his cheeks, but I suspect that is where they are. With the passing of the years, he has come to accept my invincible ignorance and even to condone it. Once, when I apologized to him for being more trouble than all his other victims put together, because of my stupidity in money matters, he replied, 'I don't understand them and I'm in the business.' What he does comprehend is that I place myself in his hands because I cannot fill in forms and not because I want my taxes to be diminished. I like my payments to the Internal Revenue Service to be large to show my loyalty to Mr Bush. I am only a resident alien and greatly fear the deportation that was forced upon the great gangsters when they defaulted on their taxes. 'Don't let them send me to Sicily,' I cry.

Having done my duty to the government, I hoped to enjoy many nights of peaceful sleep, but this was not to be. At about four o'clock one morning last week, I was awoken by my telephone bell. My totally unknown caller wanted to know if I had ever suffered from a venereal disease and whether I knew that Miss Garbo had died. I answered 'No' to the first question and 'Yes' to the second. The stranger then said with a wistful intonation, 'I suppose that means that we shall all die.'

It does.

Miss Garbo was so reclusive that it will be hard to guess if she enjoyed her later years, but, in the manner of her death, I would say that she was fortunate. Once, on-stage, when I was heaping praise on the fair name of Miss Crawford, a woman in the audience said, 'You think she was marvellous, but she died an alcoholic and alone.' I would have thought that was the ideal way to go. In old age, one of our preoccupations is how to die without violence and without pain. If we have the money to buy enough booze to deaden our senses, why not do so? Another problem arises if we expire in the presence of our friends. We have then to die and be polite at the same time. It may not be easy.

A Miss Mackenzie has presented me with a book of English crossword puzzles. I mustn't claim that they are better than those devised by other nations, but they are different in that solving them requires only ingenuity. American puzzles demand general knowledge which, as I barely live in the real world, I lack. I don't know the names of the capitals of obscure African countries; I don't know the first names of long-dead baseball players. Crossword puzzles are the aerobics of the soul. I become neurotic if I cannot complete my spiritual exercises for the day.

Nothing much has happened to me lately, except a few interviews conducted on the Mahomet Principle. That is to say that, since I decline to visit England, British journalists and photographers have to come to see me. The interviewers are lucky because, my room being at the back of the house, the roaring of the motorbikes belonging to the Hell's Angels cannot be heard. But photographers are in trouble. My living space is so small and so dark that they find themselves trampling backwards over heaps of dirty laundry or over piles of rejected typescripts to reach a spot from which more than the end of my nose comes into focus.

The number of invitations that I am able to accept is regrettably diminishing as I grow older. Some of these offer entertainment that I feel sure I would enjoy but which begins at half past ten. That is an hour at which I might still be awake, but I know that decorum forbids me to be found standing outside the doors when they open. When I was about six years old, my mother felt obliged to give a children's party; it was set to begin at three o'clock and precisely at that hour the front doorbell rang. My mother turned her head like a startled moorhen. 'Oh,' she screeched, 'who could be so ill-bred as to arrive at the right time?'

An unknown woman has telephoned me to ask if she might interview me. Removing my typewriter from my lap, I said, 'Interrogate me and I will reply.' Her first question was, 'Why is your number in the Manhattan directory?'

This is one of the great mysteries concerning which America and I remain for ever in postures of mutual amazement. What, I ask the world, is the use of a telephone if my number is unlisted? It means that no one will ever be able to call me; I will have to call him. Think of the expense. In fact, I hardly ever initiate a telephone conversation. I wait for the world to communicate with me. At least, this ensures that I am unlikely to be a nuisance to anybody.

My unknown interviewer then asked if I did not receive calls from a lot of weird people. I do, but, as I am the weirdest of them all, I can hardly complain. When, on one of his television programmes, Mr David Letterman first asked me this same question, it did instigate a lot of calls of a teasing nature and, during the next six months, about half a dozen threats upon my life. These I took calmly; I am accustomed to such treatment because, in England, I endured half a dozen such menaces a day. In America, after a while, the angry voices grew silent; nothing sinister happened until a few days ago. Then a girl called me and asked me to write on a piece of paper the words 'I love Tony', and to sign them; she proposed to come to the house where I live and collect it later in the day. I refused. Hours later, she called again, and again I said I would do no such thing. Then someone, posing as her boyfriend, called to say that if I didn't grant her request she would meet with some terrible fate. He said that he didn't know why I had been chosen for this hideous hoax.

A likely story! What can it all mean? Can any woman, however young, however carefully brought up, not know that she was trying to inveigle a self-evident gay man into signing a compromising statement? If she is innocent, who bribed, cajoled, or bullied her into such a murky situation?

Equally strange but in no way sinister was a letter I received from a gentleman living in Shreveport, Louisiana. He wants to collect drawings done of me by English art students. Perhaps he does not know how bad those efforts were. The British are not an artistic race; they go to art schools not to acquire skills in the arts but to avoid real life for a few adolescent years. My correspondent also asks if he can collect any of the book covers that I designed when I was a commercial artist some forty years ago, but these too are bad. I was forced into the arts as a way of earning a living because my appearance was so bizarre that it was totally unacceptable in the context of real work. I had no talent for anything.

The strangest part of this letter is a request for permission for a friend of his to perform the show I used to do in MacDougal Street in 1978. I am greatly flattered by all this interest in my past, and as far as I'm concerned his friend may don a blue wig, adopt an English accent, and quote me as saying anything, but there is no script; there never was. I went on to the stage and said what I thought. There are, of course, the possibilities of legal squabbles. A record of the show as done in the Village was made by a Mr Fordin and videotape produced by a firm called, of all things, Family Home Entertainment. I have no idea whether or not either of these companies would say they had rights that had been infringed. I wouldn't like to be dragged into court. What would I wear?

I have entered into the Avenue C life.

It all began with an invitation to a play by Eric Bentley. Now, as is well known, I do not hold with the theatre. For one thing, it is subject to error: at every moment on-stage something could go wrong. In the movies, by contrast, nothing goes wrong; everything is perfect. Even a bad movie is perfectly bad. For another thing, by comparison with the movies, the stage is as intimate as a football field. Our vision of a play is telescopic. We can hardly tell whether the leading lady is smiling or frowning. This handicap seduces her into multiplying her every gesture, her every word by the seating capacity of the theatre. She embraces us with semaphore gestures and tells us her secrets in the voice of a town crier while we, anxious to communicate our appreciation, clap and cheer out of all proportion to the price of the seat we have been given.

Nevertheless, I did not feel that I could decline this invitation to Professor Bentley's play. I know the professor; I once worked for him in a play entitled *Lord Alfred's Lover*. In that production I did not take my part very seriously because, at the time, I had not been told about the author's greatness. Since then, my education in this matter has been completed by a visit to a huge lecture hall on 128th Street. There the crowned heads of American literature were gathered together to honour Professor Bentley. I was frightened because I already had some inkling of how highbrow the atmosphere would be. I had received a book full of articles about him or on subjects that it was thought would interest him. I was asked to write some phrases that would enhance the value of this impressive tome, but had evaded this request on the ground that, at this exalted level of culture, praise from me would do more damage than other people's blame. Nevertheless, I attended the party for the sake of the peanuts. It was a most enlightening occasion.

It transpired that Professor Bentley is unique, and unique in many ways: he is a cabaret artiste, a drama critic, a translator, and a dramatist. His appearance is traditional; he is tall, thin, grey-haired, but to say that his manner is unexpectedly human is not enough. He is skittish. His latest play is called *German Requiem* and is what Mr Goldwyn would have described as 'freely adapted' from a work by Mr Heinrich von Kleist. Its theme is a Romeo and Juliet tale of two young lovers from hostile dynasties. It is Plantagenet in appearance, but Jacobean in style; that is to say that, by the end of it, hardly anybody is still living and those who are regret it.

This tragedy is now playing at The Living Theater, which is situated on my street but at the edge of the world. It ought to be called The Hardly Living Theater. As you look round the foyer, you feel certain it was once a shoe-repair shop. The acting space is depressingly small, but no one could deny that it has been utilized with quite astonishing ingenuity. Because there is no stage and no curtain, the various scenes (and there are many) are acted in different parts of the theatre, including halfway up one wall. As I have noticed in all such cramped and impoverished circumstances, quite inexplicably the lighting equipment is as elaborate as that of any Broadway theatre and was expertly controlled.

In spite of being totally out of my depth in such a rarefied atmosphere, I enjoyed the play. Before it began, I asked the Professor if I would understand it. His reply was, 'Only too well.' He was right. It echoes in more sonorous language than I can command my deepest convictions. I once met Mr William Burroughs. Within minutes of our being introduced, he said, 'What is worth having is worth fighting for,' and I replied, 'That which we can only maintain by force we should try to do without.'

That is what *German Requiem* is all about.

People keep asking me what I do when I'm not on television. As, even in a good year, I have never been on television more than four times, and as many interviews last less than five minutes, there is a lot of time for which to account. Obviously I must give a very long or very superficial answer. I feel more at ease with the second kind of response. 'I do what you do,' I reply, 'when you're not on television.' These words frighten some people; they blush or gasp, 'What's that?' I tell them that I wash socks, file my nails, write my letters, and fry an egg. What I refrain from mentioning is that much of the time is spent dozing.

They say that camels store water in their humps so as to be able to make long journeys across deserts without suffering acute thirst. I have never sunk so low as to drink water, but in other respects I used to be like the camel. If I foresaw that I was unlikely to be able to cadge a square meal from anybody for some time, I would immediately eat everything in sight. Similarly, if it did not seem that I would have a good night's sleep for the next forty-eight hours, I would at once go to bed and will myself into unconsciousness for as long as I could. Now that I am old, I find that I can no longer indulge in the orgies of sloth. I sleep more superficially and for shorter periods of time spread over any twenty-four-hour period. To avoid waking at dawn (never one of my favourite times of day), I retire later and later. This habit has tempted me into watching films on late-night television. I know this is a mortal sin and I have mentioned my sleep problem at some length in the hope of explaining, if not excusing, this reprehensible behaviour.

Most nocturnal re-runs are of unsuccessful movies trying to recoup their losses from hapless insomniacs. Many of them are about creatures from outer space, mad scientists, and haunted houses, but some are very immediate and very real. One such picture which I saw quite recently was entitled *Our Family Honour*. I enjoyed it enormously, but it raised the age-old, disturbing question about the pernicious influence of films upon their audiences.

I do not hold that any movie, however valid, can reverse a person's natural inclinations. For instance, I do not think that if *Scenes from the Class Struggle in Beverly Hills* were shown in a convent, all the inmates would instantly become sex maniacs. However, I do think that a well-made film can endorse and even appear to justify opinions that are already waiting for some corroboration. In this way, a movie like *Our Family Honour* can be dangerous. It is a fast-moving, vividly photographed, and well-acted story of the battle between the police family who want their father to be made commissioner and a Mafia-type organization headed by the wonderful Mr Eli Wallach. The cops finally triumph, but by brutal means of which the director appears to approve. The police are seen laying waste entire bars and pool halls. There seems to be no difference between their tactics of intimidation and those of the baddies. We all fear the police, and wisely. As the head of Scotland Yard once said, 'If a policeman is popular, there is something wrong.' In a world where another cop is killed almost every week, is it not a bad thing for a picture like *Our Family Honour* to justify our learning not to respect but to hate the police?

I put this notion forward in the form of a question, fearing that a direct statement might make me into that least accommodating of all geometrical figures – a kinky square.

When not watching films in the dead of night, I am occasionally asked to take part in one by day. I do not know why this happens, because I am not an actor, have received no theatrical training, and am always slightly embarrassed by being asked to utter other people's words. In spite of this considerable drawback, there is in existence a film of *Hamlet* in which I speak some of Mr Polonius's lines. The press said that I 'gave an unusual rendering'. That was putting it kindly. The picture was made by a Mr Coronado in the Royal College of Art, and was intended to win him a degree.

Much of the same kind of situation seems to prevail here in New York University, with one curious difference. All films made by American students or people on the amateur fringe of the movie industry have supernatural or allegorical themes: all are at some remove from reality. I have never dared to ask why; I have merely obeyed instructions. This endeavour to avoid saying no to anything has led me into presiding at a feast of freaks under Brooklyn Bridge, to sitting at the head of the boardroom table of some secret society and even to standing beside an actress called Miss Bolger on the roof of a house on Ludlow Street with our toes sticking out over the edge (Miss Gish was never more dedicated than that).

Now I have been offered another such part by a more established director. In order that I may know what is involved in this project, he has lent me a book of stories by a Mr McGrath on the first of which the film will be based. As I find that this project would oblige me to take off all my clothes, I think it is very unlikely that I shall accept the role, but my meeting with the director was by no means in vain. He gave me lunch, and the book, called *Blood and Water, and Other Stories,* has given me hours of pleasure. The author is described as 'The Poe of the '80s', but he is more than that, because a sexual element, absent from the work of the master, has seeped into these tales. Other Gothic writers seek to haunt their readers. Mr McGrath wishes to disgust us; he describes the physical and psychological oddities with such evident relish that they become hilarious. His characters and the situations in which he depicts them are like Charles Addams illustrations commissioned by Grove Press. I would recommend this book to anyone who longs for a glimpse of something worse than real life.

Summer

*

It would be less depressing to be alcoholic than to be anonymous

In a movie entitled *Ace in the Hole*, Mr Kirk Douglas said, 'Good news is no news.' Working on this principle, whenever television has deigned to show us aerial pictures of Ohio, the entire state has been flooded. We have seen pets fished out of muddy pools, children being taken to school in boats, and cars with their headlights just above the water level glaring at us like the eyes of alligators.

I have now been to Dayton and am happy to be able to allay anyone's fears. It is a bone-dry, quiet, spacious city full of the friendliest people. Having been invited there to speak at a Gay Pride festival, I was astonished to discover that Dayton has at least four hundred gay people, all of whom turned up to hear me cheer them on. I was asked by a member of my audience how Dayton compared with New York. I said that it is cosier. I hope that was the correct answer; I noticed a veiled apprehension among Daytonians that a stranger might evince a trace of condescension towards their home town. One young man said, 'You've been to Iowa. We're practically a suburb of Manhattan compared with them.'

When arriving in Dayton, the first surprise is the airport. Though not as vast as the one in Atlanta, it is large and brand-new. In the entrance there is a piece of gleaming metal sculpture symbolizing world air travel. I am so ignorant that, until my hosts enlightened me, I did not know that Dayton is the birthplace of aviation. Later, to reinforce this point, they took me to see the home of the Wright brothers, an impressive Tara-style mansion on the top of a hill. I stayed comfortably in the home of the organizers of the Gay Pride festivities and, on my first evening there, they gave a small party.

The following evening was a much grander affair than I had expected. Five long tables had been set up for dinner with vases of flowers and balloons in a vast gymnasium. On an upper floor were several tables loaded with hors d'œuvres between trays of brightly coloured condoms; it was possible to mistake them for toffee wrappers. I did not avail myself of any safeguards against contamination, but I ate salmon and signed books supplied by a local gay bookshop. By this time, I was wearing not only a rose given to me by my hosts from their garden, but also an orchid so large that later, when I spoke, wisps of maidenhair fern trembled under my chin.

On the main floor there was a small stage where entertainment was provided first by a female solo singer and later by a men's choir, who sang some of Mr Porter's lyrics. Inevitably, this made 'I Get A Kick Out Of You' sound somewhat like an anthem, but it was all very enjoyable. The main part of the evening's activities was taken up with speeches. These were about gay pride and were of a very self-congratulatory nature, but justifiably so. In spite of the fact that no alcohol was served during the entire evening, a truly joyful, friendly atmosphere prevailed. It was a well-organized event attended by nearly four hundred men and women, all presumably gay, or what a politician would call 'fellow travellers'.

Whoever would have thought there was so much happy sin in Ohio?

I returned to Manhattan with just enough time to change my socks before setting out for Tampa, where I had been summoned for much the same reason as I had been summoned to Dayton: to tell serried ranks of gay people that they must be brave. Here, though, the audience was very different – everyone was dressed in a three-piece suit – and the city was very different. As with every other city in Florida that I have seen, the general impression is one of boundless luxury (beginning with the apartment I was allowed to occupy in the absence of its two owners). My host was a lawyer most of whose clients are homosexual. Since so many gay couples start nesting within minutes of exchanging telephone numbers, he must be perpetually busy with property disputes, but for the three days of my visit justice slept, magistrates played golf, and law courts were empty while he very kindly showed me the many fascinating features of the city. I was amazed to learn what a huge business the making of cigars had once been in Tampa – an industry now kept alive almost single-handedly by George Burns.

When I expressed my awe at the splendours of Tampa, its perpetual sunshine, its wide, white streets, its bay in which the sea creeps humbly towards the expensive shore, a young woman tried to disillusion me. 'Tampa,' she said, 'is like a little girl tottering about in her mother's high-heeled shoes and pretending that she is grown-up and sophisticated.' I was surprised by this judgement; only the friendliness of everybody that I met had prevented me from feeling totally outclassed.

On the first evening, I was taken to a party at a house where we ate in a garden that ran down to the water's edge. The only hint of rowdiness occurred when the owner of the house pushed the gentleman who had driven us to the party (in a Rolls-Royce, no less) into the swimming pool. As the victim of this prank was the nicest possible man who had neither said nor done anything out of place, no one was amused by the incident; in fact, they were frightened by it and ran, squeaking, from the pool's edge, fearing that they might suffer a similar fate. I tried to remain calm, but I was bewildered. I know the rich are heartless, but this gesture seemed positively Roman in its contempt for human feelings.

I may have spoken toon soon. In a recent entry in this journal, I said that I had found Dayton to be bone-dry. I still hope it is, but I have now learned that, the very moment I left Ohio, almost the entire state was flooded again. *Après moi le déluge.*

* * *

I have now made eight flights in one month. Since going to Dayton and Tampa, I have visited Houston and Chicago. I trust that none of these fair cities will now be attacked by tornados.

I was sent to Houston a long time ago to speak to all the redeemed heavy drinkers in Texas. I did my best to utter words of comfort, but was by no means sure of my ground. Secretly I have always held the opinion that it would be less depressing to be alcoholic than to be anonymous.

Last Tuesday, with once again only time to change my socks, I went to Chicago, a city even more familiar to me than Houston because I once worked in its Ivanhoe Theater for a whole month. The high point of that earlier visit was an appearance on television co-starred with (well, seated next to) Mr T., the mountainous, muscle-bound star of television's 'The A Team'. And he truly is a star. He is so vast that I was obliged to ride him side-saddle. Though he was clanking with precious metal and bristling with diamonds, as he lowered himself majestically into a creaking chair, his first words were, 'I am a very humble man.'

On this more recent visit, I did not appear on television, but was interviewed several times on radio programmes. One of these was conducted by Mr Terkel; I had known that it would be. The first law of Chicago is that no one can enter or leave without accounting for himself to Studs Terkel. He was in his usual benign form and seemed to be able to remember every meeting we have ever held.

When not caught up in this frenzy of conviviality, I stayed in the Belmont Hotel, from the roof garden of which I could see almost the entire city. It stretched to the uttermost horizon in all directions, and the lake, of which we had a magnificent view, assumed the airs and graces of an ocean; even from the thirteenth floor, it was impossible to see the other side, and its waves crashed against a long, sandy shoreline teeming with sunbathers and even real bathers. It certainly puts the Lake District of England in its place. It also seemed to ventilate the city, which was as hot as New York but nothing like as oppressive.

Having made so many journeys by air and visited four different states in one month, it has taken me quite a while to slow down. Just as a sprinter, having broken the tape, runs on for several yards, so for about four days after my return from Chicago I did everything fast and with lunatic intensity.

The first task against which I have flung myself was answering the mail. I threw away a heap of invitations to events that had already come and gone while I was away; I tore up all requests for money (you wouldn't think that anyone whose address is East Third Street would ever receive begging letters, but they do); then I started on the more personal demands. The oddest of these came from an unknown woman living in the middle of England asking for a lock of my hair. I thanked her for her interest in my unworthy self, but I did not pander to her kinkiness. At my age, I haven't so much hair left that I can afford to distribute any among strangers. Lastly, I turned my attention to dealing with news of the dead. This is reaching harrowing proportions because, in middle age in a frantic effort to seem young, I associated chiefly with people older than I. One such person was a famous theatrical photographer called Angus McBean.

When I first met him, the Second World War had just begun. I was thirty and he was thirty-four. When he told me his age, I tried to keep my face absolutely still. I did not want to evince the least tremor of surprise, but secretly I had thought that he was about fifty. He was tall, painfully thin, bearded, and bald. Furthermore, as he himself once remarked, all the lines in his face went 'the wrong way'. I don't think that any of these defects mattered in the least to his innumerable friends, but they did to him, because he was obsessed with the notion of physical beauty. He was lucky in that he was then living in a happier time when all photographic negatives were glass and could be retouched outrageously. He – or, rather, his retoucher – even transformed Edith Evans into a great beauty.

Mr McBean retouched not only the portraits that he took, but also the houses he lived in, and there were many. He caused the doors in one of his homes to be painted to look as though they were open when in fact they were shut; ceilings were decorated to appear like beams festooned with grape vines; alcoves seemed like apertures through which the next room was visible. It would not be an exaggeration to say that he retouched his whole life. The tragic result of this wall-to-wall fantasy was that he never saw the danger he was in. When, after about a year of silence, the war began to shake London to its foundations, he moved to Bath. There, his exotic lifestyle became instantly conspicuous, and soon met with disapproval. The police broke into his house in which he had generously allowed various young men to take refuge from the bombardment of the capital. Though the youngest of the boys was living there at his mother's request, Mr McBean was charged with the perversion of minors, found guilty, and jailed for four years.

While he was 'away', his mother lived in the lodge of a large country house in Somerset where my mother was a guest. Because the lodge possessed no telephone, it was at the big house that a call from 'Angus' arrived. My mother fetched Mrs McBean and, when the telephone conversation was over, asked her if she were Mrs McBean. Seeing that the poor lady was terrified by this question, my mother added, 'You have nothing to fear because I am Quentin Crisp's mother.' They instantly pooled their disgrace and became friends.

Upon being released Mr McBean courageously went on with his life as though nothing unpleasant had happened. In spite of his misfortune, in one respect he was lucky. He worked chiefly among stage people and they rallied round him. Actresses love a gesture. He became so famous that all his early negatives now lie in the archives at Harvard (or, possibly, Yale), but I doubt that he ever became rich. He spent his money on buying large houses, altering them, sometimes to the extent of removing whole walls or ceilings, selling them, and buying even bigger premises. The last time I ever visited him, he was living in East Anglia in a Tudor mansion surrounded by a moat. I started to laugh the very moment this vast edifice came into view. While I was staying there, Mr McBean was threatening to write his life story. I wonder if that document exists; it would be well worth reading.

Now that the fever of attending to my correspondence has passed, I have returned to being my customary, slothful self. The first thing that I noticed as I resumed my meandering course through the Lower East Side of Manhattan is how dilapidated New York seems after the newness of other cities – especially Houston. There the streets are wide, straight, smooth, and absolutely free of litter, and the buildings all look as though they were erected yesterday. Manhattan, by contrast, is beginning to acquire an Old World charm. It won't be long before Grand Central Station looks like the Parthenon.

When I'm away from home, I seldom watch television. When not engaged in the smiling and nodding racket, I sleep. By the time I returned to East Third Street, I had fallen out of the television habit. Several days passed without my staring at a single frame. When, finally, I succumbed to my old sinful ways, I was so out of practice that I mistook a play for a news event. In the rather fuzzy distance, I could see some men running along a wharf while an announcer's voice told me that several people had been shot. Knowing how passionately TV loves disaster, I took this information calmly. When some advertisements interrupted this scene, my suspicions were aroused, but only slightly. I honestly cannot predict whether, when the end of the world is announced, the information will be punctuated by the words, 'Closing Down Sale. Hurry! Hurry!' I only knew for certain that what I was watching was fiction when, on being told that one of their victims had died, the terrorists displayed feelings of remorse. Zealots are totally incapable of any emotion other than rage. It is an unalterable law that people who claim to care about the human race are utterly indifferent to the sufferings of individuals.

Autumn

*

Local cockroaches are having the next-door house remodelled

Mrs Thatcher has abdicated; her acid reign is over. I shall spend my final years in perpetual mourning – rather like Queen Victoria.

Mrs Thatcher ascended the throne during one of my early, exploratory stage appearances in America. At that time, hardly an evening passed without someone asking my opinion of England's Prime Minister. I thought and still think that she was a star and I repeatedly said so. Once, after a show, while a female member of the audience was walking along the street with me, she said, 'I hope you realize that you gave all the wrong answers.' When my humble apologies finally subsided, she added, 'You are supposed to be against Mrs Thatcher.' I was obviously expected to take politics seriously; I never have.

Of course, if I had been born in China, Russia, or Cuba, I would have been shot. Then, as I stood before the line of rifles, I would have said, 'Hold your fire: I want to vote.' In Britain, going to the polls is a waste of time. There are really only two factions: the Tories and the Labourites, and whichever is in power, it doesn't take long for people to start moaning, 'What went wrong with the Labour (or Conservative) party?' It came to power: that's what went wrong. The question is as pointless as asking what went wrong with our marriage. We got married: that's what went wrong.

Politics are not an instrument for effecting social change; they are the art of making the inevitable appear to be a matter of wise human choice. Politics are not for people; they are for politicians – a medium in which a person can suspend his monstrous ego. In this respect, they fulfil exactly the same function as the stage or evangelism does for actors or preachers. The only benefit that can be derived by ordinary mortals from any of these vocations is that they present us with someone on whom we can focus our attention – even our passions – at least in a manner less fatuous than soccer. It is this human need that Mr Disraeli, Mr Lloyd George, Mr Churchill and Mrs Thatcher fulfilled so well. At first the world, and particularly the British press, tried to treat the last of these public figures as a joke or as a woman – which, in England, is much the same thing. One paper wrote, 'Mrs Thatcher arrived at the House of Commons looking dramatic in black.' These were not really words of praise, they were a cue for readers to regard her as frivolous. No one had ever said, 'Mr Wilson arrived looking commonplace in navy blue.' When the Falkland Islands suddenly loomed out of the Atlantic Ocean, the public, which had never before heard of the place, was forced to change its mind about the Iron Lady. She was the first politician in a very long time who did not try to rule the world and be loved at the same time.

For this, she has to be admired.

On Thanksgiving Day, as I have done for many years, I went again to Port Monmouth, New Jersey, where the parents of a friend of mine always welcome me. I regard this as a very special favour. Such occasions tend to be purely family affairs, and I am an outsider in so many ways. I doubt that any such thing would happen in England, but it is difficult to judge. There is no Thanksgiving Day on the British calendar. What have the English to be thankful for? In England, the eating of turkey is almost entirely confined to Christmas time; a turkey sandwich, which on the menus of New York delicatessens is a perennial item, would be regarded by Londoners as almost a blasphemy. Furthermore, apart from the differences in the history of the two nations, now that I have lived in America for many years I cannot help thinking of the southern English as a not particularly hospitable race. Of course, when I lived there, I acquired friends and they were very generous to me, but in general, public holidays and feast days, which encourage Americans to turn their attention outward towards acquaintances and even strangers, seem to cause British families to close ranks.

I have now seen Mr Attenborough's epic, *Gandhi.* I did not see this picture when it was first released on account of my deep-rooted aversion to British movies. Apparently, it won every possible award except one for costume design, presumably because sheets have only to be arranged rather than tailored. It fully deserves the praise lavished upon it. As an undertaking, it is formidable; its control of crowds is equal to that in *Gone With The Wind,* and Mr Kingsley is much more suitably cast as Mr Gandhi than Miss Leigh was in the role of Scarlett O'Hara. As a film, I did not think *Gandhi* was wholly a success, but I say this with bowed head because I know that, if I find fault with anything, I ought to be able to suggest what should have been done instead. In this instance, I can't. I can only say that, shortly after the massacre, *Gandhi* ceased to be a movie and became a documentary film. Though, very cleverly, the narrative begins with his assassination, we are not continuously drawn forward at an ever-increasing pace throughout the rest of the picture towards this climax. It is only during the final four or five minutes that our pulse quickens and, even then, we do not know why he was killed; we were never made aware of what specific danger he was in nor from what quarter disaster would spring.

It would have amounted to a kind of blasphemy to have mentioned it the other night, but, secretly, I could not repress the memory of a day when, some sixty years ago, English newspapers announced in bold letters that Mr Gandhi would 'fast unto death' if it would secure India her freedom. I overheard someone, who was surveying this announcement, say, 'It's the "unto" that will do the trick.'

*   *   *

I've now reached the age when almost every letter that I receive from anyone that I used to know in Britain contains a list of acquaintances who have recently died, and I have secretly wondered if this was ever going to pay off. Last week I thought it had. I received notification that I had been left two hundred pounds in somebody's will. As, with feverish fingers, I turned the pages of this document, my hopes began to fade. In order to get my hands on this legacy, I would have to sign for it, and my signature would have to be witnessed by a banker, a clergyman, or a justice of the peace who knows me personally. Where in the whole wide world will I find anyone with any prestige to lose who would admit to anything so incriminating?

So as to wring from anyone who may read this journal the last drops of sympathy, I will add that local cockroaches are having the next-door house remodelled and have temporarily moved into our house with their children. They sleep in my bed, eat the food from my plate, and even read the typescripts lying in a heap in one corner of my room.

In Mr Jonathan Nossiter's movie, *Resident Alien,* which is about me and New York City, Mr Michael Musto is shown saying, as if he were a dope pedlar, that he is in the business of handing out to the publicity addicts that infest this city their daily fix of fame without which they tend to become so restless. Last week, a Mr Duckett and a Mr Alig invited us to a positive orgy of notoriety: we celebrated Mr Musto's birthday at Limelight, the profane church on Sixth Avenue. As always, the music was too loud, but for the first time since the place was opened, it was lit so that we could actually see one another. We sat on real chairs at real tables and ate real food while from the stage Mr Musto introduced us to the lady who is the star of those television commercials that advertise the science-fiction gadget that helps put the helpless in instant communication with the Emergency Medical Service. She uttered into the microphone the by-now-famous line, 'I've fallen and I can't get up,' and was presented with the first Fallen Woman

Award. While we all applauded ecstatically, the girl sitting next to me murmured, 'That phrase is the story of my life.'

The guests wore clothes that ran the gamut from near nakedness, through every aspect of outrage, to deliberate dowdiness. It was quite impossible to distinguish them from the staff either by their appearance or their behaviour, since the waiters frequently kissed the diners whom they were serving. Naturally, Mr Musto looked more conspicuous than anybody else. He wore a silver topcoat over a green suit with large white stars, kinky fur shoes as big as canoes, and, of course, impenetrable dark glasses, and he embraced everyone. He really is the ideal host for such an occasion – never for a moment ceasing not merely to enjoy himself but also to be seen to do so.

During the evening, everybody photographed everybody, which prompted me to suggest that what is now needed is a periodical called *The Freeloader's Gazette*. Within minutes of my uttering these words, someone slapped on to our table a pile of magazines; I think they were actually entitled *Clubland*, but they obviously fulfilled exactly the same function as my proposed paper would do. Everybody who could reach a copy fast enough grabbed one and, at once, there was a hubbub like the noise in the parrot house at a zoo. 'Oh look,' they squawked, 'there I am and there's Tilly or Lilly or Billy or Willy.'

Whenever I make a feeble attempt to understand the financial basis on which such events are built, the glib response is always, 'It's all publicity.' I feign acceptance of this explanation, but secretly I harbour misgivings. If 'society' pictures and the accompanying gossip are only seen and read by the people featured in them, who never pay for anything, then who makes a profit, or, to pose a gloomier question, why is no one ruined by the staggering expense of it all?

When people ask me what I do when I am not involved in the smiling and nodding racket, I used to say, 'I breathe and I blink.' To these deliberately minimal activities, I must now add that I scratch. I suffer from eczema, which increases in severity with the passing years. Mr Eliot wrote that it is 'love that weaves the intolerable shirt of flame', but I'm wearing it, and I think it's eczema. Once, trying to elicit sympathy from an acquaintance, I asked him what he thought might be the cause of this strange malady. Without a moment's hesitation, he attributed it to the atmosphere in New York, and added, 'It's brought the Brooklyn Bridge to its knees and is tearing the façades from public buildings, why should it spare yours?'

Winter

*

I hate snow

Since I took up residence in the United States, so many kind people, some of them total strangers, have sent me gifts and greetings that I have come to feel acutely the lack of some easy means of expressing my gratitude to everybody in the world. Now, at last, it is to hand.

Merry Christmas, everybody!

Many who know me well may be surprised at this unaccustomed boisterousness, but, although my name has been mentioned in at least two books written by, for, and about curmudgeons, I am not really misanthropic. I merely do not have an aptitude for festivity – especially foreordained festivity – because I am by nature relaxed and happy. In the same way, I do not look forward with any special eagerness to annual holidays because, for some years past, my life has been one long vacation. Furthermore, I do not look well in a paper hat and am hopeless at what, in a time gone by, used to be called parlour games.

These are not inadequacies that have overtaken me in old age. Christmas has always been a period of acute embarrassment for me. What made the situation so absurd was the fact that, in spite of the generosity of Mr Claus, my mother used to give me two shillings so that I could buy a present for my father, and he gave me a similar sum to purchase something for my mother. On the appointed day, they both thanked me. Whom did they think they were kidding? Wishing to spare myself and my friends any reminder of such humiliating events, I have now abandoned as many rituals of the Yuletide season as possible; I try to carry on as though nothing unpleasant had happened, but, in England, it was necessary to be nice to somebody to get a square meal. Over there, the Christmas holidays may last for nearly a week. They have invented something called Boxing Day; this is the 26th of December and, in olden days, was when the dustmen, the postmen, and other public servants came knocking on the front door of the rich with money boxes and stood on the front doormat, wishing the owner a Merry Christmas until they were given a reward. If either the 25th or the 26th of December falls on a Saturday or Sunday, which for the most part are already days of rest, they feel cheated unless they are accorded some other day of idleness. During all that time England, never exactly a hardworking country, is shut. In these difficult circumstances, I have found it wise to fling myself upon the hospitality of a household where there are no children. This not only saves money, but also obviates having to crawl about on the floor, squeaking with delighted surprise, and other such humiliations.

But I have a message of hope to offer. If you ignore Christmas and all its attendant rituals, you have only about four years of disgrace to endure. If at the end of that time, anyone is still sending you a card or inviting you to a party, you can assume that his love is not merely a reflex reaction to convention, but is genuine and eternal and that, though he may expect gratitude, he will not demand from you a display of excessive merriment.

Being a sworn enemy of music – because it is the most noise conveying the least information – I have been to only one concert in my entire life, and that was many years ago and in another country. But I know Jack Eric Williams, who is a composer, a performer, and a teacher of music, and he is making continual efforts to effect a truce between me and culture. With this in view, he took me to an event infinitely more *recherché* than a mere concert – a *soirée musicale*. At least, that is what I took the occasion to be.

It occurred in the home of a Mr O'Horgan, who directed *Hair* and *Jesus Christ Superstar*, and who, on this particular evening, was a most agreeable host to about thirty people of all ages, from ninety down to a barefooted child, and of all sexes. We were assembled to hear a cantata entitled *The Child*, composed and conducted by a Mr Johnson. The singers included five or six excruciatingly fragile boys who are members of The Boys' Choir of Harlem. My ignorance prevents me from telling you if they sang well, but I can confidently assert that they behaved with the utmost decorum, considering the temptation to do otherwise. I am also unable to express any opinion of the music they performed, but the cantata was by no means the most astonishing aspect of the evening. Mr O'Horgan believes in music to an extent that I would not have thought possible. His apartment is dazzling. It is full, not of what might be called furniture, but of musical instruments. Apart from the grand piano used on this occasion, it contained another, much smaller keyboard instrument, three harps, and a huge drum. As if this did not display sufficient dedication to the Muse, the walls were encrusted with tambourines, rattles, and other devices whose function was too arcane for me to guess. Of course, this did little to make me like music any better, but it did make Mr O'Horgan the focus of my deepest interest – almost of reverence.

It is rapidly becoming a tradition that when a friend of mine, who has gone to teach in Kansas City, returns to New York for a breath of fresh happiness, we go to the theatre. Because his subject is what used to be known as elocution, we tend to choose a British play in which there is an emphasis on words rather than deeds. I think this is an aspect of the national character. In England, people over the age of thirty seem to care what they say and how they say it because their accent is a clue to class, which is so important to them. Here, there is no class and, in any case, speech has gone out of fashion. Music speaks louder than words, and in all public places, it is raised to such a volume that only a trained orator could make himself heard.

Our last visit to a theatre was to see *Lettice and Lovage*, which is a torrent of words. This time we chose *Shadowlands*. This is a play about C.S. Lewis, who wrote fantastic stories for children with one hand, and with the other, dissertations on the Anglo-Catholic religion. He was also a university teacher. This profession ideally suited him to be the central character in a drama about abstruse ideas expressed in languages festooned like a Christmas tree with glittering metaphors and similes. Indeed, *Shadowlands* begins with the hero delivering a lecture to the audience in which he tries to explain why God has made life so horrible. Though Americans mistrust words – especially unfamiliar ones – their reverence for the theatre is so great that they remained calm.

As the story unfolds, its participants are drawn at a dignified pace from the serenity of English university life into the turgid real world, from happy celibacy through awkward marriage to widowerhood, and all the while, the God of the Christians has to be appeased. It was very embarrassing, but it was never dull.

The supporting cast is good. In a sense, their task is easy because, being English, they are acting the avoidance of reaction. When Jack Lewis informs his brother that he is getting married, the reply, after a pause, is, 'You surprise me.' Miss Alexander, whom we last saw on television in *Malice in Wonderland*, plays the Eve in this academic Eden, and she is wonderful. As we sat only three rows from the stage, I cannot judge how her performance 'reads' from a distance, but to us every word was audible and every glance was loaded with meaning.

The play's fundamental problem rests on the shoulders of a Mr Hawthorne, and he carries it commendably, even heroically. His only handicap is that he has to act charm; he does not possess any by nature. Charm has little to do with being handsome; it lies in a subtle willingness to please without grovelling, combined with the ability to make decisions without a hint of tyranny.

In my lifetime, the one facet of theatre that has changed more than any other is décor. It used to be called scenery, and its only function was to suggest convincingly a place and a time of day.

When I was young and thought that going to the theatre would make me seem to be an aesthete, most drama, other than the classics, was domestic and was played in front of what that formidable iconoclast, Joan Littlewood, called 'those bloody French windows'. All that is now ended.

Being in hiding from Mr Claus, I have only attended one other public event: a party for my eighty-second birthday (billed as my eighty-first – to cheer me up?). It took place at El Morocco. I have been there once before and thought I must wear nothing but black and white if I was to seem accustomed to its zebra motif, but in fact, the festivities occurred in a bright red upper room that looked like one of the chambers in Mr Poe's 'Masque of the Red Death'.

Our hostess was the Countess Erme Klent-de-Boen, and she very graciously did the whole routine, standing by the door for about an hour to welcome each new arrival. I was deeply impressed. The guests (hardly any of whom I knew except Jack Eric Williams) arrived in droves, but hardly any of them spoke to me. Contrary to custom at such functions, photographers were few, but just as I was leaving, a gentleman who seems pleased to be known as Ugly George appeared from the nearby twitching area, wearing only a few wisps of silvered leather and carrying on his shoulder a video camera. For a few seconds, co-starred with Mr Baird Jones, I smiled and said I was delighted to be there. Then I was permitted to depart.

An English poet, probably Thomas Hardy, describes actors as 'that sad, happy race'. Translated into prose, the phrase means 'that heart-rendingly optimistic bunch of misfits'. I can think of no other profession whose members are willing to take so much trouble to create anything so short-lived – except cooks who prepare elaborate feasts decorated with all sorts of visual effects, only to have their work demolished in minutes by a horde of unheeding locusts.

* * *

It has been snowing. I hate snow, and will never understand the people who persistently exclaim that it looks pretty. This is like being glad to be attacked by a handsome mugger. Snow is, at best, tiring to negotiate; at worst it is dangerously slippery and causes one to arrive in other people's houses and sit around for hours in wet socks.

I shall try to stay in my room until the spring. This plan involves a lot of two particular activities. One of these is watching television. When I lived in England, all good programmes came from the United States. If the participants were running fast and shooting straight, the drama was American. In those days, in Britain, only two channels existed, BBC or dog food: culture or entertainment. There was no room for all these quizzes, competitions, panels, games, and above all there were fewer advertisements. Over here I find the commercials not only repetitious, but also shocking. Before Christmas, I expected feverish claims to be made on the public's every spare penny, but now that the crisis has passed, the avarice of shopkeepers has not abated. There are sales of wilting fir trees, melting snowmen, and jilted turkeys.

Moreover, these are not the worst commercials. It is generally admitted that, during the past twelve years, America has been reduced by its credit-card policies to owing money to almost every other nation on earth, but this way of thinking is still encouraged. Television offers vast loans to people who 'have bad credit or no credit at all'. Similarly, now that it might be possible to persuade even the proselytizing Dr Ruth that sex is a mistake, we are not being encouraged to think about something else, but, instead, are offered inflammatory telephone conversations with women whose smirking faces are constantly shown on our screens. All these blandishments carry warnings that no one under the age of eighteen may avail himself of them, but no suggestion is forthcoming as to how such a restriction can be enforced. If anyone were to make the feeblest attempt to curtail these commercials, there would be an outcry and the citation of any number of Amendments. Perhaps the Amendments should be amended.

Another activity that helps to occupy the time spent waiting for the snow to melt is the writing of letters. Among those that I have most recently received is one from an unknown young man who complains that, while the words 'gay community' are in frequent use, no such happy confederacy exists. His letter lists all the different factions that compose the gay population, but he pours scorn on all of them. Perhaps it may be worthwhile to write down my thoughts in this matter.

I think that anyone who feels reluctantly set apart from his fellow homosexuals must make some effort to accept their idiosyncrasies. He must party with the inveterate partygoers, scream with the screamers, and, if he grows tired of these vigorous activities, he can try visiting the closets of his less extrovert friends.

Most of the week has been spent preparing for my forthcoming visit to Seattle. I have no idea what will be expected of me there, but, on the principle of never saying no to any invitation, I shall go the Alice B. Theater and try to say the words the Washingtonians wish to hear.

Once, just before starting on a plane journey, I remember being involved in a conversation founded entirely on a misunderstanding. Someone asked me if I was in a state of anxiety; I replied that I was. This was taken to mean that I doubted that a heavier-than-air machine could stay up in the sky. In fact, this was not the cause of my furrowed brow. Of course, if a plane I was in suddenly dived towards the earth, I should squeak and cry and pray and show all sorts of signs of panic, but I do not start on a flight worrying about the forces of gravity any more than I wander around the Lower East Side thinking how I will proceed if I am attacked by a stranger. Before a journey by any means of locomotion, I am preoccupied with whether I have packed enough lip gloss to last for the duration of my stay and whether I shall be late because all the bridges leading out of Manhattan are hardly more than picturesque ruins.

In the meantime, I have received a letter from the Ronald

Firbank Society in England. Presumably, it publishes a magazine, because it has asked me to explain in 900 words what has gone wrong with sex. The answer is that sex suffers from the same malaise as television: there is too much of it, with the result that it repeats itself. Halfway through what you had assumed was going to be a new episode, you realize that it's a re-run: you know how it will end. After that, it's difficult to remain interested.

When I was about eight years old, my parents rented, more or less permanently, a cottage in a village called Pett. It was situated about a mile from the Sussex coast. On most days during our annual summer holidays we carried food prepared by my long-suffering mother to the beach where, in considerable discomfort, we ate wasp-infested fruit and sand-encrusted sandwiches. The war was still raging in France, and I distinctly remember that we stood at the water's edge and listened to what Mr Wilfred Owen called 'the monstrous anger of the guns'. Now, looking back, this seems impossible, for they must have been twenty-five miles away, but a mood of mournful curiosity returns to me whenever I recall the horrors of my childhood vacations. Whoever said that children are innocent? Because my sister and my brothers claimed to be eager to bathe, I squeaked with feigned delight whenever I caught sight of the sea, but in fact, I hated it and I still do. The ocean is not my friend. Why does it keep banging away at the helpless shore and making all that noise? What does it want?

To the west of us at Pett beach were the romantic cliffs of Fairlight and the jolly, busy seaside resort of Hastings, but to the east lay Dungeness. The very word is like a knell. If we walked in that direction, we came to Romney Marshes. Gradually the landscape became flatter, the shore grew stonier, the sky darkened, and bird calls assumed a lonely, grieving note. It is in this doom-laden terrain that Mr Derek Jarman has, for some unknown reason, chosen to live, and it is there that his latest movie is set. The landscape serves him well. The film is called *The Garden* – presumably of Gethsemane.

I didn't know that I had ever met Mr Jarman, but he assures me that we were co-judges of a beauty competition held in a London school of art. As I was occasionally a model there, and consequently an object of naked contempt, this seems unlikely, but I dare not doubt him: he is so friendly. Last week, he and his merry men came to my door with one of those vans in which moviemakers habitually travel (and, I suspect, sometimes sleep) and conveyed me to an obscure café at the corner of King and Hudson Streets. There, in a twilit upper room, we drank a few beers and met a few anonymous well-wishers before walking to the Film Forum where *The Garden* was being shown for one night. If this is the only screening in Manhattan of this film, it seems strange that so few of the crowned heads of the industry were present, and so little fuss was made about Mr Jarman, because he is, without doubt, a genius.

I have seen at least one other of his films; it was *The Tempest,* in which David Meyer walked in and out of the North Sea wearing nothing but a sword, and Elisabeth Welch sang 'Stormy Weather'. It was a deliberately skittish rendering of Mr Shakespeare's play, but, for oddity, it had nothing on the new work. *The Garden* is not impish; it is haunting . . . even harrowing.

Its style is what is glibly called surrealistic. Whatever this term suggests to connoisseurs, to real people it means that, by placing them in a deliberately inappropriate setting, an intense reality is bestowed upon objects that most of us take for granted. For instance, a kettle on a stove will be instantly recognized however vaguely it is delineated, but if it is standing in the middle of the Sahara desert, it must proclaim its kettlehood very loudly indeed if it is not to become a pyramid. In *The Garden,* almost all backgrounds are at variance with what is going on in front of them. Everything on which the camera rests its baleful eye acquires an unnatural intensity. On the way home from Hudson Street, I asked the director how this effect was achieved. It seems that it is possible nowadays to photograph people and things against a plain blue backdrop and add a quite different background later. Thus, an absolutely unruffled group of actors can stand beneath a raging, stormy sky or a harshly-lit figure can appear in a misty, nocturnal setting. It is this unreal reality that gives *The Garden* its appealing beauty.

When I returned to Seattle, the people were as friendly as they had been two weeks ago, but the weather was completely different. Having described the city as San Francisco wet, I must now say that it is San Francisco dry – especially when I recall that every morning that I was in the gay Mecca of California, if I looked out of the window when I first awoke, I saw only a dim grey wall of mist. Nothing resembling a landscape emerged until at least high noon. On this visit to Seattle, I was clearly able to see Mr Rainier's mountain; it looked like a negative of Fujiyama – a dark volcanic cone silhouetted against a pale sky.

The journeys there and back were less attractive on this second trip. The airport's spy-catching machine had become as suspicious as a parole officer. Every time I came anywhere near it, it complained loudly until I had given my keys (on which there hangs a huge metal label marked 'SUNDANCE'), my rings, my lipstick, and my money to an appalled attendant. Only then did the machine give me its approval.

Once again, the plane was nowhere near full; this was an advantage, as it permitted a kind stranger named Mr Hubbard to sit beside me and talk. It transpired that he rules an opera star, a Leonie Rysanek, whose photograph will appear on the cover of a forthcoming issue of *Opera Monthly*, so we had quite a large area of common ground to explore. My companion even managed to go a long way towards convincing me to listen kindly to opera.

Wherever I go professionally in the United States, I am always talking to audiences about happiness because it is the only thing that I understand; the only variation is my approach. In Seattle, the management suggested that I should start by explaining myself in general and, in particular, the mystery of my so-belated decision to leave England and settle – if I can call my life here settled – in

America. What seemed to amuse audiences at the Alice B. Theater most was my description of the difference between life in Manhattan and what passes for life in London.

The first thing that every English visitor to New York notices is that here everybody is his friend. Once, when I was travelling innocently up Third Avenue on a bus, a young man crouched beside me and, very discreetly, asked me to write my name on a fragment of paper. I complied with his request and he returned to his seat. Immediately, a large woman sitting on the other side of the bus asked loudly, 'Well, who are you?' Hanging my head in feigned modesty, I replied, 'Who indeed?' This apparently was not a satisfactory answer, because she then said, 'I thought he was asking for your autograph.' Simpering, I admitted that he was.

SHE: Well, why?

ME: You must ask him.

He was sitting with his head in his hands, but no one else within earshot was, so she turned to the entire clientèle of the bus and exclaimed, 'Well, who the hell *is* he?' Nobody actually answered, but they all seemed to be enjoying the dialogue immensely. When the moment came for me to alight, I passed the woman and as I did so, I said, 'I'm sorry I wasn't anybody.' Then even the driver laughed.

Nothing like this would ever occur in Britain. An Englishman once said to me accusingly, 'You're the one who lives in America permanently – why?' I explained that here everybody speaks to everybody everywhere you go. On this remark his comment was, 'I can't think of anything worse.' To demonstrate that this attitude is a national one, I repeat a story told by a friend of mine about a friend of hers.

A woman, intending to make a long journey by rail, went to a main-line terminus in London and, as she was early, entered the station canteen. There she bought a cup of coffee and a Kit Kat. Then she had to negotiate the change, the Kit Kat, the coffee, her shoulder bag, and her suitcase while she looked for somewhere to sit. The only vacant seat that she could see was at a table where someone was already seated, so reluctantly she sat there. After putting down her case and sliding her bag from her shoulder, she put some free sugar and milk into her cup. The Kit Kat was lying in the middle of the table. The moment she unwrapped it and laid it out on its sheet of silver foil, the man opposite her leaned forward, broke off a piece, and ate it. Deeply affronted, she also broke off a piece. Then, while she was taking a few sips from her cup, he took another piece, leaving her only one last bit. This she quickly devoured.

Then the stranger went to the counter and bought himself a cream bun which was a spiral confection with a little disc of pastry on the top. At that moment the woman's train arrived, so she hastily reversed the original ritual, hitched her bag on to her shoulder, took up her suitcase, and, as she passed her enemy, she snatched the lid from his bun and ate it defiantly. Then she boarded the train and, as it moved off, she put her case in the luggage rack, sat down, took her bag on to her lap, opened it, and there was the Kit Kat. The one on the table had, of course, been his, but because he and she were both English and had never been introduced to one another, neither could say, 'What the hell are you doing with my chocolate biscuit?'

The day after my return from the Far West, though as near to collapse as the Brooklyn Bridge, I reconstructed myself for an appointment in a nearby diner with a journalist from a London paper. She wished to question me about my image. Many of my answers were self-evident. There are not many occasions when I can justify my actions with the threadbare excuse, 'Everybody does it,' but this was one of them. For instance, I explained that, like everyone else, I gave up wearing nail varnish when my hands began to look like claws. I was also able to describe myself by quoting other English papers which define me as 'a scruffy dandy', but this, it seemed, was not enough. 'How do you think of yourself?' my interviewer persisted. I should have replied, 'Incessantly,' but this riposte did not occur to me. For once, words, which I have always regarded as my best friends, failed me.

A totally incongruous mystical element has suddenly entered my life. Last week, a Mr Acosta, a huge gentleman looking like Mr Michelangelo's idea of God but not so worried, arrived on the Lower East Side in a purring limousine, embraced me in the street, and whisked me away to a house of indescribable splendour on East 80th Street.

This extraordinary event resulted from the fact that Mr Acosta and I have apparently met before. On that occasion, he says, he introduced himself to me on Second Avenue, whereupon I replied, 'You must be the unicorn man' – a remark that amazed him because at that time he was involved in a film about one of these mythical beasts. I have no recollection whatsoever of this conversation, but Mr Acosta has never forgotten it, and, thinking of me as in some way in touch with the infinite, while famous names fell like rain from his fur-fringed lips, he showed me extracts from yet another picture that may be categorized as unabashed festival material. It features Mr John Hurt as a bag lady heading a cast consisting entirely of cats, photographed in slow motion and the most lurid lighting ever seen. To Comrade Prokofiev's score, these creatures represent rather than act the story of *Romeo and Juliet*, while some of Mr Shakespeare's lines are recited by real actors. It is Mr Acosta's wish that I should speak a few phrases uttered by a character called Balthasar. Now I will be compelled to read this play, which so far I have only ever scanned in a cursory manner while searching for the answers to crossword clues.

My agent once pointed out to me that if I praise absolutely everything, my judgement will soon be regarded as worthless. She is right, but it is also true that, because I can always be relied upon to say something nice, publishers continue to send me proof copies of their books for a eulogistic 'quote'. It is in this spirit of eternal optimism that Hamish Hamilton has now given me an advance copy of *Rebel Mates*, by Graham McCann.

Some years ago, when I was on a whirlwind tour of provincial cities in England, I met Mr McCann. He looked so young that I secretly thought he was a student. It was as well that I didn't say so, because, in fact, he is a professor. I have no idea what he teaches, but his abiding preoccupation is with the image-making propensities of the cinema. His book about Miss Monroe was the ultimate treatise on the movie star goddess and slave.

His latest work is about Messrs Clift, Brando and Dean. He regards these three actors as having taken over the screen from Mr Wayne and Mr Gable, those icons of total masculinity, and as representing American man's idea of himself since the 1950s – the decade in which the country began to lose its optimism and the Hollywood machine broke down. Mr McCann says that all three of the above-named actors were bisexual, and suggests that this ambiguity was at least in part the cause of that self-doubt that manifested itself in inner conflict and an outward display of unfocused rebellion – that turned Mr Dean into what Mr Kazan called 'a pudding of hatred' and made Mr Brando so perfectly suited to the part of *The Wild One* who, you may remember, when asked, 'What are you rebelling against?', replied, 'What've you got?'

I have never understood the immense popularity of Mr Clift. To me he seemed to be a shrimp with a shrimp's close-set eyes whose idea of acting was to confront the camera with a meaningless stare, but then, I was already middle-aged by the time the Fifties were in full swing; it was much too late in life for me to admire self-doubt.

About once a week, some young person writes to me or telephones me with the suggestion that we should meet. Whenever possible, I comply with his or her request on the principle that we should never say no to anything except an appeal for money, but, just in case the stranger is a murderer, I agree to a rendezvous in a neighbourhood diner. This week I was given lunch by a young man from Brooklyn who was on his way to an audition for a part in yet another of Professor Bentley's plays. We discussed many subjects, and finally talked about the vague but intense feeling that almost all men seem to have of being inhibited by the society in which they live. This is an emotion that I have never felt; I cannot think of anything important that I refrain from doing because of what the world would say.

When I returned home from this very pleasant meeting, I at once began to read Dr McCann's book about Mr Clift *et al.* It then dawned on my befuddled brain that what many men feel convention is preventing them from expressing may not be some hideous piratical urge to rape or homicide, but the feminine side of their natures. This is an idea that has never before occurred to me.

POSTSCRIPT: I have received from Mr Robert Patrick, in Stockton, California, a postcard which states that he has learned how to make a homosexual invisible. 'You may tell your readers,' he writes, 'that if you don't spread disease, exhibit pornographic photographs, or rape and kill small children, they don't know that you exist.'

Whatever will the East Third Street postman think?

Exactly one week after an extraordinary auction at the Cooper Union, in which two seats to hear the nonsense that I talk were sold to the highest bidder, I went to the New York Public Library to fulfil my half of this strange bargain. I didn't do very well, but American audiences are too indulgent to protest.

I was supposed to discourse on the subject of wit, and I have a lot to say on this theme, but I had not properly organized my thoughts. It had been a difficult week. With one hand I had tried to write something kind for *Christopher Street* about a film called *Queens Logic,* which is really a non-movie about a non-place, and, with the other, to explain censorship to the readers of a highly literary periodical called *The Hungry Mind,* which is published in St Paul, Minnesota. In my by no means humble opinion, restrictions are essential not only in society (a notion that most people seem to accept), but also in the arts (which young people find irksome, if not intolerable). It is my contention that artists, in whatever medium, produce flabbier work the more freedom they are given: all subtlety, all irony vanishes. For instance, Miss West ascended the throne in a decade when moralists grew on palm trees in Hollywood. She was compelled to use considerable skill to imply what she was forbidden to say. Proof of her greatness lies in the fact that the line, 'Come up and see me sometime,' has passed for ever into the folklore of filth because of her delivery of the phrase – which, in itself, contains not one word that a nun would be reluctant to utter. Preoccupation with these weighty matters took up much of the time and energy that ought to have been devoted to organizing what I wanted to say about humorous writing.

I had no idea that my arrival at the library would receive so much attention. On 42nd Street, an unknown woman was lurking in the shadow of the stone lions, waiting to ask me to write a foreword to a book about a drag artist of whom nobody has ever heard. I suggested that she should telephone me so that, in calmer circumstances, I could explain to her that I would gladly do almost anything (for a fee) if and when it was quite certain that this improbable biography would one day be published. At the very door of the building, another unknown woman begged me to take her in with me, although the place was rumoured to be full.

The gentleman who had organized this assignment had miraculously found for me a copy of *Vile Bodies* by Mr Waugh. It is the funniest book ever written, and I had hoped to quote long passages from it to fill the silences left by my ineptitude. I had read this book sixty years ago, when it was first published and when I still read books wantonly. I did not then realize that it was satire; I loved all those feckless bright young things. When I looked at it again, I saw that it was far too full of mordant English irony to appeal to Americans. For instance, it says of a fictitious fashionable eating place, 'Chez Espinosa . . . was full of oilcloth and Lalique glass, and the sort of people who liked that sort of thing went there continually and said how awful it was.' This single sentence encapsulates the attitude adopted by what the press used to call 'café society'. Over there, disdain is considered chic. Over here, the opposite is true; the national characteristic of the United States is indiscriminate enthusiasm. I didn't manage to put any of these opinions in an orderly manner; I merely flung myself into the well-known smiling and nodding racket.

The best part of the evening began when the performance was over. Then the organizers of the evening took the winners of the auction lot and me to a small but delightful restaurant called Tout Va Bien; it is on 51st Street between Eighth and Ninth Avenues. There we ate and drank and talked for hours without the management appearing to grow restless. Towards the end of the evening, one of the guests, suddenly deciding that the occasion must be immortalized, went to the telephone and summoned a photographer. Within fifteen minutes, two girls and a camera arrived to take our pictures. What worldly power!

I have failed. I never had much to recommend me except that I keep my word, so I am very conscientious about paying my bills as soon as they arrive, acknowledging gifts that come by mail, and keeping appointments. But last week I defaulted. Some time ago, I had received a kind invitation from the Baroness Sherry von Korber-Bernstein to a birthday celebration at Club 53. She is one of the people on the peanut circuit that I most admire and I was looking forward eagerly to the occasion. The day before the event, she even telephoned me to make sure that I would be there and I promised that I would, but, on the appointed evening, it snowed. I had even reconstructed myself and gone downstairs to the front door, but when I saw the weather in the street, I lost my nerve. I returned to my room, dismantled myself, had a good cry, and went to bed.

I am frightened of the snow. Like many people of my age, I dread slippery or uneven surfaces; if I were to fall and break even the smallest bone, it would never mend; I am no longer renewable. I would write to her a humble letter if I knew the Baroness's address, but, as with so many Americans, that seems to be a secret. I cannot, therefore, ease my conscience by making my apologies.

The following day the snow ceased to fall, so at the request of a Mr Jones I did go to the Limelight to meet all the virgins of New York. I didn't see any girls in flowing white robes carrying lilies. In fact, though the décor of the place looked different, the clientèle seemed exactly the same as last time I was there. However, I was rewarded by sitting next to a lady who told me that the love of her life was her cat and that, when one of her gentlemen friends suggested that she should transfer her affection to him, she replied that, if he was willing to undergo the operation that had been performed on her pet, she would consider his proposition.

I returned home from the virgins to find that the war in the Persian Gulf was over – at least in the opinion of various televisionaries. I personally regard all this rejoicing as somewhat premature; I think this period of American history will one day come to be called 'The Elba Fallacy'. (Elba, it should be recalled, was the island from which Mr Bonaparte returned to make more trouble.)

1991

Spring

*

Though sex seems still to be with us, breasts have once again subsided

Time passes more swiftly in America than elsewhere. If a public building is fifteen years old, plans are made to demolish it; if an actress hasn't made a movie in a whole year, she must make a 'comeback'; in England, her return to the screen would only be described in those terms if she had been absent from it for six years. This national awareness of the speed with which time is passing may be due to Americans having short memories, and that, in turn, is why they hunger for a recorded past.

To satisfy this need, Manhattan has become an island on which every fifth person is a photographer who takes at least thirty pictures of every subject, however trivial. This state of affairs is a source of amazement to me. Photography is such a complicated profession; it requires a knowledge of chemistry and of physics. Furthermore, it necessitates the buying of equipment so expensive that it has to be insured, and the renting of premises that yield a large uninterrupted space with big windows, and when all these circumstances have been assembled, the end product is only an imitation of life.

Last week, the day of reckoning came for which I had been prepared by a sumptuous tea at the Helmsley Palace given to me by my mad moviemaker, Mr Acosta (mentioned in an earlier entry in this journal). He took me to lunch at Joe Allen's restaurant on West 46th Street to fortify me for a visit to a recording studio, which turned out to be but a stone's throw away – and it was a wonder that stones were not thrown. There I spoke various lines from Mr Shakespeare's *Romeo and Juliet*. Not all of these are uttered in the play by the same character, but Mr Acosta is dauntless. He is also inexhaustibly patient.

We arrived in the torture chamber at two o'clock in the afternoon, and did not leave until after half past four. The endless re-takes were, of course, entirely my fault, but no one evinced the slightest irritation with me. My own reaction to this situation has been, from the very beginning, one of complete bewilderment. As everybody knows, my voice is as flat as a pancake, though not as palatable. Why ever was I being asked to recite poetry that has taxed the skills of great actors? I bleated the lines over and over again on one side of a sound-proof glass wall while, on the other, Mr Acosta, as though conducting an orchestra, tried to coax from my flaccid vocal cords some hint of music, some breath of magic. If he had not been due somewhere else at five o'clock, we would still be in that studio. If my performance is ultimately used, which doesn't seem very likely, it will be woven with the voices of Miss Smith, Miss Redgrave, Mr Kingsley, and other luminaries of the movie industry. How angry they will be!

When this session was over, a large white cat was released from a container, and I was photographed with it. As this movie will be acted entirely by Mr Hurt and a bunch of cats, presumably this creature was the juvenile lead. Whether this picture was a serious publicity shot or a joke, I did not dare to ask.

As long as I can wrest from the hands of fate at least one day a week during which I do not leave my room, and therefore am not obliged to devote several hours to reconstructing myself for public viewing, it doesn't really matter which day of the week it is. I do not go regularly to an office, and seldom do any serious shopping, so I don't even mind if my self-imposed imprisonment occurs on a Saturday, but if it does, there is one disadvantage. Television regards weekends as mini-Christmases. Except for the news, which never fails to regale us with stories of domestic folly and global disaster, programmes during that time tend to be very bland. Last Saturday, I spent the daylight hours trying to explain that interior decoration is folly to one magazine and, to another, that music is a sin. Then, when night fell, I watched television with half an eye. I was just about to abandon all hope of entertainment when a cops-and-robbers movie, called *Arizona Heat,* began.

At first this appeared to be a cosy but hardly original tale about a policeman who is known for his unconventional – even scandalous – methods of bringing justice to the city, but who cannot be dismissed from the force because of his high average of successful arrests. My interest was enhanced when he was given a female partner on the grounds that her presence would civilize the wild beast in him. Even then I thought this would only provide a mixture of violence and sex, but no.

One fine morning, our hero calls at his partner's home and is introduced to her flat-mate, an airline stewardess. This situation arouses his suspicions (and mine); pretending he needs to go to the bathroom, he peeps slyly into the bedroom and sees the incriminating double bed. Suddenly, the movie adds to its customary cinematographic realism an entirely different kind of human reality. Once the partner has admitted that she is a lesbian, the rogue cop cannot leave the subject alone.

Both his and her characters are exceedingly well drawn, and their dialogue is entirely free from political or poetic generalities. *Arizona Heat* survived its fatuous title and became, at least in my experience, the first movie ever to show us – nay, to force upon us – a painful glimpse of what it is like to be an unavailable woman in an obsessively masculine world. Life is much harder for self-confessed homosexual women than for gay men. If I had not enjoyed a fairly lazy day, I would never have stayed up late enough to see that film. The moral is: Never go to bed early on a Saturday night.

The letter of the week comes from a boy aged thirteen living in an unknown town in the middle of Germany. He had read some gossip about me in a recent issue of a magazine called *Stern*. He says that convinced him that I am 'a funny man' (to say the least) and he demands a long reply from me telling him what I like and don't like.

What makes this communication so remarkable is firstly that anyone so young could be bothered to write to such a freakish character as I and could be so cosmopolitan as to be interested in anyone in such a distant land. Secondly, there is not one spelling error and there are only a few erroneously used parts of speech. Almost no letter that I receive from people twice his age in any state of America is, in this academic sense, so correct. Is there something wrong with American education?

Some kind friends whom I once visited in Indiana send me newspapers that they receive regularly from England so that I may fritter away my time attempting to solve the elaborate crossword puzzles that they contain. Occasionally, I break my vow of ignorance and allow my gaze to fall on the news. In this way, I recently stumbled upon one of the funniest items of useless information that I have ever read. A rich English eccentric (famous for having taken Salvador Dali seriously) was said to have hated his mother. He can hardly be blamed for this if the following anecdote is an example of the depth of her interest in her offspring. One Sunday morning, while dressing with great care before going to church, she demanded that one of her children accompany her. When asked (presumably by a governess), 'Which child?', she replied, 'Whichever one goes with my blue dress.'

It is precisely such outlandish tales as this that give Americans the impression that the British indulge their eccentrics. They do, but with one important qualification. These human national treasures must be rich, or, if not well-heeled, at least well-born. Even in this outfield of English society, snobbery still reigns supreme. Oddity among one's social equals is regarded as 'putting on airs'. It gives rise to such questions as, 'Who the hell do you think you are that you may disregard the rules which, however irksome, the rest of us have agreed to obey?' Another remark frequently made in these circumstances is, 'What would happen to the world if everyone behaved as you do?' – a foolish query when what has provoked all this indignation is an instance of unique behaviour.

The name of Julie Harris is for ever engraved upon my heart because of a small incident that took place during my first visit to Los Angeles. In some vast building the name and exact location of which I have long since forgotten, the crowned heads of Hollywood had gathered to bear witness to the presentation of yet another award to Miss Harris. I was there with Mr Hillard Elkins, and I asked him whether she had already arrived and, if so, whether I might touch the hem of her garment. He crossed the entire room to where she was sitting and asked if she would permit this. She rose immediately and came to our table. I cannot think of any other celebrity who would have bothered to do this. Miss Harris is the personification of '*noblesse oblige*'.

When we met last week, she had completely forgotten this occasion for the simple reason that it was just an expression of the way she is all the time. I know this now because on Monday I was taken by her goddaughter to see Miss Harris's latest one-person show, *Lucifer's Child,* and afterwards we accompanied her and other guests to the Russian Tea Room, that haunt of celebrities next to Carnegie Hall, where the goddaughter spends most of her spare time, as though it were her local diner. The show, at the Music Box Theater, tells the life story of the Baroness Karen von Blixen-Finecke, who, under the pen name Isak Dinesen, wrote *Out of Africa* and whom Miss Streep played in the movie of that name. The present show takes place much later in the Baroness's life – long after Robert Redford is dead and she has returned to her ancestral home in Denmark. The woman we see now is less romantic, more cynical, and much deeper in the clutches of the disease she contracted from her husband.

Lucifer's Child is very ingeniously devised by a Mr Luce. During the first act, the Baroness packs for her visit to America, and this provides Miss Harris with a lot to do and the audience with things to see as well as hear. Like all one-person shows, this is fundamentally an exercise in lovability, and of this art, Miss Harris, though neither coy nor sentimental, is a master.

Supper at the Russian Tea Room after the show was, in a sense, an even more engaging experience. Miss Harris is totally without affectation – a trait that I find remarkable in a famous actress – and she is an amalgam of contradictory qualities: strong but almost alarmingly frail, self-possessed but able to take an interest in everything said to her. For me, the entire evening was, in its quiet way, a truly memorable occasion.

Sooner or later the time comes for almost everybody when, although he has sworn to himself that he will never utter such sentiments, he declares that the country is going to the dogs, that life has become louder, public manners cruder, and art totally incomprehensible. Where, he asks himself, will it all end? I began to lose my grip on culture with the poems of Mr Eliot, the plays of Mr Beckett, and the novels of Mr Joyce. Then one day last week, in spite of all my efforts to prevent such a disaster, I finally fell into the abyss of bewilderment.

Mr Jack Eric Williams accompanied me to the La MaMa Theater to see a play, or at least an event, entitled *Eddy Goes to Poetry City*, by a Mr Foreman. As far as I could tell, no one was given a programme and no one bought a ticket – a bad sign, but a ruse that disarms criticism. The performance space was decorated with great care to look as hideous as possible, and in it a cast of five people, obviously rehearsed with the utmost care, moved about, sometimes quite violently, and, wearing strange devices that amplified their voices alarmingly, declaimed various aphoristic phrases. At the end, a surprisingly large audience applauded enthusiastically.

As we left, someone who had driven all the way from the very edge of Long Island for this experience asked Mr Williams what the play had meant. (I'd say he had the right to know.) I did not hear the reply because I tottered home abruptly in a state of collapse, but I asked the same question by telephone the next day. I have now been informed that Mr Foreman calls his company The Ontological/Hysteric Theater, and he is concerned with the interpenetrability of everything, atomized; Mr Williams called it 'the mind/body split'.

It's such a relief to know.

When children get together, they talk about how awful their teachers are; when wives get together, they talk about how awful their husbands are; and when writers congregate, the common topic of conversation is the failings of their agents. I must have been lucky; I've had two agents and never felt the least animosity towards either of them. My first agent I never truly understood, but then he was a Hungarian and I'm grateful to him for putting me into the smiling and nodding racket. Without ever knowing it, he prepared me for my American life. My present agent is a saint and also a friend. We meet from time to time whether there is any business to discuss or not. She feeds me and occasionally takes me to parties. Last week we went to the West Side Arts Theater – an establishment not quite up to the gilt-cupids-and-crimson-plush standard, but above the dim cellar level. We were there to see a Mr Reynolds in *Only The Truth Is Funny*.

This is yet another one-man show. When I was young, in this particular field of entertainment there was only Miss Ruth Draper. She was famous to incorrigible theatre-goers, but I do not think she ever attempted the six-evenings-and-two-matinées routine; I believe she most often did afternoons on stages that, at night, were occupied by real plays.

As far as I know, it was the Edinburgh Festival that started the present rage for one-man shows; it became a hothouse for egomaniacs too uncontrollable to work with other actors. Their acts may take any one of several different forms. Miss Draper filled the empty space around her with imaginary characters; most modern solo performers imitate some famous person – Emily

Dickinson, Mr Twain, at a pinch St Matthew, or, more recently, Baroness von Blixen and Mr Capote.

Until someone invented Lily Tomlin and Jackie Mason, I do not think any stand-up comic ever tried to stay the pace for an entire evening – except, possibly, at home. Now Mr Mason has a rival. Mr Reynolds cleverly combines the typical digressions of a stand-up comic with telling us the story of his life. At one point during his performance, he divides the world into assholes and creeps. (He is not squeamish about the words he uses or the events he describes.) Assholes, he tells us, are people who enjoy jokes about physical deformity; creeps are those who do not. I must now admit, with head bowed in shame, that I am the creepiest of them all: I don't even like to hear fun made of victims who are plain or uneducated or of low degree. (In England, I hated *Punch* because in every issue it contained at least one joke about a domestic servant misusing or mispronouncing a word.)

Mr Reynolds is a self-confessed – nay, a self-proclaimed – asshole. His monologue is less depraved than even a few minutes of Lenny Bruce, but it is deliberately, uproariously coarse. In spite of this, his overall message is that life is worth living and that love is wonderful. The audience, though neither exclusively male nor predominantly young, believed him wholeheartedly. Personally, though I admired Mr Reynold's energy and his untiring voice, I was embarrassed.

On the day following my visit to the Actors Playhouse, I was invited by Mr Tony Origlio, who once undertook the hazardous task of publicizing me, to eat at The Ballroom on West 28th Street, and, after lunch, to watch a cabaret act performed by Mr Julian Clary. The food and the show were equally appetizing.

Mr Clary comes to us from a triumphant six-week stint at the Aldwych Theatre in London. He is an example of what might be termed the 'New Wave' of gay entertainers. This is not a drag show. Mr Clary makes no attempt to impersonate famous female actresses or, indeed, anybody at all; he remains invincibly himself and unmistakably English. He is as much made up as the forces of gravity will permit, and he wears clothes of no particular sex so glittering that, from time to time, rays of light from his body hit you in the eye like gleams that fall from those mirrored globes that revolve about certain dance floors. In an unashamed suburban English accent, a barrage of innuendoes falls from his ruby lips; he renders rather than sings a few numbers with titles such as 'I Want To Be A Rhinestone Cowboy' and occasionally, though he cannot be described as dancing, he raises an arm or a leg like a little boy performing in a drawing room for his mother's guests. The effect is absurd, endearing, and absolutely unique.

While I was sitting innocently in my favourite diner on East Fifth Street being photographed, an unknown gentleman approached me and accused me of doing a disservice to the movie called *Paris Is Burning* when I wrote about it for a recent edition of the *New York Times*. Since that terrible day, I have learned that almost the entire population of Manhattan (including Mr Musto, whose opinions I hold sacred) is up in arms concerning my view of this picture. I am worried by this public reaction because no such negative effect was intended. After seeing this documentary at The Film Forum, I met its director, Miss Livingston, and liked her immediately – besides which, I praise everything on principle.

I have now rolled about under the bed in my room, retrieved the carbon copy of my review, and re-read it. It says that *Paris Is Burning* is 'hilarious on the surface and, underneath the glitter, profoundly sad; it speaks with the fierce bravado that is the voice of society's permanent exiles.' These words are a somewhat high-flown paraphrase of the explanation given to me by Miss Livingston of the events in her film. Later, my review describes the picture as 'funny, frightening, and tragic'. In all that I wrote, there is not one word of opprobrium. What did I do wrong?

Naturally, I endeavoured to see this movie through the eyes of a typical Sunday *Times* reader, because that was the paper to which I was contributing. I do not pretend that journalism is an art, but I do think it is a skill to give readers what they wish to hear while claiming to present stark, unbiased truth. To justify his rage, the unknown gentleman in the diner cried out, 'The people in the film are doing what you did.' This is true, and, like them, I also was regarded by readers of the *Times* as funny, frightening, and tragic – if not downright disgusting.

Last week, I was taken by a teacher of architecture to Yale University. It was a most enjoyable outing – a drive through the New England countryside, lunch at the most oddly-designed school canteen in the world, and an unexpected opportunity to meet Mr Edmund White, whose contributions to various kinky magazines I had been reading for some years past, but whom I had never before seen with the naked eye.

We were assembled with two or three other people to comment on the ways in which about eight students of the architectural faculty had met the challenge of designing a school for 'gay' teenagers. The answers, of course, took the form of drawings, plans, elevations, and models of hypothetical buildings. Mr White had pertinent remarks to make about them. I, alas, had no idea whether these proposals were examples of good or bad architecture; to me a building is only a box in which to store one's body when not in use. Presumably, I was present in the hope that I would say something witty.

I failed. At first, my reaction was merely amazement at the skill with which the models had been constructed; it aroused in me the same wonder that I feel when I see galleons in bottles. Later, I grew surprised that the project had been set in the first place. My father never took the slightest interest in me or my education, but if he ever had moved his thin lips to ask me of what my studies consisted and I had replied that I was building a school for a bunch of homosexual children, he would at once have demanded the return of my school fees. At Yale, there was apparently neither panic nor perplexity.

Finally, on the way back to New York, I began to feel sad that, when each student tried to explain his work, he was almost unintelligible. Each must have known in advance that some verbal justification of his efforts would be expected of him, but all seemed quite unprepared. If I had taken anything seriously on that day, this would have depressed me deeply. I had not hoped for deathless oratory, but I had also not expected a flow of 'ums', 'ers', and false starts from the lips of the most privileged young men in the world.

An unknown gentleman has written to me concerning my views on American education, saying that all teaching is firstly the teaching of language. I agree with him. Muddled syntax is the outward and audible sign of confused minds, and the misuse of grammar the result of illogical thinking.

I have been approached by the editor of a magazine that I had thought extinct, but it is not and I have been asked to write an article explaining four movie actresses from the past: Jayne Mansfield, Marilyn Monroe, Diana Dors and Kim Novak.

Reading the condensed biographies of these ladies, all of whom were born either in the late Twenties or early Thirties, I realized that until the Fifties when all of them emerged into the klieg lights, apart from Miss West, who defied all the rules, no American actress had serious breasts. In the movie *Queen Christina,* Miss Garbo had to stand under a specially focused light before Mr John Gilbert could tell that she was a woman. (Miss Mansfield would never have attempted the masquerade in the first place.) Even Miss Dietrich, who represented femininity at an intensity never previously known, had legs but no breasts.

The obscene interest evinced by Hollywood publicists in what they evasively termed the 'vital statistics' of movie stars was, of course, yet another symptom of the sexual explosion that dealt the death blow of romance about thirty-five years ago. Of these four actresses, only the name of Miss Monroe now still rouses the public imagination. Miss Mansfield and Miss Dors were famous in their day, but only for the generous way in which they connived with the public at the joke about the bust measurements. For this reason, they were among the few female stars better known and better liked by men than women.

Now, though sex seems still to be with us, breasts have once again subsided. This is hard to explain. I dare not hope that we are at last returning to a less carnal era. In Miss Mansfield's day, breasts were never seen naked by the cine-camera. It may, therefore, have seemed necessary to imply by sheer bulk what could not actually be shown. Now that nudity is everywhere and almost all movies contain prolonged sequences of sexual antics, however gratuitously introduced, the mere size of any particular erogenous zone may no longer matter. (The vital statistics of male stars are not yet published, but dry your tears: the day will come.)

Miss Novak is even harder to explain than the vanishing breasts. She had neither a bosom nor legs, but at one time her appeal was greater than that of Doris Day, Grace Kelly, or even the invincible Miss Taylor. At first, unlike Miss Mansfield, she was in successful films such as *The Man with the Golden Arm*. The script for this picture was so ludicrous that, at the end of it, two cops with soppy expressions on their faces watch the lovers, both of whom are wanted for questioning in a murder case, sauntering off into the distance. But the story was about drug addiction, which at that time was all the rage. Miss Novak's later movies were less successful, but if she had been a true star, when the surrounding night darkened, her image would have glowed more brightly than ever. Unfortunately, this did not happen.

Last Friday I was sitting innocently in my room typing a review of *Miss Saigon* when I was interrupted by a telephone call from a Mr Marder who traffics in improbable movies. Only half-listening, I heard that my tickets to yet another film festival would be delivered to me immediately. An hour later, when I went downstairs to retrieve the mysterious envelope from the floor of our lobby, I found that it contained not, as I had foolishly assumed, cinema tickets, but airline tickets – and to Seattle!

This immediately threw me into a panic. I flung aside my quill pen and began what Mr Debussy would have entitled *'L'Après-Midi d'un Phone'*. I succeeded (I hope) in excusing myself gracefully from all the appointments that had been set up for Saturday, Sunday and Monday, except one, which concerned a Mr Max whose telephone number has been changed or declared null and void. As I have never been sure of his surname, I could not search for it in the Manhattan directory, and so have been compelled by forces beyond my feeble control to break my appointment with him.

I am heartbroken. If it had not been for this load of guilt that I carried with me, my sojourn in Seattle would have been most enjoyable. At this time of the year, this fair city hosts a film festival that lasts four whole weeks. Within minutes of arriving in the state of Washington, I was being interviewed by various local papers before going into the Egyptian Theater to see *Lonely In America*. This movie is about a young Indian who comes from Calcutta to live with his uncle in Jackson Heights. It is directed by that Mr Brown who edited *Do the Right Thing* and *Truth or Dare*, and it describes amusingly and wistfully the problem that seems to beset all young people arriving from India: they want to become American as fast as possible, but always find themselves living with and working for their elders who wish to remain Indian for as long as possible and even want the younger generation to enter into marriages arranged at their birth.

The real purpose of my visit to the Far West was so that I could be held responsible for the newest and first full-length 'documentary' film about me. This is called *Resident Alien*. I warned the audience that this picture shows no burning police cars and no hospital nurses being raped in car parks – nothing, in fact, that could be termed family entertainment, but I said that it would offer interesting glimpses of Mr Sting, Mr Hurt (who is my representative on earth), Miss Penny Arcade, Mr Robert Patrick, and sundry other colourful denizens of the Lower East Side of Manhattan. Between movies in Seattle, I met a Mr Whitten, who, against all odds, has secured a booking for *Resident Alien* in

August at the Village Cinema. I cannot imagine how it will fare at the hands of real critics.

Now from England comes a paperback copy of *How To Grow Old Disgracefully*, the autobiography of Miss Hermione Gingold. As she admits – nay, boasts – that at the age of eighty-one she had a twenty-six-year-old lover, this seems an apt title. I read her story with great amusement and was specially pleased to note that her opinion of the difference between British and Americans corresponds closely to mine. She says that if you wear a mink coat in the States, everyone (who isn't an animal freak) admires it, but in England, they say, 'We'll have that off your back, come the revolution.'

On Sunday, some kind friends took me to the very edge of Manhattan where we boarded *The Spirit of New York* for a mini-cruise, which included brunch and a cabaret provided by the catering staff. The weather, though shaky, refrained from behaving badly and I think we all had a pleasant afternoon. For me, the high point of the occasion came when a large gentleman came to our table to tell my host that it was rumoured that there was a celebrity on board who was 'coming out'. Turning to me, he added, 'It can't be you.'

Summer

*

Never, NEVER go to Boston

On the last Saturday in June I went with a friend to a church on Central Park West at 75th Street. We were there to join in what a programme described as a Celebration of Commitment between my friend's sister and her friend, a Miss Haney. I am not a Christian; indeed, I believe only in what I can see – and not all of that. When, long ago, I asked my niece why she was getting married, she replied that, if she didn't, she would be given no presents. So perhaps my general cynicism is a family tradition. All the same, I must admit that when I entered the Church on Central Park West I was nervous.

As soon as I stood in the chancel and saw, over the altar, a vast picture of Jesus of Nazareth washing the feet of his disciples, I remembered that I had been on this hallowed ground before. I had even taken part in a dialogue with one of the church's officials in the presence of a small congregation. I do not recall what was said on that day; I only remember adopting a minimum risk policy. On this more recent occasion, the same stratagem seemed to have been employed. Marriage was not mentioned; the commitment of the two young women to each other was described as a spiritual covenant, but echoes of the wedding service could be heard. I do not think that any but the most thin-lipped Christians could have been offended. It was a joyous but entirely decorous occasion.

Independence Day celebrates the onset of a war that, being still a part-time Englishman, I cannot claim to have won. Therefore, on previous Fourths of July I have cowered in my room, but last

Thursday, at ten o'clock in the morning, I was summoned to some recording studios on Fifth Avenue occupied by the British Broadcasting Corporation. There I took part in a programme the purpose of which was to explain to the English what makes America the way it is.

I felt totally outclassed, because I was co-starred with a Mr London, who teaches American history at New York University, and a Mr Bischoff, who is one of the editors of the *Village Voice.* I said that the uniqueness of the Americans lies in their belief that personality is the greatest power on earth and, in response to other similar questions, uttered all the well-worn aphorisms that I habitually trot out when under fire. I doubt that the British public was much impressed by anything I said, but our interviewer was kind enough to telephone me the next day to tell me that the response from Broadcasting House in London to our efforts had been favourable and that all the participants will be paid. I can't ask for more than that.

In the evening of the same day, as I was returning home from dinner with a friend, we found our block positively glittering with fireworks and, although television has repeatedly warned us all that the buying, selling or igniting of these strident emblems of merriment is illegal, we saw half a dozen policemen standing on the corner of the street and smiling benignly at the flagrant display of lawlessness.

Sad to say, last weekend I had to decline a kind invitation from Jack Eric Williams, who offered to persuade one of his unsuspecting friends to transport us by car into the countryside. I do not hold with nature, but I would gladly have overcome my revulsion from leaves and blades of grass in the hope of escaping for a while from the oven-like atmosphere of the city. This was not to be. Instead, I was compelled to choose between sitting in my room naked with the door shut, thus forfeiting even the hope of a breeze wafting past me, or leaving the door open and wearing clothes so as not to disgust any fellow inmates of the house who might chance to pass by. I tried both these courses of inaction and, in each case, spent most of Saturday and Sunday flopping about with my hair clinging to my forehead, a pool of sweat accumulating in my navel and testicles hanging down to my knees while I attempted to become acquainted with the contents of eight full pages of typescript so that, on the following day, I might be able to orate them with feigned spontaneity before a television camera. I presume my listless performance is to be part of a culture programme to be released in Britain very late at night.

The next morning, I spent the early hours blotting out the pools of perspiration on my face with powder with much the same distaste and with about the same amount of sporadic success as that with which the police cover with sand the grim signs of a street accident. By ten o'clock, a car had arrived to transport me to an address on Sixth Avenue. This turned out to be the home of a photographer and a sculptress. It covered the entire top floor of the building and was a whole world of loosely defined areas linking eating and working spaces. From the middle of it all springs up a spiral staircase leading to a flat roof so densely afforested that it was a wonder that all that exotic vegetation did not cause the edifice to topple over into the street.

With unflagging good nature, our hosts allowed not only me but also a cast of thousands of cameramen, sound-recordists, and general organizers to swarm all over their home for most of the day. When all had been said and all had been recorded, we went to Brooklyn so that I could be photographed trying to look noble against a distant backdrop of the Statue of Liberty and various ferry boats meandering hither and thither. Let no one ever speak ill of New York taxi drivers. In spite of all sorts of hazards, two of them, like charioteers in Mr Hur's movie, consented to drive abreast from the middle of Sixth Avenue to the very edge of Brooklyn merely so that I could be photographed seeming to enjoy the scenery as we sped through the city and over the picturesque ruin that used to be the Brooklyn Bridge. The entire undertaking was not completed until evening, and a benediction of rain had begun to fall upon us. Then, at last, I was released at my front door.

I slept until dawn.

At this time of year, letters fly into Manhattan from California as abundantly and with as much regularity as geese migrating from the frozen north to warmer regions of the world. These missives are all a-flutter and a-twitter with news about the various gay activities that have taken place on the streets of San Francisco. I have a spy living on Sacramento Street who informs me that, this year, the crowds attending all those parades and public events were more numerous than ever before (more than half a million by some estimates) and that the general atmosphere was happier than in recent times. He does not express any misgivings about this phenomenon, but I find it difficult to suppress a feeling of foreboding. If the rest of the population in that state ever conceives of itself as a beleaguered minority, will it not move from its present attitude of armed neutrality to a terrified and terrifying hostility?

I was in Boston last Sunday to lend my gracious presence to another showing of *Resident Alien*. It is hard to believe that my presence really makes the slightest difference to the success of this picture, but as I try never to say no to anything, I did my stint. The film was screened twice, and it is true that the first house at seven-thirty was full, but I think I ought to add that the cinema holds only a hundred and forty people.

I set out from Manhattan on this fateful mission at half past one in the afternoon to catch Mr Trump's three o'clock shuttle from La Guardia airport. (I was amused to learn that the crossword puzzle in his airline magazine consists almost entirely of the names of famous industrialists criss-crossing those of successful business tycoons and manufacturing moguls.) I was met in Boston by a Mr Mansour and his assistant. Mr Mansour rules the Boston Festival with one hand, and with the other, several New York cinemas such as Cinema Twelve and The Village Cinema.

The journey by air was so short that there was no time for the service of a meal, so we ate something before arriving at The Institute, where I was interviewed by the *Boston Phoenix, Gay Community News* (whose representative wore white gloves), and by the *Boston Herald.* All this occupied every minute until the first showing of *Resident Alien,* preceded by *A Letter to Harvey Milk,* a documentary made from a short story by a Miss Newman, who was present to introduce it. The two films constituted a double-feature lasting two hours, and Mr Mansour very thoughtfully made it possible for me to avoid seeing my film for a third time (I already knew who won). While it was being screened, he, his assistant, a heap – or should I say pride? – of journalists, and I crept away to eat at a very pleasant restaurant called Ciao Bella. We returned to our duties just in time to answer questions from the audience concerning what they had seen and to introduce the second house.

On reaching my hotel, I flopped into bed exhausted but happy, having spent the past six hours either talking or eating – my two favourite pastimes. The next morning, I arose and reconstructed myself just in time for one final interview, this time with the *Boston Globe.* The city is certainly going to know I was there.

Then the trouble began. Arriving at the airport, I found that Mr Trump had decided to take the latest hurricane warnings seriously. (Why, when he has so successfully ignored such a large number of other prophecies of doom?) When I presented my return ticket, a young woman told me that there would be no flights to New York until two o'clock. 'If then,' she added with barely concealed relish. On hearing this terrifying news, I made a great mistake. I found two other unsuspecting victims and went with them to Boston's South Station, the railway station. There I was forbidden to try to board the first available train on the grounds that it was full. Never before having heard such a flimsy excuse for being obstructive, I said that I would gladly – nay, eagerly – stand all the way back to real life. The ticket-seller did not even bother to reply; he offered me a seat on the 1.35 train or nothing.

Notoriety has its rewards. Having two and a half hours to wait, I began to wander disconsolately about the public area of the station. Half-hearted efforts have been made by the municipal authorities to give this bleak space a jaunty air. A few brightly coloured kites hang from the dingy glass roof, and here and there are small circular tables with large umbrellas sprouting from their centres. From what these are intended to shelter us I cannot imagine. While surveying this incongruous scene, I met a stranger who not only offered me a cup of coffee and a bun, but was good enough to chat with me for an hour. No sooner had he escaped than I was recognized by a self-confessed interior decorator who had seen me at the Town House in Manhattan. He looked after me and fed me during the entire remainder of our ordeal.

At about two o'clock, we were permitted to board the next train bound for New York, but even this massive, earth-bound vehicle was afraid of the hurricane and refused to take the shorter coastal route. It is true that the wind and rain were tempestuous. In fact, the only thing lacking from the scene was a glimpse of Miss Lamour, in a wringing wet sarong, clinging to a bent palm tree. All the same, I would not have expected these climatic manifestations to prompt a train driver to meander inland. There, fallen trees lay across the tracks like palm fronds placed before the feet of returning conquerors with the result that we sat in that train for nine hours.

The moral of this woeful tale is obvious: Never, *never* go to Boston.

The only actual event in my life at the moment is that I am to be made immortal in bronze, or, to be more realistic, ephemeral in clay. This is the second time I have been honoured in this manner since I came to the United States. The first sculptor to approach me saw me working at SNAFU, a dim nightclub which stood where Lox Around the Clock now flourishes. He was an extremely attractive gentleman who unfortunately decided to pare away much of his alluring roly-polyness by joining Overeaters Anonymous. I tried to teach him that people are lovable by the pound, but he paid no heed. He has now taken up residence in Los Angeles, which is, of course, 'thin city'.

The more recent sculptor who has decided to make of me a graven image is a young woman who lives on the Upper East Side, where she hires space in a large communal studio divided into small work areas – an arrangement of which I have never before heard. She very kindly spares me the arduous chore of sitting still for hours. Like most modern portraitists, she works mainly from photographs and adds a few hills and valleys to my face from life when the bulk of the work is done. In a time gone by, art and photography were enemies. Painters and sculptors despised mere snapshots, but during the past few decades, since machines have more or less made human beings redundant, the camera has been redeemed and is now as sacred as canvas or marble.

It isn't quite accurate to describe either of these two artists as sculptors; they are both modellers, members of quite a different profession. The work of a carver is eternal – more or less. He is usually a big man with huge hands and tends to be a patient hermit prepared to remain alone in his studio, wrestling with one project for years on end – one of an altogether more serious breed of men.

My bookish life continues. Mr de Luca, who rules the publicity department of St Martin's Press, has sent me two of its latest books. One, still in the form of an uncorrected proof, is called *Profiles in Gay and Lesbian Courage*, and the other, *Mother Earth*. The first is by the Reverend Troy Perry and a Mr Swicegood. Both these men seem to be wild characters – especially the preacher; he has been married, fathered two children, been divorced, and twice excommunicated. The brief biography at the back of this book doesn't tell us in what order these assorted triumphs and disasters occurred, nor does it vouchsafe into what church he was originally ordained. This is a pity, because he assures us that God loves us but doesn't indicate which god. Jehovah doesn't love us and has said so; I doubt that Allah loves us, but I won't pontificate on that theme because I don't want to have to go into hiding.

The main body of this book is divided into eight chapters; four are the stories of homosexual men who have confronted the laws of their country, and four are about lesbians who have adopted a similarly defiant stance. All these tales make fascinating, sometimes emotive reading. The murder of Harvey Milk is described again but, however often it is repeated, it remains a drama that evokes amazement and grief.

When I was young, my egotism prompted me to think of my cross as being heavier to carry than anybody else's, but, reading this book, I have become aware that being such a hopeless case had its advantages. From the moment I stepped out of my cradle, I knew what my problem was and so did everybody within a ten-mile radius. I lived in danger, but not in doubt. There is a story in *Profiles* of a Mrs Bottini, who married, produced two children and joined the National Organization for Women without being aware that she was a lesbian or that many of her friends had known this for years. Self-doubt nearly drove her insane.

The trouble with all the triumphs that the people mentioned in this book won, at such terrible risk to themselves, is that they are victories over the law rather than over life. This does not in any way lessen the admiration we feel for them, but it is necessary to reiterate over and over again that it is never the law that abruptly changes the world's attitudes: it is public opinion that very gradually modifies the law. The removal of a statute from a book does not make anybody's neighbours behave any more considerately. In England, my persecutors didn't care that I was illegal, nor even that I was immoral. They hated me because I was effeminate. A civic conscience and a sense of moral outrage are very rare but a feeling of revulsion against what seems unnatural is almost universal – no easier to eradicate than an inclination towards homosexuality.

* * *

The nicest letter of the week comes from Miss Liz Smith. It is a kind message written in the margin of a photocopy of her column in *Newsday* where she quotes a remark I made on Ronald Reagan the Younger's television show. I said that the way to improve gay relations with the straight world would be to refrain from talking about sex for a long time to come. She says that she absolutely cannot do this, and I accept that my proposal was unrealistic. When Mr Gandhi suggested that the way to decrease the alarming overpopulation of India was for married couples to practise abstinence, *Time* magazine said of this idea that it was 'long on logic, short on probability'. I am regretfully aware that the same criticism can be offered to me.

The nastiest letter comes from a gentleman in England whose signature I cannot read. I recently wrote an article denouncing the evils of 'outing' for the London *Evening Standard*. This almost illegible epistle is a reply, but says nothing about outing. Instead, it vents the writer's fury on my use of the word 'gay' for my own 'perverted and depraved use', and tries to give buggery a bad name, reminding me that it was made illegal in 1533.

I answer almost all correspondence – even the most hostile – and, in this case, I suppose I ought to point out to this indignant gentleman that many homosexual men do not indulge in this particular form of copulation. (In her very explicit book, *The Love Quest*, Felicity Mason says that none of her homosexual lovers ever tried it on her, but that several straight men made the attempt.) Somehow, I haven't the energy for trying to acquire another 'pen foe'.

Autumn

*

Perhaps I should buy a lamp and stand on a rock in New York harbour

The pace of life in the smiling and nodding racket quickens. It is now rumoured that *Resident Alien* will open in Manhattan on 18 October. This is the movie by Mr Nossiter in which I wander round the streets saying anything that comes into my head to anyone who will listen. It will be shown at the Angelika Cinema. This location places it in a twilight zone between unabashed festival material and genuine entertainment. Naturally, the attempt to shift the picture's status involves promotion, and promotion involves visits at dusk to such never-before-heard-of towns as Madison in New Jersey.

Last Monday and Tuesday, an extremely courageous gentleman called Professor Rose, who presides over something called Sneak Preview Symposium, arranged for *Resident Alien* to be shown at his local cinema and persuaded his nephew to bring me, Mr Nossiter, and one of the film's publicists out of New York into an altered state. These circumstances led me to expect an audience consisting entirely of students. I was wrong. The auditorium contained people of all ages and sexes. Sad to say, the space was not quite full. Apparently, some members of the audience departed in indignation. (One woman, as she left, was heard to hiss, 'Did you see him? He hasn't changed his clothes since the film was made!') Even those who remained were outspoken – to say the least. Someone began her remarks with the words, 'I thought the least boring part was . . .'

The most important thing I learned from this entire occasion was that I am becoming deaf. Doubtless my friends have been aware of my infirmity for some time; I hadn't noticed. I can hear easily what is said close at hand, but even in that medium-sized auditorium every question had to be relayed to me by the Professor. I shall be sorry when this manifestation of my decline is complete. I don't mind not seeing much, but I like to hear everything except music. Words are my staple diet.

The letter of the week comes from someone who is about to visit a city in Germany with his parents so that they can be united by the university with the students with whom they worked before 1939 when they left – hurriedly. Never before, as far as I know, has any country made a public act of contrition for the past sins of its rulers. It is a truly commendable civic gesture, but I cannot help adding that I hope I shall never be brought face to face with any of the little swine who made my life such hell when I was at school.

I know that the British press complains that I am boring on the subject of the joys of living in America and the kindness of its inhabitants, but I persist in my folly by recounting the following episode.

Recently, when I boarded a Third Avenue bus, I found a newspaper lying on an otherwise empty seat. Immediately I scrabbled through its pages to find the crossword puzzle, which I carefully tore out and put in my pocket. Seeing me do this, a total stranger seated on the other side of the bus, without uttering a word, removed the puzzle from his paper and handed it to me. Greater love hath no man than that he lay down his crossword for a friend.

People used for ever to be asking me, 'Isn't there *anything* in England that you miss?' I could tell from the pleading tone in their voices that they wished me to have paid a high price for my present contentment, and it was with great reluctance that I said,

'No.' Now I have thought of a way to gratify their lust for the sorrows of others. There is one small disadvantage to living in America. When real winter arrives, the radiators of Manhattan begin to clank and hiss and tenants know that happiness – or, at least, heat – is on the way, but at this time of year while in the street it is still warm, indoors it is cool – occasionally too cool. I have a fair – nay, an indulgent – landlord, but there is not much we can do about this predicament. On the days when I remain at home from dawn till dusk and beyond, I do not like to sit around fully dressed; I like to loll about in a filthy dressing gown. It is more comfortable, and minimizes the wear and tear on my few 'going-out' clothes.

This quandary does not only occur in humble dwellings on the Lower East Side. When I first arrived from the other side of the globe to take up permanent residence here, I was compelled to throw myself on the mercy of a gentleman who lived in splendour on East 39th Street. Even there, the only solution to the problem of autumn was to light the gas cooker, leave the oven door open, and sit before it in a curious, hothouse atmosphere.

In England, however lowly my station in life became, in my bed-sitter I always had a tiny, asthmatic gas fire to which I could run home and by which I could crouch until I was warm. When I ask Americans why there are no gas fires in New York, they reply in shocked voices, 'Good heavens! Think of the explosions!' But many people have gas cookers. What is the difference in respect of their potential danger? The mystery remains, and I remain curled up over my typewriter, cocooned in a blanket with only my claws sticking out, like a large mole. Of course, I could live in San Diego, where the weather is always a cool summer, but then I wouldn't be in a position to rule the world, should the opportunity arise.

I have had a week in the eye of the hurricane of promotion. I have spent a lot of time lurking in my room and a little in neighbouring restaurants welcoming visitors from England. Perhaps I should buy a lamp and stand on a rock in New York harbour.

I have also been answering a spate of letters from Britain. The strangest of these comes from a woman who first wrote to me more than two years after one of my last-ever performances in London. The reason for that epistle is no longer clear in my mind, but I think that my audience had asked my opinion of suicide and that I had praised it. My correspondent had just rescued her daughter from a suicide attempt and was disturbed by this opinion. I replied that I realized that the mother could not have done otherwise than she did (it would have been illegal), but I warned her that she might now be blamed by her daughter for every humiliation that the young woman suffered in the future. The mother showed my letter to a friend who wrote consoling her and saying that I was cruel. What else could he say?

Now, all these long, dark years later, she has sent me pictures of her house and her daughter with copies of my letter and the one from her friend. What can this mean? If her daughter's attempt to take her own life was a bid for attention, I cannot help being revolted. If it was a sincere act of desperation, and she is glad to have been restored to life, I am delighted for everyone concerned, but I am also quite bewildered. The girl must have summoned every ounce of her courage to deal once and for all with the miseries of the future, and is now once again faced with them.

The entire incident is quite extraordinary. Firstly, the mother must keep photostats of all her correspondence – even from total strangers. Secondly, and odder still, she must subscribe to the D.H. Lawrence notion that life is wonderful whatever happens. This is a fallacy that misdirects the behaviour of a lot of people – particularly anti-abortionists, although we all know that, if we are born to mothers who adore us, we may still not have a happy life. If our parents never stop reminding us that they never wanted us in the first place, we are in for a rotten time. How can anyone wish to make abortion difficult to obtain? Television shows us these publicity fiends abandoning every vestige of dignity by lying, like Arctic seals, on the pavement in front of family planning clinics, while on the same programme we are told that a garbage collector has found a baby a few hours old in a carrier bag in a dim alley.

I know that the expression of these views leads to the question of why I did not dispose of my useless self years ago. The answer is that I'm a sissy.

I went last week to New York University on Broadway. I must have passed this edifice many times, but have never noticed it. I have to say that it looks nothing like a venerable seat of learning. In England, education, which had once been decently confined, spread like a disease throughout the land. Universities sprang up in various provincial cities. Because their architecture lacked the Gothic dignity of Oxford and Cambridge they were contemptuously termed 'redbrick', and their teaching was assumed to be utilitarian rather than gloriously useless. In America, universities are evidently built of concrete, steel, and glass to indicate that they offer specifically New World, definitely twentieth-century knowledge. They even teach movie-making.

The interior of NYU is made entirely of wood with not an ink stain in sight; it looks like one vast Black & Decker project. While we sat on tubular steel chairs waiting to enter the college screening room, several young ladies passed us wearing kinky shoes and carrying gilt-tipped spears. Perhaps they were on their way to rehearsing as extras in an Equal Rights production of one of Mr Shakespeare's plays – possibly called *Henrietta the Fourth*.

In the screening room, unlike the audience to whom I spoke in Madison, there were no real people – only students, mostly male. They were either easy to entertain or, as I have found elsewhere in America, extremely polite. They did not have to be coaxed into speaking, and all their questions were technical – how long had it taken to make the film *Resident Alien*, for example. There were no questions about my life. From this I conclude that no NYU student is gay.

* * *

There is one remark which, in recent years, has been uttered by my audiences with noticeable frequency: 'Is there anyone that you particularly admire?' I have not yet found the right codified response. The expression 'role model' is comparatively new to me. In my earlier years there arose public icons, such as Mr Lindbergh, but I do not recall any exhortations from my elders to emulate such men. Perhaps such admonitions were uttered, but in my case they fell on deaf ears. Fate does not permit far-out homosexual men like me to indulge in such wishful thinking. We do not have ambitions; we have only fantasies. Like all the campy little creatures with whom I 'hung out' in my twenties, I lived in a swoon about one female movie star after another, but I never seriously expected to become like one of them, nor could I hope to reap rewards such as theirs. It may be for this reason that, while in an abstract way I greatly admire certain noble, courageous, or clever deeds, I do not seem to have much capacity for hero-worship. I hope this does not betoken any meanness of spirit. For me to want to be like some famous sportsman, some renowned philanthropist, or even some great artist would be living beyond my income of dreams.

Now I am back on the treadmill, flying from one extreme to another. On Monday, in the black of night, I was taken to the home of NBC, an impressive building in the middle of New Jersey. There I was interviewed by a Mr Matson, a gentleman of flawless respectability, for a programme called *The Real Story*. Although unaccustomed to reality in any form, I did my best to answer the usual questions in the usual way. On Tuesday, in pouring rain, I went to an office on West 26th Street, where I was interrogated by Mr Lou Maletta, whom I have met before at a different address. His fortunes have evidently improved since then. Last time we were together, we occupied a space so constricted that if I leaned forward for dramatic emphasis, I went out of focus. Mr Maletta is perfecting his image. He now has a Texan straw hat, which he wears at all times, and on this occasion was wearing black trousers so close-fitting that it was possible to see what he was thinking, brigand's boots, and a Mexican moustache. Being interviewed by him could almost be described as a sensuous experience.

On the evening of the same day, *Resident Alien* was shown at the Archives, which is a hostel for homeless movies on East Second Street. Among the audience were my favourite journalist, Liz Smith, and the movie actress, Miss Hutton, who arrived wearing a Columbo raincoat and pre-ruined jeans and swathed in an aura of reckless beauty.

The worst is over. At least, I think it is. For a while, the journeys became ever more circuitous; the limousines, longer; the interviews, more repetitive; and the parties, noisier. But, at last, two performances of *Resident Alien* have been given to the world – or at least, at the Angelika Cinema. The film is now on its own: no more publicity can alter its fate. For the director's sake, I wish this venture well, but for myself, I am inevitably somewhat blasé about its chances of making money or bringing anybody fame. Because of my great age, my future is now (if it hasn't already passed).

I have been interviewed by a Mr Castro for *People* magazine. I was somewhat apprehensive about this meeting because some years ago, for the same periodical, a young lady had photographed me and that occasion had turned out to be quite an ordeal. I had gone to a vast room, on one wall of which a huge landscape had been painted. There I was divested of my jacket which was promptly slit down the back so that two enormous white feathered wings could be attached to my rib cage through the opening. Thus equipped, I sat for about three hours in a nest of surgical cotton, moving my arms this way and that like a Hindu idol. Why the young woman didn't take any old pictures of me and paint the wings and sky around the image, I shall never know. I don't think she wanted her work to be simple: I suspect she wished it to be expensive.

My more recent encounter with a member of the staff of *People* magazine was painless – better than that, worthwhile: I was given lunch.

Even on the very day of *Resident Alien*'s release, I was sent to Washington (without the faintest hope of becoming President). There I was questioned for a television programme called *Nightwatch*. Nearly all interviews consist largely of an attempt to present my early life as a perfumed fist being shaken in the face of British narrow-mindedness – an interpretation which I always try to correct by explaining that in fact I was a helpless victim of my nature pleading with the world to forgive my difference from it. The only new subject introduced into more recent discussions is the announcement by certain doctors that the brains of homosexual men are in some way physically female. I take this discovery very calmly; I am quite prepared to accept that there is something weird about every cell in my body – let alone about what little grey matter is in my skull. (Will it now be revealed that there is something male about the brain structure of lesbians?)

I do not scour each day's papers and magazines for reviews of any of my performances, but, if people send them to me, I read them carefully. I know that all public rebuttal of adverse criticism is undignified – not to mention useless, but I would like to express a faint bewilderment at the often-voiced description of me as 'opaque'. As far as I know, I have never given an evasive reply to any question about my ideas or events in my life. My responses are aphoristic, not in order to conceal my meaning, but because they have been made so often that they have become crystallized – if not fossilized. Criticism of *Resident Alien* seems to be in the same vein; it is said to reveal nothing new about me. How can it? It is sometimes compared unfavourably with *The Naked Civil Servant*. That earlier television play was completed when I was already sixty-six – long past the age when I could be overtaken by any major change other than decay. It was never my place to ask Mr Nossiter what his intention was in making this film. I merely presumed it was an attempt to depict my life in America, to show how far it has fulfilled my dream of it, and to allow some denizens of the Lower East Side to express their opinions of me.

I have known for some months that, at the very end of October, I would be sent to St Paul to speak on the subject of ageing to whomsoever in that city's gay population would listen. I had no idea what it was hoped that I would say, but I thought that, if my powers of improvisation failed, fate would intervene on my behalf.

I rose before dawn last Thursday in order to complete the rituals of reconstructing myself without undue haste, packed a hold-all that RSVP Cruises gave me in the happy time when I worked for them, and left the house as a grey day was breaking over Manhattan. Taxis are more numerous in New York than in any other city in the world; on this, as on other occasions, I had no difficulty in finding one. I arrived at La Guardia and in Minnesota at the scheduled times. I'd 'done' Minneapolis (as touring actors say) in 1986. Now, as then, Mr Willkie (whose grandfather had been the Republican candidate for President in 1940) met me at the airport and allowed me to stay in his home. As we walked to his car, I remarked, with a jolly laugh, that I had half-expected it to be snowing, and, indeed, I saw two or three flakes frolicking in the breeze. By the time we were well on our way into the city, it had begun to rain.

As night fell over St Paul, so did the snow. At home, we started to listen to the frequent weather reports – something that in New York I try to avoid doing. News reached us every few hours throughout the evening warning motorists that, by morning, the snow might be twelve inches deep. This prophecy was fulfilled. The university was shut and Friday's gathering of all the ancient homosexuals of Minneapolis was cancelled. All during Friday and Saturday, the storm raged and the news became ever more disastrous. In spite of this, I went to a bookshop called A Brother's Touch, where a clamorous crowd of about six customers arrived to receive my autograph.

From the bookshop, I was taken to call on a Professor and

Mrs White. But this time the snow had to be shovelled from the sidewalk before I could attempt to reach their house, and I had almost to be carried everywhere. I was amazed by the patience of my escort. Our hosts fed us with gingerbread and we talked of this and that – chiefly of ageing. Then we went to a huge hotel where the hardiest members of the gay community gathered for a drink, but by then all attempts to organize a public meeting had been abandoned.

On Sunday evening, Mr Willkie gave a party at which we ate, drank, and discussed assorted gay issues. I received the impression that the homosexuals of Minnesota are in favour of the separate-but-equal solution to their problems. Mr Willkie's 'constant companion' recalled that I had once declared that, if Mr Bush announced that he was converting Indiana into a reservation for homosexual people and that we must all go and live there, I would burst into tears. It is true that I did make this statement: I would feel that I was being starved of reality. If I think about my life, I see it as a slow journey from the outer suburbs of ostracism almost to the heart of the world – assuming it has a heart. I would not wish to be shunted into a siding. Most of the guests did not share this view, but it was a really enjoyable evening at which people talked instead of merely chatting.

In a way, the terrible weather was a blessing, because I have no idea what I could have said about old age. Mrs White, the gingerbread lady, said she didn't mind ageing, but did not want to be old. She deferred this inevitable state by never looking back, on the same principle, presumably, that prompts anyone walking along a girder twenty floors above the ground not to look down. Personally, I look neither forward, where there is doubt, nor backward, where there is regret; I look inward and ask myself not if there is anything out in the world that I want and had better grab quickly before nightfall, but whether there is anything inside me that I have not yet unpacked. I want to be certain that, before I fold my hands and step into my coffin, what little I can do and say and be is completed.

Back in the real world, the routines of my life quickly engulfed me. A small television crew arrived from England to photograph me for the BBC, of all people! Apparently, a whole week of their television time is to be devoted to the subject of homosexuality.

The mind boggles.

It seems that I owe the women of America an apology. I have just received from a friend in Key West a letter reproving me for something I wrote last month concerning the Judge Thomas scandal. My correspondent's opinion is couched in phrases of such extreme indignation that I became quite frightened when I read them. I had written that I was suspicious of Anita Hill's accusations firstly because they were dredged up from the past after all other attempts to prevent the judge's nomination had failed, and secondly, because she was so obviously in full control of herself and her circumstances that it seemed unlikely that she could have found no tactful way of side-stepping, if not actually silencing, his suggestive remarks. My friend tells me that, however carefully she had tried to deal with that situation, she would have been dismissed without a reference. He adds that, though never sexually harassed, he has been repeatedly abused and humiliated by his employers.

I'm stunned. In all the long dark years that I lived in England, though the office boys giggled whenever and wherever I appeared, and though of course I was underpaid, I was never insulted or bullied by my superior in any job. Furthermore, though I knew any number of women who told me their troubles (sometimes in squalid detail), not one of them ever recounted being subjected to grossly degrading treatment by male co-workers. As for an English high court judge mentioning his sexual organs to anyone – even to God – the idea is unthinkable. I am sure that the attitude of such an august personage towards his penis would have been similar to the response in England to the question, 'Do you have a television set?' There would be a reluctant admission: 'I do have one, but of course I never look at it.'

Can it be that there are some things better managed in Britain than over here?

I have been taken to Film Forum to see a three-dimensional version of Bugs Bunny and *Dial M for Murder*. For any picture to profit from an extra dimension, it would have to be full of violent movement. To Mr Hitchcock's very neat melodrama, it adds nothing, but it didn't prevent it from remaining a very enjoyable movie. As my companion remarked, *Dial M* is hardly more than a photographed play. Apart from a few glimpses of the streets in front of Mr Milland's London house, all the action takes place in his living room. When I first saw it many years ago (in two dimensions), I accepted it all without question. Now the dialogue seems threadbare and the acting almost comically perfunctory. Moreover, the extreme unlikelihood of a convicted murderess being allowed out of prison even for a moment is a quite gratuitous addition to the story's long list of improbabilities. The trap set for Mr Milland would have worked just as well without her being present to watch it.

I have been to Atlanta, a city of which I already had happy memories. The first time I was asked to go to Georgia was so that I could attend a book signing. When I told the publicity lady for that project that I thought Atlanta had been burned down, she said, 'Well, we built it up again, just for you,' and it looked just as though they had. Every object, every building, every street that met the eye looked brand-new.

On my second visit, I really lived a little while: I met Miss Rosemary Clooney. She was performing at what, in the early 1930s, had been one of Mr Fox's cinemas, an edifice so large that its foyer was as big as the average modern movie house. What a happy era Miss Clooney's name recalls! She sang as though she understood and cared what the words of her songs meant.

On this visit, I seemed to be in an entirely different part of town. I stayed at the Wyndham Hotel, from the front windows of which it was possible to see but fifty yards away Mrs *Gone-with-the-Wind* Mitchell's home, an odd little house with a steeply sloping roof and a lot of gables.

Atlanta seems to have become publicity mad. Though it was on Sunday that I arrived, within an hour a young man was interviewing me; someone else appeared at three, and a third person at half past five. In the evening I was dined by a Mr Moon (humorously called Sunny) of the *Midtown Times*, whom I had met on an earlier sojourn in the city. The next day, there were more interviews, two of them taking place more or less simultaneously. A Mr Hopgood arrived at the same time that a young woman called to take me to a television station to be questioned by an ex-beauty queen. I followed my escort in Mr Hopgood's car. He held his tape recorder in one hand and the steering wheel with the other, but we came to no harm.

My aversion to culture is at least as strong as that of Marshal Goering. It was, therefore, with many a furtive glance to left and right that I entered the building on West 58th Street that is the self-proclaimed home of WNET, Channel 13. I was there at the request of Mrs Michael York, who had included a photograph of me in her book, *Going Strong*, to take part in a television programme ruled by a Mr Rose. In the green room, I found Kitty Carlisle, whose name is etched for ever on my memory because of a remark she made to me many years ago. I had said that I thought all Mr Williams' plays were about how awful it is to be a woman, to which she replied, 'I think they are about how awful it was to be Tennessee Williams.'

We were soon joined by a lawyer whose name I have forgotten, but, like Miss Carlisle, he was engaged in what used to be called good works and on a world scale. I couldn't help wondering how on earth I came to be co-starred with them. They are devoting their time and energy to unceasing selfless activity: I retired at birth. Indeed, I drink daily from that deep well that people like them have dug. They are striving for a better world: I am it. What do you suppose they thought when brought face to face with a living example of the result of their handiwork?

I try to prevent traditions and even habits from creeping into my way of life, but I do not entirely succeed. Every Thanksgiving Day for at least the past five years, I have been a guest at the New Jersey home of my friend's family. His uncle collects me from Manhattan and returns me. It is a very convivial occasion; the hospitality has to be consumed to be believed. I have a wonderful time, but I ought not to indulge myself in this way; I do not have the right. Not only am I not a member of this family but I am not even an American. Historically speaking, I have nothing for which to do a thanksgiving; I am only English and should, on this day, be sitting in my room doing penance for not having beheaded Charles I sooner.

There is also another, darker tradition in my life which recurs inevitably, but at more widely spaced, less regular intervals. This is a sickness which has no cause, no name, and no cure. Its symptoms are a loss of temperature, a loss of appetite, a loss of energy, and finally, a loss of hope. Once it begins, I can only wait for this malady to pass and, so far, it always has.

This year, both these traditions, the one so gay, the other so grim, occurred more or less simultaneously. On the return journey from Port Monmouth, though swaddled in a woolly overcoat and wedged cosily with four other people into a small car, I began to feel chilly. By the time I reached my front door, I was shivering so convulsively that I could hardly insert my latch-key into the lock. I almost fainted clambering up the stairs to my room and, once there, I sat for hours without removing my outer garments, shuddering.

Since then I have done almost nothing until last Sunday, when I was forced out into a mournful fringe of rain to meet a very friendly middle-aged couple who have caught glimpses of me on their television set during the BBC's unprecedented week of 'gay' programmes. (As Mr Clary remarked when he was there, 'In

England, you're much more likely to be beaten up on the street, but on the telly you can *say* anything.') Needless to say, my new acquaintances adore Mr Clary. While I lived in Britain, if I had met these two charming people in public, I would have been terrified of them, but now, because television has spun this sparkling web of amity across the whole world, I am able to talk to them and others like them without hesitation, without formality, and without reservation. I guess that I am the person who has profited more from the invention of television than anybody else.

Never again should anyone speak ill of the United States Postal Service. Someone in Birmingham, England, sent me a letter in an envelope, on the front of which were only the words, 'Quentin Crisp, New York, America,' and, on the back, apologies to the mailman and a plea begging him to find me.

He did.

Winter

*

All of society's outsiders must live in big cities

I have been a guest at a party of quite daunting elegance given by a Mr Woolley in his home on the upper reaches of Fifth Avenue. (Even Miss Fran Lebowitz was formally attired.) I sat with Miss Smith, who, having seen my room in *Resident Alien*, expressed concern for my financial status. She must be the only gossip writer in the world interested in the welfare of her victims, as opposed to wheeling above their heads waiting for disaster to overtake them. I also spent time with a young man who scolded me for saying that I was eagerly awaiting my death. Was I bored, he wanted to know. My answer is an emphatic NO: the kindness and hospitality of Americans ensures that I am never bored, but, because of my great age, I am occasionally exhausted.

At the beginning of last week, my unnamed illness re-recurred. I returned home one evening stricken by the intense cold and was just about to give way to a fit of vomiting when my telephone rang. I answered my caller in a strangulated voice which caused him to remark that I sounded different. I replied, 'Things are bad at the moment, please call me another time.' 'What's the matter?' he asked, but I could only murmur, 'Another time,' and rang off. My friend's reaction to this admittedly unusual response was to telephone his uncle, who lives in Manhattan, the paramedics, and the New York Police Department. The uncle replied at once, but I am happy to report that no one else did. If they had been able to enter the house, they would have discovered me clad only in confusion, trying to clean up the mess

I had made of myself and my room by being unable to reach the bathroom in time.

The moral in this incident seems to be that it is unwise to present to the world a façade of monumental imperturbability, because the effects are so disastrous if it ever collapses.

Another slight but strange incident occurred when I was visiting Jack Eric Williams. I forgot to wear my monocle with the result that, when I entered the apartment building where he lives, I could not read the numerals and letters engraved on the strip of metal beside the huge array of bells. As I was in New York, I imagined that all I needed to do was to go back into the street and ask the first stranger passing by to enter the building with me and read me the numbers. I happened upon a young woman. When, holding the street doors open, I explained my predicament, she declined to help me, saying, 'Oh no, I couldn't come in. I'm too nervous.' I repeated that I only wanted her to read some numbers, but she still hesitated. At that moment, two inmates of the apartment house emerged and I was able to dart forward before the inner doors closed. As I did so, I called back, 'I'm sorry I frightened you,' and, just before the doors shut, I heard her reply, 'I'm sorry I was nervous.' This young woman has the distinction of being the only uncooperative person in the entire United States.

My faith in the American character, shattered last week by the young woman who refused to help me read the numbers of the bells in a dim apartment building, has been restored. On Christmas Eve, I went to our local post office to collect four parcels that the postman had been unable to deliver at our house because there are no front door bells. One of these gifts was so large that it was in a Santa Claus kind of sack. Thoroughly dismayed, I went out into Fourth Avenue to try to persuade a taxi driver to wait while I carried all these packages on to the sidewalk. There I found an unknown young man, who had observed my predicament, waiting to assist me. Without his help, I would never have been able to transport all this load of Yuletide generosity home.

The most mysterious of these gifts turned out to be a book called *A Poet Could Not But Be Gay*, the second instalment of an ongoing autobiography by Mr James Kirkup, the first part of which was called *I, of All People*. The very title of this new volume is naughty. It is a quotation from poor Mr Wordsworth's all-too-well-known poem about daffodils and has absolutely nothing to do with the modern meaning of the word 'gay'. The contents of the book are less skittish; in fact, they are largely tragic, but they are fascinating.

There is an unalterable law that states that all of society's outsiders must live in big cities and Mr Kirkup knows this. Nevertheless, when this section of his life story begins, he is staying with his parents in Corsham, an unknown village in the west of England. He feels that the local police are watching him and, as his paranoia increases, he begins to think that he is under the surveillance of MI5 and even the CIA. He is also aware that his mother and father are suffering silently because of his eccentricities, but does not know until after they are dead that they actually received poisonous letters about their son. (To my surprise, he expresses no amazement that they kept these threatening missives.)

It was quite inevitable that he would become an object of public interest and even public scorn. He wore make-up (indeed, he describes himself as an obsessive *maquilleur*), and once peroxided his already fair hair until most of it fell out. Furthermore, his chosen profession was teaching, where he was a figure of fun to his students who were at an age when cruelty is rampant. In desperation, he went to Sweden, which to my surprise he enjoyed, and to Spain, where he was almost as frightened of the authorities as he had been of the British constabulary. Apparently, in the 1950s, when Mr Franco and the Pope jointly ruled this country, deviancy of any sort was forbidden. In spite of this, his descriptions of Spain are marvellous.

Mr Kirkup is a poet. I write these words in very small print because I know that a poet is a terrible thing to happen to anybody. Even Mr Kirkup himself didn't like poets and shunned literary cliques; he didn't much like people of any kind. He was by nature a loner, but he keenly felt his loneliness: what he wanted was what I once called 'the great dark man', and what he terms 'someone to watch over me'. Naturally, this person he never found, but he did meet an American student with whom he at first had a weird relationship in which they wrote poetry together, and later a torrid affair.

To me the only weakness of this fascinating book is that several of the author's poems are inserted into the text. They become an interruption because we read verse in a different way, at a different pace from prose.

On Christmas Day I became eighty-three, but managed to ignore the fact by visiting friends and eating other people's food. On New Year's Eve my energies deserted me and, though I received two very attractive invitations, I hid and read a novel called *Gaijin on the Ginza* by our Mr Kirkup. It is not about the intermittent quest for love, but about the incessant search for sexual gratification. It makes it seem that all Japanese young men are frustrated and that almost all will respond to overtures from whatever direction. Another distinction is that this tale is not tragicomic: it is hilarious.

Mr Kirkup has lived for many long, dark years in Japan and is rumoured to prefer it to England, which is natural enough, but also to everywhere else, which is surprising. In spite of this preference, this book makes fun of every aspect of Japanese life – the universal black clothing, the conventionality, the perpetual bowing (even to invisible listeners at the other end of telephone wires), the social hypocrisy, and the ingrained insularity. He tells us that the Japanese, in spite of all their politeness to them, will never accept foreigners as their equals. If this book is ever translated into Japanese, Mr Kirkup will be deported.

The story tells of a middle-aged and excruciatingly campy English teacher, who wears monocles tinted to match his outfits, and of his newly acquired assistant, who is a young Diana Dors type of English girl with no experience of teaching and no aptitude for it. They spend most of their time staring at the front of young men's trousers. In the end, the man is murdered by one of his pick-ups, who feels that he has been underpaid for his services, and almost everybody else dies of AIDS. I felt that this conclusion was a bit glib, but everything that happens on the way there, though extremely bawdy, is great fun.

I have had lunch with two charming young women who are working for an English movie company which is planning to produce a film version of *Orlando,* Mrs Woolf's most highbrow novel. One of these ladies is a dress designer, and the other is a wiggist. We all came back to my room so that they could measure me for one of those rigid costumes with a pointed bodice reaching down as far as you-know-what and a bright orange wig so that I can appear in this production as Elizabeth I. We all agreed that there is no portrait in existence showing Miss Tudor wearing any such highly coloured contraption on her head, but, in the movie industry, this tradition persists. Who am I to protest?

If this improbable venture ever actually comes to pass, I will be transported to Amsterdam for two weeks of next month. There is a Quentin Hotel in that notorious city. On seeing the same, a friend of mine entered the lobby and asked the proprietress if the establishment was so called in honour of me, to which they replied, 'But of course.' Whether or not I shall be allowed time to visit this place I have no idea.

My hostility to culture is at its fiercest in the matter of music because music is obtrusive – even, on occasion, inescapable; my aversion is at its mildest concerning literature, which is virtually invisible. The visual arts lie somewhere in between these two extremes; they can be taken or left. For the most part, I leave them.

Mr Cocteau once said that pictures are only the perspiration that the artist flings off while taking his exercise, and that what matters is what exercise he takes. I agree. I once shocked a teacher at the Royal College of Art by telling his students that the great painters of this century were Augustus John, Salvador Dali, David Hockney and Andy Warhol. Though of these only Mr Hockney is a great draughtsman, all these men are more famous than their work.

What a delightful hotel the Algonquin is! It is fourteen long, dark years since I stayed there, and Mr Ansbach, the owner, sat in the lobby with me and gave me glasses of port, but the staff always behaves as though it remembers me.

Last week I went there for breakfast with the gentleman who rules the display department of Paul Stuart and a charming young lady who seems more or less to rule the entire establishment. The Algonquin no longer serves creamed haddock and all those old-fashioned dishes that were available in the English country mansions featured in Mrs Christie's novels, but we ate a very pleasant meal during which my hosts talked about their advertising. Gradually, I began to realize that they wanted me to write some copy for their spring catalogue. When we were leaving, they presented me with a wooden star, though I doubt I'll ever be sheriff – even for the Lower East Side. I also dutifully took away with me samples of their previous advertisements, which I have since read, but they only convince me that this is work that I am totally unable to do. This is especially mortifying because, after breakfast, the display king was kind enough and brave enough to walk up Seventh Avenue with me in an arctic gale. I now realize that I am guilty of a crime that on the statute books will be called 'obtaining poached eggs under false pretences'.

My reason for travelling, in spite of the weather, to the upper reaches of Seventh Avenue was to undergo a medical examination at the hands of a Dr Benson on behalf of Adventure Pictures, the company that is proposing to make *Orlando*, the movie in which I will play Elizabeth I. When I was in Mr Sting's film, *The Bride*, no such ordeal was forced upon me. I mentioned to the good doctor that I had never before been medically examined, to which he replied, 'You're worth a lot of money' – and, after a slight pause – 'to somebody.' He then photographed my lungs, electrified my heart, extracted blood from my right arm and urine from my bladder, and told me my blood pressure was high. I was not surprised to hear this. My march along the freezing streets was enough to raise anyone's blood pressure. The last time that I was tested in that particular way was in Australia, when all the doctor said, in a gloomy voice, was 'It's better than mine.' What this verdict meant I was unable to judge.

Not long ago, I was asked if I would consent to appear on the cover of a dubious magazine. As it is my policy never to say no to anything, I agreed. I may now have to reconsider my policy, because on one very cold evening this week I had to endure the consequences of saying yes. I was taken by an unknown gentleman to a studio in the depths of the meat-marketing district. We arrived at about six o'clock, and were met by the owner of the place, a photographer, a make-up artist, and sundry helpers. I reckon that the effort to reconstruct my face took about an hour, during which time a huge roll of green paper was hung against one wall and spread across part of the floor. When it was deemed that nothing more could be done to humanize me, I was taken into a lavatory where I squeezed the lower half of my body into a pair of black panty hose and a pair of skin-tight black trousers. I was relieved that an attempt to force my upper half into a frilly blouse was abandoned. Then, with my trousers and my dim grey long-johns over my arm, I returned to the photographic area, where I was swathed in a mock fur stole, lined with purple fabric, and as big as a king-sized bedspread, and a weird, white woolly hat shaped like a chamber pot was placed on my head. There was even an effort made to cram my bunioned feet into a pair of black glacé shoes with two-inch-thick platforms and six-inch heels, but when it was discovered that I was unable to stand in them, this idea was abandoned. Halfway through the proceedings, it was decided that I should stand and that two unfortunate young men should be compelled to strip and stand on each side of me to support me. Their services were really needed, as the entire session lasted nearly four hours and towards the end I was ready to collapse. Everybody was extremely kind; someone fetched beer and food to sustain me, and an electric fire was found to warm me, but nothing could prevent the evening from being an ordeal only slightly less exhausting than being in a movie. Recently, Miss Lauren Hutton asked me why I didn't try to find work as a photographic model. They earn thousands of dollars a day, she informed me. I know why.

Not only does it seem likely that I will play the part of Elizabeth I in a highbrow movie, but even in real life I am beginning to resemble English royalty in that, in recent years, I have celebrated my real birthday on Christmas Day quietly with friends who live on Fourth Street, and a state birthday whenever one of Manhattan's party-givers sees fit. Last Saturday I went to the Palladium for a public birthday. After a few drinks in an almost pitch-dark bar, the chosen descended into what the Baroness von Korber-Bernstein called 'the engine room'. There I was lavishly wined and dined and given a huge birthday cake while a stand-in for Miss Monroe sang 'Happy Birthday' in an appropriately breathy, last-gasp voice.

Even better, I was seated next to the wonderful Miss Sylvia Miles, who first commanded our attention on-screen in *Midnight Cowboy*, when she refused to believe that Mr Voigt seriously expected *her* to give *him* money, and of whom Mr Warhol once said, referring to her awesome social stamina, 'She would go to the opening of an envelope.'

The only reason why I didn't ask my host to send invitations to everybody who knows me was that I could not tell and did not like to ask if all the guests had been charged for admission. Even I, egomaniac that I am, haven't the nerve to ask anyone to part with good money for the doubtful privilege of dining with me.

Now that I celebrate my birthday on several occasions round

this time of year, I receive a large number of well-wishing letters for which I am sincerely grateful. In the longer letters from total strangers, there often occurs the question, 'Who influenced you?' and, occasionally, 'What books influenced you?' To these queries I am always at a loss for a satisfactory answer. If anyone shaped my character, I suppose it was my parents – particularly my mother – and, regretfully, I admit that, because of them, I am invincibly middle-class. Apart from them, I can't think that my destiny was formed by anything but bad luck. I endured a life which offered very few options.

To speak in broader terms, the words 'role model' are not in general use in England; they express a purely American notion. As I see it, if a boy wishes to emulate Babe Ruth, he is already like Babe Ruth. All he needs is the stamina and the luck. I have admired many people, but know that I have no hope of resembling any of them or of ever receiving the rewards that they enjoyed. I am too far removed from the human arena.

On Monday evening, I went to The Book Friend's Café, on West 18th Street. I had been there once before with some friends from Dayton, so I was not frightened by the somewhat arty name of the place. There is no need to look at the books. Customers are allowed to treat the establishment entirely as a restaurant. It serves good, understandable food; that is to say that the chicken looks like chicken and has not been tortured by haute cuisine into resembling something else. Another advantage of eating there is that there is *no* music. The reason for my being there on this occasion was not so much to eat as to hear what a Mr Hoare had to say about his book, *Serious Pleasures*, which is a biography of Stephen Tennant, a famous English aesthete about whom all London gossiped when I was young. I was especially curious about the author because I had read the book and reviewed it, though I cannot now remember for what paper.

Before the lecture, Mr Hoare sat with me for a few minutes and thanked me for what I had written about his book. In appearance, he is a little like his subject, but without the languorous expression, the heavy make-up, or the pearls.

I am a great admirer of Mr Sean O'Casey. When I was about seventeen years of age, the Irish Players, whose stars were Sara Allgood and Maire O'Neill, arrived in London from the Abbey Theatre of Dublin to perform *The Plough and the Stars* and *Juno and the Paycock*. As the saying goes, they took London by storm. For weeks, theatre-goers talked about nothing else. At that time, acting in London was highly theatrical and the naturalism of the Irish Players was shattering, though I do not remember anyone discussing the contents of the dramas or arguing the rights and wrongs of Britain's occupation of Ireland. In *The Plough*, in my opinion Mr O'Casey's greatest work, when Miss O'Neill is shot, she puts her hand behind her back for a moment and then looks to see it covered with blood. ''Tis me own life blood streamin' out,' she gasps. This is the only time I can ever remember being so caught up in a play that I thought, 'She's dying,' and had to remind myself that she was only acting.

Mr Agate, the famous drama critic, could not make up his mind whether this play or *Saint Joan* was the masterpiece of the century. Their appeals couldn't be more different. Mr Shaw's play is a stimulating moral argument; Mr O'Casey's is a heart-rending document.

Though the programme sets the time of the play between 1880 and 1910, its action includes a glimpse of 'The Troubles', as they were called, in 1916, and we see the Dubliners being quelled by the British police, but this play is strictly about the life of Mr O'Casey and only marginally about the fate of Ireland. We see the playwright as a little boy with a troublesome eye disease (Mr Moyles), as a young man (Mr Fitzgerald), and in old age (Mr O'Neill). In the end they are all on stage at the same time in conversation with each other. This device gives the play a poetic and very moving unity.

While I was typing the last words of the above, an unknown

woman telephoned me to ask me for eighteen dollars and fifty cents. I told her to come to the front door, where I handed her a twenty-dollar bill. She thanked me and departed. As I walked back upstairs to my room, I wondered if I should hear from her again in a month or two. I misjudged her. Within two hours, an operator was asking me if I would pay for a call. I said, 'No.' A few minutes later, the unknown woman was telephoning me with another incomprehensible saga of misfortune. I refused to give her any more money. I hated myself for this, but I hated her even more. Since I came to America, she is the first person to drive me beyond the bounds of politeness.

Last Friday, with trembling feet, I made my way to the Warner Building in Rockefeller Plaza to record an assortment of English verses by various poets from Edward Lear to Edith Sitwell for a mad friend who teaches voice production to a heap of drama students in the middle of Kansas City. Of all the Englishmen living in America, I must be the one with the least resonant voice, but I was asked to do it and offered money, so I could hardly refuse.

Because it was a sunny day and because the entire assignment had taken only about a quarter of an hour, after it I walked all the way to The Book Friend's Café on West 18th Street to have lunch with the display king from Paul Stuart. It was foolish of me to undertake so long a journey on foot, because I arrived at my destination in a state of total moral and physical collapse. However, so kind are the people who rule this restaurant that they allowed me to loll about on a very comfortable sofa, fingering the pages of various antiquarian books, from half past eleven until high noon when my host arrived. When we had eaten some chicken pot pie, we went to the new cinema on West 19th Street to see *Final Analysis*. I have to confess that, owing to my marathon walk a few hours before, I fell asleep several times during the showing of this film, but even if I had been as watchful as an owl, I think I would still have found its story-line confusing. It concerns a psychoanalyst (Mr Gere) who probes the soul of a girl who is in a permanent rage with her more successful sister. This piques his curiosity and leads him to arrange a meeting with the sister (Miss Basinger), with whom he almost immediately begins an affair. She manages to weave into her conversation with him various psychological clues to her assumed dodgy mental condition that will make it possible for her to murder her husband and get away with it on a plea of temporary insanity. When he realizes that he is being used, he refuses to cooperate and she decides to murder him, too. Everybody ends up at the top of an extremely shaky lighthouse (don't ask me why), and only Mr Gere survives.

Final Analysis is the third in a series of movies about absolutely diabolical women. Miss Basinger, though she hasn't the frenzied look of Miss Close in *Fatal Attraction*, nor the demonic cunning of Miss DeMornay in *The Hand That Rocks the Cradle*, is perfectly adequate. Mr Gere is very good-looking – like a Chippendale stripper or like Errol Flynn with the mainspring gone – and his performance is quite satisfactory because this is one of those pictures where the plot is so elaborate that the function of the actors involved is to carry out the action rather than to reveal character. The only member of the cast who is outstanding is Mr David as a black detective who trusts absolutely nobody. I would recommend *Final Analysis* as a very pleasant waste of seven dollars and fifty cents.

The next day, like You-Know-Who, I rested, but on Sunday I went to Boston – again! This time it snowed, but at least there was no hurricane.

The purpose of this second excursion was the same as that of the first – to introduce beforehand and to try to justify afterwards two showings of *Resident Alien*. These took place in Brookline in an art house called The Coolidge, ruled by a Mr Kleiler, who positively despises movies made for the purpose of entertainment. He turned out to be a charming and generous host to me and to Mr Nossiter, the film's director, who travelled with me. I never had an unoccupied moment, and never walked anywhere.

The questions asked of me were all friendly, but more or less a matter of routine, except that one young man wanted to know what I would have done with my life if I had been under no obligation to earn money. I replied that I would never have gotten out of bed. Everybody seemed delighted with this notion.

1992

Spring

*

People who are lonely are those who do not know what to do with the time when they are alone

To hell and back. On March 9th, I set out timorously for England; I returned home in a state of total nervous and physical collapse on the 24th. The purpose of this misguided journey halfway across the globe was to make a minuscule appearance as Elizabeth I, in a movie to be entitled *Orlando* and made from a novel of that very name by the very Mrs Woolf of whom the Burtons were so afraid. All her books were highbrow, and this was certainly the *most* highbrow. It concerns a young man whom we first meet at Hatfield House in the middle of Hertfordshire (where the young Elizabeth spent much of her childhood), and who lived through the centuries until the present day, incidentally changing his sex on the way, sometime during the seventeen hundreds. This fantastic tale was said to be a tribute to Vita Sackville-West, with whom prurient literary historians claim that Mrs Woolf conducted an illicit liaison. (I, personally, don't think Mrs Woolf believed in sex; she was too much of an aesthete.)

On arriving in London, I went to stay at the Chelsea Arts Club where, at breakfast the next morning, everyone cried out in tones of deepest reproach, 'Thought you were never coming back.' I was truly ashamed, because a farewell party had been given for me there two and a half years ago. I could only bow my head and offer, as an extenuating circumstance, that I had returned for the money.

After a day or two, during which I had been fitted for a dress and a wig, Miss Tilda Swinton, the star of the film, arrived to welcome me to England with a bouquet of roses and a gift. Her most recent role was that of Queen Isabella in *Edward II,* a film directed by Mr Jarman: we can therefore assume that she is accustomed to appearing in unabashed festival material and, indeed, she seems to prefer it to real movies.

Once my part in *Orlando* began in earnest, I left the club and moved to Bush Hall, a small hotel in Hatfield, so as not to rise at five in the morning on the days when work began at seven. There I was given a room so large that I could have a party for twenty people in it, and was treated with such deference that, on the occasion when I ate lunch there, the proprietor himself served me with his own two hands.

On my first day of work, I realized instantly that I was doomed to a life of agony. Two amazingly long-suffering dressers wedged me into a costume in which two padded rolls forming a kind of bustle, a hooped skirt, a quilted petticoat, another petticoat, and finally an outer skirt were all tied round my waist before I was laced into a corset so tight that it raised a blister on my stomach. Over all this, I wore a cloak that trailed the ground behind me and on which two elk-hounds and Miss Swinton occasionally stepped, causing me to utter a cry of apprehension and to totter about the lawn. Never in the history of dress design has so much glass been affixed to so many yards of tat.

Apart from all this, I was made up clown-white with a dusting of rouge on my cheeks and eyelids and clamped into a huge red wig at times surmounted by a tiara. Apparelled thus, before I could leave the trailer, called a 'relocatable', a gentleman, appropriately named Christian, had to hold up my skirts and, watching my feet, utter instructions such as 'One step down. Now the other leg. Right. You're on level ground.' Carrying all this haberdashery caused my back to ache ferociously, and that was before I had fallen back in a high chair so that my skull crashed against the opposite wall of the make-up room and my back muscles were stretched out of shape.

Sometimes I worked in one or the other of the vast rooms of

Hatfield House, sometimes in the grounds, and once, in the middle of the night, on a lake that was really more like a pond. For this scene, real men were employed to row a small boat back and forth several times while, in another boat, a charming young man called Mr Somerville sang in a falsetto voice a song telling the world that I was 'the fairest queen'. What he thought of this assignment I did not dare to enquire.

During this ordeal, Miss Potter, the director, Miss Swinton, the star, and everyone concerned were all most solicitous and kind, but I cannot deny that I am heartily glad that it is over.

Although I try never to read books, I am now perusing two concurrently, dipping into whichever happens to be on hand when a spare moment occurs. One of these is Mr Cocteau's diary, entitled (in translation) *Past Tense*, and the other is called *Final Exit*, by a Mr Humphry, a journalist who used to write for *The Sunday Times* in London and the *Los Angeles Times*, chiefly about civil liberties, racial integration, and voluntary euthanasia.

I have now forgotten who lent me the former of these two volumes, but doubtless he will reclaim it one fine day. It has a foreword by Mr Ned Rorem, which by itself is worth the price of the entire book. He was with Mr Cocteau at most eight times during the thirteen years of their acquaintance, but says that to meet him once was to know him. He writes, 'While you were with him, you were seemingly the sole beneficiary of his charitable flood of fire. I have known few people with such infectious charm. It may be opportunism, but it can't be faked, and it can't be bought.'

Final Exit is a handbook for anyone wishing to commit suicide. This was sent to me by a Mr Hofsess who, some years ago, came to New York, like the rest of us, in the hope of ruling the world. He stayed at least long enough to do most of the work on a book of mine, entitled *Manners From Heaven*. He then returned to Vancouver and, to my astonishment, has become king of the local branch of the Hemlock Society. He wishes me to write something about this book and I will. I have always liked death, especially other people's death, but have recently been contemplating my own with a certain amount of relish. Not long ago, during a television interview, I was asked if I was worried by the idea of mortality. I replied that I was not and added that next Tuesday would do fine for my own demise. This remark caused a concerned citizen to ask how I could possibly be so bored that I was eager to die. The question was natural because he was a young man. Ennui is the disease of youth. The prevailing malady of the old is fatigue. I have never been bored since I came to live in Manhattan, but, inevitably, I am gradually becoming permanently tired.

Even before senility set in, my views about death were sanguine, or, to put the matter another way, I have never shared the prevailing opinion that life is wonderful *come what may*. I have often been surprised when someone who has suffered a permanent injury in some disaster, says, 'I'm lucky to be alive.' If I were in a plane crash, for instance, and all my luggage – let alone one of my limbs – had sunk to the bottom of the Atlantic Ocean, I would not consider myself lucky to be alive. So, if told of someone's death, I will say, 'How terrible . . .' and look at the floor for an appropriate interval, but I can't really feel it is terrible because in my view death is the *least* awful thing that can happen to someone.

It is our bodies that want to live for ever, but surely we ought to be in control of our physical appetites. However, this is a state that it is easier to praise than to achieve. Nobody wants a violent or a painful death, and this is where Mr Humphry's book comes in so handy. It is totally unsentimental, absolutely free from religious bias, and admirably practical. My only divergence of opinion from that of the author is that I do not think that the relatives of the person committing suicide should be consulted or involved in any way. They may have something to gain from the proposed death and may therefore feel guilty. In all other respects, I am full of praise for *Final Exit* and for its author.

* * *

When not writing about death, I am still answering the mail that accumulated while I was in England. In it, the most interesting letter comes from a young woman with whom I had lunch recently, but not so recently that I can remember much about her. She complains that, although we were by ourselves and she was only the width of a dining-room table away from me, she felt that she was merely a member of an audience and that I was giving a performance rather than engaging in conversation. I am rebuked. I have often been guilty of assuming that, when strangers invite me to lunch or any other occasion, what they want is entertainment. It has always seemed unlikely that anyone would wish to confide in or even to impress a stranger, but this, of course, is nonsense. Many people can never reveal themselves to anyone who knows them, their friends or, worse, their parents. I am resolved henceforth to invite confidence or, at least, communication from everybody. The only demand made by strangers that I cannot satisfy is to utter confidences of my own; I don't have any. What you see is all there is. I dare not compare myself with Mr Cocteau in any way, but I would like to think that, as Mr Rorem said of him, to meet me once is to know me.

By a quirk of fate at least as strange as any of the plot of *Howards End,* on the same day that I saw Mrs Branagh in that film, I met her in real life.

Some time ago, when Mr Nossiter's movie about my life was being shown at the New School on West 12th Street, Professor Brown, who rules that establishment, invited me to attend the screening. I couldn't accept, but last Wednesday evening I was at last free. The occasion did not start well. A car arrived at Third Street promptly at half past seven but, when I jumped into it with alacrity, it transpired that the driver had no idea where he was to take me; neither had I. We drove round aimlessly until I persuaded him to telephone his employers and find out our true destination. When, finally, we arrived at the New School, mercifully a kind young woman was waiting for me and took me into a small room in which the professor's victims are stored until needed.

There I sat drinking coffee when suddenly Mrs Branagh arrived, and I learned that she was the professor's guest for the first half of the evening. I was able to listen to her interview, which I greatly enjoyed. She is much better looking in real life than in any of her films, and she was supremely natural, speaking to the professor rather than addressing the audience, and she was eager to be understood.

When my turn came, Professor Brown was very cosy, asking no difficult or embarrassing questions, but of course the presence of an audience went to my head and I tried to give a performance rather than hold a conversation, failing just where Mrs Branagh had succeeded. What a charming woman she is! On returning to the lurking area for my hat and coat, I found that she had left me a note apologizing for not staying to hear all I had to say. She had just arrived from England; therefore, though it was only nine in the evening to us, it was two in the morning to her.

When all the interviews were over, the professor took me and two of his handmaidens to supper at a nearby Italian restaurant. There it transpired that he was surprised that I had declined his previous invitation on the grounds that I was committed to a previous engagement. He said that Americans leave messages at restaurants saying that they will not be keeping their appointments. I would never dare to do that. What do I have to recommend me to the world other than that I keep my word?

This week's entry into my diary simply must begin with a vote of thanks to Miss Liz Smith, who is the only gossip writer in the world who retails remarks that encourage self-confidence rather than spread alarm and despondency. Perhaps she should be given a different title. Mary Renault would have dubbed her 'a praise singer'. She has now sent me a glowing review of *Resident Alien*, which I would otherwise never have seen. It appeared in a Washington newspaper, and was written by a Miss Kempley, to whom

I am also grateful. Naturally, most of the praise in her article is for Mr Nossiter, who made the film, but she is also nice to me. The only adjective that she applies to me with which I would disgree is the word 'lonely'. I live alone, but am glad to do so. To my mind, the people who are lonely are those who do not know what to do with the time when they are alone. From this problem I do not suffer. When I'm by myself, I do absolutely nothing, and O, the relief!

I have read a new biography of Jean Harlow, a copy of which was presented to me by the author, a Miss Golden, when I had lunch with her at our local diner. This book has been excellently produced by the Abbeville Press on paper almost as thick as cardboard and glossy enough to offset the beautiful photographs of the actress, her co-stars, members of her family, and her friends. Miss Golden admitted this, but is disappointed by the lack of promotion arranged for her work. It is a pity that Mr Abbeville failed in this respect, because this book will appeal not only to readers who can remember Miss Harlow, but to everyone fascinated by Hollywood's happy years.

Miss Golden's main objective in compiling this book is to undo the harm done to the actress's reputation by a certain Mr Shulman who, some years ago, wrote a scandalous biography describing scenes in Miss Harlow's second marriage, to Mr Bern, accusing him of being an impotent sadist and dwelling on events of which only the participants could possibly have had any knowledge. Miss Golden's research contradicts all these sordid details, and she has even found pictures of Miss Harlow that make her look happy, healthy and natural, in contrast with the image of her looking like the head girl in a reform school, which most of us recall.

Last Friday, I was summoned by *House & Garden* to the home of a self-confessed interior decorator called Mr Osborne. This is the second time that I, who have never owned either a house or garden and who am known to be indifferent to what anything looks like, have been invited, if not to explain or evaluate, at least to describe the living quarters of someone whose tastes in the matter of décor are sufficiently refined to be of interest to the cognoscenti. Last time this occurred, my assignment was the apartment of Mr Michael O'Donoghue, who used to rule *Saturday Night Live* and who was kind enough to allow the movie crew of *Resident Alien* to invade his home. As I had met him socially, I was less intimidated by the task than by the present confrontation. However, Mr Osborne turned out to be most gracious – even cosy.

I have received a bizarre letter from a gentleman living in Cedar Grove. (Though this town has such a romantic, Mediterranean name, it is in fact in the middle of New Jersey.) He tells me that he is compiling a list of quotations on the subject of success from people who, in his opinion, have achieved this blissful state. Inevitably, this being America, most of the names mentioned are from the world of entertainment, but Mr Joe DiMaggio, Mr Arthur Ashe, and several politicians are included. Many of the sentiments expressed are slightly sanctimonious and some go so far as to mention You-Know-Who, although we all know how wholeheartedly He despises anything remotely like earthly happiness.

I have seen *The Player*, directed by Mr Altman from a book written by a Mr Tolkin and adapted by him for the screen. It is a relentless satire of the movie industry.

I like movies about movies. Usually they provide actresses with the opportunity to play actresses, which they do with special relish. This newest picture on the subject is different. There is a huge party at which we glimpse various celebrities playing themselves, but Mr Tolkin's main theme is the utter ruthlessness of executives in their dealings with frantically tenacious authors. The hero, if such he can be termed, is played by Mr Tim Robbins, who becomes increasingly desperate as his power is threatened by an even younger man played by a Mr Gallagher. At the same time that he is trying to cope with this situation, he is constantly receiving insulting postcards from a disgruntled author. Thinking that he knows who the sender is, he finds out from the man's girlfriend where he is, meets him, and murders him. At his victim's funeral, he meets this young woman who confesses that she doesn't really feel the required grief. It transpires that she is worse than a man – nay, worse than a studio executive: she has appetites but no emotion. At the end of the film, she marries Mr Robbins and they live ruthlessly ever after. The girl is played by Miss Scacchi, whose heartless indiscretions caused Mr Ackland to kill himself in *White Mischief*.

Throughout *The Player*, writers are for ever trying to interest Mr Robbins in their scenarios. They visit his office, they waylay him in corridors, they walk backwards in front of him, gibbering, as he goes to his car. One of these men tells him the tragic story of an innocent girl who is wrongly sent to the gas chamber. When we watch a preview of this film, it has acquired a ludicrously happy ending. This sequence is one of Mr Altman's funniest effects, but it is naughty. In *I Want To Live*, Hollywood *did* send the guiltless Miss Hayward to the gas chamber, and the incident contained one of the most telling lines in the history of film-making. As the prison warden straps Miss Hayward into the chair, he says, 'When you hear the capsules fall on the floor, take a deep breath.' He is trying to help her to make her agony shorter. In *The Player*, finally one of these innumerable screen writers tells the executive over his car telephone the story we have been watching. Mr Robbins likes it. Thus ends one of the neatest, most entertaining, most cynical films I have ever seen.

The very moment that Miss Dietrich's heart stopped beating, my telephone started ringing. It was almost as though she had been a member of my family. In fact, I never even met her, but in her heyday she certainly occupied almost all my thoughts. I adored her obsession with her screen image, but this opinion was not universally shared. When I saw *Morocco*, a girl sitting behind me muttered, 'She ain't 'alf stuck on 'erself.' In the 1930s, in the sad

London cafés where the more outrageous and the more helpless 'gay' boys congregated, a perpetual war of words was waged. Which was the more beautiful – Miss Garbo or Miss Dietrich? Really there was no way of comparing the two. The English press was for ever printing photographs of Miss Dietrich with captions such as 'The shadow across Garbo's path', but the two stars occupied different firmaments. Miss Garbo represented a remote, poetic yearning, while Miss Dietrich personified a worldly indifference.

Miss Garbo, though almost reverentially admired in Hollywood, was not popular there. Miss Davis said that this was because she invested most of her money outside the United States. Miss Dietrich, on the other hand, while claiming that she never liked making movies, loved America, and enriched her patriotic image by going to Europe to entertain the troops, often in situations fraught with danger. Hedda Hopper, who hardly ever praised anybody, said of her, 'That woman can do no wrong.'

I have been given a copy of *Marlene*, Miss Dietrich's autobiography. It is a fascinating book presenting a person very different from her screen image. In real life, she was highly emotional, but cynical; very feminine, but by no means frail; hard-working, but resentful of exploitation. Mr Siman, who wrote *Pizza Face*, a study in physical hideousness, has now turned his attention to the subject of beauty. He took me to lunch at Jerry's on Second Avenue to question me about my thoughts on this topic. To my surprise, he had been told by someone else whom he had interrogated that the most beautiful is that which arouses the greatest sexual excitement. I formed my ideas on beauty from movie heroines, and none of the women I admired had anything to do with sex. (If snowbound for a night in a wooden shed with Miss Garbo, all the men I have ever known would have been terrified.) What she and Miss Dietrich and Miss Del Rio radiated, at least from the screen, was a slightly sorrowful nobility, and that, to me, is an essential ingredient of beauty.

* * *

On Wednesday, I was invited by Mr Cook, who used to rule the Actor's Playhouse, but who now reigns over the Cherry Lane Theater on Commerce Street, to see a play called *Hauptmann* by a Mr Logan. I was privileged to sit next to Miss Kim Hunter, whom I have admired ever since I saw her co-starred with Mr Niven in a movie entitled *A Matter of Life and Death*.

Hauptmann I found interesting, but it worried me. Firstly, I thought its title a mistake. While no one will ever forget the name of Mr Lindbergh, I doubt that many people now living recall that the man who may not have kidnapped his baby was a Mr Hauptmann. Once it dawned on me that the play was about this famous court case, I couldn't help wanting to know if the accused was guilty or innocent. In a programme note, the playwright says that it is not the purpose of his play to refute the prosecution's case. This left me wondering what exactly its aim is.

After the show, there was a first-night party in a neighbouring bar which, for a few hours, became a mini-Sardi's with all the customers applauding the entrance of the star. While there, I was able to discuss the play with Mr Cook. He has always disapproved of the Lindberghs on the grounds that they were fascists. I felt that their attitude and that of other aristocrats such as the Duke and Duchess of Windsor was less a political stance than a hideous social snobbery – that all they wanted was for the world to be ruled by gentlemen. Mr Cook's dislike of the Lindberghs led him to suggest that it was they themselves who had murdered their baby. What a play that idea would have made!

On Monday evening, with Mr Cook and his constant companion, I was invited to an evening meal in the home of Miss Hunter and her husband. They live near the Cherry Lane Theater. Among the guests were a Mr Zindel and his wife. I didn't know until later that it was he who wrote *The Effect of Gamma Rays on Man-in-the-Moon Marigolds*, and that he is a Pulitzer Prize winner. Never before have I luxuriated in such a cosy, and, at the same time, rarefied atmosphere. Mr Cook questioned Miss Hunter closely about the experience of playing Stella in *A Streetcar*

Named Desire. She told us some fascinating things – among them that, during a scene with Miss Leigh, there were so many takes that, after a while, she rushed over to the director to ask him what was wrong. He replied that he was hypnotized by seeing that tears came into Miss Leigh's eyes at exactly the same moment of each take. It was a truly fascinating evening.

Summer

*

I am becoming more American

In my neighbourhood, traffic was in chaos this week because some kind of street fair was in full swing. Someone explained that the same objects are offered for sale at all New York's open-air markets. The vendors simply pretend that they and their wares are Italian one week, Ukrainian the next, and so on all summer long. I found this information hilarious.

The week has been shrouded in failure. On Thursday evening, I had been asked by a Mr Gordon, whom I do not know, to go to the Astor Place Bookshop and to read to its clientèle. It was fortunate that I telephoned before setting out for this illustrious emporium because I was informed by a member of its staff that Mr Gordon no longer worked there, and when I asked if, in that case, my presence was not required, the young lady said, 'I guess so.' She seemed slightly amused and offered no apology. I was surprised: I regarded this somewhat offhand method of dealing with what was, after all, a mild betrayal, as almost un-American activity.

The next night, I was supposed to hear one of the remaining Beatles perform at Radio City Music Hall. I reconstructed myself elaborately and sat, with one ear cocked towards the telephone, like the dog on the famous 'His Master's Voice' gramophone record label, but silence reigned throughout the evening. It has since transpired that I was given the wrong date by my proposed escort's brother.

I was therefore broken and disillusioned as I set out for Providence, Rhode Island on Sunday morning. However, the train journey cheered me up. I like travelling by rail: it is a situation in which no one can blame you for doing absolutely nothing but looking out of the window for several hours. Rhode Island is mostly water, but what landscape there is is picturesque, and Providence is quaintly Puritanical. The houses are made of wood, except for a few beautiful pseudo-classical public buildings such as the courthouse, in which I imagine that, with any luck, you might be condemned as a witch.

At the station, I was met by a fully representative group of three people – a white man, a black man, and a woman, the latter of whom explained that she had only been invited because it was her car we were using and her credit card with which everything was paid for. She appeared to accept her fate with surprising calm. As it was about half past three in the afternoon, we immediately went to a café for an all-purpose meal over which what was expected of me was explained.

The purpose of my visit to Rhode Island was to try to justify *Resident Alien,* which was being shown at the Avon Cinema, an 'art house' which the gay and lesbian folk of the city had taken over for several days of 'unusual' films. When, after signing a few books, we left the premises, people were lining up to see Mr Jarman's *Edward II.* The audience was extremely friendly and only asked benign questions, chiefly about my life rather than about the movie. I was on familiar ground and gave the usual answers in the usual way.

The following day, I arrived back in New York just in time to rush home and telephone a Mr Vincent, whose fair name was written in my sacred book in the space designated June 15. I had never met him and could not remember what on earth I had promised to do for him. The number he had given me was of a department in the United Nations building. I was terrified, but he turned out to be a very cosy gentleman who only wanted to take me to the elegant home of an elegant gentleman named Mr Kooder. The occasion was a party given for some of the members of a group called ILGA – International Lesbian and Gay Association. This is a formidable organization, but the party was extremely urbane: I don't think an outsider would have been able to guess anybody's guilty secret. However, they fully intend to change the world.

In the taxi on the way to the party, the conversation of my escort had already given me an inkling of the devastation likely to be caused by his iconoclasm and that of his friends. His view of what is usually meant by the words 'consenting adults' is a case in point. He thought that the age at which this hazardous status could be deemed lawful is thirteen. Another conventional notion that he challenged was the meaning of the phrase 'in private'. He wished it to include sequestered areas of public parks. Where, I asked myself silently, would it all end? Though I did not voice my misgivings to my kind companion or any of his friends, I could not help wondering if a worldwide gesture of defiance of the established order would not one day be regarded as based on what could be termed 'the Spartacus Fallacy'.

Yesterday evening I went to that frightening section of East 9th Street that is just beyond Revolution Square. My steps might have faltered in such a benighted neighbourhood had not a total stranger by some occult process divined what my destination was and led me almost to the very door. I was going to the home of a Miss Sharif who, from time to time, very generously transforms her living room into a mini-theatre. Some time ago, I saw a production there of *No Exit* by Mr Sartre.

The offering this time was *The Lover*, by Mr Pinter. It is about a married couple that tries to keep their sexual interest in one another alive by enacting various charades in which he pretends to be all sorts of different types of men whom she meets in bizarre circumstances, or he plays the husband jealous of these men. Though I am sure it was not intended by the playwright, this plot has relevance to the love lives of many homosexuals. In those far-off days when there was still a marked difference between the sexes, homosexual men frequently played at a heterosexual relationship with one partner parading a worldly competence that he did not really possess, and the other, an excruciating femininity which was sometimes a considerable handicap. Later, different masquerades emerged. Young men who had never seen a horse began to wear full Western gear; boys who couldn't even catch a fly – let alone hurt one – donned stormtroopers' uniforms. I have never understood how these disguises can hold up for more than ten minutes. When a pseudo-Westerner is asked by a prospective partner about his ranch, or a fake stormtrooper is questioned about his regiment, does not the entire subterfuge collapse? Moreover, what is the use of desire provoked by or admiration bestowed upon someone whom you are not? Even while watching *The Lover*, I couldn't help wondering when the married couple would stop pretending and collapse in totally asexual laughter.

On Sunday afternoon I was taken to East Hampton. It was a long journey – so long, indeed, that halfway through it we had to change cars like the coachmen of Wells-Fargo changing horses. At about five o'clock, we arrived at a clearing in the jungle ominously called The Swamp, but which turned out to be two picturesque barns with an open-air space between them occupied by garden furniture and one sumptuously upholstered chair that someone must have transported from her home specially for me. On this I sat for some hours and, though the sky was cloudy from one horizon to the other, no rain fell.

The occasion was a gathering of members of Thursday's Child, a benevolent organization devoted to the care of people with AIDS. Raffle tickets and T-shirts were for sale and there was an abundance of food and liquor to consume. I sat beside the ticket seller, ate and drank everything that I could lay my hands on, and talked with anyone who approached within a mile of me until about seven o'clock. Then my throne was carried into one of the buildings which transpired to be a pitch-dark twitching area where a Miss Rapp sang with great gusto some highly subversive political songs and a Mr Cohen read a passage from one of my books. Thereafter

I answered questions from the audience until it was about nine o'clock and time for me to go home.

The task of driving me back to Manhattan was nobly undertaken by a second Mr Cohen, the older, bigger, bolder brother of the first. I had been offered the opportunity to stay overnight in East Hampton, but had declined it because it is now very difficult for me to sleep a night away from my room. Because of my eczema, large areas of my wretched body have to be swathed in bandages to prevent me from clawing myself until the blood gushes out of my wounds and down the stairs with a gurgling sound. This, naturally, I did not mention to my escort. He did not complain, but my feeling of guilt was great and increased as time crawled by and progress became slower and slower. Everybody in America seemed to be converging on New York.

In prehistoric times – that is to say before I began to write this diary – I was once transported by car to Danbury in the middle of Connecticut. There, a movie, which it would be polite to call experimental, was being made. The scene in which I took part happened in a disused shop that, for the film, had been disguised as the canteen of a mental hospital. The only piece of action that I can now remember occurred when two handsome young men in white coats appeared and dragged the star of the picture out of the room. Now, many long, dark years later, a soundtrack that will narrate the entire story is being prepared, and what a wild tale it is!

I gather that several versions of this saga have already been attempted. The one in which I was involved was recorded in an upper room in that part of New York University that is situated on Broadway and Waverly Place, and that, from the outside, looks like a very modern cathedral and, from within, like a newly-erected shrine to the gods of DIY carpentry. My reading was supervised by two (presumably) superannuated students who, considering my various inadequacies, were positively indulgent and who took me to supper in a nearby café when the ordeal was over. The contempt felt by the young for the old which so disfigures English society seems to be totally absent from life in America.

One mystery arising from this assignment remains unsolved. Why did the makers of this film ask me to record its soundtrack? When, in a play about Mr Wilde by Professor Bentley, I played the part of the elderly Lord Alfred Douglas, critics described me as sounding like 'a nasal Mr Magoo'. It was not a kind description, but it is funny and undeniably accurate.

As though this new profession of being a 'voice-over' were not bizarre enough, I have now entered another unexplored kingdom: the comics.

In that restaurant on the corner of Second Avenue and East Fifth Street that has become my dining room, I met Mr Russo and Mr Wong who, between them, produce a comic magazine called *Jizz*. They presented me with a copy of its ninth issue. In captioned pictures, sometimes at the rate of twenty to a page, this tells the story of an attempt by an enemy of Mr Russo to incriminate him in a plot to kill the President by sending to the White House a letter signed with Mr Russo's name. Some of the wording is hilarious – e.g., 'questioning my parents about me is like asking a blind man about colour.'

Even more amazingly than the contents of this magazine was its cover. There, printed in full colour on glossy paper, was a picture of a gathering of people warming themselves at a fire in a dustbin, and most conspicuous among them was me. Does this mean that, after seeking recognition so vigorously and so unsuccessfully from so many sources, I am at last to take my place beside Mr Mouse and Mr Abner?

While we ate, Mr Wong, the magazine's illustrator, drew from a vast canvas bag a large sketch book filled with 'life' drawings. I have never deliberately read 'the funnies'. But, by chance, I have caught sight of a strip cartoon called 'Big Ben Bolt', and I was quite amazed by the skill and accuracy of the drawings. Mr Wong's work is also astonishing: it is far from naturalistic like the old-fashioned cartoons, but not because of any lack either of observation or competence. It is distorted by a consistent and highly stylized vision. However, my admiration turned to stark terror when I realized that Mr Wong was showing me these drawings not merely to solicit my approval, but also in the hope that they would persuade me to pose for him. I hastily explained that the time for me to pose nude was long since past, and this sad fact he graciously accepted. It was decided that he should take pictures of me fully clothed and work from them. He wishes to make huge paintings of The Seven Deadly Sins, and he thinks that I would be the ideal personification of Pride. I did not protest: he was paying for my lunch.

I am becoming more American. This is a change that I have always earnestly desired, but I now realize, alas, that it is the more blameworthy characteristics of my adopted nation that I am acquiring. Everyone, including Americans themselves, is for ever accusing people in the United States of having short attention spans – a phrase that, until a few years ago, I had never heard, but which, to my shame, I am now aware applies to me.

In the course of a single evening spent watching it on television, I tired of the Democratic Convention. It seemed to me that the same vaguely optimistic, self-congratulatory sentiments were uttered over and over again – that I was hearing what Mr Macbeth would have called 'a tale told by a Democrat, full of sound and fury, signifying nothing.' Friends tell me that, on subsequent evenings, these notions were expressed with considerable eloquence, but by then I had turned my eyes and ears elsewhere.

The Japanese recovered from being literally flattened by devoting themselves body and soul to their employers, by working harder for longer hours for smaller wages. But Americans think the solution to their nation's bankruptcy lies in demanding more from their government and by striking when their requests are not met.

* * *

All male homosexuals are missionaries at heart, and are for ever implying, if not actually stating, that everyone is really gay and either does not know or does not admit it.

The English branch of this enclosed order is now pecking at the long-dead corpse of poor old D.H. Lawrence. As part of this process, a Mr Robinson, who rules a company laughingly called Wall-To-Wall Television, and two of his merry men recently arrived in America to conduct interviews on this subject. One of these confrontations was with me and it took place at the Player's Club on Gramercy Park. This is a hushed, dignified institution full of old-fashioned portraits of people famous in the world of entertainment. I couldn't help wondering if whoever allowed these premises to be used for our programme knew what we were discussing.

The new argument about his sexual orientation is based on the undeniable fact that Mr Lawrence lavished much more enthusiasm and many more words on describing the physical splendour of his male characters than on the beauty of his women. Except for a paragraph in a story called 'The Ladybird', I cannot call to mind a single passage in praise of the features of a girl, whereas, when he discovers the gamekeeper's arm in *The White Peacock* completely fills his sleeve, he is deeply impressed. Personally, I do not think that this proves that Mr Lawrence was homosexual.

As I see it, he longed for the locker-room set-up, that celebration of manliness from which he was for ever excluded by his frail physique and his illness. Many people who suffer from tuberculosis have voracious sexual appetites, but this was apparently not so in the case of D.H. Lawrence. Mrs Lawrence described her husband as almost impotent. Once you have seen that famous photograph of the two of them standing side by side – she so huge, so self-confident, he so thin, so haunted – you understand his entire literary output. He never got his wife to do a damned thing he wanted. His novels compensated for his failure. Halfway through each book, we come across the sentence, 'She trembled before his dark beauty.' As with so many writers of lurid fiction, his writings describe the unlived life. Nevertheless, for all his iconoclasms, his insistence on using the shortest words for the longest things, the exhibition of paintings, so pornographic that they were seized by the police, I think he would have been horrified if any of his dream heroes had ever tried to use him as the instrument of their sexual gratification.

Last weekend I went to Baltimore. Every time I undertake one of these journeys out of Manhattan, I think it will be the last gesture that I am obliged to make on behalf of *Resident Alien*. Then another excursion is proposed, and I stagger on. This one was not difficult because Mr Nossiter and his newest true-love, a charming French girl, came with me and guided my steps towards the right train and led me from it at the right station. There we were met by a Mr Udel, who looks like the movie actor Sam Jaffe, but without the frenzied stare. We all rushed immediately to a radio station for a lively interview with a Miss Semione, who more or less rules the cultural channel of Baltimore, after which I was taken to a very grand hotel called the Colonnade, while Mr Nossiter and his friend were distributed among the poor.

Dinner was served at the strange hour of half past five in a restaurant of great splendour, whose staff remained admirably calm although our party of more than a dozen guests rearranged the furniture several times before finally settling at a table of da Vincian length. There I sat next to Mr John Waters, who is king of Baltimore and makes all his films there, including *Pink Flamingos* and *Hairspray*. He and Mr Nossiter indulged in a disparaging dialogue concerning field distributors, which might have been positively venomous had not Mr Waters been aware that I might repeat everything he said.

Incidentally, he told me that, in a time so long ago that the television play of *The Naked Civil Servant* had not been made, he paid me a visit in my room in Chelsea. I'm ashamed to say that I have no memory whatsoever of our meeting.

* * *

Last Friday, I was taken to lunch at the Café des Artistes by two young women who had come from England to test the climate of fashion in the United States. For some unknown reason, they thought that I would be knowledgeable about this subject. I explained that I am impervious to fashion – indeed, to change of any sort. This they found difficult to believe until I explained that I have not only been dressing in the same way for the past fifty years, but am still wearing the actual garments that kind friends gave me all that time ago – that I have never bought clothing since I came to America. In spite of this shocking admission, my hostesses remained calm and even paid for my lunch.

Behind me, as we sat and talked, a great deal of movement was going on. Lights were being adjusted; cameras were being focused. The centre of all this activity was Mr Charles Kuralt, the televisionary. For the entire time that it took us to eat, drink and talk, he sat at a nearby table with a plate of food before him (which he never touched). Whether this photographic session was intended to advertise him or the restaurant, we were unable to ascertain, but, at least to some extent, this incident compensated my hostesses for my lack of useful information on the subject of American fashion.

A few evenings ago I went to John's Restaurant on East 12th Street, where I found Jack Eric Williams and a coach party of his friends. There we ate as much as possible to fortify ourselves for a visit to the ruined public school on First Avenue, called Performance Space 122, where Miss Penny Arcade is doing a revised version of her show called *Bitch! Dyke! Fag-Hag! Whore!* This event has been reviewed in the *New York Times* without mentioning its title, which was considered too wicked to name. We all had a good idea what we were in for but our most unnerving expectations were not merely fulfilled; they were surpassed. There were more dancers, more nearly naked, twitching more violently to louder music than ever before. It was like *Hair* but angry instead of jubilant. Miss Arcade hates everything except sex. Her rage extends as far as the critics because they do not mention the names of her dancers.

At one moment, everyone, including some members of the audience, was jumping up and down. It was, as someone remarked, a 'very Sixties' event. I am happy to say that the dancers had been warned not to try to involve me. Even so, I was frightened. For me the show was saved by some wonderful lines such as 'Lesbians don't like you if you're a straight woman – unless you're battered' and 'If you're bisexual, lesbians think it's because you're not trying hard enough.'

Mr Jon Winokur is a complier of books rather than a writer of them. In modern times, he is a recycler of phrases. In the past he has been kind enough to send me *Writers on Writing*, *The Portable Curmudgeon*, an anthology of unkind remarks about the world, and *The Curmudgeon's Garden of Love*, a collection of cynical observations on human relationships. Now I have received *True Confessions*, a goldmine of revelations about famous people by themselves.

In this latest book, needless to say, Miss Madonna is the richest source of self-revelation: pages are devoted to her utterances while only paragraphs or single sentences are contributed by others. Among other confessions, she says she is not really a sex maniac – that she would rather read a book. Perhaps she is thinking of her bank book.

Many of the quotations are very funny but few are really peculiar. Perhaps the oddest comes from Miss Kinski, who says she used to eat her eyebrows. (Should she have been called Nastassia Kinky?) To me the most interesting piece of gossip is divulged by Jackie Cooper. He says that, when he was seventeen, he had a brief affair with Miss Crawford, who at that time would have been in her early thirties.

On Thursday afternoon, I went to meet two young men who had come to New York to climb the Empire State Building and to see me. In England, they had been performing a stage version that they had written of *The Naked Civil Servant*. The day was so crowded with engagements that I had to ask them to accompany me to the Ziegfeld cinema to see *Death Becomes Her* with Jack Eric Williams and sundry friends. To my relief, my new acquaintances were well received by Mr Williams. To my horror, he asked them if they were lovers, but they took this intrusion upon their privacy calmly. What they thought of the movie, I have no idea. My own feelings about it were worse than mixed. Mr Williams has a genius not only for discovering restaurants where the food is uneatable but also for finding cinemas and dim cellars where the shows are unwatchable.

The story of *Death* is about an ageing actress (Miss Streep) who visits a sorceress who gives her a potion that will make her young again. Her arch-enemy (Miss Hawn) receives the same rejuvenating treatment. Then both women try to nag Miss Streep's husband (Mr Willis) into trying it. He refuses, wisely regarding eternal life as something no one would wish on his worst enemy. Miss Streep, as always, flings herself whole-heartedly into the part, sings a cabaret number and nearly dances. She does not have a natural flair for comedy but she is better than adequate. The special effects are nothing short of miraculous and the editing is superb, but the plot is so farcical that, about halfway through it, it becomes impossible to care what happens to anybody. As our party was almost the entire audience at the Ziegfeld, what the world will think of this film, I have no idea.

I have a friend who rules Bloomfield in New Jersey and who, from time to time, sends me nuggets of eternal wisdom. Recently, I have received from him a clipping out of a paper called *The Star-Ledger*, describing experiments conducted by two scientists working at the medical school of the University of Southern California in Los Angeles. The article states that they have found that the brains of homosexual men are structurally different from those of heterosexuals: an area called the 'anterior commissure' is larger. This news has prompted my friend, who is an unquenchable optimist, to prophesy that these findings will instantly change the world's opinion of homosexuality – indeed will cause it to realize that gayness is innate and not a matter of wilful perversity.

I doubt it.

Firstly, scientific experiments take years to be accepted even by the experts and centuries pass before any new knowledge seeps into the consciousness of the man in the street of small-town America. Secondly, the objection raised by Pauline Christians to the gay community is less to its nature than to its behaviour. Whatever our instincts may be, we are expected to control them. In any case, prejudice is like a cactus: it flourishes without any discernible source of nourishment. I have conveyed these depressing opinions to my friend but I doubt that they will dim his rosy vision of a universally tolerant future. Surprisingly, I have received no reaction to this scientific information from any other quarter.

Occasionally I receive invitations to events taking place at the Public Theater on Lafayette Street. I seldom accept them, fearing they will be cultural in nature, but recently I pulled myself together and went to a screening of *The Water Engine* by David Mamet. When I've watched movies before at Mr Papp's theatre, they have always been quiet, slightly off-beat affairs. This occasion turned out to be rather grand. When I arrived, I found a large audience already wandering like caged lions around the vast entrance hall where three photographers were taking pictures of almost everyone. And Miss Miles was there.

The film is good. It has a beautiful colour constancy though it seemed to me too dark, but that may have been the fault of the projection at that theatre. The story, set in Chicago in the 1930s, is of a humble factory worker who invents a machine that requires no other fuel than water. This he tries to patent but, from the very beginning, his efforts are frustrated by agents of Big Business who are secretly determined to destroy his invention. Clandestine meetings are held with large men in huge limousines parked in deserted places. Offers are made for the machine but its creator does not want an outright sale: he is aiming at a royalty. Slowly the situation passes from the eerie to the grim. 'They' blackmail the inventor by kidnapping his blind sister and, when he still does not give in, they kill both of them. We did not see the victims die; we were merely told that their bodies had been found. I accepted this tactful finale and assume that when this film is released the world, which is for ever complaining that television is too violent, will rejoice.

When the picture was over, a reception was held for Mr Schachter, the director, and, presumably, for Mr Mamet who, on the Hitchcock principle, has a small part in the film but, as I have no idea what he looks like, I cannot say if he was there. Miss Miles and I sat together and gobbled up whole handfuls of *hors d'oeuvres.*

I have been to hear Peggy Lee in cabaret at the Hilton Hotel on Sixth Avenue and 53rd Street. Never before have we been treated with such deference. The manager of the cabaret came to our table, soon after we arrived, to welcome us and, after the show, introduced us to Miss Lee who sat in another part of the hotel to receive her fans. She was wonderful. She hadn't the faintest idea who I was but, after a flicker of bewilderment directed towards the manager, she graciously pretended that she did. When I praised her performance, she replied, 'It could have been better,' with just that hint of self-mockery reminiscent of Mae West – whom, minus the sexual undertone, she greatly resembles.

Her audience was mostly middle-aged couples who obviously knew her and her repertoire well. Before she had uttered the first words of such favourites as 'Fever' and 'Is That All There Is?' they were already applauding. She was in complete and effortless control of her audience, her material and the microphone (in spite of the fact that, at one moment, it fell apart in her hand). She did not sing one decibel louder than audibility required, but every possible shade of meaning was expressed.

In a humbler setting I have met an unknown relative. I only ever had one cousin whom, because he was fatherless, my mother said that my brother and I must treat with special kindness. Needless to say, we instantly decided to give him hell. He survived this treatment, grew to manhood, married a woman I only met once and sired four daughters whose names I never knew. One of these girls married an American artist whom she met while, as is the custom in the US, he was waltzing round Europe at the taxpayer's expense. They settled in Baltimore, where they raised three children.

Suddenly, after half a century of silence, the son of this couple telephoned me to say that he and his girlfriend would like to see me. We met in my local diner, where I asked how he knew of my existence since I have changed my name, my country of residence and so much else. 'We've all known about you for years,' he said. 'You were the homosexual in the family.' On hearing these words I had one of those rare glimpses of myself as others see me. I had never before thought of myself as the family's dark secret, the black sheep, the skeleton in the cupboard. I recalled that television conversation between Mr Harvey Fierstein and an interviewer in which he growled, 'Well, Barbara, every family has one.'

On Wednesday evening I went to the Rainbow Room on Rockefeller Plaza to meet Jack Eric Williams, who had managed to secure us a table at *Say It with Music,* the Irving Berlin revue. The Rainbow Room, though very grand, is not an entirely satisfactory setting for a cabaret performance. It is wide rather than deep and therefore compels singers to divide their attention between diners to their right and left, and the stage is so small that, what with a grand piano, played by a fabulous gentleman called Fred Wells, a double bass and a set of drums, it leaves very little space for the four singers. They had decided to add a visual component to the show by dancing about and waving their arms, which I found a little embarrassing. Nevertheless, *Say It with Music* provided a very enjoyable evening and the baritone, a Mr Raines, has a truly powerful and beautiful voice.

I once read an article which said that some of Mr Berlin's songs had been written so long ago that youngsters thought they were traditional airs. I avoided that mistake but I didn't realize that most of his earliest work consisted of wistful lyrics about lost love – *What'll I Do?* and *Remember.* The bolder songs in 4/4 time – *This Is The Army, Mr Jones* and *You Can't Get a Man with a Gun* – came later.

Autumn

*

How different Hollywood is from New York!

These last few days should really have been a time of mourning for me. My eczema has now begun to attack my eyelids, in consequence of which I rub them so furiously that one morning I woke up to find that I had a black eye. I could not hide my head in shame until the discolouration had, if not disappeared, at least diminished, because hardly a day has gone by this week without my being invited to a meal of some sort by a stranger – an occasion never to be missed. I do not know if these windfalls are occurring because September is the month when visitors flock to New York from altered states or because news of my infinite availability has been spread across the length and breadth of the land. I accepted the challenge at first by wearing dark glasses, though I knew people would laugh me to scorn thinking I was trying to stage a Garbo, and later by painting out the bruise with a stick of Erase given me by Jack Eric Williams. It was worth it. All my unknown hosts had amusing tales to tell.

A Mr Barefoot recounted how, when he went to England to stay in a private house, his hostess met his plane, did not greet him, drove him home in utter silence and only when the front door was shut behind them, spoke. Then her first words were, 'You are a great disappointment to me: I had expected you to be an American Indian.' Let that be a lesson to all travellers thinking of going to Britain.

A young woman I met in the Thompson Square Restaurant told me an even more delectable anecdote. When I mentioned that I live on the same street as some Hell's Angels, it reminded her that she had a friend who once occupied the very next house to theirs. After her home was vandalized by burglars, she appealed to one of the Angels to board up a window for her until it could be repaired. This he did. She repaid his chivalry by baking him and his confederates a heap of cupcakes which she decorated in icing with skulls and crossbones. I hope they appreciated that this must have been the first instance ever of witty cuisine.

Some time ago, Miss Arcade asked me to return to the public speaking racket at the ruined school on the corner of First Avenue and Ninth Street which will one day be renamed The Penny Arcade Theater. When I declined on the ground that I have already said it all – and often – she offered to interview me. This meant that I would be relieved of the burden of having to decide what on earth to say. I would merely be required to answer questions asked by her and possibly from members of our audience, if any. On this condition I agreed to her request and a series of five Sunday afternoons has been set aside for these public conversations. The first of them occurred last Sunday.

Dressed all in white like a Pierrot but without the huge black buttons and the black skull cap, Miss Arcade arrived at about half past three to collect me from East Third Street and take me to our destination. There I found a cosy setting complete with mock fireplace, two armchairs, a table, a tea trolley and a tea service. The performance, if such it can be called, began almost imperceptibly. A small audience of about forty people had arrived and we started to talk to one another and to them. Very graciously it transpired that what Miss Arcade longs to unearth in the course of this series of two-hour sessions is some hitherto hidden aspect of my nature. She obviously doesn't believe that my one desire in life is to please the public. She thinks – nay, hopes – that underneath my sickeningly ingratiating image there is another angry self waiting to burst forth. I am infinitely willing to cooperate in this voyage of discovery but I fear there is no hidden treasure at the end of it. What little you see is all you are likely to get.

* * *

Just as religion is for evangelists, not for congregations, and education is for teachers, not for students, so politics are for politicians, not for voters. The people who enter these professions are those who cannot live within their income of admiration. Most men search, in their spare time, for a woman who can be relied upon never to let a day go by without saying, 'How clever you are', or 'You're going to win – in the end.' This woman they marry and if, after a while, she ceases to utter the essential adulatory phrase, they move on to somebody else. There are, however, some men for whom, from the very beginning, the praise of one person is not enough. They become actors or, if the stage seems too hazardous a profession, they take to education, evangelism or politics. Such a man is the hero of *Bob Roberts*.

Bob Roberts is another political picture, not quite as fascinating as *JFK* but it features Mr Robbins, whom we last saw in *The Player*, and here he is even better. He plays an extremely right-wing candidate for the Senate who will stop at nothing to secure his election. He even contrives to stage an attempted assassination of himself and plants the gun on a persistent agitator. It transpires that this poor man has a withered right hand and, since the weapon in question is found in his right-hand pocket, he cannot possibly be guilty of the crime. He is acquitted and therefore has to be silenced by more direct means.

The critics have described this movie as hilarious and I cannot deny that the surprisingly sparse audience at the Paramount did laugh, although uneasily. I found it grim. It is very well and completely realistically acted, especially by the ill-fated revolutionary and by Mr Robbins, who plays a guitar at least as expertly as Mr Clinton plays the saxophone, and sings a number of songs, some of which are first-rate.

Two evenings later, I was taken to the Cocteau Theater on the Bowery to see *Under Milk Wood* by Dylan Thomas. I once met this strange man in Chelsea during the Second World War. Even in those far-off days he was famous, but chiefly as a drinker rather than a thinker. He was a tiny creature looking like a permanently surprised cherub. The programme notes tell us that he described *Milk Wood* as 'an extravagant play about a day's life in a small town in never-never Wales' and that is exactly what it is. It has no plot: it only narrates, in highly idiosyncratic language, how various townsfolk – the postman who knows the contents of every letter he delivers, the local wicked woman, a man for ever plotting the murder of his wife and so on – wake up, spend their day and go back to bed. The poetic language took some digesting but we became acclimatized and enjoyed the evening enormously. Ultimately it is a sad play. I have been to Wales: it is a dreary country – even worse than England – and, throughout *Milk Wood,* the audience is made inescapably aware of the monotony and the limitation of these people's lives in those days. Now, doubtless, they all have television sets and fax their love letters to one another.

The other day I was invited by the *maître d'* of a posh hotel to his home on the Upper East Side where he lives in mini-splendour. I had been asked to bring with me a picture of myself. I took two – one in black and white and another in colour, which is a postcard made from a painting done of me by a student when I was an art school model in about 1943. The purpose of all this was so that my host could embroider a likeness of me in coloured silks. I was shown a portrait done in this way of somebody else and very impressive it was. The stitches are so small that the shading on the face passes by imperceptible stages from light to dark. At a distance it could be mistaken for a painting. In my youth, I often day-dreamed that one day I would be sculpted by somebody famous and become monumental in bronze. I never imagined I might become immortal in silk.

My sessions with Miss Arcade at the ruined school on East Ninth Street continue. To my amazement, every week the audience is larger and Miss Arcade becomes angrier – not with me so much as with the world in general and the people of Oregon in particular.

In that state, she tells us, it is a punishable offence knowingly to employ a homosexual person. I had no idea the tide had turned so drastically.

As with Mr Noah and his dove, when I did not return to Britain any more it became known there that I had reached dry land and that therefore it was safe for all the other malcontents of the lost ark of London to fly westward. Among those who made the hazardous journey was a painter whom I had known for a long time in the days when I was only English. Over there, he had often resorted to giving his pictures away; once he alighted in Malibu, his work began to sell like hot cakes – almost like hot Hockneys.

Last week, on learning that a friend he had made on the West Coast was coming to New York, he asked him to telephone me when he arrived and this the young man did, calling himself Mr Stallone. He is really someone quite different but he has a Mexican name too difficult for ordinary mortals to pronounce. However, he is travelling with Mrs Stallone, who really is the mother of the movie star. She was here to rule a stall at the Whole Life Expo, which occupied two entire floors of the New York Hilton.

Mrs Stallone is an absolutely splendid being, festooned with ropes of pearls the size of chicken's eggs. She looks like a fortune-teller and, in a way, she is. She traffics in horoscopes. Within a few seconds of our meeting, she had asked me on what day I was born. When I told her my birthday was Christmas Day, she exclaimed, 'Ah, a Capricorn.' When I enquired if that was a good thing, she pointed out that it was the birthday of Jesus of Nazareth but did not say if that meant that I could save the world. I then went with the new Mr Stallone to another part of the hotel where he very kindly bought me a drink and gave me news of my friend in Malibu.

The Whole Life Exhibition was unbelievable, full of every brand of hazy philosophy, all manner of systems for prognosticating the future and any number of bogus diets and cures. I passed several people being massaged in all sorts of peculiar ways and in public. I even sat for a few minutes with a glorious black gentleman who passed his hands backwards and forwards within a few inches of my body and told me the story of my life. I loved every minute of it.

On Tuesday of last week, at the request of a Miss Metzler, I set out for Los Angeles. Never before have I travelled in such splendid style. A purring limousine arrived on East Third Street and took me to Kennedy Airport. There I took the MGM flight on which I found myself seated next to Mr Niederlander, who told me that he owned two theatres in Los Angeles and three in London, one of which was the Aldwych, where, in a time gone by, I saw Mr Shakespeare's *Antony and Cleopatra,* featuring Miss Suzman.

On arriving on the other side of the continent, I was met by an even grander limousine and whisked away to the Mondrian Hotel on Sunset Boulevard. There it transpired that I was to work for a German advertising agency, one of whose clients manufactures West cigarettes. I am happy to say that no attempt was made to turn me into a Marlboro Man. Next day I was taken in a trailer, together with some dressers and two real photographic models, to a side street off Wilshire Boulevard. There, as I have come to realize is customary in America, two policemen were waiting to supervise the parking of our fleet of vehicles and to sit around during the proceedings. One of these handsome gentlemen wore a black eye patch and, according to Mr Goldammer, who ruled this wild venture, asked him to make a movie in which he could appear as a pirate.

How different Hollywood is from New York! When we were making *Resident Alien* (which, to my amazement, was being screened in Los Angeles while I was there), bystanders on the Lower East Side of Manhattan took a keen interest and many of them tried to get into the act. When I sat on a canvas chair in the middle of the pavement on Wilshire Boulevard, strangers hurried by with averted gaze.

After a while, we all crossed the street and, on the other side, I was photographed refusing a cigarette from a typically good-looking young man. Apparently the utter improbability of such an overture being made to me was the whole point of it all. Later, though I was no longer involved, another similar young man was pictured offering a cigarette to a mermaid. For this escapade, the entire crew went to the beach but I was allowed to return to the Mondrian. The homeward journey to New York was just as splendid as the voyage out but, on it, I did not sit beside a potentate. In fact, the seat next to mine was empty. Does this mean something?

I have also been to Chicago, where I had a simply wonderful time. The weather was like summer: in the streets people strolled about, staring into the sky and smiling seraphically. Mr Guy Ruggeri, who had arranged the entire trip, met me at the airport and took me to the Belmont Hotel, where I had stayed the last time I was with him. There a friendly atmosphere prevails and the staff is willing to 'do' my room with me still in it. I merely lifted my feet in the air while the carpet was vacuum-cleaned.

I did not work (if you can call it work) on the day of my arrival but, instead, was given an evening meal at Mr Ruggeri's home and shown a videotape of *The Boy Friend*, the stage version of which I had seen many years ago in London. The movie is much better. It recreates to perfection the look of a 1920s glossy magazine illustration. In those days, it was not possible to manufacture 'fast' dyes of really bright colours. Therefore fashion houses told women that to wear a bright red dress or a screaming blue coat would be vulgar. All furnishing fabrics and dress materials were in 'art' shades – phlegm green, old rose, ice blue – and these are the colours used in this film.

I started to perform at the Halsted Theater Center on Wednesday, did two shows on Saturday and finished on Sunday evening. I was supposed to explain the royal family of England and the politics of America. I have no knowledge of either subject but fortunately a local journalist had prophesied, in a very witty article, that I would digress from my theme.

I did. I explained that the folly of all politicians in this country is that they want to rule the world and be loved, and this is not possible. The problem facing America at this time is purely financial and it is useless to offer voters more policemen, more teachers or a comprehensive health service, all of which will further deplete our already meagre resources. Japan, which was flattened at the end of the Second World War, has now become the most powerful country in the world because every Japanese man of employable age agreed to devote his entire life to his employer, and work for longer hours for smaller wages. I suggested that, if the United States is once again to become the great creditor nation, its politicians must offer their constituents starvation. Mercifully, nobody hissed. From this kind reception, I do not conclude that anyone agreed with me. I already know that American audiences are the most indulgent in the world.

In recent times I have made the slight acquaintance of a gentleman called Mr Regan. He is of Irish descent but, unlike the rest of his unruly race, he adores the English. He used to rule a bar called The North Star where from time to time he staged events recalling wartime Britain. At one of these he managed to secure the presence of Millicent Martin. He now reigns over the Spotty Dog Bar and Unisphere Cocktail Lounge on Eleventh Avenue at 43rd Street, to which he invited me for a Halloween party. I endeavoured to decline because I try never to become involved in occasions of public jollification. It is a long time since I tricked and I have never treated but I did not offer these facts as excuses. Instead I told him that I couldn't put on funny clothes, to which he replied, 'But you're always wearing funny clothes.' So I went.

As a special inducement, he sent one of his helpers to collect me from East Third Street. This young man explained to our taxi driver that we were in no especial hurry. He said that, though he did not expect to live for ever, he would like to survive the next two hours. His words went unheeded. We careered through the streets, stopping, starting, swerving with alarming violence. However, we arrived at our destination with only our nerves shattered.

The Spotty Dog, completely renewed, was opened three weeks ago. It is now a spacious, well-lit restaurant, serving large portions of pleasant food. What kind of clientèle will habituate an establishment so far from civilization, I have no idea. On the evening I was there, very few of the customers were recognizable because of their masks and strange costumes. Even the waiter had, perched on his shoulders, a toy rat which squeaked when pressed in the right places. (Who would not?) Mr Regan wore white painter's overalls and a bowler hat. How he will appear on subsequent occasions I cannot say but he is always a very agreeable host.

Today an unknown gentleman telephoned me to tell me that he 'works out' for two hours a day at his local gymnasium because, if he did not, fat would begin to surround his pectoral muscles until he would need a brassière. He seemed to be apologizing for his habit of taking regular exercise but I don't know why he thought it necessary to excuse himself to me. I think everyone should spend hours daily in a gymnasium and I have often explained that a man cannot be considered handsome unless his neck is thicker than his head (think of Mr Tyson). The only reason why I have remained such a feeble specimen is that, when I was young enough for my shape to be capable of augmentation, I lived in England where bodies are never mentioned.

Last week I received an invitation from an unknown gentleman living on the Upper East Side of Manhattan. I took the Third Avenue bus up into the rarefied seventies and with some trepidation walked westward. The nearer I got to the park, the more daunting my journey became. Houses gave way to mansions. When I finally arrived at my destination, I found the door open because a man in overalls was tampering with the lock. A doctor appeared as I entered the marble hall but he retreated almost immediately, probably realizing that he couldn't cure me. I proceeded to an upper floor where I found my host living in slightly constricted splendour with a young man who absented himself from our meeting to cook vegetables for a delicious meal to which I was later invited because I had talked so much that night had fallen while my lips were still moving.

The conversation was chiefly about a movie called *The Queen*. This is a documentary about a drag contest that my host had organized in a time gone by. From 1959 to 1968, he had traversed the length and breadth of the United States and (himself in drag) presented this show. Only Dallas had refused to condone the spectacle of 'deviants' having a jolly time. The word 'deviant', which I would have taken calmly, caused him to fly into an ungovernable rage.

Now many long, dark years later, he wishes to re-release this movie and his dearest wish is that I should become some kind of spokesperson for the film. I will, but I felt it was only fair to explain that when, for the *New York Times*, I reviewed *Paris is Burning*, I incurred the undying hatred of the entire homosexual community, though I genuinely thought I was repeating what Miss Livingston, who made that excellent picture, had told me. This information did not daunt my host. He feels that my equable nature in the face of what he considers the false naïveté of interviewers equips me for this touchy assignment.

Unfortunately, the demon machine which was to have shown me *The Queen* had broken down so I cannot, at this moment, say what the film is like, but my guess is that it will be different from modern drag shows in that it will be less bizarre. In olden days men donned female attire in the hope (not always fulfilled) of looking attractive. I myself only put on a dress once in my entire life because I soon realized that it accentuated my maleness – what there was of it. In a suit and wearing a collar and tie, I looked effeminate – appallingly so – but in silk stockings my ankles looked like chicken's legs. Also, in a dress my collarbones were shockingly visible. Many of my friends seemed unaware of this adverse effect or perhaps they didn't care. They may have worn women's clothes for the feel of them rather than their effect on others. They felt beautiful so to hell with public opinion.

Nowadays, beauty is no longer the point. This sad fact was brought home to me last Saturday when I went to Limelight where a party was being given for Screaming Rachel. There, amid deafening music, the lurid lighting and the decorations that prevented anyone from having a clear view of anybody else, was a motley assortment of guests, nice young men casually dressed as though for an evening at home, real women scantily clad and a throng of beings from outer space, glittering with sequins and fluffy with ostrich plumes. They wore shoes with heels so high that they could no longer brace their knees and fishnet stockings through which whole haddocks could have escaped. Their faces were clown-white and their lips were the colour of uncooked liver. The wish to allure had given way to the desire to appal. Drag artists no longer wish to make us sigh: they want us to gasp.

Towards the end of my lifetime in England, I was introduced by a mad child psychologist to a married couple who lived outside London. After a while the psychologist faded from the picture but I continued to know the two schoolteachers. They seemed a cosy couple, exceptional only in their willingness to know me. When I left England, our association came to a quite natural end.

Suddenly, about a month ago, the wife telephoned me in great distress to tell me that her husband had announced that he was homosexual. I do not imagine that she expected advice; I think she wanted comfort. As they have no children, I asked, in a cautious tone of voice, if their marriage had been 'satisfactory' until now and she replied that it had. Two Sundays ago, she called again. The situation had become worse. Among her husband's possessions, she had found a videotape which she had watched and found 'disgusting'. Whether she had challenged him with her discovery she did not say, but he is obviously now in agony – either of guilt or of frustration. (He recently thrust his arm through a glass door and is now minus half a thumb.) The wife says they will separate. I replied, 'The sooner, the better.'

When I asked how, in an English suburb, her husband had made any homosexual contacts, she replied, 'Through his computer.' I was both amazed and appalled by this. I was aware that the once-so-antiseptic telephone had recently become tainted but if computers have given way to sex, then all is lost.

On Sunday afternoon, a transvestite came to East Third Street to escort me to a dim cellar beneath a Unitarian church in midtown where, on every second Sunday in the month, a gathering takes place of all the people of ambiguous gender in New York. There were men disguised as women; men disguised as men; women disguised as almost everything. What to me was so remarkable about this meeting was the total absence of bitchiness, of wrangling and of showing off. We celebrated my forthcoming birthday with a delicious cake and I was presented with a tiny lamp which, when rubbed, emits a faint, tinkling melody. I was delighted and humbled by the hospitality lavished upon me.

The following day I went to that part of New York University that is on Broadway at Waverly Place to try to re-do the soundtrack of a film that I have never seen. It has been made by some young men who may once have been students at NYU or may merely be pirates who hire the recording equipment available in that extraordinary seat of learning. However, by this time my voice had sunk to an unsteady croak and the whole assignment had to be cancelled.

I went home, had a good cry and, towards nightfall, was collected by an unknown man who had been dragooned by an unknown woman into taking me to her home in Brooklyn. Apart from Mr Cherry-Garrard's voyage to the South Pole, this was the worst journey in the world. Though we implored about eight of them, no taxi driver would take us on such a desperate trek. I couldn't blame them. Brooklyn is a terrible place and all who live there know they have entered an enclosed order. In desperation, we walked to the subway station at the corner of Broadway and Houston Street where we waited for a train that did not come for a long and dangerous time. When it did appear, we forced our way on to it and stood swaying perilously but unable to reach any fixture on which to hold. I have to report that this motley throng of strangers, though pressed into disgusting proximity, remained surprisingly calm – even cheerful. Arriving at our station, we still had a long, dark way to walk over pavements that have not been repaired in a hundred years. By a miracle, when we reached the right house, our hostess was just that minute arriving. Had we not been delayed by so many difficulties on our journey, we would have been compelled to stand in the bitter desolation of a Brooklyn street for some time.

It transpired that our hostess did not really know the gentleman she had obliged to collect me. She had imagined that he owned a car – a notion which he dismissed with a self-deprecating laugh. When he had delivered me, he went away, presumably to recover. The unknown woman and I entered her apartment and I drank tea while she tidied up the place and herself. She was obviously expecting a great throng of guests. Only one arrived. To him and me, she read her poems while my escort, who had by then returned, played a trumpet. This situation, in a muted way, was as bizarre as a James Purdy story, the strangest element being my presence. Why had I been invited? Did my hostess imagine I was a poet, a musician, a critic? For me it was, though harrowing, an enlightening experience but I'm sure that, as a guest, I was a complete failure.

A gentleman who lives in this house, on the same floor as I, used to put dead mice under the door of my room. Then the young lady who lived on the floor below me acquired a cat with the result that my tormentor ran out of ammunition. Now the woman and her pet have moved and the rodents have returned. This may mean that my journal will become even emptier than it habitually is. I may find myself living under 'mouse arrest'.

Winter

*

For that one mad day, I lived a charmed life

Another Christmas. Even as a child, I did not believe in Mr Claus. I used to humour my parents in the preservation of this embarrassing myth. 'How long,' I asked myself, 'are we going to keep up this charade?' However, that cynical posture has never caused me to denigrate other people's participation in the season's festivities nor has it ever prevented me from partaking of their Yuletide hospitality. Nevertheless, it is a slight relief when Christmas is over. I now return to the serious business of re-acclimatizing my much-abused stomach to its customary bed-sitting-room diet of baked beans on toast. I also begin the lonely task of replying to at least some of the kind cards and letters that I have received from friends and strangers during the past month.

This takes longer than you might expect. If you purchase a large number of overseas stamps, the post office clerk hands you a block of strange yellow stickers on which are printed the words, 'PAR AVION AIR MAIL'. Since these are a gift, I do not feel that I have the right to refuse them and, if I accept them, I must use them. It isn't easy. To protect the gum, each of these small labels is backed by a piece of white paper exactly the same size as the piece in front. It takes about five minutes, inexhaustible patience and long thumbnails to separate the two so that the front half can be affixed to an envelope. So far I am managing to reply to four letters a day.

Communications have arrived from near and far. One has come from Auckland in New Zealand. It tells me that over there girls are sexually molested at a rate of one in four and that one boy in ten meets the same fate. Almost all the letters from Britain congratulate me on having escaped and say that England is deteriorating daily with more and more homeless people lying on the pavements of the West End of London. Compounding this generally gloomy view, a parcel was recently brought to me by hand. It contained gifts and a long letter purporting to prove that AIDS is a genocidal plot against minorities being hatched by the government. As I am neither a doctor nor a pharmacist and, as I do not consider sociology a legitimate science or think that politics make the slightest difference to the lives of real people, I was powerless to endorse or disprove this notion; but it worried me until, reading further, I found that the writer suspected her telephone of being tapped and herself of being 'tailed' as she walked about the Lower East Side of Manhattan. These suspicions relieved me of taking her medical theory seriously. I offered to return the gifts but was told to keep them.

Of the parties that I attended the most enjoyable was a birthday celebration for the long-time companion of a photographer who once made a videotape of a conversation between me and Lord Montagu. In a time outworn, his lordship was mixed up in one of those scandals that the English public likes best. It concerned a gentleman of high degree. Though the English have a fatuous reverence for their aristocracy, they also envy it and secretly wish to see it brought low. Furthermore, this case involved kinkiness. Lord Montagu had given a party at which some young airmen had danced with one another. Oh fie! (This event took place in an era when a man held his partner instead of merely twitching in front of her.) The newspapers nearly turned pink with shocked excitement. The photographer says that the videotape of my talk with his lordship can never be shown even to a limited public while either of us is still alive because it contains some 'heavy stuff'. I have no recollection of anything that we said but I accept my host's judgement.

More recently I have attended a party that lasted more or less all day. On this occasion my hosts were a gentleman who went to Kansas City to teach what used to be called elocution and his sister who works for a record company in Los Angeles where she deals with what her visiting card terms 'artist relations'.

They are both dauntless. They had hired a purring limousine – complete with cordless telephone – to transport them from Virginia to New York where they collected me from my humble abode and took me to lunch at the Jockey Club, though none of us has ever so much as seen a horse other than the poor old nags that stand in the rain on the south side of Central Park. There I expected to be asked to leave but, instead, we were given a delicious lunch over which my friend's sister and I tarried while he visited a publisher on whom he hoped to foist a book telling drama students how to make a loud noise for a long time without becoming vocally tired. Of this project I wholeheartedly approved. I have never believed that people can be taught to act, but they can be told how to declaim and, in happier times before anyone was ever 'wired for sound', that was what they had to do. Nowadays, when actresses do not wear hidden microphones, they tend to scream, which simply will not do.

When we did not dare to linger in the Jockey Club any longer, we walked to the Plaza, of which I was slightly less frightened because I had been there on two previous occasions without mishap. There we were not expected to queue with the ordinary mortals but instead were ushered to a special table where, though we had only just stopped eating lunch, we embarked upon a sumptuous tea. I have always thought that supplying background music in public eating places is the saddest job in the world so we loudly applauded the tea room's resident violinist. This he noticed and came to our table to ask what selection we would like to hear. We suggested the songs from *The King and I,* the words of which were known to the drama teacher, who went so far as to sing them. Even this did not cause us to be evicted. For that one mad day, I lived a charmed life.

A few days ago I received an invitation to go to an address at the bitter end of 23rd Street. On the very morning of the chosen day, another message came explaining that the original venue had been closed by angry creditors. I was asked instead to go to 45 West 21st Street. This turned out to be a sort of annexe to Tramps and is a grim building showing no sign whatsoever of festivity, but I bravely pushed open the big black door and found myself in a lobby lit only by the light from a box office window no bigger than that opening in the door of a speakeasy through which customers used to murmur, 'Al sent me.' To one side of the box office, a tinsel curtain thinly veiled a long room furnished with a bar and a lot of small tables. At the far end was a small stage on which, on this occasion, stood two more little tables. I was reminded of SNAFU, a dubious cabaret setting where I worked in a time gone by. The bar is situated so that only the person nearest to the stage can see anything; his fellow drinkers could only see him.

The event that I had been summoned to watch was a play being presented by The Two Per Cent Solution called *Jungle Winter*. There were no programmes, but a leaflet explained that this is a modern adaptation of *The Seagull* by Dr Chekhov. It is set in what might be East Hampton in the off-season but that is not the only surprise. Some of the characters are black and a woman who is hopelessly in love with the young playwright has turned into a man – an innovation that the rest of the cast and the audience seemed to accept with unusual calm.

I saw *The Seagull* in England so long ago that Miss Ashcroft, last seen as the elderly English lady in *A Passage to India*, played the ingénue, as aspiring actress seduced and abandoned by a successful writer much older than she. Dr Chekhov was a country physician whose view of his middle-class provincial clientèle was cynical to say the least. He thought that their idleness was what caused them to take their broken hearts so seriously. However, English audiences regard all his plays as tragedies. Even a woman justifying the perpetual wearing of black with the words 'I am in mourning for my life' does not raise a laugh.

* * *

On Friday morning at half past six, a total stranger telephoned me for a chat. On hearing my slightly drowsy response, he said that he had not looked at his watch and therefore did not realize it was so early. I would have thought the fact the world was still in utter darkness might have warned him. At half past seven someone telephoned me from England to ask me the difference between right and wrong (I am not making this up). I quoted the hero of one of Mr Munro's stories who admits that he has forgotten the difference between good and evil but excuses this lapse by adding that his mother also taught him three ways of cooking lobster and that 'you can't remember everything'. My friend seemed content with this anecdote and rang off. At half past eight someone called me from Australia. Realizing that it would be foolish to hope for any more sleep, I got up – which was sad because my only appointment was not until nightfall.

Many weeks ago I went to a recording studio to speak some lines from *Romeo and Juliet* for a movie of that name. Now the hour has arrived when this film, which is acted entirely by Mr John Hurt and a bunch of cats, has been shown at the New School on Twelfth Street to the students of Professor Brown. Whether this picture will ever be shown to real people in a real cinema I have no idea, but a lot of publicity is being accumulated, presumably in the hope that it will. I have become involved in all this activity to a surprising extent in view of the fact that my voice is used for the smallest number of lines. I assume that this is because I conveniently live in Manhattan and adore publicity – even other people's.

The furore began last Tuesday when I was taken to a television station on Eighth Avenue at 34th Street. I have only seen a fragment of *Romeo and Juliet* on somebody else's television set and had to confess that I didn't understand it in the sense that I could not imagine for whom it was made. The young lady who was interviewing me smiled uneasily because I was not trying to 'sell' her the movie. I too was slightly embarrassed.

Last Tuesday I went to the New School to be interrogated by Professor Brown. The evening, which was almost like a vaudeville show but which I suppose should be called a class, began with the professor asking the students what they had thought of *Romeo and Juliet*. One girl was even allowed to read a short poem which ended with the words, 'I go to the movies to escape my pets.' Another student scored a big laugh by saying that the film was miscast. In general it seemed that the picture had not been well received. The professor did not chide the class for its negative reaction. In fact, he explained that the purpose of his tuition was by no means to force the students to like whatever they were shown. I have never dared to ask what it is he is actually teaching.

Yesterday, in one last effort to promote *Romeo and Juliet,* I was taken to the Whitney Museum. I had been there once before to attend the Absolut Vodka party given for Keith Haring by Mr Warhol. On this more recent occasion, the long trestle tables had been replaced by small round ones among which what I should now call a guest wrangler walked with me until we found someone who knew me and with whom I could sit and drink champagne. Later, we were shown about half an hour of the movie whose total running time is more than two hours. I am happy to report that the interest of the audience was aroused. A moment comes in the film when a cat, which has forced its way into a cage and snatched up a bird in its mouth, is compelled to release its victim on being hit by a car. On seeing the bird fly away, everyone cheered. On realizing the cat was dead, everyone groaned.

This week my agent said I must go to Philadelphia in spite of all the terrible things W.C. Fields said about that entirely inoffensive city. She explained that I was to receive more than is usually paid to extras in movies, so I went. I believe that it was Miss Cher who said that being in a film was like being asked to swallow broken glass and I endorse that impression. Everybody was extremely kind to me, finding a chair for me to sit on during breaks, but the experience was absolute hell.

I was made to do the 'Madison', of which I had never even heard. It turned out to be one of those old-fashioned dances involving an *enchaînement* of complicated steps which have to be learned. Actually, I stood in the background and moved minimally to and fro because I am now too old to learn anything. Mr Drake, who was once kissed by Larry Kramer and who wore solid gold boots and a false moustache but very little else, managed to learn the steps with astonishing ease: he even executed them as though he were enjoying the exercise, but then, as we all already know, he is an accomplished actor.

All the extras were appearing as guests at a conspicuously sinful fancy dress party. A member of the crew asked a woman disguised as a cowgirl if she was looking to lasso a cowboy, to which she replied, 'Not at *this* party.' Among those present were a bishop, a Monsignor, the Mona Lisa, a circus ringmaster and sundry other ingenious masqueraders. This scene was photographed at night in the apartment of two of the guests who surveyed the situation benignly, though it is certain the place will never be the same again when the movie colony has departed. To this vortex of kinkiness Mr Tom Hanks, dressed as a naval officer, invited Mr Denzil Washington, who will spend most of the film defending Mr Hanks in a discrimination suit against a firm that has terminated his employment because he has AIDS. The picture will be called *Philadelphia* and is being directed by Mr Jonathan Demme, a charming man who visited all his cast in their trailers to thank them for appearing in his movie.

I think we began work at about seven in the evening, though it is hard to guess the time because there is so much waiting to be done. We were allowed an hour for 'lunch' at midnight and crept home at four in the morning. Strange to relate, it is not really cold in the middle of the night in the middle of January in Philadelphia, though there are other hazards. One young man was mugged on his way to the set.

A large room had been booked for me at the Omni Hotel, which is not quite so vast as the Omni in Atlanta but is very grand. I tried not to show that I felt out of place. When we all foregathered in the lobby, it transpired that a Mr Nyswaner, who wrote the script for *Philadelphia,* and a Mr Stoddard were also guests of the hotel. The latter gentleman was on his way to North Carolina to explain to the inhabitants of that state the new laws acknowledging the rights of gay couples. I forbore to explain to him that *The Last of the Mohicans* was made there and that he might be attacked by savages wielding hatchets.

On Saturday morning I returned to New York in a train crammed with passengers: evidently people leave Philadelphia more often than they visit it. In the evening of that day, I attended a party celebrating the thirtieth year of a partnership between two of my acquaintances. I was not alone with them for long enough to ask them how they felt about the new laws relating to 'significant others'. I sat next to a handsome escaped policeman who believes in acupuncture but, even so, this party seemed normal compared with the one in the film.

On Monday I returned to Philadelphia and reached the Omni Hotel just in time to fling my luggage into my room before being whisked away to the film set. This session proved to be less exacting than the previous one. I was allowed to sit down almost all the time – as a wallflower while others 'did the Madison' or as an amused spectator while entertainers performed. These were The Flirtations, a quintet of gentlemen who sang, 'Please, Mr Sandperson, bring me a dream' (decorum prevents me from describing what dream they had in mind) and Lipsynka, who was required to do her act four times. It never varied by so much as the twitch of a feather boa, which shows how highly professional she is.

I was released in time to snatch seven hours' sleep before returning to New York a second time. I now have a cold and am a nervous wreck but no one can accuse me of failing in my duties as a butterfly on the wheel. Despite my cold, I pulled myself together sufficiently to keep an appointment at my very own local diner with a Miss Goodkin, who works for *The Times* of London. She wanted chiefly to know about my childhood, a time now so distant that my memories of it may be only partly true, but I did my best. It is difficult to imagine readers of *The Times* being interested in me. That august paper has never enjoyed a reputation for sprightliness. One of Mr Coward's plays begins with a wife arriving at the breakfast table where her husband is engrossed in a morning paper. 'Anything exciting in the paper?' she asks brightly, to which he replies, 'Don't be silly. I'm reading *The Times*.'

On the evening of that day, I went to Mr Musto's birthday party, held this year at USA, a relatively new twitching area, situated on West 47th Street. Appropriately, the first person that I met when I arrived was the unquenchable Miss Miles. We proceeded to the bar where our host greeted us. His birthdays have become an annual excuse for a gathering of people in the 'fame game', at which he is an expert. He was wearing platform shoes, a suit made from some metallic fabric and a wild Afro hairdo. He seemed as tall as a tree – the one God did not make. Every time another guest arrived, more lights flashed. As someone remarked, there were more photographers present than victims.

After a while, we all proceeded upstairs to an eating area where Randy Allen appeared as Bette Davis. I did not think the performer was very well treated. For one thing, half her audience was behind her and, for another, the hideous music never ceased. But perhaps this jaundiced opinion was due to the fact that, by this time, I had begun to feel really ill. I'm ashamed to say that I left without saying goodbye to Mr Musto.

On Saturday morning I was interviewed by the BBC. If the interest in my childhood taken by *The Times* was not enough proof that the walls of British respectability have been breached, let this incident be added. The BBC used to be called 'Auntie' by those who worked there – a snide reference to its posture of perpetual avoidance of anything shocking. Moreover, it cannot be claimed that pressure is being brought to bear on it by the public. When a young friend was last in London, he was asked by a stranger if he had been in *Resident Alien*. He admitted that he had been, which evoked the comment, 'We're a bit tired of him over here but in America . . .' In spite of all this, I was summoned to 103 Second Avenue at eleven in the morning where a handsome Welshman questioned me about glamour. Why me? I said that glamour exists where all is present but not all is given. This seemed to please the organizer of the programme, so I repeated it several times and the interview passed pleasantly – especially since, at the end of it, I was paid in cash.

One morning at the beginning of last month, I stood for a moment at the open window of my room and, except for the very faint wail of a distant police car siren, there was no sound to be heard. I thought it was the snow that had hushed the usually strident city. Then I sat down and began to turn the pages of a newspaper in search of its crossword puzzle and it was as though I was handling some kind of flannelette. At last it dawned on me that I had become almost totally deaf. My agent, who also has hearing difficulties, says that I'm not missing much but I think she might be considered cynical. I liked the noise of Manhattan. It is said that we should beware of the ambitions of our youth because, in old age, we may achieve them. When I was young, at a time when my brothers wanted to be ships' captains or steam engine drivers, I only wished to be a chronic invalid. Now I am, but in a way that deprives me of the pleasure of long telephone conversations – especially with strangers.

In spite of this and other serious handicaps to communication, I went, at the invitation of a Miss Sherrer, to a branch of the School of Visual Arts on West 21st Street to speak to some students. They were gathered on the second floor, which has been partitioned into a honeycomb of small cells. Presiding over one of the slightly larger areas was a cosy professor who, to my amazement, had heard me when I spoke at the Players Theater on MacDougal Street some fourteen long years ago.

I tried to explain to the audience what an art school is like from a model's point of view – that the students have entered the college, not running eagerly towards art but creeping backwards, trying to avoid real life, and that they hate the model. When father asks his daughter what she intends to do when she leaves school, she thinks, 'Oh my God, it's a reasonable question,' and then, after a moment's panic, 'I know: I'll do art.' She then sits in the college canteen, necking, playing a guitar and smoking pot for four years, after which she becomes a typist. Though I detected no sign of consternation on the faces of my audience, fearing that this picture might seem unduly gloomy, I explained that these years need not be wasted, that they can become a time during which a young person decides who he or she is and how to process, package and market an image. It was hard to tell whether this message was understood, believed or even heard. There was certainly no outcry.

My contact with current events now comes less from actual experience than from reading letters and newspaper clippings sent to me by kind friends. Of these the most elating took the form of a letter from my spy for Key West. He tells me that many long dark years ago the Royal Academy of Dramatic Art staged a version of *Orlando*. At a small cocktail party after the show, the young Australian student who had played the lead said to Lord Kinross, one of those queer peers who gave the British aristocracy such a bad name, that she had acted 'a peculiar role in which she kept changing her sex.' To this his lordship replied, 'Not peculiar at all. People like that are all over London.'

The most distressing news refers to Mrs Riva's biography of her mother, Marlene Dietrich. We all know that, while a child's parents are alive – especially if the son or daughter still lives at home – never a day passes without renewed vows of vengeance upon either the father, the mother or both, but when the offending parent is dead – when the worst is over – cannot calm be restored? Cannot the past be forgiven and public memories, though largely untrue, be allowed to linger on the air like a fading perfume?

Miss Dietrich was not really such an indestructible beauty as, say, Miss Del Rio, but she was presented to us by Mr Sternberg and by herself with such hushed reverence that we believed in her beauty absolutely. As Mr Beaton said, 'What does it matter if she is really beautiful? She *feels* beautiful enough to convince anybody.' Even Mr Hitchcock, who never forgave any woman for not being Grace Kelly, called Miss Dietrich 'the supreme screen being'.

I have now seen *Orlando*. It is, as I guessed, unabashed festival material and can never be shown to real people. It is a slow but very beautiful pageant with long, sustained close-ups of the exquisite Miss Swinton in costumes ranging from Elizabethan through Queen Anne and Victorian to the present day. For me the most exciting moment at the screening came at the end when the new Mrs Sting, who was in the audience, introduced herself to me.

1993

Spring

*

In the rest of the world, fame is something that happens to you but in the United States it is something you do

I have been trying to understand how Miss MacLaine manages to suppress all feelings of weariness when she so enthusiastically embraces the idea of reincarnation. Imagine falling out of your mother's womb with the words, 'Here again.'

On the first Sunday that the weather was like spring, I was taken to Chinatown to be interviewed by an English television company. When I arrived, they were on Elizabeth Street in a vast, extremely busy restaurant owned by a Mr Fong. They explained that they had chosen this noisy, difficult venue because of the décor which, as in all Oriental eating houses, is in bright red and yellow. I was not interviewed there but, after the customary interval spent drinking coffee in a van, I was transported to another street and questioned standing on a sidewalk thronged with Chinese shoppers. I have no idea whether the streets were so crowded because this was a special day in the Chinese calendar or because it was the first day in a long while that it had been pleasant to be out of doors or because this district is always so populous. It was hell. I was asked what was wrong with the world. I managed to refrain from saying 'the people' and said 'the music'. I have no idea if I said the words the interviewer wished to hear.

I am not a dedicated theatre-goer but, in my late teens, I thought I was and went to see a lot of highbrow shows. That was nearly seventy years ago. Since then I have noticed a lot of changes in show business – not all of them for the better. In recent years there has been no play as great as Mr Shaw's *Saint Joan* or Mr O'Casey's *The Plough and the Stars.* There has been no actress with the panache of Edith Evans and no singer as good as Gracie Fields, though this has not mattered because all performers are now wired for sound.

However, two components of theatre are better. One of these is the dancing. When I was young, a chorus boy (almost a term of abuse in England) was only required to put his arm round a girl, which he did with little conviction, and to kick his height, with which demand he had no trouble at all. Now young men are turning unsupported somersaults in the background while the leading lady is singing centre-stage. The second aspect of modern theatre which has improved is the staging. In the Twenties, it was as well for a dramatist to arrange his plays to require only one set because it took so long to change the scenery. Now, in no time at all and without even lowering a curtain, miracles are wrought: back-projections glow and fade, lighting re-focuses on different areas of the stage, props slide effortlessly back and forth.

The *Washington Post* has sent me a copy of Mr Shipman's biography of Miss Garland. The subtitle of this work is 'The Secret Life of an American Legend'. I would not have thought she had a secret life. Her behaviour was so outlandish that almost everything she did became instant public knowledge, but in these pages a few strange facts are revealed. Her father, though he married and sired three children, was homosexual and so outrageous with it that schoolboys in Grand Rapids made jokes to his daughters about how to obtain a pass into his cinema.

Unlike so many show business biographies, this is not a work of deconstruction; praise and blame are handed out with an even hand. All the same, it becomes impossible to like Miss Garland. She seems to have possessed no humility. She was placed under contract to Metro-Goldwyn-Mayer by the time she was thirteen years old and was a movie star at sixteen but she never seems to have been grateful. She wanted not the wages that would meet her needs, but a salary which would prove that Mr Mayer valued her as highly as Miss Durbin was thought to be worth to her studio.

After reading the book it becomes clear that Miss Garland was not naturally suited to being in the movie industry. She could not cope with the long hours and was for ever affronted by the peremptory commands of her directors. She needed a live audience whom she could bamboozle into thinking of her as a helpless waif who must be given all the applause in the world to get her through a single number, when in fact she was as tough as old boots but not as comfortable. I once saw her at an extinct cinema in London. She was a dumpy little thing wearing a suburban party dress and singing in a rangy, brassy voice in constant danger of cracking, but the audience went wild. When the orchestra had played the first few introductory phrases of a song that begins, 'I'm gonna love you like nobody's loved you . . .' people sitting near me were already sobbing audibly.

On Tuesday evening I went to Mr Papp's theatre on Lafayette Street for a symposium on fame, moderated by Mr Clive James, an Australian masquerading as an English televisionary, who has written a book on the subject. His guests were Mrs Ivana Trump, who, as someone remarked, has proved that there is life after Donald; Miss Liz Smith, who made the distinction, not usually appreciated in America, between fame and notoriety; Mr Harold Evans, who rules Random House, which will publish Mr James' book; Miss Anna Wintour, who described the spread of fame from fashion models to their photographers and even to their hairdressers; Mr Norman Mailer, who told various stories against himself and finally Miss Fran Lebowitz. Naturally she was the most interesting speaker. She said the best kind of fame was a writer's: it secured its possessor a good table in a restaurant but didn't provoke anyone to interrupt him while he was eating.

Sitting in the audience, I whispered to the young lady next to me that no one had pointed out that, in the rest of the world, fame is something that happens to you whereas in the United States it is something to do – a career in itself. The next day, this remark was quoted in Miss Smith's column. Her spies are everywhere!

I've been to Los Angeles.

I was frightened because, the day before I was to embark upon my journey, no airline ticket had arrived. When I told my agent that it seemed unlikely that I would go, she flew into a panic so great that she uttered the words, 'Buy a ticket.' This I thought would be going too far. Money is for saving, not for spending. However, our difference of opinion never degenerated into an unbridgeable rift because, on the very morning when I was due to depart, a kind lady arrived in a purring limousine and escorted me to Mr Kennedy's airport. On the other side of the world, I stayed this time at the Bel Air Hotel, and the high spot of my visit came when in the lobby I met Miss DeMornay, who was the star of one of my favourite movies, *The Hand that Rocks the Cradle*.

While I was in Los Angeles, my trembling steps were guided by a Miss Korenbrot (whom members of the hotel staff, apparently unaware that publicists are with you always, sometimes called Mrs Crisp). With her help, I was interviewed by the *Los Angeles Times* and many more papers and radio shows. At the final party to which I was invited while there I realized that almost all the men in Hollywood are lawyers and to be with them is like visiting a zoo just before feeding time. There are few exchanges of ideas; almost all conversations are deals.

I was worn out, but it was fun. Los Angeles is New York lying down.

The actual purpose of my visit to California was to meet Mr Jay Leno and to be on his television programme. He was charming and, on being told that if you can live on peanuts and champagne you need never buy food again, he handed me a bowl of nuts and opened a bottle of champagne. My spies tell me that he seemed nervous, but I did not notice this. I had a wonderful time.

I have now seen *Jurassic Park*. I enjoyed this film. The special effects, which are now the main attraction in all modern films, were spectacular. At one moment, a prehistoric flightless bird is seen to jump from ground level onto a counter. But it all remains 'kid's stuff'. It typifies a disturbing trend. Within living memory, I have seen a musical about broken hearts of railway coaches, managed to avoid another musical in which the entire cast wears cat-suits, and lived through a play, regarded as serious, at the end of which two grown men play with a balloon. It is no good claiming that this descent into puerility is a pandering to American tastes, because many of these shows originated in England – once the home of jaded sophistication. Nursery entertainment is now a universal vogue.

Now that I am a blasé veteran of two first features, I watched all these epics to see how much the actors have suffered. In *Jurassic Park,* two children and one adult spend about a quarter of the film covered with mud and drenched with rain. I could imagine them enduring this state of humiliation for at least two weeks – in which, every morning, a make-up artist, holding in one hand a Polaroid photograph of yesterday's final take and with the other smearing their cringing faces with some kind of brown paste and squeezing a wet sponge over their heads before pointing them toward the set. However, you can dry your tears: they were thinking of the money, the beautiful money.

Summer

*

The only way to avoid being photographed in Manhattan is to keep moving

I have been to Cleveland – again. The last time I was there, it snowed. On this occasion, the weather was sunny and pleasantly warm. I was met by a charming young woman who works for Landmark Theaters and who took me to a hotel where the woodwork is always wet because it is owned by a Mr Glidden, who invented house paint. I was interviewed by a Mr Dooley and, later, by a Ms Connors. It seems that all journalists in Cleveland are Irish.

In the evening *Orlando* was paraded before the amazed eyes of the local inhabitants while I was given a pleasant outdoor meal, after which I faced the audience and tried to justify my appearance in the film.

At dawn the following day, I went to a television station, where I said the usual things in the usual way. Then a handsome gentleman called Mr Harris took me to his office, which is situated in a strange building that I dimly remember from my previous visit to Cleveland; it is a huge arcade covered by a glass roof and lined with chic shops on two levels. I was deeply impressed.

I have also been to Toronto – again and again. My original invitation to that fair city was my first intimation that the world had gone mad. In those days, I was only English and was asked to go to Canada at once just for the day. The second visit lasted two or three weeks, during which I worked (if you can call it work) in the Toronto Workshop Theatre. On my third sojourn, I was accompanied by Mr Nossiter, who had directed *Resident Alien*, which was being shown to the crowned heads of the festival circuit (including Mr Jaglom wearing his funny hat). This time I was there at the invitation of Reliance Releasing, personified by two delightful young women who housed me in the Four Seasons Hotel in great luxury. There I was interviewed from ten in the morning until five in the afternoon. I know I have a bad reputation for saying the same things over and over again, but what else could I do? I had a wonderful time but, as always, the greatest pleasure of travel is that it makes you so glad to be home – however dreary that might be.

My slavery to Mr Sony continues. I have now been sent to Miami. Before I set out, I was in some bewilderment as to what I would find at the end of my journey. Recent television pictures of the enduring damage from last year's hurricane had shown me Florida as a few water-logged planks lying beside a deserted road. When I mentioned my apprehension to my agent, she said, 'Those were the remains of the homes of the poor. The rich *never* get blown away.' I thought this remark unduly cynical, but she was right. The rich live on an island clearly visible from the mainland and there not a leaf has fallen, not a tile is cracked, not a brick has been dislodged.

I stayed at the Century Hotel on Ocean Drive, which also had remained unharmed. The proprietor told me that, until recently, the entire district had been a den of thieves and murderers; now it is a line of Art Deco hotels. The weather was burning hot, but the room in which I slept was cool. I remained comfortable until I was dragged on to the beach where, amid wind and sand, though fully clothed, I was photographed holding a surfboard. Where such a picture could be used I cannot imagine. *Orlando* was not yet showing in any of the local cinemas, so I was not expected to address an audience. Instead, I merely answered questions put to me by a local journalist and returned to New York.

* * *

Since then, I have been to Dayton in Ohio. There, once again, I found that the weather had been restrained for my sake. The river was not in flood. This engagement was not engineered by Mr Sony. It was a private event set in motion by the kind friend who, some time ago, took me to see *I Hate Hamlet*. In Dayton, *Orlando* was being shown at an art house called the Neon Cinema, to whose denizens I tried to justify the film. I really like Dayton: its inhabitants are inexhaustibly friendly. If I were not still waiting for the opportunity to rule the world, I could live there. During my stay, I was taken by my hosts to see *The Fugitive*. It is an excellent film: the excitement never flags, but its plot is so complicated that none of us could decide why Mr Ford's wife had been murdered. Mr Ford starts out with a beard, but soon shaves it off in an effort to avoid being recognized by his pursuers. This is a pity, because he looked very attractive when he was fully woolly.

Finally, I have been to Staten Island. It is riddled with culture and with history, of which the Islanders are justly proud. The occasion of my visit was a picnic organized by a politically active lesbian group called Lambda, in front of whose banner I was photographed. This event was sufficiently civilized for me to be able to avoid sitting on the ground, but the music was as loud as if everyone had been heterosexual. The members of Lambda are pinning their expectations of a happy future on the re-election of Mr Dinkins. I regard this as a forlorn hope, but did not say so – at least, not loudly.

On home ground, I was taken some time ago to the Helen Hayes Theater to see *Shakespeare For My Father*. This is a one-woman show performed by Sir Michael Redgrave's younger daughter. It does not hint at any of the gossip about him that so intrigued the English – his illicit liaison with Dame Edith Evans, for instance. Instead, it concentrates on the relationship between Miss Lynn Redgrave and her father, which greatly resembles the relationship between Mr Lear and Miss Cordelia. It took her most of her life to gain his attention, to say nothing of his affection. This fact helps the show, because it allows her appropriately to quote *King Lear*.

The evening is fully cultural, but never boring. On the contrary, it is both touching and funny. Miss Redgrave offers hilarious impersonations of Maggie Smith and Sir Noel Coward. She couldn't quite manage the prolonged wail, like the whistle of a distant train, for which Miss Evans was so famous, but perhaps it is a little unchivalrous to mention that, as she had already spent two hours reciting fragments from a number of Mr Shakespeare's plays.

The only way to avoid being photographed in Manhattan is to keep moving. The fact that I've been photographed between each of the above-mentioned events would not be worth recording if it were not for the fact that one session was so extraordinary. A young man came to my home to conduct me to an upper room on East Seventh Street where he placed thin strips of sticky tape across my face (as though he were preparing to execute a hard-edge abstract). Then he painted almost my entire face black. When this coating was dry, he added a few dabs of white and the result was photographed by his friend.

That was the easy part. The difficult stage of the proceedings was trying to remove the paint. Though it was watercolour, it could only be removed with soap. I tried not to complain, though, obeying laws set down by Helena Rubinstein, I have not washed my face with soap in the past sixty years. To my surprise I do not seem subsequently to look any worse than usual.

Of course, I consider that beauty is a complete waste of time – principally because, without even knowing it, we still cringe in the shadow of classical ideals of beauty. The Greeks were mad about the human body – so much so that during its heyday Athens must have looked like an outfitter's window during a weavers' strike. But it was no help: not one of the great classical statues has the least physical individuality which would make it desirable or even interesting. I regard the human body neither as the image of You-Know-Who nor as the temple of Miss Aphrodite. I would describe it as a gravity-resisting mechanism of extreme vulnerability in constant danger of going wrong.

Autumn

*

I thought I was in a jolly film. I was wrong

I have received a book of drawings by Mr Cocteau called *The Passionate Penis.* I cannot refrain from expressing a faint regret at finding that this man, whose movies I loved for their all-pervading but delicate poetry, was just as obsessed with the idea of the economy-size you-know-what as all those tiresome homosexual men I met when I was young and only English.

My term of slavery is drawing peacefully to its close. I have been sent to Austin and Tampa, on each occasion to try to justify the movie *Resident Alien.* Both these fair cities I have visited before. The last time I was in Austin I stayed in the home of a gentleman whose name I have sadly now forgotten, but whose garden I remember well because it was mostly vertical, descending by steps cut in the cliff face to a landing stage at the edge of the Colorado River. Apparently, this river was once a trickling stream, but has now been broadened by a dam into an impressive waterway on which, from my hotel window, I could see oarsmen sculling to and fro, whether singly or in crews of four, and at dusk could watch swans gliding by. The hotel was a very grand establishment called The Four Seasons, and was where the Queen of England (the other one) stayed when she graced Texas with her presence. I spent most of my three days there sleeping or eating – including an open-air breakfast. Between meals, I was taken by car to survey the surrounding landscape: mostly parched grass and crumbling rock.

The last time I was in Tampa it was to address all the gay businessmen in Florida – as someone recently remarked, a room full of sodomites in suits. This time it was to introduce *Resident Alien*, which was part of Tampa's Gay and Lesbian Film Festival. The cinema manager hit on the hilarious idea of my coming into view of the audience by sitting beside the organist who arose through the floor playing a shaky version of 'Rule, Britannia,' on the huge cinema organ. It must be one of the last of those Jurassic instruments still in existence.

Tampa is a strange city, almost devoid of inhabitants. When my escort kindly drove me to a broadcasting station at the very edge of town, we overtook a bus on which there was only one passenger, and, apart from her, we saw no one. The radio station was a small shack in a jungle and was manned by a staff of beachcombers. They were very kind to me, but it was a slightly eerie experience. Needless to say, I now have a cold caused by travelling from chilly Manhattan to warm Texas back to New York, then almost at once to steamy Tampa and home again. It will pass.

My hosts from Dayton have invaded New York and taken me to Radio City to see Miss Midler. Her show is long, lavish and lewd. It was exactly what the audience should have expected, but apparently some people left in a marked manner because of the raunchiness of her jokes. Every possible bodily function was mentioned.

We sat in what in happier times would have been called the 'upper circle' and saw Miss M, as she would say, 'from a distance'. Naturally, she looked tiny, but the surprise was that she is now so thin – a fact on which she commented with pride. We attended this performance towards the end of its run, and inevitably Miss M's voice was a little tired, but her spirit – a kind of bawdy valiance – remained undiminished. I think it was this quality that so obviously appealed to the audience: they applauded every song as soon as they recognized the first few bars. Miss Midler is the archetypal music-hall artist.

I have been back to Montclair in the middle of New Jersey to attend a screening of *The Naked Civil Servant*, which was being shown to a heap of lesbians and gay men in a building attached to a Unitarian Church. By now I am accustomed to this incongruity. A transvestite once told me that if ever I found myself unaccompanied in a strange town (which heaven forfend) and wished to meet a bunch of homosexual people, I should make for the Unitarian church. The screening in Montclair was very pleasant and I sat through the movie without becoming restless.

I have also seen a secret screening of *Zelda*. This is a picture about Mr and Mrs Fitzgerald, a subject in which I am deeply interested and which, as far as I know, has never before been treated in a movie. Someone once said of this famous couple, 'They didn't want elegant surroundings; they didn't want witty companions; they just wanted something to *happen*.' This film accurately depicts their lust for excitement. For instance both Scott and Zelda jump off the roof of their house into their swimming pool while all their guests scream at them that it is too dangerous. He survived his lifelong sensation safari by taking to drink; she succumbed and went mad. The film, directed by a Mr O'Connor, makes it clear that if Fitzgerald didn't actively drive his wife insane, he certainly made no effort to save her. He is played by Mr Hutton, who looks just right and acts well, but has no natural charm and therefore cannot be seen gradually losing it. She is portrayed by Miss Richardson, who is too large for the part. In movies, if you are a victim, you have to be small. Nevertheless she is fascinating to watch. It is her film, and she never lets the audience off the hook. The weakness of this picture lies in the direction or possibly in the script. The camera does not go inside Mrs Fitzgerald's skull: we do not see her hold on reality gradually weakening. When finally she thinks she sees a huge spider walking across the piano, the hallucination seems too sudden.

After the screening, to which I went alone but at which I met a young woman who seemed to know me, the two of us, with some trepidation, attended a party at the Algonquin Hotel. There we were asked if we would like to sit among the VIPs. Never having been a VIP, I was eager to bask for a moment in their rarefied atmosphere. First I was photographed with a gentleman about my own age who turned out to be Douglas Fairbanks; then I sat beside a lady who proved to be Miss Warrick – Citizen Kane's first wife. When we were asked to be photographed together, to my delight she sent up the whole absurd situation by holding between us a few lilies from a vase on her table. I tried to look virginal.

Since then, growing ever more brazen, I have attended two fashion shows. At the first of chese, I had the audacity to totter along the runway among a regiment of women wearing see-through shifts and silver boots. At the second show, I behaved a little better and remained a spectator. The models were glorious creatures, who paced to and fro in dresses no one would ever wear and kinky shoes. They moved at a brisk pace, always keeping at least two girls in view at any one time. At the end of this event, the designer, a Mr Oldham, appeared looking like a schoolboy, shorter and a little wider than any of his victims.

In the same week, never letting go of my shaky hold on the high life, I went to the Ambassador Gallery on Spring Street to the opening of an exhibition of the art work of Mr Tony Curtis. He is America's answer to Mr Matisse. When I told him this, he admitted that there is in his work a little Matisse and added, 'A little Matisse goes a long way.' He is a really nice guy. When Miss Miles (who, of course, was at both *Zelda* and the Ambassador Gallery) introduced me to him with the words, 'Do you know Quentin?' Mr Curtis replied, 'Yes. We were in a movie together.' There was no hint that he was one of the stars and I was an extra. This is American democracy at its best.

I nearly strayed beyond the limits of my newfound VIP-hood when I was invited to the first night of a play entitled *Any Given Day*. It is by Mr Gilroy, advertised on the invitation as a Pulitzer Prize winner. I was frightened, but I went. The play is truly Pulitzer material; that is to say it is grim. By this I do not mean that *Any Given Day* is bad. I mean that things do not turn out well for anyone on the stage. For instance, a bride and groom part on their wedding day. (Mr Pulitzer does not like happiness.) The audience was also Pulitzer material. It contained a lot of bespectacled men with thinning hair waving to other bespectacled men with thinning hair. I took them to be critics employed by conservative newspapers.

The invitation to this impressive event included supper at Sardi's restaurant. I realized that I was insufficiently Pulitzer to attend, so, when I left the theatre, I walked determinedly in the opposite direction from Sardi's but, almost immediately, I came face to face with the young woman with whom I had gone to the Algonquin only a few days previously. 'Come with us,' she cried. 'Free food.' And she led me to a huge place on Broadway. We managed to slink past a few members of staff and were given plates of food. When I had eaten everything in sight, I crept out into the gaudy night of Broadway. Fortunately, no one asked my opinion of the movie that my companion had just seen.

Finally, I have seen *Philadelphia* at a screening for the cast and crew of the film. Before it began, Mr Demme arrived, greeted his mother, and apologized for some fault that no one noticed in the print we were about to watch. When I was an extra in the party scene of this picture, I thought I was in a jolly film. I was wrong.

Philadelphia is one of the most tragic pictures I have ever seen. It concerns a court case brought by Mr Hanks against his employers because they have dismissed him, pretending he is incompetent but really because he has AIDS. He wins his case but loses his life. The lawyer defending him is Mr Washington, who, to the naked eye, seems slight but, to the camera, is monumental. He is a truly great actor. As with Miss Garbo, filming him is like photographing thought. With the use of a few words, we see him start out hating homosexuality and end up at least sorry for Mr Hanks.

Winter

*

My body was handled as though I were already dead

Mr Claus and I have never been on the best of terms. At this time of year, I tend to hide from the public scrutiny that on other occasions I cultivate. Even so, I enjoy receiving Christmas cards. A newspaper, the name of which I forget, has telephoned to ask me what was the best and what was the worst Christmas present I had ever received. There are, of course, no worst presents because no generosity must ever be disparaged. However, I do remember imploring an unknown woman, who used to telephone me in the middle of the night, *not* to send me any useless emblem of Yule-tide. In spite of this prohibition, she caused me to trudge through the snow all the way to the post office to collect an evergreen wreath which weighed a ton and which I had no means and no intention of hanging in my very small room.

The most unexpected gift of this year was twelve bottles of champagne sent to me by Mr Naim Attallah, who recently interviewed me for a magazine called *The Oldie*. I had never heard of Mr Attallah, but when I mentioned his name to some friends who had just arrived from Britain for a glimpse of happiness in New York, it transpired that, over there, he is well known.

Occasionally, the pseudo-contemplative life into which I retreat at this time of year has been punctuated by telephone calls from various English newspapers expressing indignation that I have presumed to record an address to the nation to be broadcast on Christmas Day at the same time as Her Majesty's annual speech. I have refrained from quoting Miss West, who, when told her radio programme was obscene, replied, 'They could've turned it off.'

While hiding from all the jollification, I have read a number of books. The most recently received was called *Masked Culture*, published by Columbia University Press. It says that it is our duty to take part in Halloween parades and to try and ensure that they are celebrations of gender ambiguity. The text is serious – nay, philosophical – but the illustrations are outrageous, a strange combination.

A long time ago, I received a copy of *The Diary of Jack the Ripper*. Now, at last, I have read it. The author is at great pains to establish the authenticity of the manuscript. Chemical tests and other procedures have been applied to it, none of which had any interest for me. I have never paid more attention to television dramas because they were based on actual events. What is absorbing about *The Diary* is the life of Mr Maybrick, who, the book claims, was Mr Ripper. He was a cotton merchant who became an arsenic addict. I had always thought that if you gave anyone a teaspoon full of this stuff, he dropped dead on the spot. It seems that I was wrong. In happier times, men took repeated doses of arsenic to increase their potency, but it was so habit-forming that it became impossible either to continue or to desist from taking it. In the end, Mr Ripper died of this practice, but his wife was accused of murdering him. Her trial was sensational and was the most egregious miscarriage of justice imaginable. Mrs Maybrick, a pretty American woman, was condemned to death. Her sentence was later commuted to life imprisonment and she served fifteen years, emerging at the age of forty-one. This is a tragic but fascinating story.

One of the strangest episodes of my life occurred the other day. I was sitting innocently in my room when the phone rang and an unknown voice said, 'We can't get in. There are no front doorbells.' (This is because I live in a rooming house. Traditionally, in Manhattan, to live in a rooming house is to be part of an enclosed order.) It was the police. I was very frightened, but I was brave. I went downstairs, opened the front door, and three young policemen burst in. They stood about in my room (there is only one chair) and talked among themselves, but searched my living space for signs of sin. While they were doing this, the telephone rang again and a voice said, 'The ambulance is here.' I disclaimed all knowledge of such a request having been made, but went downstairs a second time. In the street, I found my landlord, half the denizens of the Lower East Side, and a Mr Sorrentino, who is a performance artist famous for imitating Elton John. I talked for some time, smiled and nodded at the assembled throng, until one of the policemen said, 'It is snowing,' and suggested (forcefully) that we board the ambulance. So I, one policeman, and Mr Sorrentino were whisked away to hospital in no time.

Once there, my arrival was treated as though long-awaited, but never welcome. My body was handled as though I were already dead, flung unceremoniously on to a wheeled stretcher, raced into an elevator where the other passengers stared down at me coldly, making me long to reach a bed where I thought my privacy would be restored. How wrong I was! Once I was turned on to my bed like a bale of shorn grass, a nurse stripped me of my clothing, which included two bandages around my ankles (without even asking why they were there), and threw them in the rubbish bin. Then she seemed interested in my pair of small white underpants and their contents. When I retreated from this prurient intrusion, which shocked modesty, the fiend, with shrieks of Filipino glee, said she thought I was wearing diapers . . . as if that made any difference!

I have often wondered why a young woman would adopt such an ugly career as that of hospital nurse. Now I know. They are penis-choppers. They only wish to spend their days among people who are physically unprotected and weaker than they. I have never known such sadism. She jabbed me with needles and, when I began to scream, said with feigned surprise, 'I understand you would rather take this stuff orally' – as if preferring to swallow a small black pill to having its contents passed into the veins of my arms were one of my funny little ways.

Now that the episode is mercifully over, I still don't know how or why it happened. I still don't know who rang for an ambulance, or what was supposed to be wrong with me. All I know is that when there is anything wrong with you, go to a faith healer, go to a witch doctor, go to a herbalist, go to a chiropractor, go to an analyst; but don't go to hospital.

As if calling on me to define my politics, I returned home to find a letter waiting for me from the *Sunday Times* of London, asking me to review a book called *The Politics and Poetics of Camp*. This is a collection of abstruse essays by the crowned heads of academia. Miss Sontag is, surprisingly, not among those contributing. It was she who elsewhere suggested that such an enterprise was in itself a form of camp.

But who is the book for? Not other professors; it is too frivolous. Not other gay readers; it is too serious. Even the cover of the book is misleading. It is a soft cover edition showing a photograph of a young man posing on top of a malachite pillar, wearing nothing but a jock strap while, with his back towards you, another young man, also wearing a jock strap – inferred by the hazardously thin straps that can just be discerned running round his hips and between his buttocks – kneels at the foot of the pillar in an attitude of adoration. It is innocent. Only Senator Helms could take exception to it. All the same, this book could not be read on a subway train.

What *are* the politics of camp? In England, it is a three-dimensional word: a verb meaning to behave in a deliberately or unconsciously effeminate manner; an adjective meaning displaying one's effeminacy in possessing it, wearing it, doing it; an abstract noun signifying the intention to display one's effeminacy. In the Twenties, it was a secret word used by low-life street people. By the Forties, it had been taken up by the theatrical profession – well known by the English public to be of dubious morality (unless you played Shakespeare) – to mean a style of acting that could be seen by the audience to be acting (or, more accurately, a style in which the actor can be seen enjoying acting). Now it means anything done not for the intrinsic value of the action, but in order to demonstrate one's individuality in doing it – showing off.

Politics, being the art of making the inevitable seem to be a matter of wise human choice, is therefore a form of camp. This homosexuals perceive and applaud because they are not involved in the process, or indeed in anything. A homosexual is standing on the bank watching other people swim. So, as far as I'm concerned, there can be no *Politics* in *Camp*, and what am I to say to the editors of the *Sunday Times*?

Whatever those Filipino fiends spent so many agonizing hours pouring into my veins in hospital I do not know, but it has shattered my memory. Twice in one week I have forgotten to take my keys with me into the outer world and have been compelled to ask our concierge to let me into my own room in the middle of the night. He is what Katherine Mansfield would call a man without a temperament and never complains, which makes me feel more ashamed. I forgot my teeth and brought humiliation to Beef Steak Charlie's. I forgot my money and was driven to roll on the floor in squirming self-abasement at the feet of the ruler of our local diner because I couldn't pay for my lunch. I forgot my 'bus money' and had to take a taxi all the way to 60th Street to the Church of St Paul the Apostle, where a memorial service was held for Jack Eric Williams.

I arrived in a rage. But my mood soon thawed in the cosiness of the situation. St Paul's is a huge church, hideous, and in a constant state of being repaired. A few people, some of whom I knew, were gathered together. They sang some of Mr Williams' songs and reminisced informally about the deceased. I kept quiet for once. There was not the embarrassing whitewash job that you might expect to prevail at such an occasion, but I didn't recognize

Mr Williams in any of the portraits painted by his students and collaborators. They described him as cantankerous and difficult on the debit side and as boyish to his credit. To me, though he was at least thirty years my junior, he was fatherly, quiet and amenable – even when I said music was a mistake. (Mr Rorem said the remark was sweeping.) To me, he was like a slow-moving bear of a man, constantly eating. One thing I would have agreed with his friend about was his brazenness. He kissed my hand in a well-lighted restaurant, but I couldn't have mentioned that in a church, however Unitarian.

I mention all this at some length because it supports the oft-repeated opinion that we all present different aspects of our personality to different people. So far, I have disagreed with this. I never caught myself doing it and would be deeply shocked if I did, but Mr Williams evidently did. He was a master at it.

The only good that has come from all this wintry weather is that it inclines one to stay indoors and therefore to work. I have written for *The Hungry Mind*, a slightly arty magazine published in St Paul, a piece about role models. The phrase didn't exist when I was young, so originality flourished. Now uniformity is all the rage because everyone is encouraged to be like someone else, the future is held captive to the past since models must be sought in history, and the great must be trimmed – nay, 'Bobbitted' – to fit some standard that children have of adults (or are supposed to have) by thin-lipped magistrates who are for ever telling famous people who come before them that they cannot drink or take drugs or sleep around or kick policemen's shins because they are 'role models to the young' (a position they never sought). This is precisely the Louis B. Mayer fallacy that the talented must be pure. In short, role models are a mistake.

But I did go out into the snow. I went to the Museum of Natural History to my first Jurassic party. This event was in celebration of the Grammy Awards. I have no idea how I got mixed up with Time-Warner, but someone I did not know was desperate for me to attend. Two charming young people came to fetch me in a purring limousine and took me through the snowy night to Central Park West. There the police and the photographers were gathered together. An unknown man, addressing me by name, led me along a white canvas tunnel into the entrance hall, where the brontosauruses greeted me. They were the only animals who knew me. We wandered through a solemn crowd of people dressed in black drinking and talking, elderly men in faultless evening dress (high-ups in the offices of Time-Warner), black women (singers), black men (orchestra), and very black men (drummers). I recognized no one and was greeted warmly only by the catering staff. The talk was all about Mr Sinatra having been cut off (not Bobbitted), but he is no longer a Time-Warner star, so it mattered little. When we left, we discovered standing on the kerb the huge man who had invited me. We were photographed together to his great satisfaction and my bewilderment – an enigmatic tableau. I reached home at half past two.

Miss Miles was not at the party.

Who is Tom Stevens? A cosy male voice at the other end of the telephone wire asked me if I knew him. I replied that I did not remember the name, but that was no reason to suppose I didn't know him intimately. I was born, I explained, with Alzheimer's disease. The voice then asked me what I did for a living. I replied that I was in the profession of being. I had to repeat that several times. Mr Stevens, the voice then said, had my name, telephone number and address in his pocket when he was arrested. This piece of news aroused my curiosity. I envisaged living my whole life on the telephone like Miss Stanwyck in *Sorry, Wrong Number,* but there have so far been no other calls relating to this intriguing incident. Mr Stevens was described as a heavily-built man with red hair. I nearly cried out, 'Ooh, another lovely man already!' but thought this might confuse the issue. I remained by the telephone fearing to miss the next instalment and because it was then so cold outside.

The snow brought out the best in everybody – except me. When I stood tottering on top of a pyramid of ice, hands reached out to help me down. People say that New Yorkers are indifferent to strangers. I have not found this to be so. I would say that everyone in this metropolis who isn't shooting you is your friend.

1994

Spring

*

I once told Comrade Nureyev that the charm of ballet was that someone might break his neck

In all big cities, I suppose, there is a fringe theatre. In London, it is called 'Fringe Theatre'; in New York, it is called 'Off-Off-Broadway'. This secondary entertainment is usually too risqué (filthy) or too cultural (boring) to be presented at great expense to the public, which will reject it, but it serves the purpose of employing actors, set designers etc., and prevents them from becoming desperate. Now nothing can possibly be too risqué for modern audiences, so 'kinky' has become the mainstay of fringe theatre.

Mr John Glines has established a cartel in kinkiness at the Courtyard Theater on Grove Street. I went there to see four 'gay' plays gathered into something called *Adjoining Trances* by a Mr Buck. This is very different from its last theatrical offering, which was a hilarious play about a televangelist tempted by the devil, who appears in drag for this purpose. The present play is a sober affair, an imaginary conversation between Tennessee Williams and Carson McCullers. It is only gay in that we know both parties were homosexual. It is cultural in that nothing happens. We see both writers sitting at their typewriters struggling with the strain of composition, which they endeavour to alleviate by the use of alcohol and pills. Finally, Mrs McCullers passes out and is carried by Mr Williams to a place where she can rest. The play's virtue is that it presents the extraordinary tenderness with which Mr Williams regarded women, unlike so many gay men who think of them as rivals – even enemies.

From there to Wings Theater to see *In a Land Far Away* by Mr Jefferies, who rules the place. This is a musical about the fall of Troy, with an emphasis on the 'alternative' relationship between Achilles and Patroclus. The lyrics contain rhymes that would please Mr Sondheim (there can be no higher praise). Achilles is made to rhyme with 'This place gives me the willies' and 'We're in a fix' with 'The River Styx'. The actors sing themselves to bits. They should have been warned that the space at Wings Theater is, to say the least, intimate, and they could have spared their tonsils or whatever part of your anatomy you use for singing.

Finally leaving the fringe for a real cinema, I saw *Serial Mom*. It features a real movie star, Miss Turner, and is the part she was born to play. She looks so pretty and she is so tough. In this film, she flings herself with the utmost gusto into a series of murders of anyone who disappoints or thwarts her. She is caught, but in an uproarious court scene provokes, or seduces, all witnesses who give evidence against her into behaving badly, and she is acquitted. Of course, since this is a John Waters film, the murders are as gruesome as can be, with blades withdrawn from victims dripping with blood and entrails. Even a fly that she swats is shown smeared across a plate.

After the secret screening of this picture, the entire audience was invited by *Paper* magazine to a party at Match, an unmarked grave on Mercer Street. There I found Mr Waters buried among his fans. It is always a delight to see this master of degradation looking like the head assistant in a boys' outfitters shop, dressed in a conservative suit, a sleek hairdo, and a pencil-thin, pencilled-in moustache.

It might seem from the foregoing that I have had no time to venture into the real world, but I went to the State College of Pennsylvania. I made the journey by plane – or, rather, by planes, first boarding a real flying machine to Philadelphia, and from there by a small plane made of oiled silk and matchbox wood which I found standing in a field at the airport. The passengers could feel this frail toy fighting valiantly with the elements to gain height. It succeeded and landed shakily in a town built purely to house the college and inhabited entirely by students and professors.

In addressing them, I told them that education was for teachers, not for students, and that nothing worth knowing could be taught. As usual, they remained calm. I realized that I am becoming like Miss Madonna. The more desperately I try to shock, the more hopelessly routine my act becomes.

Mr Roddy McDowall, who seems to bounce from side to side of the continent like a shuttlecock in a game of badminton, returned to New York from Los Angeles recently and took me to lunch at Sardi's. Like all restaurants in this city, though crowded to overflowing at night, it is empty at lunchtime. Nevertheless, he spotted Miss Tammy Grimes in the distance and rushed to her table to greet her in the theatrical tradition for which the place is famous. He had chosen Sardi's because it is almost next door to what is now the Helen Hayes Theater, where Miss Joan Rivers was playing *Sally Marr.*

This is an extraordinary play about the mother of Lenny Bruce. (She is still living.) It is not so much a barrel of laughs as a funeral urn of laughs. Miss Rivers flings herself into the show with an air of desperation, shouting mordant one-liners at other actors, none of whom speaks. I have no idea what Mrs Marr is really like, but this performance is straight Rivers; the same appearance that we know so well, except that her hair is red, and the same aspect on which the cost of having to be funny all the time is etched. The exhaustion was real, not acted, because not even Mr McDowall could see her afterwards. She had to recover before a second performance that evening.

I have since become aware that Miss Rivers additionally participated in a made-for-TV movie in which she plays herself and is blamed loudly by her daughter (also playing herself). All comedians are desperate people, and Miss Rivers, because of her painful thinness, her harsh voice, and her tragic private – or rather, flagrantly public – life is a cartoon of a comedian. While one laughs at what she says, one weeps for what she is.

This is the American dilemma. The neon lights of Broadway lure us like moths. We dash ourselves against them again and again in search of we know not what until we have crippled ourselves, and in this desperate flight we are abetted or rather exploited by television. Television loves disaster. To watch it regularly is to be given the impression that all children are beaten by their drunken stepfathers, all schoolgirls are raped by their escorts, all policemen are corrupt bullies, all politicians are either embezzlers or lechers or both. So we live our lives courting disaster that will bring us on to the screen into the glare of the neons. To other countries, we must seem to be a nation bent on self-destruction. It is useless trying to frighten us by telling us the world will come to an end in the year 2000, because we think of such an event only as a great television play and we hope to secure a leading part in it.

In view of all this, it is no wonder that Mrs Onassis seemed in the public mind like a calm island in the midst of a raging sea. She was sanctified not by what she did, but by what she refrained from doing. The English, who think they invented class and regard all Americans as vulgar, would do well to compare Princess Diana's behaviour in the face of Prince Charles's infidelity with Mrs Onassis's discreet way of dealing with Mr Kennedy's priapic behaviour.

I was taken by my doctor to see the hundredth season of the New York City Ballet at Lincoln Center. It was a huge success. However, Americans are not such balletomanes as the English, whose fatuous enthusiasm was parodied by Miss Gingold, who, as a ballet-goer in a revue, said, 'I clapped right from the end of *Swan Lake* to the beginning of *Sylphides*.' The audience at Lincoln Center was large and enthusiastic, but sane. The ballets were stripped to the minimum. There was no glitter – no fairy princesses, no distraught princes. The dancing was energetic but not breathtaking. I once told Comrade Nureyev that the charm of ballet was that someone might break his neck. At the Center there were no fantastic leaps – no dangerous lifts. If I sound disappointed, that is because the ballet is for the very young. Years ago I loved it, though I can't now remember whether I loved the ballet or loved loving it. I was full of aesthetic pretensions, and loved talking ballet jargon loudly in public places. All that is ended now. I am a self-made Philistine.

Onward and upward, I have flown into the presence of a Mrs Krim. I was invited by AmFAR, of which she is chairperson (co-starred with Miss Taylor, who was not present). Mrs Krim lives on West 69th Street in an elegance and splendour I have never seen rivalled. I trod over carpets as thick as pampas grass up a spiral staircase to two spacious rooms on the first floor. There were gathered tall thin men in dark suits with collegiate ties. Food was served to us by handmaidens in black dresses. The delectables offered were arranged so meticulously that I trembled to destroy the symmetry of the layout by subtracting from it. The occasion was a commemoration of the death of Mr Mapplethorpe, whose foundation has given a million dollars to AmFAR. (How did he ever get so rich?)

In a high clear voice, Miss Sischy, editor of *Interview* magazine, described to the assembled guests some of Mr Mapplethorpe's photographs in painful detail, including a picture of someone thrusting his fist into someone else's rear end. The young men did not blush, or giggle, or faint. I very nearly did all three. Like Mr Bruce, by dying, Mr Mapplethorpe has become one of the saints of pornography – a title you can only earn in this decade in this city.

Summer

*

Never open a letter written on pink paper

I have received a letter written on pink paper. Never open a letter written on pink paper. Furthermore, it was from a woman called Francesca. Another bad sign. Obviously her real name is only Frances – if not Lizzie or Ruby or worse. She claimed to have been an art student when I was a model and hankered to be remembered, though that was fifty years ago, and she was one of up to twenty students a day for thirty-nine weeks a year. She cited various touching incidents that would jog my memory – for example, she bought me cups of coffee in the mid-morning breaks – in return for which, she now wanted me to meet her at La Guardia airport. There are no free coffee breaks.

I positively refused to flaunt a card besmirched with the word FRANCESCA, but I have other means of making myself conspicuous, and I stood at the entrance to the baggage claim area. She recognized me instantly. We went to Days Hotel on Eighth Avenue, and up to her room. There, though she was so small as to be hardly visible to the naked eye, she seized me in an iron grip and demanded that I kiss her. At this point, I must remind you that we are both English and that physical contact is an embarrassment among married couples, let alone perfect strangers. I lay my cheekbone against hers in the manner adopted by touring actresses when greeting people they do not know, and left hastily.

The next day, though she is at least seventy and I am at least eighty-five, undaunted by my coldness, she demanded that I cuddle her. 'Don't press your luck,' I warned her. She said she won't. But she will.

Yet she is not a fag-hag. Fag-hags are all plump, sophisticated, middle-aged ladies who use a lot of outmoded 'gay' gestures and utter all the traditional 'gay' catchphrases at parties where they are the only female present. This woman is worse. She is artistic, loves animals (which is always a fatuous claim, as some animals are lovable and others are downright fiendish), does not want sex but likes to stand as near the edge of the cliff as possible. Naturally she took me to the ballet – not to the same company as that which I had watched only a week before with my doctor, but next door in a theatre that was just as full. We saw *The Red Shoes*, dazzlingly staged. I was interested to see that the mechanics were at work even in this dusty backwater of art, and I imagine that all the high jinks would shock true balletomanes – the prima ballerina on wires, the red shoes dancing eerily by themselves in a spotlight, and so on, but my companion, though cultural as hell, seemed not to mind.

Is it not amazing that two theatres next door to one another, both five tiers high, should be full on the same evening in New York?

I have also seen *An Inspector Calls*, where the set received a round of applause when the curtain went up. Perhaps in view of this, I should mention that it was the work of a Mr MacNeil. It is truly impressive and actually takes part in the play, expressing the dramatist's personal views. J.B. Priestley was a Yorkshireman, which is not only to say that he came from Yorkshire, but that he shared all that county's prejudices. He was a no-nonsense man, who held that the poor were more 'real' than the rich. In this play, we see poor children playing in the rain-drenched streets and the rich eating, drinking and laughing smugly in an ornate, warmly-lighted interior. Towards the end of the drama, the lower middle class invades this interior silently, an underlying wish of Mr Priestley.

The set is so elaborate that much of the action of the play takes place in the street, obliging the lady of the house to throw herself down in the gutter, which seems a little unlikely, but no matter. It was all high drama and greatly appreciated by the audience.

Gay men are like the children of the damned: if you tell one of them anything, spontaneously the whole bunch knows it. Having whispered to someone that I didn't watch basketball because the men who play it are pathologically tall people with huge hands and feet, I was invited to an upper room on West Third Street, where the 'gay' basketball team was gathered together, to see for myself that they were of normal height with itty-bitty hands and feet. As they play against one another, this will not be a disadvantage, but in the great big outer world, they would never win. They take no exercise other than walking up five flights of steep stairs and twitching invitingly to rock music. Perhaps the hoop is lower in 'gay' basketball.

When, like Mr Alexander (the Great), you run out of worlds to conquer, you invent a perfume. I would claim that they all smell alike, but, when I took a taxi up Park Avenue, the driver said, 'Somebody's wearing Joop.' I was accompanied by two other passengers who denied the charge, so it was up to me to say, 'Forgive me, driver, for I have sinned and am no more worthy to be called thy passenger.' So they *are* all different and easily recognized. Now Mr Klein has concocted 'CK1' and a lot of men and women foregathered on Mr Roosevelt's Island, in a studio so large it would have been possible to film the Charge of the Light Brigade, to advertise this mysterious scent. No one held a glass bottle of quaint design under his nose, dilated his nostrils, and shut his eyes in feigned ecstasy or any of that rubbish. We huddled together, talking airily of this and that, while a half-naked young man crawled between our feet. It is a politically correct perfume: it is for everybody, but more than that I cannot say.

All that seems to have happened in another life, though it occurred only last week. Since then, I have been plunged into social activity so hectic that I would describe the intervening time as the worst week in my life if it didn't seem ungracious. I went to the Supper Club to watch a cabaret act staged in my honour by *Paper* magazine, starring Joey Arias, who appeared on platforms that double his natural height, and a black dress so tight that I was reminded of the words uttered by Danny La Rue at the opening of his own drag show: 'I bet you're wondering where I've put it.'

Some time ago, I posed in a white suit provided for me by a photographer who wished to take a picture of me thus clad seated in an armchair (which he carried on his head to a stagnant pool in the middle of Central Park). There I sat trying to look like a Twenties academician's illustration of a poem by Tennyson – languid, mournful, effete. He gave me the suit and at the time I wondered when I could possibly wear it but, as the hottest June broke over us like a bowl of warm molasses, I thought, 'This could be the time.' It paid off. In it, I sat in a restaurant on Second Avenue and was complimented by a middle-aged lady. 'You remind me of Quentin Crisp,' she said. I simpered, lowered my eyelids, and sighed, 'We all try to dress like him. He was such a wonderful role model.'

I was invited by Mr Origlio, the most ingenious publicist in the world, to The Ballroom. As a stunt to advertise a forthcoming play, adapted from a book by Mrs Fuller called *Me and Jezebel*, about a month-long visit by Miss Davis to the author's home, a Davis look-alike competition was being held. You would have thought that there would be a line all the way down Eighth Avenue for such an event, since none of us can be restrained from going into his act when the lady's name is mentioned, but there were only five contestants. One was very good and managed to waddle across the stage on her heels to a tee, but no one spoke with her mouth worn upside-down, which is the trademark of what one might call Bette Noire. The play should be a riot, because the book is very funny. I didn't see it, because I was sent to San Francisco.

I went with some trepidation, because it is the only city where I have received bad notices. This is because the gay population of that city seemingly cannot understand my refusal to be an apologist, much less an evangelist, for homosexuality. Nonetheless I went, and explained yet again that I was hired to be there and that my function was to sell theatre seats. Furthermore, I noted that in my opinion a theatre-goer was a middle-brow, middle-aged woman with a broken heart and it was to this vast body of people that I addressed myself. Homosexuality was never mentioned.

Disaster struck. I had been hired by a charming woman called Miss Olsen. She knew what to expect. I was but a small part of an event called Unity Expo. I think it was her object to stage a gay show to which real people were invited. I applaud this idea. It is useless to put on a gay show which is attended only by gay people. It is more of the separate-but-equal rubbish. Unfortunately, Miss Olsen's scheme did not work.

There was no publicity. No one interviewed me except one radio channel, and that was aired only when the event was safely over. Only one person photographed me. He arrived with his daughter (aged about two) in his arms. While he operated his camera, she picked his nose, smoothed his hair, repositioned his spectacles. In spite of her attentions he remained firmly focused, but I do not think the pictures were for immediate use. No one knew that I had arrived – except all the waiters in the cafés near the Cartwright Hotel where I stayed. I think that it was due to them that anyone came at all to the Fashion Center where the Expo was held. It is a huge building on Eighth Street like a luxury liner inside-out, five decks high, and with a floor space at least a thousand feet across. The basement was occupied by a sort of fair with all the usual mountebanks present – offering strange liquids said to be life-enhancing, telling fortunes, and administering invigorating rituals by laying their hands on your solar plexus. Everyone except Sylvester Stallone's mother was present.

That was all great fun. It was on the ground floor that the trouble started. In a huge auditorium, a sea of empty chairs was aligned before a small stage on which, presumably, on happier occasions, unknown fashion models strutted and swished. On the evening I was there, performers read the works of unknown writers. There was a real actor who read a real short story. I stumbled through what I think it would be polite to call an allegory by a Miss Russ.

Public readings are always a mistake. You focus your eyes on the printed page and not on the audience. I remember that, at school, it was during the classes when the master read to us from a dreary textbook that we all went to sleep, giggled, or tampered with the boy sitting next to us. When the teacher addressed us directly, we listened or at least sat still. On the stage there was a microphone. When you look at the page before you, your lips are not oriented towards the microphone. When they are, you cannot remember a word of what you have just seen and so fail to convey its meaning to a bewildered audience.

That was on Saturday. On Sunday evening a huddle of gay men attended, and I must say they were very appreciative. They were eager to ask questions. One person wanted to know if I had ever desired to have a family of my own. That startled me and the rest of the audience. I had never been asked that before. The idea of family life looms large in the minds of everyone in America, but everyone must know how awful family life is. The trouble with children is that they are not returnable. You take them out of the box and they say 'Dada' and 'Mama' and all is well – for a while. But they grow up to be larger than you are and to hold views with which you disagree.

In my book *Manners From Heaven,* I wrote that bad manners begin at home. A televisionary called Mr Boggs questioned this statement, but when I asked him if, in adult life, he had ever been so continuously and acrimoniously insulted as he had been by his brothers when he lived at home, he bowed his head. I rested my case. Not only are all the wounding words used by our siblings, but all the grimmest murders are perpetrated by relatives of the victim. Yet no one in America realizes this fact or reacts wisely to it. The one place you cannot send runaways is home. As Miss Stanwyck has remarked, 'Home is where you go when you run out of places.' I can endorse that statement, but, in fairness to my family, I must admit that I was a most objectionable child.

In spite of all the foregoing remarks, I had a wonderful time in San Francisco. The weather was perfect: no fog in the mornings, no earthquakes in the afternoons.

Autumn

*

I have been auctioned off at Christie's

I have been on a grand tour. Firstly I visited Minneapolis, summoned thither by an Organization for Human Rights. Needless to say, that meant gay rights – not because homosexual men have more rights than other people, but because they complain so loudly and so continuously when they are deprived of them. When asked why I was there if I didn't believe in gay rights, I said, 'because I never say no to any invitation if my fare is paid.' That reply seemed to satisfy my inquisitors.

This time I really saw the city, because I was welcomed by a Mr Pufkin. (I thought it was an affectionate nickname, Poofkin, but it was his real name.) He took me in his car to see the many lakes and beautiful green parks of which Minneapolis consists. Minneapolis, like St Louis, is much more verdant than most American cities. At nightfall, we went to a real beerfest in a real beerhall with wooden walls and a stone floor such as I have only seen in travelogues of Germany. The only things lacking were the fat thighs bulging out of leather shorts and a drinking song.

On my second night in Minneapolis I was taken to a huge convention centre, where nearly a thousand guests dined and were entertained by some half-hearted dancing and some rousing speeches. It was in fact a political meeting, but that aspect of the occasion went over my head, as I do not believe in politics. From Minneapolis, I went to Chicago, and from there to Los Angeles, where I was met by a Mrs Johnson and her brother (whom I know) and taken to an even larger convention hall, where I read in a faltering voice from my autobiography to a small huddle of people who looked quite bewildered. A few more people turned up on Sunday evening and questioned me about my love life. I explained that I didn't have one and that I would never have come to America if I was still active (like a volcano) because I thought that in order to be registered as a resident alien, you had to take an oath that you would not engage in moral turpitude, which I assume means kinky sex.

After the question-and-answer session, I went to dinner with a heap of wonderful people, including a gay banker (I didn't know that such a thing existed) who has interested Wells Fargo in the finances of the gay community, and Miss Patricia Nell Warren. I had never heard of her, but she is apparently America's answer to England's Mary Renault, having written in a time gone by a novel called *The Front Runner* about a gay athlete and his male partner. She was signing copies of a sequel called *Harlan's Race* at Unity Expo. She gave me a copy, but, like a fool, I forgot to bring it home.

Miss Warren is a wonderful person, looking like a lesbian but not mannish, looking like a writer but not aesthetic. We went on a disastrous bar crawl in which each place we entered was darker, louder, and more depraved than the last one. She did not flinch, but she did not join in. She accepted compliments, but was not in the smiling and nodding racket. I regret to have to say that my patience wore out and finally I broke down and refused to be introduced to one more person. I much deplore this shattering of my image.

The following morning I rose at dawn to be photographed for an advertisement for some spectacles (which I never wear, knowing that I would be socially washed up if I did) and returned home to answer a pile of all the usual letters asking me the usual questions, such as how does one succeed in the profession of being, what do I think of AIDS, and what is Crisperanto.

* * *

Miss Arcade has come home with her 'world-wandering' feet, as Francis Thompson would have said. She had been publicly taking off her clothes in Australia, Scotland, Ireland, Germany and Austria with great success. Though mortally tired, she never rests. She took me to hear Mr Albee read. Having seen *Three Tall Women,* I was curious to see what he looked like. He was surprisingly mortal – almost humble. I had expected (him being a dramatist and all) that he would jump from side to side of the rostrum and back again, squeaking one line and growling the next to indicate 'dialogue', but, instead, he read a strange story about a dog which he recited in an unemphatic but audible voice. Miss Arcade says the tale was taken from one of his plays, but what an odd play it must be, for this monologue lasted at least half an hour. The event took place in Wooster Street, in one of those huge rooms that are a characteristic of New York.

When I was young, no one who visited Manhattan talked about anything but the skyscrapers. Gertrude Stein said, 'It isn't the way they rise into the sky. It's the way they spring out of the ground.' Now every city has skyscrapers – even dreary old London. What makes New York unique is that district between Houston and Canal Streets in which all the buildings contain huge rooms – not just on the ground floor, where they are art galleries, but at all levels. These huge salons have ceilings as high as churches, and beautiful dance floors, all of laths of wood the same width, polished to the same colour, and all installed on the same day. They have never been walked on.

Having heard Mr Albee in one such venue, I tottered along brick roads in a terrible state of disrepair (by which the district is also characterized) to 20 Greene Street to the Kisslinger Gallery to see the latest paintings of Mr Iain Potts. There is something very appealing about this young man. Having been told that I had said: 'When people say, "What have you got against pictures?" I reply, "What have you got against the wall?"' he has now painted on transparent sheets of plastic and hung them in the middle of the room. The walls remained their untarnished, beautiful, blank selves, like the faces of film stars.

Thy say that if you criticized the music of the late Jack Eric Williams, he took it away, altered it, and brought it back to play for your approval. In England, artists only toss their manes and say, 'You don't understand what I'm getting at,' or some such rubbish.

When not rushing about from one form of entertainment to another, I have been trying to catch up with the books that various publishers have kindly sent me. Here I must mention that I received from The Crossing Press a book by Mr Gary Stern called *A Few Tricks Along the Way*. Not having time to do more than glance through it, I replied, as I do to all publishers whose books I haven't read, 'Please feel free to quote me as saying anything that will promote the sales of this excellent book.' Most firms receiving such a letter trot out adjectives of a generally affirmative nature for my approval to which I give my royal consent, but The Crossing Press has joined those few witty enough to print my response verbatim.

The face of the Lower East Side is darkened. The restaurant in the window of which I used to sit on exhibition like a Dutch prostitute has been shut by the authorities. This not only means that I starve, but also that there is no place where I can meet all the strangers who telephone me. The system of dealing with the outer world has broken down.

There are no front door bells where I live. I don't know why. It may be a caste symbol. Apartment dwellers have bells. Roomers do not. Therefore, if I judge that the stranger calling me on the telephone is of low degree, I ask him to call me from the corner of Third Street and Second Avenue, so that I can rush helter-skelter down the stairs and jump up and down in front of the house to make myself conspicuous. If I suppose him to be of high degree, I dare not ask him to do this and suggest that we meet in the diner on Fifth Street. It was humble, but it was also the only restaurant where there was *no music*, and tape recorders could hear me. All this, it goes without saying, is so as not to invite a stranger into my room, and avoid the charge of folly when my body is found by the police with my throat and various other parts of my body slit. All these rituals are no more.

Of course, if the strange caller suggests a place of rendezvous such as a theatre or cinema, we can meet, but even that is not simple. At every event in Manhattan there are not only the people wishing to attend, but also all the people wishing to see the people attending. This produces such a crowd (in fact, almost the entire population of Manhattan) that it is difficult to find any one person – especially as, quite often, I don't know what he looks like.

There is no limit to the oddity of the invitations that I have received lately. One evening, I found myself at a farewell party for a Mr Benoit, who was going to Nevada. When I asked him what he would do there, he said he would rally the gay community. I implored him not to do that. Left alone, a gay person is hardly gay at all, but put two such people together and they are four times as gay as they were separately. Four gay people are sixteen times as gay as two, and so on. The progression is geometrical rather than mathematical. We shall have them marching down the roulette table and demanding the *rouge et noir* be changed to straight and gay.

At the party for Mr Benoit, his late employer, Mayor Dinkins, slipped quietly into the room. When I shook hands with him, I was aware that he is a kind of saint. How did he ever get caught up by the political machine? I didn't ask him, though I travelled home with him in his limousine. His term of office must have been torture for him.

I have been auctioned off at Christie's. It was the rowdiest auction ever. People came and went, waved to one another, talked to one another, embraced, kissed – all as though nothing serious was going on, but thousands of dollars were being thrown away (should I say spent?) on a week's holiday in Belize, or a photographic session with Mr Francesco Scavullo. It was all for the people of El Salvador. Who won me and what my duties as a slave will be I never found out in all the hurly-burly.

Winter

*

That's the wonderful thing about Manhattan. You are never without friends

I've gone into mourning. Jerry's Diner on Sixth Street is shut. Soon the Lower East Side will be like one of those silver-mining towns in Nevada that are now only piles of dusty planks, and I shall emerge from one of them with a battered hat with the brim turned up in front and a fuzzy beard to point a crooked finger to show travellers where once the dancing girls and the miners sang and danced and fought.

What precious substance did we mine here? I think it was diversity without pretension – a natural individuality not bolstered by claims of artistic achievement. A brand-new eating place called the Bowery Bar has opened on East Fourth Street, but that is on the other side of Third Avenue – almost beyond redemption. The first time I went there, I knew it was an important meeting and eating place because Miss Miles and the Baroness Sherry von Korber-Bernstein were there.

I went with a Professor Connolly to the Gershwin Theater to see *Show Boat*. Professors in America are very different from English purveyors of wisdom and truth. There they have pointed white beards and walk with a stoop, weighed down by their knowledge, I presume. Here they are friendly and human and what they profess is not known. When I asked Professor Newton what he professed, he replied, 'My sin.'

Professor Connolly doesn't go that far, but he is sufficiently human to know Miss Stritch, who at the moment is playing the captain's wife in *Show Boat*. What an odd play it is! The miscegenation for which it is famous takes place at the side of the stage very early in the show, and is only the means of getting rid of the two characters who were to be the stars of the show on the boat. We do not hear of them again until we reach Chicago, where the girl is singing 'He's Just My Bill'. Miss Stritch described the show as a series of pop-up cards and music, and it is. When we went round to see Miss Stritch in her dressing room, she was dressed only in a bra and panty hose. We talked for a while and she suggested that I should perform my one-man show in Canada – as a two-man show with Professor Connolly. He, to my surprise, agreed, so I'm getting my act together and I'm taking it on the road.

As a sort of dress rehearsal, I went to Barney's dress shop to take part in a literary breakfast. I was questioned by Mr Evans about Mr Wilde. When it transpired that I heartily disliked Mr Wilde, Mr Evans was nonplussed. 'You have taken the wind out of my sails,' he cried. I offered to put it back, but he declined.

The thing that I deplore about Mr Wilde was that he never came to grips with how sordid his life had become. When the names of five or six boys whom Mr Wilde knew only in Braille (they were procured by Lord Alfred Douglas and met Mr Wilde in darkened rooms in Oxford) were read out at his trial, he was still bleating about love and invoking the fair name of Mr Plato, who died a Greek philosopher and came back as a spinster's alibi. We were asked how he would fare in today's society and I said he would never be off television. Someone compared him with Gore Vidal, which I found strange. Mr Wilde was a gross human being trying to enter English society. Mr Vidal is an elegant American trying to get out of society. Mr Wilde once said there was only one thing worse than being talked about, and that was not being talked about. He was a sort of male Madonna. All this discourse took place with us sitting on a small raised dais facing inward in the middle of a restaurant full of respectable middle-aged ladies eating toast and sipping tea. For incongruity, the situation took a lot of beating.

I have sinned in accepting an invitation from a Mr Utne to address a multitude of readers of the *Utne Reader* (of which I had never heard). He sent me a letter telling me I was one of a hundred 'visionaries' and invited me to the New York Town Hall. I accepted because I never say no to anything on the grounds that, as I lie dying, I shall not regret anything that I did – only what I didn't do. But it is a sin to accept challenges you know you cannot meet. First of all, we went to the Harvard Club, where immediately I was outclassed by the furnishings. Then, after a lot of eating and drinking and speech-making, we all sauntered to the Town Hall. Really it was an august occasion on which a lot of men about my age, in rumpled suits to show they were serious-minded, spoke words of universal and eternal wisdom. Then I went on stage and endeavoured to entertain the audience on the principle enunciated by Miss Stritch that the thing to do was to get them to like me, which was beside the point when grave prophecies were being uttered about global warming (though we could have done with some of that), ozone layers, deforestation, ecology, and various forms of religion.

I have now written to Mr Utne apologizing for my transgression, but the harm is done. Worse than that, I have now said yes to a Mr Stevens who has invited me to go to the Young Republicans Club. When its various members discover that I do not believe in politics, blame will fall on my host and it will all be my fault. So now I publicly state that I have not a serious thought in my head and cannot be inveigled into speaking on any world-shaping or world-shattering subjects. I long ago renounced serious relationships. Now I renounce serious topics.

The trouble with whatever is written from any angle about what is loosely called life is that it has all been said before. In the days when I had the temerity to traverse the globe telling the secret of happiness to anyone who would pay to listen (an occupation that

I have now abandoned and for which I apologize), I was harshly criticized for being insincere, which I deny, and for being unoriginal, which I freely admit. I was merely domesticating the high-flown precepts of the great thinkers of the past.

I have survived February. Mr Engel, a sculptor who made me immortal in bronze, said that more suicides occurred in February than in any other month. I did not go to that extreme, but then, I was given a 'flu shot', on the instruction of Miss Arcade, by a doctor who came all the way from Connecticut to administer it. I've had a cold ever since, but I have not been to hospital or the morgue.

There have been some dark moments, it is true. I was taken to the Palladium, where it was thought that my presence would help to launch a new magazine called *Wilde*. There, amid universal gloom and incessant din, we were shown a television programme in which some unprepossessing men were trussed up like chickens and lashed by gentlemen of dubious nationality, and I was interviewed by the ubiquitous and indefatigable Mr Barry Z, who asked me what I thought of the content of the magazine. I said that I had been shocked, but that I had remained calm. Whether such remarks will help to launch or sink the periodical in question upon the treacherous seas of debauchery, I cannot say, but shortly after midnight we were allowed to leave, bewildered but relieved.

I found myself at a banquet after seeing *Uncle Vanya*. The play was at Circle in the Square, and the supper at Gallagher's. *Uncle Vanya* received bad notices from the professional critics, which was precisely what the feast at Gallagher's was designed to prevent. They complained of the ages of the various actors. Mr Courtenay (as Uncle Vanya) says that he is forty-seven, and I thought he looked it, allowing for the fact that he was playing a Russian. In the 1880s, no man took the enormous trouble to seem young, as they now do, especially not in Russia. Nothing is more ageing than living in Russia. It was the women in the play to which I took exception. Yelena should have been dreamy, self-possessed, and self-absorbed, moving about in slow, graceful dance among her admirers as women did before they regrettably decided to be people, and Sonia should be fluttery. The difficulties imposed on the cast by the performance space may account for a lot of their defects. The stage is so vast that, in order not to hold up the action, they felt compelled to run off it, making the production feverish instead of mournful. When the play was over, I ate at Gallagher's with a charming young woman whom I had met before the show while wandering about trying to find the theatre.

That's the wonderful thing about Manhattan. You are never without friends.

AFTERWORD

BY QUENTIN CRISP

ONE IS NEVER WITHOUT FRIENDS, especially in America, and particularly in Manhattan. I have survived the rigors of New York City life for nearly twenty years and have made it a nesting placc for my weary bones and failing body. I have never truly felt my age, at least not until I turned ninety. And now, I am falling apart as I write this for you. Yet, I try always to remain calm.

Since the publication of *Resident Alien*, I have lost the use of my left hand to carpal tunnel syndrome. Doctors suggested I should have my wrists cut. But I said when I cut my wrists it will be forever! So I have not had the operation and can no longer type. I can write because I am right-handed, but I cannot use both hands to type. My friend Mr. Ward has become my fingers and he types the words I speak.

The papers for which I worked have folded. I worked for the *New York Native* and for *Christopher Street*. They were part of the kingdom of a very resourceful man called Tom Steele. His whole empire crumbled because kinkiness is now mainstream. There is no need to read the shocking things they said between brown paper covers, because they are now printed in *The Wall Street Journal* or the Sunday *Times*. So there was no need for his papers and they aptly disappeared. It is a pity that all came to nothing.

At the same time, Connie Clausen, my longtime agent in America, died. I took these things as a sign from You-Know-Who that my writing career was ended. Miss Clausen was a wonderful lady. She took care of many of my needs. I miss her very much, but luck has played an enormous part in my survival and I am rarely without work in the speaking and nodding racket. Mr. Mays and Miss Tahan have taken full control of what Miss Clausen left behind. They make sure that I have something to do and a means to earn a living. I owe it all to them, actually. They have been so very kind to me.

Now I go to various places and work in tiny arty theaters, telling the inhabitants how to be happy. I have been to some most extraordinary places. Like Portland, in Oregon. And Seattle, which is a strange city full of lesbians and Christmas trees. I have been to Chicago, Cleveland, Atlanta, Key West. I have also been to San Francisco, Los Angeles, Philadelphia, Baltimore, and even to Texas. I still enjoy Americans wherever I go. They remain a wonderful people. Americans have always welcomed and even embraced me since my arrival in America.

On my ninetieth birthday, I was put in a theater called the Intar Theater by Mr. Glines. There I performed my act for six weeks. I became ill with a horrible cold and almost died, but I still went on and gave the audience what they came to see and hear. Mr. Ward collected all the questions the audience had asked so that we may make a manuscript of all my dusty answers. The book will also include a transcript of my act and will most likely be published after I am dead. I will rest assured that Mr. Ward will make it all happen.

Now there is a theater and a museum named after me. Why, I just don't know, but they do exist. The theater is in Los Angeles and the museum is in Kansas City, Missouri. I live in New York City and why these two venues exist, I haven't any idea. What does it all mean? Also, I have been made immortal by Madame Tussaud! Why they have decided to put me in her museum, I can't imagine, but they have. When Madame Tussaud flings open the doors to her Times Square museum, my wax image shall hold court, but I shall not be there.

When I was younger and was not ill, I didn't mind how long I lived. Now that every step of my life is painful, I long for death. Even when I long for it to end, I start to remember other times and other people. I had a difficult and unhappy life in England, but it prepared me for the gold-covered streets of America. My life in America has been a wondrous wealth of joy. I have always lived my life in the profession of being. Living in New York City has prepared me for the glorious state of not-being. In my present condition, I look forward to being extinct.

When asked what it meant to be human, I was very sorry that I was not a scholar and had no philosophical point of view to express. More than not being a scholar, I am not really a human being. I do not seek the company of another person, but only of people. People are my hobby. And I do not mind spending long hours alone, and I never find something to do. Why should I have something to do? This is part of my nature. I have to be excluded from what is human so that I may look at humanity with a sense of detachment. It is then that I guess at its motives and what makes it the way it is. Be assured that when we say a thing is human, we are condoning it, not praising it.

As I have mentioned earlier, my body is falling apart as I write this missive to you. My weary bones speak each time I lift my legs to climb the stairs to my room. I am very ill with prostate cancer, an enlarged heart, and eczema (to mention only a few of my afflictions). So, I don't expect to live much longer. However, I would hate to leave this world without saying that I have had a good ride of it all. Luck has played an enormous part in my life, I realize looking back. And I have no regrets with my life's adventures. I made it to the Big Time with an abundance of smiles and I have only you, the reader, to thank for helping make it happen.

I have stood on this planet for nearly a century where people regarded me with amused curiosity, some with open mockery. My tale has not been a happy tale. But I hope you have enjoyed reading it. As I have said many times, nothing is more pleasant than reading about other people's misfortunes.

My life in New York City has been infinitely wonderful. I have been very happy living my winter years here. I remain very busy going here and there telling people everywhere how to be happy. I am always approached to appear in movies, and my agent continues to book me for appearances across the country. Mr. Ward makes it especially easy for me to continue to write articles for various magazines and newspapers. So, despite rambling on about my body's decline, I've gone on living. At least for right now, I am too busy to die! As I approach my ninety-first birthday, I am just as active as I have always been. I am at the age where all the people my age stay home and sit in their rockers. Not me!

Lastly, I hope you have enjoyed reading this book. And I take heart that it hasn't frightened you away. Instead I hope it has inspired you to live your life as carelessly as I have done. I have lived my life the best way I know how and I regret nothing.

QUENTIN CRISP was born Denis Pratt on Christmas Day in 1908 to middle-class parents in a suburb of London. He worked as a commercial artist and an art-school model ("the Naked Civil Servant" of his landmark autobiographical work) for thirty-five years. In 1931 he came-out on the streets of London wearing makeup and attired in a flamboyant fashion, outwardly signaling to the world his refusal to don a traditional masculine persona, a refusal to hide his homosexuality. He received rave reviews and garnered hordes of fans with his portrayals of Queen Elizabeth in the film *Orlando*, Lady Bracknell in the stage production of *The Importance of Being Earnest*, and his inimitable self in his acclaimed one-man show, *An Evening with Quentin Crisp*.

Beginning with the 1938 work *Color in Display*, Mr. Crisp's literary output has taken several forms. This includes the autobiographical writings *The Naked Civil Servant*, *How to Become a Virgin*, and *Resident Alien* (collected here for the first time, and accompanied by a new Preface and Afterword written by the author shortly before his death); film commentary published in *Christopher Street*; travel articles for *The New York Times*; observations on manners and society in the *Advocate*; and party-going advice in *Out* magazine.

Mr. Crisp, who had moved to New York in the late 1970s, died in November 1999 (while in England touring his one-man show) just as this edition was going to press.